Jacobitism
and Tory Politics
1710-14

For Jan and Anna

Jacobitism
and Tory Politics
1710-14

D. SZECHI
Department of History
University of Sheffield

JOHN DONALD PUBLISHERS LTD
EDINBURGH

ISBN 0 85976 116 9

Exclusive distribution in the United
States of American and Canada by
Humanities Press Inc., Atlantic
Highlands, NJ 07716, USA.

The publisher acknowledges
the financial assistance of
the Scottish Arts Council in
the publication of this volume.

Phototypeset by H.M. Repros, Glasgow
Printed in Great Britain by Bell & Bain Ltd., Glasgow.

Acknowledgements

For permission to publish extracts and citations in this book I am indebted to: Her Majesty the Queen for her gracious permission in allowing me to use the Stuart papers microfilm held at Cambridge University Library; the Duke of Hamilton; the Duke of Atholl, the beauty of whose seat at Blair Atholl I shall not soon forget; the Trustees of the Winchilsea Settled Estates for the use of the Finch Hatton MSS.; the Trustees of the Lamport Hall Preservation Trust, for the use of the Isham MSS.; the Scottish Catholic Archives for the use of the Blair letters; the Chaytor papers in the North Yorkshire R.O. by courtesy of the late Sir William Chaytor and Mr. W. D. Chaytor; Lady Ravensdale for the use of the Panshanger MSS. in the Hertfordshire R.O.; the Keeper of the Records of Scotland for his permission to use the Breadalbane Papers, Mar and Kellie MSS, and the Morton Papers; Lincolnshire Archive Office for the use of the Massingberd collections; the Department of Manuscripts at the University College of North Wales for the use of the Baron Hill MSS.; the Earl of Dalhousie for permission to use the Dalhousie Papers; Lady Anne Bentinck for permission to use the Portland Loan at the British Museum; Lord Hampton for the use of the Pakington papers; Sir John Clerk for the use of the Clerk of Penicuik MSS. kept at the Scottish R.O.; Staffordshire R.O. for the use of the Dartmouth MSS. and the Bradford muniments; Lord Polwarth for the use of the Home of Marchmont papers; Lord Newton for the use of the Legh of Lyme MSS. deposited at the John Rylands University Library of Manchester; Mrs C. Methuen-Campbell for the use of the Penrice and Margam collection held at the National Library of Wales; Sir John Hanmer for the use of the Bettisfield collection held at the National Library of Wales; A.R.I. Hill Esq. and the Downshire Settled Estates for permission to use the Trumbull MSS.; the Marquess of Cholmondeley for the use of the Cholmondeley (Houghton) Papers kept at Cambridge University Library.

I must also thank the staff of all the record offices I have visited in the course of my research for this book, in particular those of the Bodleian, the British Museum and the Quay d'Orsai in Paris, for their courtesy and patience.

A special debt of gratitude which I must acknowledge is due to Dr. Eveline Cruickshanks of the History of Parliament Trust for allowing me free access to the transcripts she and Dr. David Hayton are amassing for the 1689–1714 volumes of the History of Parliament, as well as the use of the microfilms of the despatches of Kreienberg and Bonet. For permission to see the Kreienberg microfilm I must also thank Professor G. S. Holmes.

Contents

Note on Dates and Abbreviations

Except where otherwise stated, all dates are given in the old style calendar used in Britain during this period, but with the year assumed to begin on 1 January rather than 26 March.

Abbreviations

Add. MSS.	Additional MSS.
AAE	Archives du Ministère des Affaires Etrangères, Quay d'Orsai, Paris: Correspondance Politique, Angleterre.
Baschet	Public Record Office, Chancery Lane, London, Baschet transcripts 31/3/-
Blair Lett.	Scots Catholic Archives, Columba House, Edinburgh, Blair Letters: James Carnegy to Bishop Nicolson of the Scots mission (unless otherwise stated).
Blenheim	British Library, Blenheim Papers.
Bodl.	Bodleian Library, Oxford.
Bol. Corr.	*The Letters and Papers of Henry St John, Lord Viscount Bolingbroke*, ed. G. Parke (1798).
Bonet	Zentrales Staatsarchiv, Dienstelle Merseburg, Rep XI (England), Frederick Bonet (Prussian resident in London) to Prussia. Microfilm kept by the History of Parliament Trust.
BL	British Library.
Bull. Inst. Hist. Res.	Bulletin of the Institute of Historical Research.
Carte	Bodleian Library, Oxford, Carte MSS.
CJ	*Journals of the House of Commons*
Dalhousie	Scottish Record Office, Register House, Edinburgh, Dalhousie MSS. GD 45.
Eng. Hist. Rev.	*English Historical Review.*
Fieldhouse	H. N. Fieldhouse, 'Bolingbroke's Share in the Jacobite Intrigue of 1710–14', *English Historical Review*, lii (1937), pp. 443–59.
Gaultier	University of Pennsylvania, French MSS.
Gualterio	British Library, Additional MSS., Gualterio Papers.

Hermitage	British Library, Additional MSS. 17677: G. de l'Hermitage (Dutch resident in London) to the Estates-General.
Hist. Journal	*Historical Journal.*
HMC	Historical Manuscripts Commission.
Hist. Today	*History Today.*
HPT	History of Parliament Trust transcripts.
Hunt. Lib. Bull.	*Huntington Library Bulletin.*
Hunt. Lib. Quart.	*Huntington Library Quarterly.*
Journal of Brit. Stud.	*Journal of British Studies.*
Kreienberg	Staatsarchiv Hannover, Calenberg Briefe 24 England, C.F. von Kreienberg (Hanoverian resident in London) to Hanover. Microfilm kept by the History of Parliament Trust.
Legh MSS.	John Rylands Library, Deansgate. Manchester, Legh of Lyme letters.
Lockhart	*The Lockhart Papers*, ed. A. Aufrere (1817).
Macpherson	*Original Papers; Containing the Secret History of Great Britain from the Restoration to the Accession of the House of Hanover*, ed. J. J. Macpherson (1775).
Mar MSS.	Scottish Record Office, Mar and Kellie MSS., GD 124.
Nic. Diary	*The London Diaries of William Nicolson, 1702–18.*
ns	New style date.
Portland	Historical Manuscripts Commission, *Portland MSS.*
R.O.	Record Office.
Scott. Hist. Rev.	*Scottish Historical Review.*
Stuart	Historical Manuscripts Commission, *Stuart Papers.*
Szechi	D. Szechi, 'Parliamentary Jacobitism and its Influence in the Tory Party, 1710–14' (Oxford D. Phil thesis, 1982).
Welsh Hist. Rev.	*Welsh Historical Review.*
Went. Corr.	*The Wentworth Papers, 1705–39*, ed. J. J. Cartwright (1882).
Wickham-Legg	L. G. Wickham-Legg, 'Extracts from Jacobite Correspondence, 1712–14', *English Historical Review*, xxx (1915), pp. 502–18.

All printed works should be assumed to have been published in London unless otherwise stated.

Introduction

This book is an attempt to deal with an intractable problem. Jacobitism has proved to be the bane of early eighteenth-century British historical writing since the profession came into existence over a century ago. In part this stems from the near-mystical nature of much of the Jacobite world-view. Because God was on their side, they had to win, and since they must be winning, every cloud had to be searched for a silver lining, which because it was sought was always found. Such a determined sense of unreality is uncomfortable to twentieth-century minds, accustomed to so much that is familiar in eighteenth-century society. Jacobitism is closest in spirit to medieval ideas of loyalty to the monarchy and the sovereign as Christ's vicar upon earth, attitudes which seem strangely out of reckoning with the age of Rousseau and Voltaire, Palladian mansions and the beginnings of the industrial revolution. Moreover, it failed, visibly and catastrophically, for its adherents. Political movements which fail are always more stringently analysed for the seeds of their own destruction than successful ones are for the rickety tendencies which they nevertheless overcame. Consequently, analyses of Jacobitism have been dominated by a feeling of impending doom and futility, and this has masked the impact of their activities or consigned them to the dustbin of history as unimportant. Popular opinion may find poignancy in the slaughter of dumbly loyal clansmen on Culloden moor, but in historians it rarely excites more than contempt and disgust for the cause which put them there. These factors have combined to leave the historical profession with little time for Jacobitism — a penchant increased by the addiction of romantic novelists and amateur enthusiasts to the perpetuation of a myth of tragic but noble failure in a virtuous cause. This dismissive attitude has generally been rationalised on the grounds of failings in the sources, the unreality of the Jacobites themselves, the difficulty of researching underground organisations with any accuracy and the ultimate irrelevance of it all.

There are definitely failings in the sources. A Jacobite letter which has survived to the present day has done so only because someone was too stupid or too careless to burn it — and this means that very little direct evidence remains at the British end of affairs. The eternal optimism of the Jacobites pervades much that is still extant, making research in the field either an amusing or an irritating experience, depending on the mood of the student. Yet these barriers to serious study are not insuperable. Most Jacobite activity was carried on from abroad, which means that the Jacobite Court's end of most correspondence has survived to the present day. The Jacobites also had no hesitation in plying their host nations with information about their friends and adherents, much of which can still be found in foreign archives. For all that the

Jacobites were undoubtedly prepared to magnify their own strength and influence in order to excite interest in the recipient, they were more careful in their assessments and plots than has been usually credited. The host nations' foreign ministries were not staffed with idiots, and the Jacobites knew better than to insult their intelligence too obviously.

Secrecy engenders uncertainty which, allied to optimism, creates fantasies. All secret and illegal organisations suffer from over-zealous supporters who will interpret almost everything in the most favourable light. The Jacobites were no exception. This does not mean that their leadership's responses were necessarily naive or unintelligent. The earl of Middleton was no-one's fool, the duke of Berwick was one of the better generals of his day, the duke of Hamilton was a competent second-string political manager and James, the Old Pretender, was able enough. Nor does misperception preclude effective political action. In our own era the German Communist party contributed not a little to the destabilisation of the Weimar Republic, despite its strategy being founded on a fundamental misunderstanding of the situation. Sir John Pakington and George Lockhart may have been trying to restore a golden past which had never really existed, but that is not to say that they could not appreciate the best way of going about it.

Actions are more important than policy documents in showing what a politician wants or an organisation can achieve, and plainly, underground organisations are reticent about revealing themselves without good cause for fear of suppression. Jacobitism in the form of overt military activity was something naturally ridiculed and denied by nearly all Jacobites when in public, right up to the actual moment of rebellion — just as the crypto-Cavaliers denied their attachment to Charles II in 1658-60 or the 'Immortal seven' theirs to William of Orange in 1687-8. Political activity was, of necessity, something overt and hence lends itself to observation and analysis by the historian. Thus, the activities of traceable Jacobites at Westminster can tell us a great deal about the Jacobites, their connections, policy and effect.

Irrelevance is a charge which no historian can sustain for long against Jacobitism. However ephemeral the Jacobite 'threat' may have been, the Government's response to it from the time of Nottingham and Danby to that of the Pelhams was of considerable importance for the development of British political and legal institutions and hence the rest of society. Five rebellions, six near-invasions and innumerable scares, engineered or spontaneous, cannot seriously be thought to have had not a jot of impact on British society and institutions. It is fair to say that the impact of Jacobitism was almost uniformly negative, apart from some fine theological and historical scholarship among the Nonjurors. But it should be remembered that this is a direct consequence of its failure, rather than any intrinsic fault peculiar to it.

Of all its manifestations, the political aspect of Jacobitism is the easiest to study. The period 1710 to 1714 was one crucial to the development of Britain as a whole and the Tory party in particular. Because of what happened in these years Britain became destined for domination by a Whig oligarchy for nearly half a century. The role of the Jacobites both inside and outside Parliament in these events has often been alluded to, but never examined in depth. Such examination can shed new light on the motivation behind the manoeuvres and machinations of these years, which have hitherto tended to be regarded as something of a headlong and headstrong rush to embrace its nemesis by the first Tory party. Because it is necessary for such a study to focus on those for whom their Jacobitism was a guiding principle, it must be concentrated on the Jacobite Country Tory element of the Tory party, those who owed allegiance to none of the Tory chieftains and were beholden to no ministry for their livelihood. If Jacobitism had any influence in the Tory party, it was these men who represented it in a practical sense.

The Jacobite Country Tories did not exist in a vacuum. There were many conflicting interest-groups at Westminster, of which they were only one. Within the Tory party they represented one extreme of the political spectrum but were in no way divorced from the interests and ambitions of the rest of the party. To arrive at some understanding of the Jacobite role in the movements and events of these years, a broad examination of the context in which they operated is required. Without looking at the Hanoverian Tories, the October and March clubs, and the final struggle between Oxford and Bolingbroke for leadership of the ministry, no true appreciation of their significance can be established. In practice this amounts to a re-examination of the political developments of the final years of Queen Anne's reign from the point of view of one group of Tory backbenchers. This is not a disadvantage but an advantage, as it allows in the process much conventional wisdom about the part the Jacobites played in the discrediting of the Tory party with the incoming Hanoverian dynasty and the events of 1710 to 1714 to be tested by comparing it with the part played by their peers.

Just as the Jacobites in Parliament remained Tories throughout, they also continued to be attached to the Jacobite organisation operated by the exiled Court. As an element in it, they were subjected to its stresses and inefficiencies and exerted their own influence in return. Hence, the Parliamentary Jacobites cannot be divorced from their Jacobite background either without impairing our understanding of them and their behaviour. Thus the Jacobites at Westminster can be used as a tool with which to gain a better insight into both the first Tory party and the workings of the Jacobite movement.

The historiographical orthodoxies which can be tested by a study of Parliamentary Jacobitism are of wide-ranging significance. The fierce controversy of the 1960s over the structure of Augustan politics has long been settled in favour of the model suggested by Professor G.S. Holmes. An essential part of his paradigm was the existence of ideologically motivated splinter groups within both of the parties.[1] Because these groups formed around issues of principle, they intrinsically denied the reality proposed by Professor R. Walcott, in which dynastic connexions were the basic stuff of politics.[2] The period 1710 to 1714 gave rise to several such groups, among them the Jacobites, which makes it ideal for studying the implications of

Professor Holmes's theories. The intemperate politics of the Tory party during the Harley ministry, exacerbated by these splinter groups, steadily eroded the moderate basis on which Harley founded his ministry in 1710. As a result, he found himself increasingly isolated and driven to find desperate expedients in order to stave off the growing discontent of his backbenchers. One of the measures he adopted to this end is generally thought to have been an approach to the Jacobite Court offering it a restoration, and this offer events transformed into a sincere proposal.[3] New light has recently been shed on this episode by Dr E. Gregg's invaluable re-assessment of Queen Anne, which has finally disposed of the idea of the queen as a timid cipher, and has convincingly shown that she wanted no truck with any kind of Jacobite restoration.[4] As Oxford and Bolingbroke cannot have been unaware of this attitude, the way has thus been opened for a complete revaluation of their motives in contacting the Jacobite Court with proposals to restore the Old Pretender. A more general theory, of profound significance for the whole of the post-Revolutionary period up to the 1720s, is that of Sir John Plumb on the development of political stability from 1675 onwards.[5] Plumb argues that the preconditions for the type of political stability established by Walpole were steadily developing from the Revolution onwards. A detailed study of the state of the party battle just before the triumph of the Whigs is a suitable test of this interpretation.

It will be readily apparent from the assumptions and framework used in this book that I have leaned heavily on the work of the great men who have gone before me. The theories and findings of Professors G.S. Holmes, W.A. Speck, H.T. Dickinson, H.L. Snyder and Sir John Plumb have all left an indelible impression upon my own thoughts which can be seen throughout my writing. Of no lesser impact have been the researches of Dr E. Gregg and Dr G.V. Bennett. Any perusal of this book will also reveal a debt that can never be adequately repaid. If all scholars were as generous and helpful as Dr Eveline Cruickshanks and Dr D. Hayton of the History of Parliament Trust, and Clyve Jones of the Institute of Historical Research, the historical community would be a much richer one. Without their advice and criticism, inexhaustible patience with my half-formed ideas and fund of sound common sense I could never have completed this book so quickly. I hope all these scholars will forgive me for not citing every idea and finding which I owe to them, but which are the accepted wisdom to me, in my footnotes. Instead, I leave it to my bibliography to bear witness to my obligation to them.

NOTES

1. G.S. Holmes, *British Politics in the Age of Anne* (1967), pp. 217-84 and *passim*.

2. R.R. Walcott, *English Politics in the Early Eighteenth Century* (Oxford, 1956), *passim*.

3. For the best exposition of this viewpoint see: E. Gregg, 'The Protestant Succession in International Politics, 1710-16' (unpublished London School of Economics Ph.D thesis, 1972), pp. 106-12, 119-25, 171-85, 189-205. I differ with Dr. Gregg on this point, for which see Chapter 9 in particular.

4. Gregg, *Queen Anne* (1980), *passim*; 'Was Queen Anne a Jacobite?' *History*, lvii (1972), 358–75.

5. J.H. Plumb, *The Growth of Political Stability in England, 1675-1725* (1967).

1

'A strange confused chaos': Jacobite organisation, 1710-14

Parliamentary Jacobitism was always inseparable from the rest of British Jacobitism. It was not and cannot be distinguished in organisation or adherents from the rest of Jacobite activity. Without consideration of the nature and functions of the Jacobite network from 1710 to 1714, a study of the Parliamentary Jacobites would be distinctly two-dimensional. As they were an intrinsic part of this organisation, so they were affected by its tensions and problems, and in turn their attitudes and behaviour caused repercussions throughout the associated structure. Placing the Jacobite M.P.'s in their Jacobite context also throws new light on some of the more obscure antagonisms and tensions which arose between some groups of backbench Tories, just as it enables us to glimpse the continuity of such vexed questions as the religious debate (basically over the attitude James, the Old Pretender, should adopt regarding the Church of England).

The network of agents and sympathisers which the exiled Court ran from St Germain was the feature which marked it out from the other dispossessed French clients such as the Elector of Bavaria and the Prince de Vaudemont. That, and the fact that Jacobite subversion was aimed at France's major enemy in the War of the Spanish Succession, made it a potentially decisive political tool for the French Court. Conversely, once peace negotiations had begun, its sacrifice was a valuable bargaining counter for which concessions could be extracted from the victorious Allies (it should never be forgotten that, Whig propaganda to the contrary, the Grand Alliance won the war handsomely). As far as the exiled Stuarts were concerned, the organisation gave them not only status in the hierarchy of French clients, but also sources of information independent of the French, and, at least potentially, the ability to pursue their own ends. The way in which St Germain used the network, then, related directly to how well the network was doing its job, or was capable of doing it.

The actual structure of the organisation is the first element in this background. The efficiency with which it was run follows from this. The tensions inherent in Jacobitism naturally influenced whatever use was made of the network, and undoubtedly affected its efficiency too. The value which was put on the activities of the organisation, and hence the use which was made of it by the exiled Court, stems from all these. By investigation along these lines a picture of Jacobite organisation in Britain and the role played in it by the Parliamentary Jacobites can be established.

Jacobite organisation was extremely hierarchical, and the intrigues and jealousies at St Germain and later Chaillot and Bar-le-Duc sometimes rendered it top-heavy as the various factions tried to develop the authority of the few positions that carried any real power: those which operated the Jacobite network. Only one man actually directed the lower echelons at any given time, with direct responsibility to, and under orders from, James 'III' and his intimate family. This consisted of: James; his illegitimate half-brother, James Fitzjames the Marshal-Duke of Berwick; and the queen mother, Mary of Modena, who was always influenced to some extent by her own coterie, amongst whom were Dicconson the treasurer, the 'duke' of Perth and the queen's own secretaries John Stafford and, after his return to Britain, James Dempster. The earl of Middleton, as secretary of State, was already in control of most of the direction of the network by the time of 'lord' Caryll's death in September 1711, whose functions he had steadily accumulated during Caryll's long, wasting illness. The duke of Perth tried to succeed Caryll, but Middleton effectively excluded him from all correspondence with Britain, leaving him with nothing but the conduct of formal diplomatic business, primarily with Rome.

Between Middleton and his undersecretaries, David Nairne and Sir William Ellis, and the actual correspondents in Britain, there were no further organisational tiers. Within Britain itself no-one was nominated to coordinate activity, and where one person did act as controller of several correspondents, it was an *ad hoc* affair. In November 1713 James was reluctantly obliged to remove Middleton by 'promoting' him out of the Secretaryship to become Queen Mary's master of horse. In his place James appointed 'Sir' Thomas Higgons, whose sole recommendation for the post, as Dempster freely admitted to cardinal Gualterio (a friend of the exiled Stuarts at the Holy See and future Protector of England), was his religion: 'Comme il est Protestant de la Religion Anglicanne, cela aura fait plaisir aux amis du Roy en Angleterre'.[1] In fact, Higgons, who could not even write proficiently in French, was ignored, and his function was carried out by the duke of Berwick.[2] Berwick apparently had no peer of equal capacity, so that when he was ordered to go to Spain in June 1714, to take command of the siege of Barcelona, correspondence and direction from the Jacobite Court to Britain seems to have largely lapsed until his return in November.[3]

Jacobite correspondents were an extremely motley group. There were a few salaried 'official' agents such as James St Amand, John Menzies and Captain Henry Straton.[4] These three seem to have written the most regular reports, and to have undertaken official missions on behalf of St Germain when required. They also provided a channel of communication by which British Jacobites could send their opinions and requests to the Jacobite Court. Allied to these were a host of lesser 'unofficial' reporters who supplied St Germain with reports of wildly varying optimism and accuracy. Prominent amongst these were: Robert Ferguson 'the Plotter'; James Plunket; John Netterville; and sundry less frequent writers such as the duke of Buckingham and Charles

Leslie.[5] The regular agents seem to have had defined areas of responsibility within Britain. Menzies usually received St Germain's instructions for the Parliamentary Jacobites, as in November 1711 when Nairne noted: 'I told him again to get all Susan's relations [Scots Jacobite M.P.'s and peers] and Proby's [English Jacobite M.P.'s and peers] to favour Phipps [peace].' He is also mentioned by George Lockhart M.P. in his memoirs as 'Mr John Meinzies (who received the dispatches commonly from St Germain)'.[6] Henry Straton seems to have been responsible for Scottish matters, as can be seen from a typical note of Nairne's concerning him in December 1712:

> As to advice or directions the K[ing: the Old Pretender] could give none to his friends in Scotland at present being advis'd by his best friends to do nothing at present for fear of spoiling any good intentions some persons may have for him, that all depended on H[arley: the earl of Oxford] who being a dark man, nobody knew well what to reckon upon and how to act therefore in the uncertainty, nothing seemed more prudent than to wait to see how things will turn.[7]

Straton is also mentioned in Lockhart's memoirs.[8] St Amand's area of responsibility, as far as can be ascertained, was restricted to England, but as he was ill for much of the time between 1710 and 1714 he seems to have usually just supplemented Menzies's efforts. All the available or suitable correspondents were used when it was necessary to contact leading political figures, regardless of these apparent operating zones. A typical case of this occurred in December 1710 when Middleton instructed Menzies to contact lord Dupplin:

> I was surprised to hear that Miss Honiton [Harley] had marry'd a Mirmidon [Jacobite sympathiser], that you should be ignorant of it or conceal it, let us know the particulars, ply the son in law with the more effectual promises for himself and his father in law, he being foreman of the jury [leader of the ministry], as without him we cannot hope for a favourable verdict.[9]

And in 1713 Berwick used the then amateur agent Thomas Carte in the same way, to contact the duke of Ormonde.[10]

A third type of agent were those sent directly from St Germain on special missions. Though some were despatched by the incumbent senior Secretary of State, others were used to bypass the regular organisation. Colonel Nathaniel Hooke was sent to Gertruydenberg in 1710 in the first of these roles, to advise the French plenipotentiaries negotiating with the Allies there on Jacobite interests, and to publish an official protest should, as was expected, terms detrimental to the Jacobites be agreed. Hooke also acted in the second of these roles when he was sent to Germany in 1714 to try and find a State willing to hire out its troops to the exiled Stuarts as mercenaries. Apart from their use on unusual missions by the Secretaries of State, 'special' agents could be used to circumvent the usual channels by other members of the Jacobite leadership, as was the case in August 1713 when, with James's permission Queen Mary sent an agent named Tunstal to contact Marlborough in Flanders, confiding to Dicconson that Berwick (and presumably Middleton) was not to know of it.[11]

This predeliction for 'special' agents outside the regular channels could cause considerable uncertainty and confusion amongst St Germain's adherents in Britain, and was open to abuse in the course of Court intrigues. The worst such case occurred early in 1713 when the Abbé Butler appeared in London, told all who would listen that James was a Deist at heart, and tried to persuade Netterville, who was an acquaintance of Oxford's, to influence him to write to the earl of Melfort (a former Jacobite secretary of State dismissed in 1694) rather than Middleton, 'but Mr Netterville would not, knowing it would do the King harm; and if said man stays long, he will do hurt', warned the worried Plunket. The Jacobites in Britain were not the only ones confused by this penchant: in February 1712 Nairne was obliged to write an embarrassed letter to Menzies, asking if Hooke was there, as the regular organisation had no idea where he was or what he was doing.[12]

Such organisation as did arise spontaneously in Britain among the Jacobites was usually centred on a correspondent who enlisted others of like sympathies to gather news for him. Ferguson, Plunket and Mrs Jean Murray all followed this pattern, only Netterville standing out among the more frequent writers in not doing so. An obvious exception was the Parliamentary Jacobite group formed in August 1713, but even that had its own established correspondent: Netterville.[13] Ferguson seems to have aimed at establishing a private network of his own, including his own links to the Government, in 1711-13. In March 1712 he wrote to Ellis to introduce one of his recruits, 'Mr Sheridan', whom he implied the Protestant Jacobites would like to see employed.[14] In May 1712 he followed this up by capitalising on Plunket's discoveries of Whig intrigues to establish his own credit with the Government:

> Mr Peregrine [Ferguson] did acquaint Mr Tom West [Buckingham] of Mr Rogers [Plunket's] business, unknown to Mr Rogers; for he had taken measures to have it laid before the friends in Mr Medlicot's family [Jacobites in Parliament]; and the pleading first council [Cabinet], both at a time, when he found Mr Hans [Oxford] concealed all from them; but when Mr Peregrine had taken that way, Rogers was satisfied, though he was not privy to the doing [of] it, for it had the end he wished.[15]

Ferguson was awarded £100 for his services by the Cabinet. An inexorable slide from judicious leaks to outright betrayal followed, and by 1713 Ferguson was to be found whining to Oxford for money and spying on his former friends.[16]

Rivalries and jealousies between these groups of agents were common. In late May 1712 Plunket feared that Sheridan was going to let the Government have some valuable papers that Plunket had entrusted to him. In the same vein Netterville warned St Germain against entrusting Ferguson with sums of money. Ferguson himself used his knowledge of an admonition Menzies had received to try and undermine his position in Britain and at the Jacobite Court.[17] A more serious problem than these petty feuds was the mutual hostility of the two main national groups into which the Jacobites in Britain instinctively divided: the English and the Scots. The tone of the Jacobite

Court's periodic soothing letters on the subject, assuring the Scots of its reliance on them, is ample testimony to their sensitivity:

> as to his [Middleton] neglecting Stirling [Scotland] whoever thought so, were very unjust to him for on the contrary Joseph [James] and he had a true value for Stirling and more confidence in him than in their richer relations, but in that nice conjuncture they could not trade neither with Estmor [England] nor Stirling because Joseph was bid ly quiet and say nor do nothing till he shall see clearer into the dark doings of the chief director of trade, least in clashing with them he should ruine himself.[18]

Though *ad hoc* groups did arise among the British Jacobites, these were transient phenomena, dependent on the enthusiasm of the correspondent at the core. Only the national alignments had any permanence. Instead, most Jacobites found congenial homes in High Tory organisations such as the October Club and the Board of Brothers. This remained the case until the emergence of the Parliamentary Jacobite group in August 1713.

The main route by which Jacobite agents and letters moved between the Court at St Germain and Britain was, surprisingly enough, via Holland rather than France, even after the Franco-British armistice of June 1712. The route was not altered until November 1713 when it was shifted to pass through Dunkirk. In both Rotterdam and Dunkirk a 'dead letter box' was kept by a friendly merchant: Mr Hacket in Rotterdam and Jacobus van Eassel in Dunkirk. On average it took ten days for a letter from Britain to arrive at St Germain, and it presumably took a similar time on the return journey. The ordinary Jacobite correspondents do not appear to have used French covers at all, but the upper echelons, especially after Berwick took control, relied extensively on French diplomatic channels to convey their letters, which cut down the travelling time to four or five days.[19] Other formal diplomatic correspondence travelled quite regularly under French covers, so that Middleton could casually instruct Gualterio in September 1712, as the Jacobite Court prepared to leave France, merely to continue to direct his correspondence for the Court to the French Secretary of State, the marquis de Torcy, who would pass it on.[20]

The security measures taken by the Jacobites were haphazard and primitive even for the time. A sublime confidence was apparently felt in the antiquated system of writing under cant names known only to the writer and the recipient. Number codes (the only contemporary technique offering any real security), in which a number was substituted for each word in the message, were used only occasionally, and then mainly in diplomatic correspondence. So complete was the Jacobite Court's confidence in its codes and routes that even in January 1712, when four consecutive posts from Britain had failed to arrive, Stafford merely remarked in a letter to Gualterio, 'mais nous en a receu des nouvelles a Versailles par Calais'. Middleton did advise a Mr 'Boine' how to warn the Court if he felt the mail was being tampered with, but no reply has survived and there is no sign of further concern.[21] Government penetration of Jacobite security was spasmodic but deep when it occurred, and it appears to have been limited only by a lack of sustained official interest.[22] Interception by the British Government was an inevitable hazard for the Jacobites, but their reliance on French conveyance of the most revealing diplomatic correspondence was a subtle threat to their security they never even considered. Torcy openly vetted all letters conveyed by French channels, in effect monitoring all Jacobite diplomatic initiatives and plans.[23] This did not represent a real threat unless French and Jacobite aims diverged, but it was certainly unwise to assume that they could never do so.

Jacobite finances were based on two pensions. The major one was from the French Court, and was technically for the upkeep of Queen Mary's household. The other was probably smaller (about 42,000 livres) and paid to James directly by the Pope. The total was just sufficient to keep a small Court with economy. However, the numbers of destitute hangers-on and old servants attached to the Court quite precluded any accumulation of a surplus that could have been used for the purchase of arms and equipment, or for paying troops. Indeed, in 1712 James was so hard pressed for his removal expenses in transferring the Court to Lorraine, that he literally refused to move until he or his mother were paid the pensions they had been promised by the French Court.[24] Although an account survives for the last six months of 1714, it is impossible to extrapolate from this the annual income of the Jacobite Court, due to lack of other evidence. The British Jacobites did offer James a 'loan' of £20,000 in 1711 but, after consulting the French Court, he refused it as politically inexpedient. In general it would appear that, because of the growing inability of the French to pay the Court's pension, the exiled Stuarts found themselves in increasingly dire financial straits during this period.[25]

Of what was available, as much as possible seems to have been sent to Britain. Apart from the wages of the three regular agents, there were also sums sent over to be distributed among the British Jacobites at irregular intervals. Menzies was sent £1,400 in 1712, to cover 'expenses' in the next session of Parliament, and money was being sent into Scotland at about the same time.[26] An itemised account also survives of John Fisher's journey to Scotland in late 1714 which reveals £4,000 disbursed as gifts and pensions to the marquis of Tullibardine (the duke of Atholl's heir), the marquis of Drummond, the bishop of Edinburgh, Straton, William Gordon, 'Forbes' and lord Nairne.[27] It is difficult to say whether these were the accustomed recipients of the exiled Court's bounty, though the presence of the bishop of Edinburgh would seem to support such an assumption.

The conduct of diplomacy was always the preserve of James's personal circle. Purely technical or formal matters, such as the annual application to the French for another attempt to invade Britain, or calling upon the Dutch to support Jacobite claims in peace negotiations, were left to the secretaries of State.[28] There was not really much necessity for the use of diplomacy by the Jacobite Court while James was in France, could speak to Torcy and other ministers easily, and had little or no contact with any other State except the Holy See (nor envisaged the need for it). Once James had been removed to

Lorraine, and denied official access to the French Government, the necessity for surreptitious diplomatic activity came to the fore. Berwick was obviously the best man to negotiate with France, and it is his dealings with Torcy which were the prime focus of the Court's interest and activity. Gualterio, described by James as 'le maistre de mes affaires a Rome', continued to represent the Jacobite cause at the Holy See, as he had done since the death of Cardinal Caprara in June 1711.[29]

Continued close relations with France and the Papacy could easily have been foreseen. What was more unexpected was Jacobite attempts to enter into friendlier relations with the Emperor and the Elector of Saxony. Charles VI was approached at the end of 1713 through Duke Leopold of Lorraine's envoy at Vienna, with the project of a marriage between James and one of his sisters. The Austrians were politely sympathetic, but refused to get too closely involved, the Lorraine Envoy reporting that 'his Majesty appeared to relish the proposal, but found the times too critical to come to a determination'. James, who was conducting the negotiations personally, responded with commendable vigour, and tried to persuade Charles to receive a letter from him as 'King of England', before other business forced the suspension of the contact.[30]

The attempt to win over Augustus the Strong of Saxony was conducted by Hooke, who was sent to Dresden in late 1712. Though he worked painstakingly on the project for several months, Hooke was evaded by the Elector himself as much as possible, and was reduced in the end to proposing chimerical projects involving the reconciliation of Charles XII of Sweden and Augustus under Jacobite auspices (a patent impossibility given Charles's intransigence), in return for which Augustus would aid them.[31] Though indicative of a certain spirit of independence, the failure of these two initiatives served in the end only to reinforce the Jacobite preoccupation with France.

All organisations dedicated to political ends are ultimately judged by their effectiveness. Given its clumsy organisational structure and its failure ever to achieve its aims, the Jacobite Court was in fact surprisingly successful in commanding the obedience of its supporters. The Jacobites in Parliament were dutifully compliant with St Germain's directives, except on a few occasions when Harley's pusillanimity pushed them too far. Berwick wrote in his memoirs, recalling the inception of the exiled Court's directive to the Parliamentary Jacobites to support the Government, that it was

> pour faire voir que nous ne vouliens rien omettre et pour montrer notre bonne foi, nous ecrivimes à les Jacobites de se joindre à la Cour; ce qui ne contribua pas peu à rendre la parti de la Reine si supérieur dans la Chambre Basse, que tout s'y passa selon ses desirs.[32]

He overrates the Jacobite contribution to the successes of the Harley ministry, but it is noticeable that those identifiable Jacobites who can be traced throughout the period between 1710 and 1714 do seem to have been remarkably reluctant to attack the ministry from 1711 onwards, despite their natural inclination to do so. Their High Toryism put them on the October Club wing of the party, and they were far from averse to supporting extreme measures originating there, but though they grew to detest the Government heartily, they still followed its line for most of the time.[33] The St Germain 'whip' had to be repeated occasionally so that the Jacobite Parliamentarians could not convince themselves that it had lapsed, but kept the same format from 1711 on:

> get all Jainon's relations [Scots Jacobites in Parliament], & Proby's also [English Jacobites in Parliament], to favour Phipps [peace], as also to keep well with Prior [ministry], to know all he could from him, and send account here.[34]

Only after sustained disappointment in their expectations of Oxford did Berwick finally unleash the Jacobites in February 1714, after which they rapidly evolved into an independent political force.[35] Supplementary directives had also to be issued during three political crises in which Jacobite Parliamentarians were involved: the boycott of Parliament by the Scots Representative Peers after the Lords' decision on the Hamilton peerage case; the October Club's attempt to 'Tack' the Grants Bill past the Lords; and the Scots' attempt to harry the Government into dissolving the Union in 1713.[36] It would be facile to maintain that 'whips' such as this were the only, or even the crucial, factor in the ministry's repulse of these three attacks. Harley's Parliamentary management was extremely shrewd, if short-term, and other Parliamentary and interest pressures played their part in the ministerial success in each case. Nevertheless, each of the Jacobite Court's supplementary 'whips' coincides remarkably well with the subsidence of the trouble in question, and while its influence must not be exaggerated, it should not be ignored.

A piecemeal organisational structure such as that operated by the Jacobite Court was liable to create competing, if not inimical, groups of its own accord. Inherent divisions compounded the problem. Each tended to intrigue against the others for what it felt was its due share of attention at St Germain, and to influence the Court's policies (or their application). The example of Ferguson, cited above, is a clear case of the organisation engendering its own disruption, while the latent antagonism of the English and Scots Jacobites was a more deep-rooted problem. Their shared loyalty usually overcame their national hostility, but on national issues friction was almost inevitable. George Lockhart coolly remarked that after the united English Tory opposition to the repeal of the Union in 1713, 'there appeard some little dryness, occasiond by it, betwixt the Scots and English Tories in the House of Commons'.[37] The care which the Jacobite Court had to take in soothing the two sides' endemic jealousies is indicative of the seriousness of the problem:

> I am also ordered to tell you that Joseph [James] thinks it necessary that all Snell's family [Scots Jacobites] should know that his haveing had no occasion for some time to trade with them, do's not proceed from any neglect either in him or in his partner Robert [Middleton] on the contrary he has always had an entire confidence in that family and is very sensible of the affection they shew'd him all

along; trade has beene of late such a mistery and is so still, that in the nice conjuncture he is in, he can not with prudence give any directions either to Snell or Edgebury [England], and has been positively advis'd by his best lawyers [Ministers] to be quiet, and neither say nor do any thing, least speaking or doing in the dark might do him more hurt than good.[38]

It must always be remembered that the elements making up Jacobitism in Britain, particularly in Parliament, were basically hostile to each other. English and Scots nationalism, and High Toryism and Roman Catholicism, were fundamentally inimical. Their only common ground, of substance, was the cause of the exiled Stuarts. Hence, St Germain had to be extremely tactful and devote a good deal of its energy toward coaxing continued cooperation from them all. The Irish Roman Catholic lobby could have further complicated matters, but the Jacobite Court avoided this by simply ignoring their claims to influence. Control of Britain was what mattered, so it was the British Jacobites who had to be humoured. After all, the Irish Roman Catholics had little choice but to look to St Germain for succour and therefore could be taken for granted.

Control over such a motley and suspicious collection was bound to have lapses. The surprising aspect of these, given the feuds which riddled the network, was that so few elements did try to operate outside the 'official' aegis. When it did occur, the Jacobite leadership was quite phlegmatic about it:

M. de Torcy told me two dayes agoe at Versailles that M. Harley had writt him word that your Majesty had sent lately into England some puckles [spies] whose behaviour very much embarressed the government. I told him that I believed it was a mistake, but that you were not master of all the Jacobites' actions and discourses which very often were indiscreet.[39]

The main challenge to the 'official' organisation came from a clique centred around the ageing and bitter lord Melfort, who ascribed all his woes to Middleton, his successor as secretary of State. It was from Melfort that at least one of the two spies mentioned above came. By early 1713 the Abbé Butler (technically a French agent) was trying to convince the British Jacobites and their contacts to communicate with Melfort rather than Middleton.[40] This initiative collapsed in March when James wrote a letter denying that he had sent Butler, who was accordingly shunned by the British Jacobites and drops out of sight thereafter.[41] Melfort seems to have revised his tactics after this, and next appears in summer 1713, when his henchmen in London began spreading rumours that Middleton was incompetent, lax in security, or even a traitor, which, Netterville thought, 'deters and frights the great traders from engaging their stocks'. Meanwhile, in Paris, the French Minister of Marine, the marquis de Pontchartrain, was assiduously upholding these allegations when questioned by visiting Jacobites (Middleton was his *bête noire* too). The upshot of Melfort's new plot was revealed when he tried to persuade lord Fingall to communicate with Middleton's rival, the duke of Perth, instead of Middleton, having obviously decided that even if he could not supplant him personally, he could still ruin him and have him replaced by the more sympathetic Perth. Initially this created considerable confusion and doubt in Britain, so that the loyal Netterville had to extract a promise from Plunket that in his forthcoming visit to France he would only go to see Middleton, the unspoken alternative being Perth.[42] By August Netterville, presumably with help from St Germain, had managed to discredit Melfort's rumours and could write with relief of lord Fingall: 'now this lord is convinced that all this is occasioned by malice and designs and desires'. Melfort returned to the wilderness after this, shunned even by his old friend the earl of Ailesbury, until his death in 1714.[43]

Melfort was trying to blacken Middleton's reputation and thus intensify calls from Britain for his removal. Though petty and damaging, it was essentially a Court intrigue and limited to Jacobite circles. A potentially more dangerous independent move occurred when a Colonel Parker tried to get to England with a scheme of his own, apparently based on old plans and probably of a military nature. Berwick promptly denounced him to Torcy, who had Parker arrested:

> M. de Torcy was entirely against his going to England and has even writt to the commandant of Calais not to lett him stir from thence. Tis certain it would be in Coll. Parker's power to doe great mischief, especially at the present time when the Whigs desire no better than a plott, besides the old ones are not proper to be renewed.[44]

Parker was later pensioned off by the Jacobite Court, but on condition that he live inland, well away from the coast, and his pension was deliberately set at a level that would prevent him travelling.[45] An equally ill-timed independent move, which St Germain did not hear of until it was too late, was the gratuitous use of James's name and cause by French recruiting officers in Ireland in 1713 and 1714, in order to swell their drafts. When discovered, the practice triggered a wave of fear among the Irish Protestants, and a spate of executions and wild stories resulted which had repercussions in England. The damage was further exacerbated when French recruiting officers using the same ploy were found in England. The Jacobite Court was far from pleased:

> Nous devions veritablement garder plus de mesures sur un point si delicat, et la Cour de France ne devoit pas permettre qu'il passat des officiers en Angleterre pour de pareils enrolemens. Les Irlandois seroient venus d'eux mesmes en nombres plus que suffisant sans qu'il fut besoin d'envoier les chercher avec tant de bruit et de danger. Il n'estoit probable que le Gouvernement d'Angleterre permit ces levées, et en general c'est un crime capital d'enroller du monde dans les Estats d'un Prince sans son consentement.[46]

These incidents, though serious, were unrepresentative of the Jacobite leadership's otherwise firm control of their supporters. Overall, the Jacobite network and its adherents were very much instruments of the leadership's will.

St Germain's effectiveness in relation to its object, the restoration of James to the throne, corresponded directly to the capacity of the men who acted for it in Britain. As channels of communication to the British Jacobites the regular agents were relatively efficient. As we saw, the Court's instructions were usually obeyed, which implies that they were received, so the transmitters of these general orders, the regular agents, must have been doing their job fairly conscientiously. In their other function, as sources of information, they seem to have been less punctual. The reports of the 'unofficial' correspondents who supplemented their efforts were, moreover, of very mixed quality and regularity.

The number of correspondents *seems* to have increased between 1710 and 1714, although this impression may arise from uneven survival of the evidence. The regular agents' reports, however, remained those that the exiled Court appears to have valued most. The most graphic illustration of this is the way an agent who did not send in regular or detailed enough reports was liable to be severely admonished. In February 1711 Middleton wrote to Menzies advising that he compile a daily journal to help him write more thorough reports, ending with the comment, 'you should make best use of it that we may not be three months of hearing of Mr Grace'. This does not seem to have had the desired effect, for Nairne felt it necessary to write to him again in August: 'To [Menzies] to tell him his not writing fully and frequently enough was not well taken'. And again in May 1712: 'That he was desird to write *often and fully*'.[47] Unfortunately, none of the regular agents' reports survive for this period, so it is impossible to assess their reliability as opposed to their desirability. But they cannot have differed greatly from the tone and content of the unofficial correspondents' reports, as the leadership's responses accord broadly with the version of events put forward by those correspondents whose letters survive.

The surge of new correspondents — which the increase of source material suggests occurred in early 1712 — varied greatly in calibre. Two in particular accurately reflect the extremes of reliability among these 'amateur' writers: James Plunket and John Netterville. Plunket's vainglory is typified by a letter written to Middleton in November 1713 in which he boasted: 'I have given several hints of late, that did put some people of power on the tantrums, and made them jealous of each other, and will spur them on to serve the consul [James] better than they have done hitherto'.[48] This amply justifies Netterville's summation of him: 'Mr Rogers is an ill figure of a man, and as ill an utterance; but what he has fallen into, by chance, is very extraordinary, and I believe that silly appearance has been of great help to him in doing what he has done'.[49] Plunket's claim to fame was that he appears to have stumbled upon some compromising Marlborough-Junto correspondence with the Allies, in effect urging a repeat of 1688 to prevent the Tories making a separate peace. Oxford silenced him by taking him into Government service as a spy against the Whigs, and extending to him hopes of an eventual Jacobite restoration.[50] Plunket let this success go to his head and by April 1713 was producing portentous rubbish based on nothing more than popular rumour:

> I must tell you, by the by, if Egleton [the Emperor] would but close with Knox [Louis XIV] the Duncans [Dutch] will be forced to vomit up what they are to get

by this portion [treaty], and of course will be glad to give a helping hand to Kennedy [James].[51]

In complete ignorance of French politics Plunket also tried to persuade Oxford to conduct his correspondence with France via the duc D'Aumont rather than Torcy in 1714, eliciting the cutting comment from the Abbé Gaultier (the French agent in London negotiating peace with the Harley ministry) that he was 'le plus indiscret de tous ceux qui sont icy et qui pretendent avoir quelque correspondence avec la cour de B[ar-le-duc] y ils font grand tort a notre chevallier [James] par leurs discours'.[52] Netterville tended to offer better grounded opinions, as in January 1713 concerning Oxford's negotiations with the Whigs, which he based on a conversation with lord Cowper's brother:

> My council hates him [Oxford] and uses to repeat all his unfair practices; yet at this time, owns he has so warded against a storm, that few beside himself could have done; and added that it was the opinion of all of his sort, that if he gave the proofs which he had promised and order'd it so, to have the family of Medlecot [Parliament] to be such as they had been some years past, he will be in esteem with those that now hate him.[53]

Paradoxically, both agents, and in fact virtually the entire Jacobite network, were tricked by Oxford's bland affability into believing him well-inclined towards the Jacobite cause. Plunket confidently wrote to Ellis on the subject:

> the partners [Parliament] will carry on their business smoothly and roundly, with little or no noise, but with caution, and manage that of the sape [succession] as they did the portion, and take their own time to do it, and it will be left entirely to them. This I know to be Overton's [Oxford's] mind, and his scheme which will be put in execution, when things are ripe for it, which will be before the new partners meet.[54]

Netterville was more guarded, but to the same effect:

> I cannot change my opinion of him I have named [Oxford]. On Mr Jenkins' [James's] account, he would engage all; but keeps the balance in his own power, to give a turn the way he thinks will prove the most suitable to continue for his own private account.[55]

That the network's reports did influence the views of the Jacobite leadership is apparent from the effect this unanimity of opinion had on the Jacobite Court's view of Oxford. In spite of the fact that he had not made a single overt gesture in their favour, Berwick could still write to James in October 1712 with touching faith in Oxford's sincerity:

> I do realy believe that they [the Government] meane well for your interest, and that they intend to act with all speed immaginable, but they are so afraid of its being known before the conclusion of the peace, that they are unwilling of trusting anybody with the secret.[56]

Though the reports to St Germain were of mixed quality, they do seem to have been effective in shaping the leadership's appreciation of events and personalities in Britain. There were occasional gross errors, such as Stafford solemnly informing Gualterio in October 1712 that General James Stanhope had defected to the Tories, but a reasonable understanding of the mainstream of British politics could have been built up from them, albeit with partisan leanings.[57] As with most sets of reports, what mattered in the end was the reader's preconceptions, and hence his interpretation of what was presented.

Theoretically, the Jacobites had two ways of achieving their ends. One was by a Parliamentary restoration, in which the Parliamentary Jacobites would necessarily play a leading role, the other was by a successful invasion or rebellion. How real this choice was depended on the military capabilities of the Jacobites' organisation. These were not tested until 1715, and then under an entirely different set of circumstances. During the period 1710 to 1714 it was generally assumed that the French would mount and support any invasion, with the Jacobite Court only being called on to provide officer cadres and James at the head.[58] Though there were occasional interludes of doubt as to France's ability to give such support, independent Jacobite military planning was not usually conceived of as necessary during this period.[59] The earliest discernible show of concern lest the French might not be forthcoming at all was as late as April 1713, when Nairne wrote to Straton enquiring about the acceptability of such an attempt:

> he [James] desires you to take the prudentest methods you can to let them [Scots Jacobites] know that in case Mr Dumbar [Queen Anne] breaks [dies], and that nothing be done by him to secure Knowles debt [James's restoration], he is resolved to have immediat recourse to Mr Stuart [Scotland] and trust his law suite entirely into his hands, but that he can bring no effects with him of any kind, I mean neither wine nor brandy [munitions or money] for he deals no more in these commoditys, nor can his factors Aiselby or Masterson [France or Spain] come with him for they are both sick, so he'l only bring a few servants with him. He would be glad therefore to know whether he'l be wellcom in that condition to Stuarts relations.[60]

St Germain's concern is not even certain to be genuine at this point, as the letter was sent at a time when the Scots were feeling resentful at what they considered to be undue attention to the English Jacobites at their expense, so that it may have been nothing more than a placebo.[61] By early 1714, however, more serious consideration was being given to the possibility of an independent attempt. The Jacobite Court favoured a scheme proposed by the Jacobite M.P. Colonel George Douglas: he was to raise a Scots regiment for the French (and presumably on occasion Jacobite) service, and an entry on a memorandum from this period — 'none of those who came lately from Scot: desird ye K: to come with a Page: they all requird ye D. of B[erwick] some mony, & wt armes they could ... Procure promises to manage ye D of B' — shows that the Jacobite Court was trying to give itself a military option.[62] In March Berwick received permission from the French Government to accompany James, should an independent attempt be made to invade Britain.[63]

The lack of progress in the political sphere in Britain soon engendered a more elaborate plan once the initial step away from purely political measures had been taken. In June Berwick first broached the idea of using German mercenaries to stiffen the raw recruits expected to flock to the Jacobite army:

> What I writt to your Majesty last post about, was about endeavouring to gett M. Alexandre [troops] from M. Allain's house [Germany], for certainly that first gentleman would be much the properest person to employ in M. Raucourt's [James's] affaires, either for having a fair tryall at Alencon [England] against M. Horne [Hanover] or even for facilitating M. Albert [Queen Anne] to settle his concerns according to our desire.[64]

Hooke, whom Berwick had consulted, thought it was possible, and proposed to use his German and Russian connections to gain the Czar's support for the scheme. The main problem, as Berwick saw it, was financial. He accordingly consulted Torcy, who was eventually persuaded to approach Louis XIV for funds, while Berwick himself resolved to ask Philip V for money while in Spain.[65]

Hooke did set out for Germany, as Dicconson mentions his expenses as still outstanding at the end of 1714, but nothing came of the scheme before Anne's death in August.[66] It is actually difficult to think of any German state (including Denmark, which Hooke himself favoured) that would have been willing to incur Hanoverian wrath for such pay as the exiled Stuarts could offer, or how such troops would have been got to Britain. Put together, it looks as though Berwick was once again looking to the French to provide port, ships and diplomatic cover for the enterprise.

Within Britain preparations for a rising in Scotland in the event of Anne's death were put in train only after February 1714. Brigadier William Mackintosh ('Old Borlum') returned to the Highlands from France in March with commissions for the Highlands' Jacobite chieftains, and Berwick told James in late February that he was soliciting men and money from Torcy for a Scots expedition.[67] On receipt of the news of Anne's death many of the Jacobite chieftains suddenly went hunting and were unobtainable for a time, and the earl of Breadalbane promptly retired to his most defensible castle, Kailholm, presumably to await the arrival of James at the head of a French army.[68] James undoubtedly enjoyed a great deal of popular support in Scotland, as shown by the scale of the celebrations on his birthday (10 June) in Edinburgh and Leith in 1712 and 1713, but it does not seem likely that such casual enthusiasm could have supported a serious rising such as the '15 without having first been hardened by the Whig purges and impeachments which followed the Hanoverian succession.[69]

Ireland was never seriously considered as a target for invasion, or as a place to begin a Jacobite insurrection. Although there would certainly have been a great deal of popular support for either of these, an Irish rising would have cost the exiled Stuarts the support of their Protestant sympathisers in Britain, without which the British throne was unattainable.[70] James II's debacle in Ireland in the 1689-90 invasion and insurrection had shown that Ireland could not be held without Britain, so that Britain became both the most logical and the most expedient target thereafter.

An independent Jacobite military option seems only to have been actively considered as late as 1714, in frustration at the lack of progress in the political sphere. Even then, flaws and discrepancies in the plans show that the French were still being looked to for financial and diplomatic help. It would appear, therefore, that although the Jacobite leadership became keen enough on the idea of creating an independent military option of some kind, they were unable to do so. This in turn meant that they were forced back into reliance on political action, which meant that the Parliamentary Jacobites remained the only effective weapon the exiled Stuarts possessed with which to achieve their aims.

So far, Jacobite divisions have only been noted, not explored. Apart from the national division already touched on, there was a religious divide, as well as the inevitable personal rivalries of any eighteenth-century Court. All of these were influenced by the position the Jacobites in Parliament took, for as there was no military option, these were the adherents to whom the Jacobite Court had to at least appear to pay heed. In turn, their involvement in these factional pressures produced repercussions which affected them, in the form of official directives from St Germain and attempts by the Jacobite Court to evade the necessity of compliance with their wishes. Even when they were not directly involved, as in the case of personal rivalries at the Court, the parties concerned could only hope for success if they were acceptable to this group.

The principal division at St Germain was religious. From the end of 1710, when the last significant attempt to convince the French to support an invasion of Scotland failed, the dominance of the Roman Catholics at the Jacobite Court began to be thought of as counter-productive.[71] At that time Sir William Ellis was the only Protestant of any importance at St Germain. Since there was no longer any hope of French help except if France faced a dire emergency, the emphasis in policy at the Jacobite Court was obliged to shift towards winning political support in Britain. It was also patently obvious that a Roman Catholic dominance at the Court was distasteful, politically and personally, to many of those St Germain hoped to use. From late 1710 to late 1713 ostensible Catholic control of the Jacobite network was slowly eroded, culminating in the fall of Middleton. Berwick replaced him in practice, but Higgons's installation as figurehead Secretary of State ensured that Protestants were seen to be favoured.

The displacement of Catholic control of the Jacobite network by the Protestant lobby occurred largely as a by-product of the campaign by the British Protestant Jacobites, principally those in Parliament, to oblige James to convert to Anglicanism. Charles Leslie initiated this campaign with an explicit hint in a memorial of April 1711: 'Je ne veux rien cacher, la seule objection contre le Roy est celle de religion, et cela ne luy pas impute comme sa faute, mais comme son malheur et le notre'.[72] St Germain perceived his meaning clearly enough and returned a polite refusal in a style and with a format which was to characterise such replies until long after 1714, and is worth seeing at length as it summarises the consistent attitude of the Jacobite Court to the question:

> In answer to yours, I cannot at this distance, and in my present circumstances, enter into disputes of religion; but those of the Church of England have no reason to doubt my favour and protection, after the early assurances I gave them in my instructions, bearing date 3rd March 1702, which you have seen, and I am resolved to hold good. Experience fully sheweth, that the Crown was never struck at but she [the Church of England] also felt the blow; and though some of her chief professors have failed in their duty, we must not measure the principles of a Church by the actions of some particulars.
>
> Plain dealing is best in all things, especially in matters of religion; and as I am resolved never to dissemble ... so I shall never tempt others to do it; and as I am well satisfied of the truth of my own religion, yet I shall never look worse upon any persons, because in that they choose to differ with me; nor shall I refuse, in due time and place, to hear what they may have to say upon this subject. But they must not take it ill if I use the same liberty I allow others, to adhere to the religion which I, in my conscience, think the best; and I may reasonably expect that Liberty of conscience for myself, which I deny to none.[73]

Though this temporarily silenced overt demands for conversion, the issue inevitably revived as the Jacobite Court became more dependent on Protestant British Jacobites to show its goodwill and strength to those with whom it was negotiating. The Protestant British Jacobites, particularly those in Parliament, gradually realised the advantage this gave them in pressing their demands, and duly made what use of it they could. The change is apparent by the time the next such request occurred, under the guise of a plea for dissimulation by the otherwise circumspect Netterville, but now directly from the Parliamentary Jacobites:

> the best part of the gentry, and half the nobility, are resolved to have the King; the parliament would do it in a year, if it could be believed he had changed his religion. They would not impose it, but would have it reported, to give them a handle: for to change, on that account, would render him unworthy of wearing what he has so got; but they tell me, they do not desire it to be done, only said to be done.[74]

St Germain replied to this request in a manner which was to become customary: it ignored it. A glimmer of unease at the revival of the issue so soon is discernible, however, in Nairne's repetition, in letters to Menzies, Straton and St Amand, that no Jesuits would be accompanying James to Bar-le-Duc.[75] But a more explicit response was made necessary by the duke of Buckingham's letter bearing Queen Anne's response to a Jacobite approach through him:

> I would have Harry [James] remember he is not the first of his family who have thought a good estate worth changing an opinion for, and ten thousand pounds a year is a pretty thing for a young fellow to play withal; but if his scruples are so

very strong, that he cannot go this length, let him endeavour to make his uncle [Queen Anne] believe at least, that he is in himself desirous to come back, but is ashamed, lest the world should think he changes his religion for an estate, which he will hardly get quietly, if at all, without it.... Tell him likewise, and I have pretty good means to know it, that my brother [Anne] and his best servants are now so angry at Dick's [Hanover's] late insolence, that if Harry will put it in their power to help him, they will do all they can for him.[76]

St Germain at length replied in August with a pamphlet setting out the advantages which would accrue to the Church of England from a Catholic King. An open letter repeating James's reasons for not wishing to convert was also draughted but not sent, and Nairne bluntly told Menzies in September that James did not wish to discuss the matter.[77] Even such a firm response could not lessen the pressure this time, and intermittent refusals, and instructions to suppress such demands, punctuate Nairne's letters with the principal agents for the rest of the year.[78]

By late 1712 the constant harping on the subject began to have its first discernible impact at the Jacobite Court. Berwick, irritated by what he felt was Protestant bigotry, advised the removal of Ellis from St Germain, so as to deny Protestant Jacobite visitors a sympathetic channel near Paris, 'for he is alwayse full of politick and will be medling in affaires he ought not'.[79] Ellis certainly was abetting such demands, as he explained in detail to Lewis Innes in January 1713 that the Tory demand for conversion stemmed from their belief that Charles II was a secret Catholic long before his deathbed conversion in 1685. He then covered his actions by solemnly admonishing the astonished head of the Scots College for attempting to convert James, repeating 'that the King should be no more teazed upon that subject'.[80] At the end of January the following year, Richard Hamilton, long attached to the Jacobite Court, was peremptorily dismissed for his effort on behalf of the Protestant lobby, even though he may have been directed to exert himself by the Abbé Gaultier.[81]

By the time of Hamilton's dismissal, it was increasingly apparent that the Protestant lobby was blaming Middleton for James's refusal to conform, and demands for his dismissal began to arrive.[82] In response, Queen Mary and Berwick gave him their unflinching support, which was enough to sustain him through this first crisis.[83] This could only be a temporary reprieve, though, as the implications of the policy he was pursuing were his departure from office, and the Protestant Jacobites saw him as their arch-enemy, which made him the prime candidate for a scapegoat if one was required.[84] Meanwhile, allegations and innuendoes directed against Middleton continued to arrive in a steady stream. Captain William Philips, Sir Thomas Hanmer's secretary, having implied many were afraid to trust James because of Middleton's presence, was equally venomous when questioned by viscount Galmoy on what the general opinion was of Middleton: 'He answered, that he was in very good esteeme, and thoght very capable of businesse, but that since he changed his religion, they had not soe good an opinion of him'. In another interview, Philips advised James to 'shew kindness to protestants, and have as many of them about him as his present condition will allow', and to ram home the point he later told Innes, 'by way of exclamation, how many ways were taken to mortify honest Sir William Ellis, and to keep him from the King'.[85] Ellis was now the Protestant candidate to replace Middleton, and though he continued to pay lip service to the official reluctance even to discuss the issue, such rumours as Philips mentioned can have continued to circulate only with his connivance.[86] Despite official discouragement the stream of requests for conversion continued to flow in, culminating in August with what appeared to be a hint to convert from Oxford himself. Nairne, dismayed, wrote back demanding further details:

> You say that Hales and Johnson [Buckingham and Mar?] have strong wishes and strongest views that way, but do's the story say that Mr Hugh's [Oxford's] free thought went that length to advise John [James] to comply with these strong views and wishes by dissimulating or abandoning; this seems to bee insinuated, but is certainly a calumny upon Hughs, invented to John and Robin's [England's] prejudice, and therefore you are desir'd to explain the dark hints you give upon this subject by telling us plainly how farr it is said that Mr Hughs carry'd this free advice of his concerning Mr Renny [religion] to which they so unjustly attribute his misfortune.[87]

A spate of attempts to highlight James's natural toleration, and zealous compliance with a ministerial request to order the Jacobites to support Tory candidates in the general election, accompanied this.[88] The Jacobite Court plainly hoped these measures would avert such a demand, or else soften the impact of James's inevitable refusal. But in the event, Oxford denied any such wish, in a letter in his own hand according to the relieved Nairne.[89]

However, the decision had been taken by then to give the Protestant Jacobites a douceur to ameliorate their disappointment at their continued failure to persuade James to convert. James was very loth to dismiss Middleton to provide this, as he feared (correctly) that this would simply lead to redoubled pressure on him to convert, but French pressure finally persuaded him:

> A l'egard de Mylord Middleton malgre les raisons qui se presentent en foulle a mon esprit pour le retenir sa fidelite inviolable sa capacité, son experience et ses longs services, les reflexions que le monde pourroit faire en me voyant abandonner un serviteur si fidele a l'importunité et a l'injustice de ses ennemis qui peutestre ne s'arresteront point encore la, en voyant la succes de leur premier projet malgre dis je toutt ces raisons, je suis cependent tellement convaincu de la sagesse du Roy et ma defference pour ses conseils est si entiere que je me determine a les suivre...[90]

The removal of Middleton also had the advantage of removing someone whom Oxford was by now insinuating represented the main obstacle to direct negotiations with the Jacobite Court.[91] Higgons ostensibly took over the running of the Jacobite organisation, symbolising the Protestant success. In fact, as already noted, Berwick took over the business of the Secretary of

State's office in practice, which rendered the Protestant 'victory' more than a little ironic, as he appears to have had far more reservations about their value to the cause than Middleton. It is significant that it was Berwick who first attempted to find an independent military option for the Jacobite leadership, so that they would not be so absolutely committed to the political sphere alone. His attitude is made abundantly clear in a letter he wrote to James describing Hanmer's secretary, Philips:

> lequel est un homme d'espirit me paroit fort zelé pour V. M. mais parle comme tous les autres de sa sorte et de sa cotterie, les Lesle les Floyds, etc de maniere que je ne trouve pas qu'il y aye grand fond a faire sur luy plus que sur les autres, a la verité il est bon de luy marquer de la bonté et de la reconnoissance pour son zele, mais je doute qu'il faille luy fier de secret, car il m'a la mine de tout dire a ces autres messieurs ses amys, y compris le Chevalier Ellis.[92]

St Germain's increasing reliance on the Protestant Jacobites, principally in Parliament, due to its inability to operate in any sphere other than the political after 1710, gave them, for the first time since Middleton's conversion, considerable political weight at the exiled Court. They chose to use this to try and effect James's conversion, but failed. Instead, no doubt aided by Oxford's vague promises of direct negotiations when Middleton was dismissed, they brought about the fall of the despised apostate and his replacement by a Protestant Secretary of State. Berwick's succeeding *de facto* might make this appear a hollow victory, but in reality (given James's absolute refusal to convert) this was the best they could hope to achieve as long as they failed to penetrate James's inner circle: the ultimate centre of power in the Jacobite organisation. This they were not to achieve until the Jacobite earl of Dunbar's heyday.

The religious prejudices of the British Protestant Jacobites altered the nature of the organisation as their value to it increased. But this group was itself divided along national lines between English and Scots: a division which in turn centred on the pursuit of factional interest within the organisation's upper echelons. Jacobite political policy was profoundly Anglocentric, and however much this could be justified from past experience, was duly resented by the Scots and Irish Jacobites.[93] As in the military sphere, the Irish interest carried very little weight at the exiled Court, but the Scots had to be conciliated as they (or rather the Jacobite clans) were usually felt to be the mainstay of James's hopes if the Jacobite political initiative at Westminster failed to procure his restoration.

Consequently, it was a rude shock when, just as his position came under increasing pressure from the Protestant lobby and Melfort's latest intrigue, the Scots Jacobites declared they could no longer work under the direction of someone who favoured England and the Union, and, they implied, might even be a secret supporter of Hanover. Middleton responded with a soothing letter from James, explaining the position and justifying himself:

> You was and are still desir'd to assure all Knowls relations [Jacobites] that he is very sensible of Stuart's [Scotland's] kindness and of the particular marks he has

given him thereof all along that he could send no directions to him of late about his affaires because he is in the dark himself and has been advis'd by his best friends to ly quiet and not to say nor do any thing till he sees clearer what Dumbar [Queen Anne] and Gooldings successor [next Parliament] intend to do, so he hopes Stuart will not attribute this necessary prudence of Knowls [James] to a neglect or want of friendship and confidence in him.[94]

What made Middleton vulnerable to this kind of hysterical nationalist malice was that in his supra-national devotion to the Stuart cause he tended to be a little too dispassionate when it came to subjects of particularist interest. Thus part of the Scots diatribe against him may have been based on knowledge of the sentiments behind a memorandum he sent James in 1711 in which it does appear that he favoured both England and the Union, for the sake of Stuart Government convenience, even at Scots' expense:

So that all considered I think it remains still a probleme, and as such I leave it to the King himself to decide, whether sixty one sure votes in a Brittish Parliament may not be more useful to the Crown, than a barren independancy when experience shews how doubtful it is whether in troublesome time they'l appear for or against the King, since the same fanatical party [Presbyterians] and other influencing motives which have prevail'd in that Kingdom more than once may prevaile yet again.[95]

The Scots Jacobites could not bring Middleton down on their own, but they could and did add to the pressure already on James to remove him.

There were other factions at St Germain besides the Scots and Protestant groups, but they possessed so little political interest as to be virtually invisible for most of the time. The campaign against Middleton in 1713 was a rare exception to this, and these groups duly appeared to throw what little weight they possessed in the scales against him. The Irish at St Germain felt much the same about Middleton as the Scots, presumably on the same grounds, and took the opportunity offered by his increasing difficulties to encourage the Protestant lobby in its denunciations of him:

They [the Irish] say Jonathan's [James's] friends desire this removal: these good friends have of late found themselves mightily disappointed in their threatening Jonathan, as they have done, unless he complyed, or as they term it, temporized in point of religion. It is very probable, they think Mr Massey [Middleton] has contributed to his being fixed in that point, and may, therefore have been glad of any pretext to get him removed.[96]

An even less prominent group who joined the attack on Middleton were the English Roman Catholics. They appear to have turned against him because they too believed he was obstructing James's temporisation, which, very pragmatically, they regarded as their best hope of a *de facto* toleration.[97] Prompt action by Middleton seems to have removed them from the lists. In a letter to Menzies in February, Nairne revealed Middleton's awareness of their intent:

> I told him no ground was given from hence for the Colleges [English Roman Catholics] jealousy against him, Robert [Middleton] having kept no correspondence with the College since the advice Abram [Menzies] gave of the proposal they intended to make concerning Renny [religion].[98]

This completely disconcerted them, and Innes reported a few days later that they were denying ever having intended to press for James's conversion, and that as regards Middleton all the plotters were 'so much ashamed that they will disown their ever having meant a removal'.[99]

The contribution of such minor factions to the Protestant lobby's success was no doubt slight. However, their appearance and return to obscurity in the context of the campaign against Middleton amply illustrate the significance that was by now attached to the views of the Protestant Jacobites throughout the Jacobite movement.

It is an old cliché to emphasise the personal nature of much of eighteenth-century politics. Like many clichés, however, it is inescapably valid, and the Jacobite Court was as prone as any to the problems of personal animosity between those in authority. At St Germain the main clash of ambitions was between Middleton and the duke of Perth. The rivalry between the two men extended to almost every sphere of Jacobite activity, in most of which Perth felt Middleton was actively excluding him.[100]

Since there was so little 'business' at the Jacobite Court for the various officers of state to do, those posts that still had a function tended to be jealously guarded.[101] Perth built up a separate correspondence with Scotland by 1710, an area over which he had no pretence at jurisdiction, and in that year made a further bid to encroach on Middleton's preserve by backing the approaches of a Scotsman named Ogilvie to the French Government for support of an alternative plan to that proposed by Middleton, for an invasion and rising.[102] Out of well-grounded suspicion, or pique, Middleton swiftly procured Queen Mary's agreement and wrote to Torcy denouncing Ogilvie as a spy (which he was), and urging his arrest:

> The Queen believes it will be necessary to send him to the Bastile. He shall be sent to you, as if it were to give you an account of his business. He will have a letter from me to introduce him, in order that you may dispose of him as you choose. But I hope you will reflect upon the mischief which his return may occasion to a number of honest men.[103]

Middleton was gambling that James would reach the same conclusions when he met Ogilvie as he had, and in the event was proved right:

> he [Ogilvie] pretends to have seen Ld Athol, Bradalbin, etc, and they say that if the King of France cannot be brought to help them, they will do my business themselves, provided I come to them; but then he brings no other security of what he sayes but his own word, and ample credenshul from Ld Drummond [Perth's son], whom he affirms to be sent by the rest... This man is certainly employed by the government to betray my friends.[104]

Perth was not even informed of the collapse of his scheme, as in August he was still writing to Middleton recommending Ogilvie as a courier.[105]

Perth emerged from this farce with little credit, and refrained from challenging Middleton again until 1713, when Melfort used his agents in London to try and persuade the British Jacobites to communicate with Perth rather than Middleton (his own hopes having been summarily dashed earlier).[106] This intrigue made little impact, though, as few of the British Jacobites seem to have known much about Perth. Netterville recorded of Fingall, one of the leaders of the Jacobites in London, and hence one of the main targets of the intrigue, 'he laughs with me at that'.[107]

Perth's attempts to oust Middleton were pointless, as he obviously planned to succeed him as Secretary of State. Given the burgeoning influence of the Protestant Jacobites, this was a hopeless ambition. Having ousted the despised but competent apostate Middleton, they were hardly likely to support the appointment of an incompetent apostate to succeed him.

By far the most serious division in the Jacobite network had nothing to do with religion, nationalism, or personalities. This was the gradual detachment of the leadership from its supporters in Britain by the lure of direct negotiations with the leaders of the Tory party. Dazzled by the glittering prize Oxford seemed to be offering, the Jacobite Court neglected to reinsure by using its Parliamentary strength. Though it is unlikely that serious concessions could have been extracted, at least the Jacobites would have found out earlier just how sincere the Tory leadership was in its offers to them.

The process began in 1711 when Gaultier first approached the Jacobite Court with promises of restoration from the British Government. Berwick recalled:

> En effet il me dit qu'il avoit ordre de me parler sur les affaires du Roi Jacques, et de concerter avec moi les moyens de parvenir à son rétablissement, mais qu'avant d'entrer en matiere, il avoit ordre d'exiger promesse; 1/ que personne à Saint Germain n'en auroit connoissance, pas meme la Reine; 2/ que la Reine Anne jouiroit tranquillement de la Couronne sa vie durant, moyennent qu'elle en assurat le possession à son frere apres son mort; 3/ que l'on donneroit les assurances suffisantes pour la conservation de la Religion Anglicane et des libertés du Royaume.[108]

The restriction of this information was ignored as far as Queen Mary was concerned, and the other members of the Jacobite leadership were soon in the secret as well: Middleton by 1712, Dicconson by 1713 and Perth by 1714.[109] The importance these negotiations quickly assumed is apparent from the alacrity with which Middleton leapt to Gaultier's defence when criticism arose at the Papal Court of the terms he was negotiating in Britain, as inimical to Catholicism:

> Le Roy mon maitre ayant eté informé que le Pape s'est laisse persuader que l'Abbe Gaultier a travaille a un Traitté contraire et prejudiciable a la Religion et

au retablissement de S. M. Brit.. S. M. prie V. Emce d'assurer S. S. qu'elle est tres perusade que cet Abbé n'a rien negocie en Ang[leter]re au prejudice ni de la religion ni de son service, mais qu'au contraire il luy a rendu services on ce pays là, et qu'elle a tout lieu d'etre convaincüe qu'il est tres bien intentionné pour elle, et fort zele pour les interests de la religion.[110]

Middleton offhandedly finished the letter by remarking that he would not forward a newsletter as the French knew as much as he. This would normally have been a damning admission, had it not been patently untrue. Middleton was pursuing political connexions in Britain, orchestrating the next session's Parliamentary activity by the Jacobites, and was obviously in receipt of a quantity of 'analysis' of British political events which would have had considerable interest for the Jacobite candidate for the Protectorship of England and James's 'maistre de mes affaires a Rome'.[111] As far as is known, Middleton had no particular antipathy towards Gualterio, so what was really being expressed was a lack of concern about political events in Britain. If restricted to Middleton alone, the trait would have been serious enough, but the correspondence of the entire Jacobite leadership is riddled with the same lack of concern. The reasoning behind this attitude is obvious: since the business of James's restoration was being handled at the highest level, that of Berwick and James, other ways of pursuing Jacobite aims were merely auxiliary.

The gist of all the Jacobite Court's directives to Britain, from the end of 1711 to February 1714, was to keep quiet and follow the ministry's lead. The network was kept functioning, and its information was perused and undoubtedly influenced the Court's view of events, but its potential was disregarded as irrelevant to the negotiations in hand. The danger of relying on a single route to their aims only dawned upon the Jacobite leaders quite late. Perth wrote to Gualterio in dismay in June 1714 after he had heard Queen Anne was ill again:

il est vray que l'on la croit un peu soulagé mais pas tout a fait hors de danger et dans l'estat ou il se trouve il est a plaindre, il est sans avoir un partie beau lieu; sans armes; sans argent; et sans un correspondence en Angleterre capable de luy conseiler ce qu'il falloit faire dans un telle conjoncture; sa plusieur retraitte (jusqu'a ce que ses fideles sujets en Ecosse pouvoit s'assemblé autour de say Majte pour le sauver des insultes de ces troupes qui sont en Ecosse sous les ordres du Gouvernement present) vient de la manquer par la mort de ma soeur la Comtesse d'Erroll veuve de feu Connetable Hereditaire d'Ecosse, et son fils est actuellement en France. Il y a un act de pretendue parlement contre sa Majte que ceux qui avoit la toute puissance entre leur mains n'ont jamais annullé quoy que dans leur pouvoir de l'avoir fait. Si la situation des affaires de sa Majte ne sont pas en tres mauvais estat l'on peut facilement juger. Mais si la Psse [Queen Anne] pouva eschaper cette fois, l'espere que l'on aura soin de ne pas estre si a l'improvist.[112]

It appears that Perth was as yet unaware of Berwick's attempts to give the Jacobites a military option, but in general he was correct. It was too late by this time to rearrange the whole bent of Jacobite policy, and Berwick's absence in Spain from the end of June redoubled the organisation's inertia, reducing it to the role of an impotent onlooker on events in Britain in August. All that was left to Perth was to lament to Gualterio:

> Mon chagrin mieux que je me puis l'exprimer pour moy je croyay que l'on avoit preparé un projet de ce que le Roy devroit faire quand ce cas seroit arrive, mais rien de cela. L'on se flattoit que ce Tresorier d'Angleterre avoit des designs pour servir le Roy, que sa soeur l'aimoit, et qu'il avoit un partie capable de soutenir ses interests en cas de besoign. Mais je suis persuadé que le Tresorier a trompé l'Abbe Gaultier, et l'Abbe a amuse Monsr de Torcy et le Roy mon maitre s'estant reposé sur la Cour de France pour son interest, a negligé toute les autres moyens. Et nous voyla perdue sans resource.[113]

The Jacobite Parliamentary group was the main operational arm of a very cumbersome organisation: the Jacobite network's structure was so rigid that its own leaders often had to bypass it in order to achieve their ends (a custom open to abuse in Court intrigues); the nature of Court politics at St Germain was such that the decentralisation of power from the exiled Court to Britain, which would have minimised the dangers of interception and the inevitable delays in decision-making, was inconceivable; and the piecemeal nature of Jacobite organisation in Britain tended to create rivalries between agents and adherents to exacerbate the inevitable frictions of an organisation already composed of antagonistic elements. Parliamentary Jacobitism was an integral part of the rest of Jacobite activity in Britain (mainly the collection and transmission of information), and in consequence suffered from the same feuds and jealousies. As the Jacobite leaders were forced to adopt political measures from 1711, the Parliamentary group, as a result, became of increasing importance. Its response to this was to try and alter the nature of the organisation to favour itself, by converting James. It failed in this but secured the palliative of at least nominal Protestant control of the network. In reaction to this and the apparent stalling of its political initiative by 1714, the leadership began to try to reorientate the organisation towards an independent military option should the need arise. This alteration had barely got underway by the time of the death of Queen Anne, so that the Jacobites were unable to do anything more than look on as the Hanoverians peacefully succeeded to the throne.

The Parliamentary Jacobites first came to dominate the Jacobite network in Britain between 1710 and 1714. Yet, at the same time, they were increasingly estranged from their leaders — to whom they nonetheless remained obedient — who chose to use them merely as a douceur in the 'negotiations' with which they were engrossed. The leadership's ignorance of the Parliamentary Jacobite group's potential was the crucial failing which led to this, but even had they been aware of it, the organisation's overcentralised structure would have precluded sustained, and hence effective, use of its Parliamentary sympathisers without drastic reforms first.

NOTES

1. Gualterio 46495, f. 43: 31 Jan. 1714 ns.
2. Stuart, i, 287-329.
3. *Ibid.*, i, 329-30.
4. Carte 212, f. 26: Nairne to Menzies ('Abram'), 3 Mar. 1712 ns; f. 46: Nairne to Straton ('Scot'), 10 Dec. 1712 ns; Cambridge University Library, Stuart Papers microfilm 1215/2: undated warrant.
5. Macpherson, ii, 295-7, 313-5, etc: 'White' (whom I infer from circumstantial evidence to have been John Netterville) to Ellis; 386-7, etc: Ferguson ('Lilly') to Middleton; 309-11, etc: Plunket ('Rogers') to Ellis; 327-31, etc: Buckingham to Middleton; Carte 180, ff. 286-96: Charles Leslie to Middleton.
6. Carte 212, f. 22: Nairne to Menzies, 29 Nov. 1711 ns; Lockhart, i, 368-9.
7. Carte 212, f. 46: Nairne to Straton, 10 Dec. 1712 ns.
8. Lockhart, i, 401-10.
9. Carte 212, f. 15: 18 Dec. 1710 ns.
10. Stuart, i, 285-6: Berwick to James, 15 Dec. 1713 ns.
11. Macpherson, ii, 148-9: Hooke's instructions, Apr. 1710; Stuart, i, 274: Queen Mary to Dicconson, 31 Aug. 1713 ns.
12. Macpherson, ii, 387-94: Plunket to Middleton (Ellis's extracts), 9-27 Feb. 1713; Carte 212, f. 24: Nairne to Menzies, 14 Feb. 1712 ns.
13. Macpherson, ii, 306-7: Ferguson to Ellis, 9 May 1712; ii, 307-8: Mrs. Jean Murray ('John Scrimger') to Middleton, 9 May 1712; ii, 398-400: Plunket to Ellis, 7 Apr. 1713; ii, 427-8: Netterville to Middleton, 7 Aug. 1713.
14. *Ibid.*, ii, 291-2: 10 Mar. 1712.
15. *Ibid.*, ii, 313-5: Netterville to Middleton, 12 May 1712. *Bol. Corr.*, ii, 146-8n: 'Extracts delivered to the Committee in Council by the Lord President [Buckingham]', 20 Mar. 1712, confirms Netterville's story.
16. BL, Portland Loan 29/135/2: Ferguson to Oxford, 22 June 1713.
17. Macpherson, ii, 312-3: Plunket to Ellis, 11 May 1712; ii, 424-7: Netterville to Middleton, 30 July 1713; ii, 233: Middleton to Menzies, 8 Nov, 1711 ns.
18. Carte 212, f. 48: Nairne to Straton, 25 Jan. 1713 ns.
19. *Ibid.*, f. 34: Nairne to Hacket, 13 June 1712 ns; f. 45b: Nairne to St Amand, 14 Nov. 1712 ns; Stuart, i, 251-2: Berwick to James, 20 Nov. 1712 ns.
20. Gualterio 31257, f. 129: 4 Sept. 1712 ns.
21. Gualterio 31258, f. 36: 8 Feb. 1712 ns; Carte 238, f. 228: Middleton to Boine, 28 Jan. 1712 ns.
22. *Bol Corr.*, i, 189-90: St John to Lord Raby (Ambassador at the Hague), 6/8 May 1711; i. 180: St John to the Earl of Orrery (Ambassador Extraordinary to the Hague and Governor of the Spanish Netherlands), 1 May 1711; *The Letters of Henry St John to the Earl of Orrery, 1709-11*, ed. H.T. Dickinson (Camden Soc., 4th Ser., xxvi., 1975), pp.153-4, 164-5, 172-3, 181-2: St. John to Orrery, 20 Mar., 6 and 10 Apr., 22 May and 20 July 1711; BL, Add. MSS. 31135 (Strafford Papers), ff. 345, 399-400: John Drummond to St John, 7 May and 13 June 1711 ns; ff. 367, 384: Raby to St John, 22 May and 2 June 1711 ns.
23. Stuart, i. 280-1, 284: Berwick to James, 25 Oct. and 10 Dec. 1713 ns.
24. Carte 211, f. 324: Dicconson's accounts for the year 1715-16; Baschet 200, f. 311: James to Torcy, 23 Dec. 1712 ns.

25. Baschet 197, f. 363: Queen Mary to Torcy, 2 Aug. 1711 ns; Macpherson, ii, 184: [Lady Middleton] to [Middleton], 2 June [1711] ns.

26. Carte 212, f. 45: Nairne to Menzies, 4 and 14 Nov. 1712 ns; f. 46: Nairne to Straton, 10 Dec. 1712 ns.

27. Carte 211, f. 320: John Fisher's account for his trip to Scotland, 1714. For Fisher's instructions, see: HMC, *Hodgkin MSS.*, pp.225-6.

28. Carte 180, ff. 255-63: Middleton to Torcy, 29 Aug. 1710 ns; ff. 228-9: Middleton to the Estates-General, 12 Mar. 1710 ns.

29. Stuart, i, 247-328; Gualterio 31255, f. 11: James to Gualterio, 23 July 1714 ns.

30. Macpherson, ii, 523-4: Envoy at Vienna to the Duke of Lorraine, 22 Feb. 1714 ns; ii, 524-5: Lorraine to his Envoy at Vienna, Mar. 1714.

31. Bodl., MSS. Add. D 26, ff. 454-94: Hooke's report on his negotiations in Saxony, 1712.

32. Berwick, *Mémoires du Maréchal de Berwick* (Switzerland, 1778), p.127.

33. See pp.93-4, 101-3.

34. Macpherson, ii, 234: Nairne to Menzies, 19 Nov. 1711 ns; Carte 212, f. 49: Middleton to Menzies, 13 Feb. 1713 ns.

35. Stuart, i, 299-300: Berwick to James, 21 Feb. 1714 ns.

36. Carte 212, ff. 29, 33, 56: Nairne to Menzies, 3 Apr. and 26 May 1712 ns and 22 June 1713 ns.

37. Lockhart, i, 417, 437.

38. Carte 212, f. 53: Nairne to Menzies, 27 Apr. 1713 ns.

39. Stuart, i, 250: Berwick to James, 4 Nov. 1712 ns.

40. Carte 212, f. 44: Nairne to Menzies, 21 Oct. 1712 ns; AAE 248, f. 247: 'Extrait d'une lettre d'Ang[leter]re', 10 Mar. 1713; f. 277: Butler to Torcy, 13 Mar. 1713.

41. Stuart, i, 260: Berwick to James, 28 Mar. 1713 ns; Macpherson, ii, 400-1: Ellis to Plunket, 9 Apr. 1713 ns.

42. Macpherson, ii, 423-4, 424-7: Netterville to Middleton, 30 July 1713; ii, 428-30: Netterville to Ellis, Aug. 1713.

43. *Ibid.*, ii, 427-8: Netterville to Ellis, 7 Aug. 1713; ii, 424-7: Netterville to Middleton, 30 July 1713.

44. Stuart, i, 268: Berwick to James, 26 June 1713 ns.

45. Stuart, i, 274: Queen Mary to Dicconson, 31 Aug. 1713 ns.

46. Gualterio 46495, f. 140: Dempster to Gualterio, 12 Aug. 1714 ns.

47. Carte 212, ff. 17, 20, 32: 26 Feb. and 30 Aug. 1711 ns and 8 May 1712 ns.

48. Macpherson, ii, 449-50: 15 Nov. 1713.

49. Macpherson, ii, 424-7: Netterville to Middleton, 30 July 1713.

50. Macpherson, ii, 309-11, 311, 311-12, 317-18, 451-61: Plunket to Ellis and Middleton, May 1712 and Nov. 1713. For a full account of the evidence for such a conspiracy, see: E. Gregg, 'Marlborough in Exile, 1712-14', *Hist. Journal*, xv (1972), 593-618; Gaultier 139, ff. 248-60: Gaultier to Torcy, 28 Oct. 1713 ns.

51. Macpherson, ii, 404-5: Plunket to Ellis, 20 Apr. 1713.

52. Gaultier 122, p.34: Gaultier to Torcy, 28 May 1714 ns.

53. Macpherson, ii, 379-81: Netterville to Middleton, 26 Jan. 1713.

54. *Ibid.*, ii, 406-8: Plunket to Ellis, 24 Apr. 1713.

55. *Ibid.*, ii, 369-71: Netterville to Ellis, ep. arrived at St Germain 19 Jan. 1713 ns.

56. Stuart, i, 247-8: 23 Oct. 1712 ns.

57. Gualterio 31258, f. 185: 9 Oct. 1712 ns.

58. AAE, Mémoires et Documents 24, ff. 108-15: 'Responses Aux Questions proposées sur l'Ecosse', 23 Jan. 1710 ns; Stuart, i, 284-5, 287-8: Berwick to James, 12 and 24 Dec. 1713 ns.

59. Carte 212, f. 5: Middleton to Menzies, 30 Jan. 1710 ns; f. 12: Middleton to Leslie, 9 Oct. 1710 ns.

60. Carte 212, f. 55: 30 Apr. 1713 ns. A French translation of the Scots' response (which was largely negative) is in AAE 249, ff. 166-8.

61. Carte 212, f. 53: Nairne to Menzies and Straton, 27 Apr. 1713 ns.

62. Portland, v, 339: Douglas to the earl of Mar, 30 Sept. 1713 ns; Stuart, i, 284, 285-6: Berwick to James, 10 and 15 Dec. 1713 ns; Stuart Papers microfilm 1215/3/54: anonymous memo [early 1714].

63. Stuart, i. 305-6: Berwick to James, 4 Mar. 1714 ns.

64. *Ibid.*, i, 326-7: Berwick to James, 8 June 1714 ns.

65. *Ibid.*, i, 327-9: Berwick to James, 22 June 1714 ns.

66. Carte 211, ff. 318-19: Dicconson's accounts for the last six months of 1714; AAE 262, ff. 297-8: [Hooke] to Torcy, 31 July 1714 ns.

67. Hermitage HHH, ff. 213-14: 7 May 1714; Stuart, i, 299-300: Berwick to James, 21 Feb. 1714 ns.

68. W. Michael, *England Under George I: the Beginnings of the Hanoverian Dynasty* (1936), p.59.

69. Carte 238, ff. 233-5: Middleton to Torcy, 13 July 1712 ns; Hermitage FFF, ff. 259-60: 24 June 1712.

70. This did not stop the Irish lobby at St. Germain pressing for an attempt there, on the grounds that it stood the best chance of simple military success: Gualterio 20311, ff. 68-70; Bibliothèque Nationale, Paris, Nouvelles Acquisitions Françaises 7488 (Collection Renaudot), ff. 228-31.

71. Carte 212, f. 12: Middleton to Leslie, 9 Oct. 1710 ns.

72. Carte 180, f. 293: Leslie ('Lamb') to Middleton, Apr. 1711.

73. Carte 210, f. 409: open letter by James, 2 May 1711 ns, cited in M. Haile, *James Francis Edward: the Old Chevalier* (1907), p.111.

74. Macpherson, ii, 295-7: Netterville to Middleton, 18 Mar. 1712.

75. Carte 212, f. 32: 12 May 1712 ns.

76. Macpherson, ii, 327-31: Buckingham to Middleton, 1 July 1712.

77. Carte 212, ff. 38, 40: Nairne to Menzies, 7 Aug. and 1 Sept. 1712 ns; ff. 41-3: draught letter by James, Sept. 1712.

78. *Ibid.*, f. 45: Nairne to Menzies, 14 Nov. 1712 ns; ff. 47-8: Nairne to St. Amand, 31 Dec. 1712 ns; AAE 242, ff. 137-8: [French copy of a memo sent to St Germain] [late 1712].

79. Stuart, i, 353: Berwick to James, 25 Nov. 1712 ns. James agreed: Baschet 200, f. 294: James to Torcy, 4 Dec. 1712 ns.

80. Macpherson, ii, 365-6: Innes to Middleton, 2 Jan. 1713 ns.

81. Gaultier 139, ff. 208-20: Gaultier to Torcy, 15 and 28 Feb. 1713 ns; Wickham-Legg, pp.502-3: Gaultier to Torcy, 16 Feb. 1713 ns; F. Salomon, *Geschichte des Letzen Ministeriums Königin Annas von England, 1710-14* (Gotha, 1894), pp.328-9: James to Torcy, 5 Jan. 1713 ns.

82. Wickham-Legg, p.502: James to Torcy, 5 Jan. 1713 ns; AAE 243, f. 68: the duc D'Aumont (French Ambassador to London 1712-13) to James, 28 Jan. 1713; Blair Lett: 1 Nov. 1712.

83. Macpherson, ii, 376-7: Queen Mary to Middleton, 28 Jan. 1713 ns; Stuart, i,

258: Berwick to James, 10 Mar. 1713 ns.

84. Legh MSS: Dr. Roger Kenyon to Peter Legh, 15 Nov. 1712; Lockhart, i, 396-7.

85. Macpherson, ii, 377-8: Galmoy to Middleton, 29 Jan. 1713 ns; ii, 378-9, 384-5: Innes to Middleton, 5 and 18 Feb. 1713 ns.

86. Macpherson, ii, 400-1, 403: Ellis to Plunket, 9 and 20 Apr. 1713 ns; Carte 211, f. 91: anon. to Middleton, 20 Feb. 1713 ns, may be a secret report on Ellis's conduct at this time.

87. Carte 212, ff. 57-8: Nairne to Menzies, 20 Aug. 1713 ns. See also: Macpherson, ii, 398-400, 402-3: Plunket to Ellis, 7 and 13 Apr. 1713; ii, 442-3: anon. to Nairne, 20 Oct. 1713.

88. Carte 212, ff. 51, 60: Nairne to St Amand, 26 Aug, and 19 Sept. 1713 ns; f. 60: Nairne to Straton, 19 Sept. 1713 ns; AAE 249, ff. 29-30: Torcy to James, 14 May 1713 ns.

89. Carte 212, ff. 61-2: Nairne to Menzies, 25 Nov. 1713 ns.

90. Gaultier 121, f. 45: James to Torcy (Gaultier's transcript), 2 Dec. 1713 ns; AAE 250, ff. 119-28: James to Torcy, 2 Dec. 1713 ns.

91. Wickham-Legg, p.502: James to Torcy, 5 Jan. 1713 ns; p.506: Gaultier to Torcy, 19 Dec. 1713 ns.

92. Stuart, i, 251-2; Berwick to James, 20 Nov. 1712 ns.

93. For example see: Carte 212, f. 53: Nairne to Menzies, 27 Apr. 1713 ns.

94. *Ibid.*, f. 53: Nairne to Straton, 27 Apr. 1713 ns.

95. Carte 180, ff. 349-50: Middleton to James, 1711. Even ultra-Catholic Scots Jacobites detested Middleton, on the grounds that he was encouraging James to compromise too far with the Protestants: Nouvelles Acquisitions Françaises 7492, ff. 5-6.

96. Macpherson, ii, 371-2; Innes to Middleton, 9 Jan. 1713 ns.

97. AAE 251, f. 209: the duc D'Iberville (French Ambassador to London, 1713-17) to Torcy, 23 Mar. 1714 ns.

98. Carte 212, f. 49: 1 Feb. 1713 ns.

99. Macpherson, ii, 378-9: Innes to Middleton, 5 Feb. 1713 ns.

100. Gualterio 31256, f. 45: Perth to Gualterio, 29 Feb. 1712 ns.

101. Carte 212. ff. 21-2: Nairne to Menzies, 11 Oct. 1711 ns.

102. Carte 210, f. 379: Ogilvie to Middleton, 1710.

103. Macpherson, ii, 156: Middleton to Torcy, 5 July 1710 ns. See also: Portland Loan 29/395: Ogilvie's reports to Harley.

104. Carte 210, f. 344: James to Middleton, 4 July 1710 ns.

105. Macpherson, ii, 156: Perth to Middleton, 14 Aug. 1710 ns.

106. Above, pp.14-15.

107. Macpherson, ii, 428-30: Netterville to Ellis, Aug. 1713.

108. Berwick, *Mémoires*, p.126.

109. Stuart, i, 266, 271-2: Queen Mary to Dicconson, 17 May and 9 Aug. 1713 ns; Gualterio 31256, f. 79: Perth to Gualterio, 1 Apr. 1714 ns; Gualterio 31257, ff. 111-12: Middleton to Gualterio, 24 July 1712 ns.

110. Gualterio 31257, ff. 127-8: Middleton to Gualterio, 28 Aug. 1712 ns.

111. Carte 212, f. 38: Middleton to 'Watson' (probably the duke of Shrewsbury's half-sister, Mary Stonor), 28 July 1712 ns; f. 38: Middleton to St Amand, 4 Aug. 1712 ns.

112. Gualterio 20296, f. 19: 29 June 1714 ns.

113. Gualterio 31256, ff. 88-9: 19 Aug. 1714 ns.

2

'Our rebellious kingdoms': the Jacobite perception of British politics

Jacobitism and Toryism shared the same principles and many symbols. At first glance many Jacobites appear to be simply uncompromising Tories, a little outmoded by 1710 but by no means anachronistic.[1] Jacobites who were active within the political nation could easily and convincingly pass themselves off as Tories, and indeed considered themselves as no different from other Tories in most respects. Yet there was plainly an ideological divide between the austere Catholic monarchism of St Germain and the Country Toryism of Sir Thomas Hanmer's 'Whimsicals'. Each found the other strangely aberrant, and neither could understand how the other could be justified in the eyes of its adherents.[2] It is only by throwing the anti-Jacobite extreme of the Tory party and the most reactionary element in Jacobitism into contrast that such a sharp distinction can be obtained. Between Jacobite and anti-Jacobite groups in the Tory party at Westminster the difference was more subtle but as profound. All Tories believed in the danger to Church and State posed by the Whigs and their Nonconformist allies. By 1710 an equally potent Tory article of faith was that peace was vital before the backbone of the nation, the country gentleman, was destroyed by grinding taxation brought on by Whig war-profiteering. The Jacobites tenaciously and zealously upheld all these views. A Jacobite Tory's outlook differed from that of his more respectable associates in little more than nuances of interpretation of certain classic events in Tory mythology: the restoration of Charles II in 1660 and the Revolution of 1688. The effect of this difference in emphasis and interpretation on the attitudes of Jacobites in general goes far towards explaining their behaviour in Parliament and at St Germain, which often seems contrary to their interest.

Just as there was a spectrum of opinion within the Tory party on the succession and other issues, so there was a spectrum of opinion among the Jacobites. The various strands of Jacobitism differed in their attitudes to problems associated with securing a restoration. Thus there were internal ideological conflicts centred in such issues as: when and how military force should be used; what kind of religious compromise was acceptable; how far exploitation of Parliamentary Jacobitism could yield results; and what trust could be put in France. There was also a basic problem of a more intangible nature: the growing incomprehensibility of much that went on in Britain and at Westminster to the exiled Court.

Jacobite peers and M.P.'s in themselves represented the ultimate form of compromise which Jacobitism could comprehend. They reconciled their oaths against James with their consciences by arguing that to succeed they must infiltrate the political establishment; or that they were merely deferring action on James's behalf until Queen Anne died.[3] Hence George Lockhart and others found no contradiction in devoted personal loyalty to Anne while striving to achieve James's restoration on her death. As Captain John Ogilvie, Harley's agent in the Highlands, put it: '[they] love her for her father's sake'.[4] Less compromised in theory, but inescapably compromised in practice, were the English and Scots Episcopalian Nonjuring communities.* Though they refused to take oaths of loyalty to post-Revolutionary governments and many were heartily involved in all Jacobite plots, the exigencies of life under the Revolution settlement forced concessions on them, in that they were not constantly in rebellion and did pay their taxes to what they believed was a usurped government. Beyond them in the spectrum of opinion leading to the exiled Court were the British Roman Catholics. They too were obliged to make concessions to the established order but from their position as political pariahs were more inclined to favour any decisive solution that might rescue them quickly. Finally, there were the uncompromising Jacobites of the type found at St Germain, those who were at war with all post-Revolutionary governments, though policy or circumstances might force a suspension of it in practice. Without exception those who shared this attitude had long since left Britain, mainly in the years immediately following the Revolution.

In terms of outlook the separation between St Germain and the Parliamentary Jacobites was of crucial importance. The Jacobite Court's understanding of British politics was based on the experience of men who had terminated all contact with it in 1688, or shortly thereafter, so that by 1710 their interpretation of events was both idiosyncratic (in that those concerned were old men by 1710), and often wildly inaccurate.[5] This became a source of conflict between the leaders at St Germain and their followers in Britain and affected the behaviour of both. Much that the Jacobites in Britain, especially in Parliament, conceived of as necessary to achieve a restoration was felt to be demeaning, pointless or downright offensive by their superiors. This was of considerable importance for the Parliamentary Jacobites who, in the final analysis, were unlikely to defy the exiled Court once it issued a decree based on its interpretation of the situation and the best course of action. In practical terms this meant that the Court's perception of events in Britain was almost as important as that of the Jacobite peers and M.P.'s who would in the end, however reluctantly, obey St Germain's orders.

---

*A cogent new analysis of Scots Episcopalian nonjurors has appeared since this was written; see: B. Lenman, 'The Scottish Episcopal Clergy and the Ideology of jacobitism', in *Ideology and Conspiracy: Aspects of Jacobitism, 1688-1759*, ed. E. Cruickshanks (Edinburgh, 1982) pp. 36-48.

Since we are concerned with practical politics, Jacobite propaganda will not in general be considered here. When dealing with the way politicians behave in a given set of circumstances, the credence they put in certain images and concepts is more indicative than the polished rhetoric of the polemicists. No man can read another's thoughts, but by cautious correlation of the images and concepts, and the stress put on them, in a politician's speeches and correspondence, with his actual behaviour, it is possible to reach some tentative conclusions on how he perceived his aims, situation and hopes. In such an approach most use can be made of letters and utterances written or delivered in an unguarded moment, such as to a close friend or in a fit of passion. By further correlating this with the subject's actual behaviour, unrepresentative evidence can be eliminated. In this way an insight can be gained into how Jacobite politicians perceived their situation, to what extent their understanding differed from that of the exiled Court and how it was different from the understanding of the rest of the Tory party.

Easily the most far-reaching difference in interpretation between the Jacobite Tories and the rest of the party concerned the Restoration of 1660. In an age which still believed in a cyclical progress in human affairs, it was inevitable that parallels would be drawn between the events of 1659-60 and 1710-14.[6] These were not even the exclusive property of the Jacobites: the Whig pamphleteers who accused Oxford of planning a second restoration with himself cast in the role of Monk, implicitly assumed that their audience was cognisant with the parallels they were drawing.[7] Similarly, a friendlier source, French newsletters, credited the most absurd rumours in favour of the exiled Stuarts because of this 'parallel': 'Mr Menager avoit dit à une personne de Distinction, qu'il esperoit de voir bien tôt le jour qu'on rameneroit le Prince de Galles en Angleterre avec le meme empressement qu'on fit autrefois le Roy Charles second'.[8] Yet, for all that the image was common currency, it was to the Jacobites that it signified most, both as an example of rectitude rewarded in the past and as a vision of hope for the future. There were three tangible manifestations of the hold their vision of 1660 had over the Jacobites, which can be summarised as: Charles II-come-again, in the form of James the Old Pretender; the belief that some wise and powerful 'Great Man' must eventually see a second restoration as the only way to restore political harmony, as Monk had; and that divine providence would ensure that the natural order was restored, as it had done before.

The Jacobite conception of a new Charles II returning to restore order in 1714 in the manner of 1660 had two components: a straightforward likening of the situation in 1710-14 to that of 1660, and a conviction that civil war must follow if James were not restored. At its simplest the Jacobite equation of Charles II and James took the form of remarking on their physical similarity in Jacobite propaganda.[9] In more ceremonial displays of Jacobitism, such as the riots in Edinburgh and Leith on James's birthday in 1712, it took the form of singing 'the King shall enjoy his own again', and, also in Edinburgh, during the 1713 general election, of ostentatiously saluting the memory of Charles II:

Edinburgh, September 10 — This day was a very great meeting of the barons and freeholders of this county, where their former representative, George Lockhart, of Carnwath, Esquire, was unanimously chosen to represent them in the next parliament, and after the election they went to King Charles the Second's statue in the Parliament Close, and to the Cross, and in both places, with trumpets sounding and the huzza's of a great number of people, drank the Queen's health and to all true Scotsmen.[10]

In the minds of prominent Jacobites golden memories of 1660 and the eventual ease of Charles's restoration dominated their expectations of James's probable reception should he return to Britain. In a letter directed at the duke of Shrewsbury via 'Watson' (probably his half-sister, Mary Stonor), Middleton asserted that, 'those who never had a good thought of Richard [James] would crowd to embrace him, and tell him as they did his Unkle, that it is the happy day they had allways wish'd for'.[11] In a similar vein Sir William Whitlock implicitly threatened both the Government and the Whigs with eventual retribution for persecuting James when he spoke in the Commons in 1713 against an unopposed address to the Queen asking that measures be taken to secure James's expulsion from Lorraine. Defiantly he

told them he cou'd not be for that Address because he remember'd in Oliver Cromwell's time, when he obliged France to banish the person Charles Stuart, it hastened on his Glorious Restauration, w[hi]ch follow'd in a year and a half afterward.[12]

Queen Mary's secretary, James Dempster, also found comfort in drawing such parallels in a letter to Gualterio in 1714: 'Les extremites se tiennent et ce fut ainsy que sans que les Anglois y pensassent, Charles second fut retabli dans son Trosne, lors meme qu'on le persecutoit avec plus de fureur'.[13] The most complex manifestation of Charles II 'parallels' was over the question which preoccupied the Jacobites most: that of James's religion. Many Tories appear to have believed that Charles II was a secret Catholic throughout his reign. The Protestant Jacobites adopted and expanded this idea to justify their pressurising James to dissemble his Catholicism and thus regain the throne, as they argued Charles II had done. Innes described this myth and the plans based on it to Middleton, from a conversation he had had with Sir William Ellis:

He said their encouragement proceeded from their reflecting that King Charles had been Catholic long before the restoration; yet that he temporised and never declared himself Catholic, till upon his death bed; and that this encouraged them to hope, that the King, seeing the impossibility of his being restored without temporising in the same manner, might be persuaded to it.[14]

Oxford and Bolingbroke both seem to have been aware of this widespread belief among the Jacobites, and judiciously manipulated it when they made their ritual demands for James's conversion in 1714, by including appeals to the memory of Charles II.[15]

Fear of again unleashing the social forces which had so nearly triumphed

during the Great Civil War, and of another period of such dislocation and
destruction in general, was still ingrained in British politics at the Revolution
and continued until well into the eighteenth century. The Jacobites' conviction
that the continued exclusion of the rightful line was certain to lead to civil war
was a concomitant of this, in support of their aims. All of them seem to have
been convinced that Britain was about to lapse into civil war between the
Whigs and the Tories and that the inability to sustain a stable government for
any length of time would necessitate James's recall just as it had done Charles's
in 1660.[16] Perth explained this to Gualterio in 1712:

> Les affaires du Roy mon maitre sont bien brouilles dans ses Royaumes. Mais les
> changements continuels qu'y arrivent donnent sujet d'esperer qu'on voira a la fin
> la necessite de s'establir sur des fondements solides et justes: car sans cela il n'y a
> point de paix pour ses gents enfatués.[17]

This belief contributed directly to the Jacobite willingness to bide their time
and wait for their opportunity, 'there being reason to think these jealousies
and divisions would in the event turn to his [James's] account'.[18] Indeed, to an
extent, no Jacobite believed that any form of government not based on
hereditary monarchy could have any durability. The upshot of which was that
the Revolution settlement could not long survive such an enfeeblement of the
monarchy and infringement of the principle of hereditary right as was inherent
in the Hanoverian succession, and might even collapse in the face of it.

If James was Charles II come again and the Revolution settlement was
breaking down in the way the Republic had done before it, then to complete
the 'parallel' a 'Great Man' was needed to do the actual work of the
restoration: someone to play the part of Monk. A prerequisite of belief in the
need for such an actor was the assumption that Queen Anne was a cypher, as,
if she had a policy and will of her own, the 'parallel' would no longer be viable.
Throughout her reign, but particularly in the period 1710-14, the Jacobites
firmly believed that Anne was a timid woman, well-intentioned, but entirely
ruled by favourites: 'Esq. Young [Anne] is so entirely in Goldsmith Baker's
[Oxford's] power that we cannot tell what judgement to make of him'.
Sentiments with which Perth concurred: 'le Tresorier... a un pouvoir absolue
sur l'espirit de la Psse de Dannemark.'[19] Having removed Queen Anne from
their political picture of Britain, except for a minor background part when it
was convenient, the next problem was to find a suitable 'Great Man'. The most
obvious, due to his considerable power and great military prestige, was
Marlborough, with whom the Jacobites kept up an intermittent
correspondence throughout 1710-14, in the hope that he might eventually be
forthcoming in deeds as well as promises. This can be seen in Queen Mary's
letter to him in July 1710, begging him not to resign:

> I beseech you, therefore, to reflect well, before you deprive yourself of the means
> you have in your hands, to support yourself and to assist your friends. But, as
> you are lost, if you quit your employments, I see likewise, on the other hand,
> that it will be very difficult for you to keep yourself in office as things are now

situated, so that your interest itself declares now for your honour. You cannot be in safety without doing justice, nor preserve your greatness without discharging your duty, and the time is precious for you as well as for us.[20]

Despite their repetition, not much trust was put in his protestations of fidelity and contrition. Though the Jacobites were always ready to try again, their consistent demand for a concrete demonstration of his loyalty always led to an impasse and the exchange of nothing more than 'words for words'.[21]

The next man chosen as their deliverer by the Jacobites was, logically enough, Robert Harley, earl of Oxford. The exiled Court was decidedly wary of him at first, and admonished Menzies for making too eager an approach to him which had gained nothing, 'nor indeed is there anything to be expected from honyton's shop but pump and banter.' His secret promises of restoration made through Gaultier had won them over by 1712, however, and by then Middleton was seeking his opinion on how the Jacobites should conduct themselves.[22] The Jacobite willingness to believe in their chosen 'Great Man' is nowhere better exemplified than in the trust they put in Oxford, which at times verged on the purblind:

I confess I cannot see any prudent reason for Baker's [Oxford's] dilatory proceedings, but he being the chiefest lawyer [minister] and his own interest so much concern'd, Manly [James] must be govern'd by him and comply with what he can not help, and in the mean time have patience and hope the best.[23]

Disillusion only gradually set in. As late as October 1713, Nairne was still repeating the same message to Menzies:

Tho all this (I say) be very melancholy and disheartning, yet y[ou]r unkle continues still resolv'd to try what time patience and all good offices on his side will produce, leaving (as you say very well) the event to God alm[ighty]: and to Charl. [Anne's] and Hon: [Oxford's] consciences. But when Proby [Parliament] comes to town we shall be better able to judge how matters will go, for tis raisonable to beleeve yt then or never some people will show themselves.[24]

Oxford's unacceptable demands of February 1714 angered the Jacobite leaders. Accordingly, within less than a month he had been dropped for a more suitable candidate for their trust: the duke of Ormonde.[25] He had first come into regular contact with the Jacobite Court in October 1713, and was initially only very cautiously encouraged for fear of offending Oxford.[26] As their confidence in Oxford waned, however, Ormonde was pursued with increasing determination, so that by December 1713 Berwick was already trying to involve him in a plot for a French-backed *coup d'état* in the event of Anne's death.[27] By March 1714 Berwick was vowing that he would 'leave no stone unturn'd to gaine Orbec [Ormonde].' Though they agreed to keep up the polite formalities that were by now usual with Oxford and Bolingbroke, the man whom they were now clearly set on winning over was Ormonde:

one must keep fair with them, for there is no remedy, but one must at the same time endeavour to gett other friends to work, who will not speake of unreasonable as well as impracticable conditions. The Duke of Ormond would be certainly the most proper person, the difficulty is to gett at him and conduct him.[28]

This courtship continued until Queen Anne's death altered the political situation entirely.

Though they were agreed that a 'Great Man' was necessary to restore James, the Parliamentary Jacobites were not always in agreement with St Germain's current candidate. Probably due to the fact that Jacobite Tories were among the staunchest of Tories, by 1710 they detested Marlborough. The depth of this loathing surprised even the Abbé Gaultier, who commented to Torcy in December 1710:

Dieu Garde ce Grand General et son parent et amy Godolphin car, malgré les grands services qu'ils ont rendus tous deux a leur nation, si la Reine disoit seulement un mot, ils eroient bientost perdûs l'un et l'autre, tant le Parlement est invité contre eux et toute leur famille.[29]

William Shippen and Sir John Pakington, both prominent Jacobites, were among the most violent speakers against Marlborough in the bread-money debates in early 1712.[30] In the summer of that year Godolphin was warned by a friend:

the Jacobites cannot so well contain themselves but that now & then in ye heat [of] argument or wine they lett dropp what they know & think & tis not only my own remark but that of other Gentlemen in this countrey that their principal malice is levell'd against ye D[uke]. of M[arlborough]. & yr L[or]d[shi]p but especially the D. who (ye gentlemen of that persuasion say) must of necessity be persued even to blood.[31]

In this particular opinion they were joined by the other Jacobites in Britain, who indicated their feelings in some venomous pamphlets.[32] The next difference of opinion came over the Jacobite Court's adoption of Ormonde as the new candidate for deliverer after Oxford had been discarded. Ormonde did not have a significant following in Parliament, except in the general sense of being 'the Tory hero', and some of the Jacobites in the Commons preferred to look to Bolingbroke, arguing that he 'was a good man and a wise man, and knew what was fitt to be done and when to do it', which occasioned a schism in the Parliamentary Jacobite ranks.[33] The source of their differences with St Germain over this issue really lay in the Stuart Court's inclination towards military figures, with whom it felt a natural empathy, and the Parliamentary Jacobites' natural inclination towards politicians.

As they believed that they were retracing Charles II's path back to the throne, the Jacobites had no doubts that it was impossible for such a just (and from their interpretation of history, divinely sanctioned) cause to fail. After all, if God appointed hereditary monarchs to rule his flock, he was hardly likely to countenance their overthrow except as a punishment for the rebels. As far as the Jacobites were concerned, 1660 had shown the way; if they tried they could not but succeed in the end. They displayed this conviction in two distinct forms. One was an unshakeable belief in Queen Anne's tender concern for her exiled brother, the other was an equally unqualified faith in divine sanction of the Jacobite cause. The first of these illustrates both the depth of their faith, and the ability of committed zealots at any time blithely to ignore uncomfortable facts when they are confronted with them. Thomas Smith, the Whig M.P. for Glasgow Burghs, remarked on this phenomenon in March 1713:

> I have often admired [how] ye Jacobites [with] us could please ymselves [with] telling us that her Ma[jes]ty was inclined to the pretender, [which] after soe many declarations in favoure of ye H[anoverian]. succession is to use her very ill.[34]

Queen Anne could in fact only be seen as a Jacobite by those determined to force all her actions into such a mould. This included virtually all the Jacobite Tories.[35] Correspondents with St Germain calmly assured the exiled Court that, 'Whatever you hear, let it give you no trouble... Her lawsuit [cause] and yours are now so linked that one cannot subsist without the other'.[36] Even veteran campaigners like Lockhart could never believe the Queen had herself been opposed to James's restoration:

> That the Queen did of a long time design her brothers restauration, I do not in the least question, but was prevaild with to postpone and delay it, partly by her own timorous nature, partly by the divisions and discord of her Ministry, and partly by the tricks, intrigues, and pretences of the lord Oxford, in whom for a long time she plac'd entire confidence, and cou'd scarce at last be perswaded that he did not deserve it.[37]

This sublime confidence in Anne's concern for James among the Jacobites in Britain duly had its effect at St Germain, where Middleton confidently assured Torcy, following the fall of the Godolphin ministry:

> la Princesse qui est en possession prennant les Anglicans rigides en sa confiance, et leur donnant les meilleurs emplois semble declarer assez intelligiblement quelles sont ses inclinations pour son frere. Et voila ou la maine invisible de la providence a deja conduit cette affaire, se servant meme de plus grands ennemis pour l'avancer sans qu'ils s'en appercoivent.[38]

As much as the Jacobites were convinced of Queen Anne's good intentions, so they were even more assured of divine blessing. After the Jacobite case had been aired in the course of the Sacheverell impeachment, Middleton submitted a memorandum to James asserting that since the Revolution had now been revealed as a rebellion, 'then [there] is no presumption to relye on providence, rather than to embarke in a desperate affair, which may serve only to reconcile yr ennemys'. James was himself influenced by this attitude, as can be seen from a letter he wrote to Torcy in 1714 lamenting his failure to elicit a response from Anne and the issuing of a proclamation against him: 'il n'y a plus rien à faire que laisser a la grace de Dieu et a la nature le soin de la mettre dans le bon chemin'.[39] In part, this belief's appeal arose out of the austere Catholicism practised at St Germain, and the necessary faith in their own righteousness which all exiled governments must retain in order to survive. Devout Catholics like Perth and Nairne did not hesitate to proclaim their belief that James's firm adherence to Roman Catholicism would bring its own reward in the end.[40] This conviction of divine sanction and predestined success was virtually unshakeable until after Anne's death, even when confronted with calamities such as the death of the duke of Hamilton, one of St Germain's most powerful and committed adherents:

> Votre Eminence verra dans le feuillet cy joint la noirceur de l'assassinat du Duc d'Hamilton; les combinaisons qui sont soupconner que c'est un attentat des Whigs, et le nouveau ferment qui irrite de plus en plus les deux partys. Il faut croire que la Providence disposera le tout pour le mieux et que nous en verrons enfin eclater les miracles pour la consolation des bons et a la confusion des mechan.[41]

Nor was the attitude of the Jacobites in Britain in any way divergent on this score. In Scotland Defoe found 'the poor highlanders and other people in the country ... do not look for their Saviour's coming with half the assurance as they do for that of the [Pretender]'. While in England, Marlborough was well enough aware of the Jacobites' predisposition to believe 'analysis' encouraging them to quietly await the working of providence to make ruthlessly cynical use of it in his contacts with them, so as to encourage them to do nothing at all to help themselves.[42]

The differing Tory and Jacobite Tory interpretations of even so momentous an event as the Restoration would not normally have been expected to have produced such a significant divergence. Other factors such as the devout Catholicism of the exiled Royal family and the staunchly Country-Tory *cum* Anglican beliefs of the majority of their adherents must have played their part. But whatever its basis, the belief in the need for a 'Great Man' and the ubiquitous references to Charles II which are obviously casting James in the role of Charles-come-again, show how fundamental the image of themselves as re-enactors of a divinely ordained sequence was to all Jacobites. Such was the hold of the concept on them that until Anne's death they could never really believe that it was possible for them to fail. The consequence of this was a strong tendency towards putting an unquestioning trust in those professing themselves friends of the cause, and a similar tendency towards inflexibility. After all, why compromise when success was assured? The Jacobite perception of themselves and their situation was such as to put a premium on obstinacy and optimism.

A symbol on the significance of which the Jacobite Tories were bound to differ with the rest of the party was that of the Revolution. To High Tories like Francis Atterbury, Bishop of Rochester (from 1713), and his ilk, the Revolution was an act of divine providence in favour of the Church of England. This was the most commonly held Tory view of the Revolution, as, thanks to Atterbury's carefully argued polemics, it allowed the Tories to make believe that therefore they had not been guilty of resisting their anointed monarch in 1688.[43] A Jacobite simply could not at this time accept the

Revolution as a justifiable or divine act (except as a punishment for the nation's sins) and remain a Jacobite. Events altered this after 1714, but that lay in the future. As far as the Jacobite Court was concerned, there was no case to answer: 'And no body can be ignorant how unjustly the late King our father, of blessed memory, suffer'd by this unjustifiable revolution'.[44] Even in their private correspondence the Jacobite Court never questioned the validity of James II's acts or the continued vindication of him by the exiled Court. Indeed, if anything St Germain's veneration of his memory deepened, culminating in an attempt to have him canonised in 1734.[45] In the eyes of the exiled Court James II had been grievously wronged, and the Whigs and Dutch were still to be seen and understood in the light of their actions in 1688:

> Les frequens attentats des Wiggs devroient enfin determiner les Thorys a les prevenir. Ces premiers en viendroient a une rupture ouverte, si leur bons amis les Hollandois estoient en liberté de les appuyer comme ils ont fait dans touttes les revolutions.[46]

Herein lay a slight but perceptible difference between the attitude of the Jacobites in Britain and that of the Jacobite Court. Though at first glance they may appear the same:

> En parlant du Roy Jacques, il dit, que quoyque depuis plus de vingt ans (parmy beaucoup d'etrange modes) celle la principalement avoit esté fort practique, de denigrer la reputation de ce Prince, Que neanmoins il osoit dire sans craindre la moins censure, que ce Roy avoit esté en tout point le meilleur des tous les qui ont jamais esté assis sur le throsne; qu'a la verite il etois trop honest homme et trop sincere pour un Roy d'Angleterre, que sa bonte avoit esté scandaleusement abusee par les fripons ausquels il se froit et lesquels (a la honte eternelle de l'Angre) ont esté recompensez pour leurs trahisons et infamies, pendant que le seul Prince a esté puny luy qui par la loy que nous avoüons, est impunissable.[47]

Shippen's speech at least tacitly implied that there had been faults with James II. In other Jacobite utterances originating in Britain, it was more explicit:

> And as we were loyall in the time of the royall Martyr we continued to be so in the reigns of both his sons and tho your Royal father of ever blessed memorie (whom as a curse upon our rebellious practices God in his wrath deprived us of) seemed to commit some Irregularitie we willingly submitted to his Maj: opinion and that of his parlia[men]t.[48]

The shift in the balance of power within the Jacobite movement during 1710-14, to favour the British and Protestant elements, brought with it a corresponding ideological shift (at least temporarily) at the Jacobite Court. St Germain was obliged to accommodate the ideological views of the Jacobites in Britain by moving towards their interpretation of the Revolution in particular. Hence, in April 1714, the exiled Court was forced to admit that James II might have been mistaken on some points:

> He [James] has inform'd himself of past miscarriages, and knows well ye difference between ye Office of a King and a Missionary, he will concern himself

with no man's Religion, but is resolv'd yt w[hi]ch is legally establish'd, and whose principles are true to Monarchy and safe for Government, for whose satisfaction, & for his own restauration, he thinks himself oblig'd to do every thing that is consistent with Conscience and Honour.[49]

St Germain had not had a real change of heart, though, and in the first official statement after Queen Anne's death and the collapse of the political initiative returned to its former, uncompromising, position.[50]

In accordance with the Jacobite belief in the justice of their cause, their leaders had a predilection for a military solution to the problem of restoring James. James himself was an enthusiastic proponent of such schemes.[51] The reasoning behind this is straightforward: Britain (especially Scotland) was thought to be just waiting to welcome James (as would his sister if she had the opportunity and was freed from the tutelage of self-seeking men), so why not take the direct approach, the military one? Initially, this inclination may have arisen from sheer lack of any alternative, and the faint, but always real, hope that the French might risk such a desperate venture. After 1710 any chance of this swiftly diminished, but St Germain's penchant for military action had become ingrained. At first they signalled their continued predilection and frustration by irritable criticism of what they felt was French stupidity. Once they had become reconciled to the development, it was expressed less overtly, in the form of annual 'schemes' and in the speed with which a new plan could be presented whenever some crisis in the peace negotiations offered hope that the French might have a change of heart.[52] On this subject it appears that most Roman Catholic and Nonjuring Jacobites endorsed the exiled Court's stance. Leslie wrote a long memorandum on this subject to the Jacobite Court in 1711, in which he claimed that an invasion by a mere 5,000 men would have a good prospect of success, for all the crypto-Jacobites would declare themselves and the post-Revolutionary establishment collapse. The Parliamentary Jacobites already appear to have been keeping their distance from such schemes, for the only support Leslie had managed to extract from them was both low-key and very guarded:

> Je suis fort assure de quelques membres de Parlement qui parleroient fortement en ce cas la, et j'ay lieu aussi de croire qu'il y a encore plusieurs autres qui ne manquent qu'une pareille conjoncture pour s'expliquer, et que le feroient cordialement.[53]

This reluctance to consider military adventurism gradually spread from the Parliamentary Jacobites to their fellow Protestants, the Nonjurors, at the very time that the Roman Catholics and the Jacobite Court drifted in the opposite direction, in favour of a military solution. The Protestant Jacobites were in the ascendant during this period, so it was their views on the subject which held sway. This made the military alternative which the leadership intrinsically favoured even more attractive, because if they did manage to manufacture a military option, not only did it offer all the prospects of a quick solution but it also meant that no more distasteful concessions to Protestant sensibilities would have to be made at St Germain. By late 1713, however, the disinclination of the Protestant Jacobites towards such plans had become virtually insurmountable: 'You have reason to be kind to the Liddells [Highlanders] for they are the only forward friends Sir John [James] has, I've lost patience yea and it has made me sick to find Mr Mark [Jacobites] so pusillanimous and inactive'.[54] Carnegy was not exaggerating. Some of the Protestant Jacobites were so disinclined to take military measures that they even contacted the French Government privately to beg them to prevent an invasion attempt, lest their cause be lost by foolhardy action.[55] Though hampered by this reluctance to become involved among the majority of the Protestant Jacobites, the prospect of assured success without compromise still led Berwick into ambitious plotting designed to arrange a Jacobite *coup d'état* on Anne's death:

> I suppose Walters [Gaultier] in saying "je crains que vos lettres n'auront pas le sort que vous attendes", meanes that the difficulty about M. Rolland [religion] will make people silent, but I hope M. Orbec [Ormonde] will not stick at that, hitherto he has not, and by the last letter M. Belley [Berwick] has had he finds Orbec is just going to settling his friend M. Alexandre's [the Army's] affaires in spight of M. Oleron [Oxford].[56]

In essence this battle of wills within the Jacobite organisation was occasioned by two certainties juxtaposed. The Court in advocating a military solution was basing its thinking on the confident knowledge that as soon as the Jacobite invasion arrived all the crypto-Jacobites would rush to join it, Queen Anne would welcome her brother, and so on. Conversely, the Parliamentary Jacobites, and eventually the Nonjurors too, based their opposition on their certainty that Queen Anne would restore James peacefully if guided and helped.

It is always difficult for governments in exile to avoid becoming entirely dependent on their hosts, even when they are averse to doing so. The Jacobite Court was far from averse, rather the opposite: it was admiring and grateful. Many exiled Jacobites unselfconsciously identified themselves so completely with their hosts as to become naturalised Frenchmen, as was the case with Berwick, Hooke, Galmoy and many others. Those who did not still implicitly trusted and relied on the good intentions of the French Government. Nowhere is this better exemplified than in James's parting letter to Louis XIV on leaving France in 1713:

> What terms shall I employ to express my gratitude to your Majesty, before I leave the asylum which you have been pleased to grant me, almost ever since I was born, and which you do not permit me to leave, but in order to procure for me another more suitable, in the present state of your affairs and of my own? Words fail me to express how my heart is penetrated, by the remembrance of your Majesty's beneficence and former kindness towards me. The care you are now pleased to take of me, and whatever concerns me, crowns the whole, and encourages me in the sad condition I am in, from the confidence I have in the

generosity that has no example for its continuance, in a wisdom which is to accomplish the greatest designs, and in a bounty which unweariedly extends itself to me and my family... When I have assured your Majesty of my most sincere and fervent wishes for your prosperity and happiness, I have nothing further to say, but to conjure your Majesty to be thoroughly persuaded, that you will always find in me the respect, attachment, and if I can presume to say, the tenderness of a son, a will always ready, not only to follow but even go before your own in all things, during the time of my exile; and if I shall ever see myself restored to my dominions, a faithful ally, who will make it his glory and his happiness to concur with the first designs of a King, who does honour to royalty.[57]

The exiled Court's frankly adulatory attitude towards France was demonstrated not just by servile letters. Such was the deference shown to the French Government and French interests in all St Germain's activities during this period that at times it resembles nothing more than an ancillary department of the French State. It was accepted practice for the French to be consulted on all the Stuart Court's plans.[58] The conduct of the Jacobite Court's diplomatic agents was not only vetted by the French, but their activities were dictated by them, at St Germain's own request.[59] More insidiously, the Jacobite leadership seems to have identified its own interests with those of France, and behaved accordingly, as can be seen from the way Marlborough was told in 1713 that if he desired Jacobite assistance against the impeachment he claimed to fear, he must not only support them, but, 'no more blow the coals against M. Rethel [Louis XIV]'.[60] Even when faced with outright betrayal by France, the Jacobite Court's complacency was barely touched. In 1714, after the French Government had peremptorily ordered James back to Bar-le-Duc after he came to Paris seeking aid for an attempt to invade Britain, Queen Mary was still finding excuses for them:

mon fils estoit resolu de tout hazarder et aller en Ecosse, mais le Roy lui à fait entendre, que non seulement il ne vouloit (c'est a dire qu'il ne pouvoit) pas lui doner le moindre secours mais que mesme il seroit obligé de le faire avertir, si il alloit plus loing, et qu'il n'avoit pas d'autre part à prendre de s'en retourner à Bar.[61]

St Germain's identification with France contrasted sharply with the prevalent attitude among the Jacobites in Britain. The Roman Catholics, whom the French Ambassador, D'Aumont, reported looked to Louis XIV for protection, and who were usually closest to the exiled Court in their sympathies, were distinctly cool on the subject of deference to France in Jacobite planning:

I humbly think it was ill advised the consulting of Mr Morgan [France] when he [James] intended to writt last since Morgan does every thing without communicating the least of his intentiones to him, and has forsaken him in every respect, its the oppinion of most part here.[62]

As for the Protestant Jacobites, at times their attitude verged on the hostile. Lockhart recalled Marlborough's despatch against the French in 1711 in tones of approval; Netterville felt France should be obliged to grant whatever terms Britain asked for at Utrecht; Ferguson openly doubted if they could be relied on; and Plunket found the French held in contempt by the Jacobite M.P.'s.[63] This divergence in attitudes was largely founded on patriotic pride in British achievements during the War of the Spanish Succession, from which even Jacobites were not immune. St Germain's identification with France was alien to most of its adherents in Britain, which created a conflict between the two as St Germain tried to maximise French involvement against the wishes of its supporters.

The issue on which the Jacobite Court differed most with its British supporters was religion. It was not simply a clash of devout Roman Catholicism and devout Anglicanism, but a basic inability of the Jacobite Court to comprehend the degree of religious feeling in Britain, particularly among its own adherents. It was never able to understand just how detested Roman Catholicism (as opposed to individual Roman Catholics) was among those whom it hoped to win over. From this incomprehension stemmed much of the internal struggle over which religion was to be seen to dominate the Jacobite network. From it too stemmed the facile statements with which the exiled Court confronted queries about a future religious settlement: 'I think it demonstrable that neither Edward [Church of England] nor Aylmer [Queen Anne] have any interest to oppose Old Cotton [Roman Catholicism]'.[64] A corresponding impatience was also felt at Protestant Jacobite concern over the lack of facility for Protestant worship at St Germain, as in 1713 when Innes blithely brushed off Philips's request that Leslie be summoned to the Jacobite Court to hold Protestant services, with the answer that he was too old and too useful in Britain.[65] A similar response was made to the suggestion by the Protestant Jacobites that James should settle in a Protestant country on leaving France, in order to prove that he was not bigoted: 'Les amys Anglicans de sa Majte la conjure d'aller pour un temps dans un pays Protestant. Mais c'est ce qu'elle ne feroit pas. Car il ne veut pas donner lieu de supsoner qu'elle est capable de changer de religion'. Even the intervention of the British Roman Catholics in an attempt to persuade St Germain to make some gesture to ease Protestant Jacobite fears, by Leslie holding services or something similar, proved unavailing.[66] The source of such profound misunderstanding was probably once again in the nature of the pious Catholicism which permeated the Court. This was imbued with more than a little of James II's blind zeal, which had regarded all other religions as opposed to Catholicism because of ignorance or self interest.[67] With such an attitude dominant it was hardly surprising the the Jacobite Court could not credit the Protestant Jacobites with genuine religious concern, and were astonished when the Protestants flatly stated that James's Catholicism was a hindrance, or demanded his conversion. This soon turned to annoyance as the Protestants became more persistent and explicit, which led to the exiled Court refusing even to discuss the matter.[68]

However much the exiled Court wished the issue would go away, or misunderstood the depth of Protestant Jacobite religious feeling, such feelings remained strong and insistent. Virtually all the Protestant Jacobites wished James would convert, as can be seen from the eagerness with which the slightest rumour of it was seized upon:

> Depuis quelques semaines le bruit s'estoit repandu icy que le pretendant avoit change de religion et qu'il faisoit profession ouverte de la protestante, mais on n'en a pas esté bien eclaircy, quoy que quelques Jacobites le debitoient avec joye et grande confiance dans l'esperance que par la, ils viendroient au comble de leur desirs.[69]

Even the Nonjuring clergy, who ostensibly tried to remain aloof from the campaign to force James's conversion, and dutifully made some show of discouraging it, were privately hoping he would accede.[70] This is evident in a letter from 'J.H.' to Richard Rawlinson, asking what was the present position and,

> Hopes of our young P[rince]. ye 3d of yt Name, with what grounds there are for his & our Hopes. We are told here, yt he has sent into London for one of our Comon prayer-books hav[in]g a Chapel in Lor-n wherein they are to be us'd by Him & his Domestics, very good news, if True.[71]

There were also Leslie's attempts to convert James when he went to Bar-le-Duc. Outside Parliament too, prominent lay Nonjurors, who had carefully remained silent before, began discreetly to signal their fears for the future security of the Church of England.[72] The Parliamentary Jacobites constituted the main means of applying pressure on James to convert, and had no hesitation in expressing their commitment to this goal. Arthur Maynwaring, the Whig M.P. for West-Looe, had a graphic demonstration of this when he dined with two October Club men in the summer of 1711:

> one of them being ask'd if it was true that the Chevalier St George was turning Protestant, as was given out in one of Roper's Papers, reply'd that if it was in that paper, it was possible there might be something in it: And he wish'd to God it might prove true, for then, said he, there will be an *End of all our Troubles.*[73]

The religious controversy within the Jacobite movement was of the worst possible nature for such a body. The Protestant Jacobites were reluctant to ask James to convert as it was self-evident that a politic conversion would be of little value in safeguarding the Church, yet they were constrained to do so by their religious sensibilities. James and the Court in general were offended that they should think him so insincere as to try, and therefore swiftly lost patience and returned brusque replies, which in turn irritated the Protestant Jacobites, who vented their displeasure by blaming the Roman Catholics at St Germain, whom they convinced themselves were thwarting their plans. In effect this created two feuding camps within the Jacobite network: those in Britain against the establishment at the Jacobite Court, each convinced of the other's bad faith.

Another area of misunderstanding between St Germain and its followers in Britain lay in the former's expectations of what could be achieved by political management. St Germain's hierarchy had carried into exile the presuppositions and framework of reference of pre-Revolutionary political management, and it was in the main these same men who still ran the Jacobite network in 1710-14. They had no other means of interpreting the information they received than by these old memories, which by that time were dangerously misleading. Apart from this, political development in Britain was moving in an entirely separate direction from that at the exiled Court, where tendencies which may be called absolutist were naturally encouraged by the exigencies of running an extremely loose organisation in which the only real authority was that of the monarch. The idea that the Tory party was just the same as its pre-Revolutionary antecedent was possibly the single most misleading notion held at St Germain. The success of Atterbury and others in accommodating the Revolution within High Tory principles seems to have gone entirely unrecognised:

> Deux partis animez a outrance l'un contre l'autre etablissent evidemment le droit de ce Prince dans leurs ecrits publiques: Les Anglicans rigides soutiennent comme un principe de leur religion qu'il n'est jamais permis de resister a son Roy pour quelque cause que ce soit, et que la succession hereditaire est une loy si fondamentale que Parlement meme ne peut pas la changer.[74]

This summary of the basics of Toryism is fairly typical of the general view at the Stuart Court, and is so inaccurate as to verge on caricature. Old chestnuts like Non-resistance and Indefeasible Hereditary Right did still have some use in party battles in Britain, but they had long ceased to be the major issues in the party battle, which by 1710 centred on such issues as the necessity for peace and the security of the Church of England. Non-Resistance and Indefeasible Hereditary Right had also changed their meanings, as far as most Tories were concerned, between 1688 and 1710. Non-Resistance was held only to apply to the legislature as a whole: the monarch-in-parliament, and though Indefeasible Hereditary Right remained a tenet of Toryism, it was limited to the Protestant line. This was understood by the Parliamentary Jacobites, hence the pressure on James to convert, but the Jacobite Court in no way appreciated the magnitude of the change. With all its faults, Middleton's perception of the principles of Toryism, cited above, was incomparably closer to reality than that of some of the other officers at St Germain. Caryll consistently referred to the Tories and Whigs as Episcopalians and Presbyterians and characterised Godolphin's administration as having been Presbyterian. Stafford followed him in this, while Dempster contentedly thought all Tories wished to restore James, and with him the natural order in society.[75] From this misleading view of the nature of the two parties came an overestimation of the capacity of contemporary political management to achieve their aims. Most of the more chimerical Jacobite schemes were largely based on the premise that such a mercenary Parliament (from their point of view if it did not espouse their principles it must be corrupt) would acquiesce in whatever its managers thought fit. Hence, if James suddenly appeared in London and was presented by Queen Anne to Parliament, they were certain it would welcome him, just as if he landed in Scotland and raised a rebellion, Parliament could easily and swiftly be wrought upon to recognise him as her heir.[76] The practical result of this overestimate, when interwoven with other Jacobite 'certainties', was to exaggerate their trust in their major articles of faith. Thus Dempster believed that because Queen Anne wished to restore her brother she would do so (given time and the requisite 'Great Man') and could do so.[77] Parliament did not figure in his calculation at all. This is not to say they ignored Parliament completely, but that they did not appreciate its significance or independence within British politics. In turn, this suggests that they did not grasp the value of the Parliamentary Jacobite group to any Tory ministry, or what could be extracted in return for its support.

There was obviously a significant difference between the attitudes of the Tory party in general and the Jacobite sub-group. Yet of equally immediate relevance to the Parliamentary Jacobites were the differences in attitude between them and their leaders. Though they were united in a common cause, they were still the 'nonjuring jurors', and as such, a different beast from the rest of their kind. Parliamentary Jacobitism never had a separate, stated set of aims or policies of its own, so its general principles and where it stood in relation to Toryism in general can only be drawn from the statements of its leading members and their communications with St Germain.

Even as regards the Revolution, the disowning of which must seem to be characteristic of all Jacobites, there was a perceptible limitation of their condemnation to the revolution-of-1688, by these Jacobites, which was a typically pragmatic piece of 'Country' thinking. The Parliamentary Jacobites might technically be upholders of Non-Resistance, Passive Obedience and Indefeasible Hereditary Right, but they clearly had no intention of foreclosing their options for use against future administrations of whose actions they did not approve. Lockhart, in his own introduction to his 'Memoirs', in which he set out to discredit views of his former friend, the Court Whig pro-Union M.P. Sir David Dalrymple, makes several revealing statements on the relationship between rulers and ruled:

> And now taking it as he would have it, that is, that the Union was undertaken on no other view than what I have mentioned [to secure Scotland's liberty, religion and constitution], and yielding that the Cavaliers [Jacobites], in opposition thereto, designed the restoration of King James, who would certainly oppress and harass his own faithfull subjects, and impoverish and ruin his own flourishing dominions, — I say let us suppose matters stood thus, the question naturally arising from it is, which of the two schemes was most detrimental to Scotland? Why, for my own part I truly think the former, because King James might change his mind, and be persuaded by reason and interest to act otherwise: if not, he might be controlled by the Parliament, resisted by the people, and sent a-packing, as was his father; and for certain he would sooner or later die, and a better prince perhaps succeed him... King James had a right before and untill he was actually deprived of the crown legally; but the Elector of Hannover had none before and untill it was given him; and if for my country's service I may turn him

out that actually is, I may much more keep him out that only aims at being my King. On the other hand, if I was a Cavalier believing that King James and his issue were unjustly secluded from the throne, might I not very consistently with my principles be against the Union, even tho' he or one of his posterity whose title I own was on the throne and advanc'd the measure? because tho' I own his right to rule over me, I deny that he or any power under God can dissolve the constitution of the kingdom; and therefore I might fairly oppose it in a lawfull manner, nay think my aledgiance loosed as to him my soveraign if he was accessary to the subversion of the monarchy, as happened in the case of Baliol, who without doubt had the best claim to the crown.[78]

From this it is readily apparent that Lockhart had thoroughly absorbed the post-Revolution Tory party's revision of its principles, so that the stress was not on loyalty to the monarch so much as loyalty to the monarch-in-parliament. Lockhart was not a Jacobite Tory because he believed in the divine right of Kings, but because he believed in the 'ancient constitution' and that a mistake had been made in 1688. In this he was quite typical of Parliamentary Jacobite opinion. Thomas Strangways junior, M.P. for Dorset from 1713, expressed the opinion of his peers on the results of the Revolution when he lamented to lieutenant Adam Ottley

how many a noble fortune and antient family have been reduced since this war, and how many of these men yt now surprize ye Town with their misfortunes [bankruptcies] were worth sixpence at ye revolution nay how many even of those yt surprize all thinking men with yr riches. I think ye nation can never wth greater reason bemoan her poverty yn wn she considers the characters of those who have been ye cause of her ruin and prosper at her expense.[79]

Sir John Pakington had no hesitation in attacking what he felt was unconstitutional use of the Royal prerogative over the Bewdley Charter in a manner which amply demonstrates the stress he felt should be put on the 'ancient constitution':

how great soever the discouragements are to freedom of speech, I think myself obliged, as an English gentleman, who never will comply with an arbitrary ministry; as a member of this House, who have been always zealous to support the constitution of parliaments; as a neighbour to this borough in question in the case now before us, to speak my mind with that warmth I used to do, when the liberties of my country, or any part of it, seemed to be touched.[80]

Shippen, speaking on the same subject two years later, claimed, ' 'twas arbitrary and illegal and tended to the destroying the constitutions of Parliaments'.[81] Within this framework there remained room for undoubted veneration of the monarchy and respect for what remained of the royal prerogative — provided it kept within bounds of which they approved. Charles Eversfield made a brief speech on the 'No Peace Without Spain' clause in the debate of December 1711 which is redolent of this attitude:

par deference pour ce que la Reyne avoit declare dans son discours, il ne voteroit pas pour cette clause, mais qu'il ne vouloit pas qu'on entendit par là, qu'il

consentoit à une mauvaise Paix, et qu'il ne voyoit pas comment l'omission de
cette clause pourroit mettre un Ministre à couvert, qui aviseroit la Reyne de faire
un Paix prejudiciable au Royaume.[82]

Given such stridently constitutionalist principles with respect to their
Jacobitism, it is hardly surprising to find the Jacobites at Westminster among
the most fervent believers in 'Country' principles in general, and, in accord
with the view that corruption and management had allowed the executive to
exceed the bounds set by the 'ancient constitution', determined reducers of the
powers of any government. Hence the stance of prominent Jacobite Tories on
issues like the Bewdley Charter, where Pakington had also claimed:

if it be in the power of the crown to dissolve old corporations, and erect new, in
so exorbitant a manner, we may bid adieu to liberty and property, and to all that
has cost so much blood and treasure to maintain and defend; there will be no
difference between a parliament of Great Britain and a parliament of Paris.[83]

And hence the presence of Lockhart, Shippen and Henry Campion on the
Commission of Accounts set up in 1711. Thomas Strangways senior and
Shippen also led the October Club's presentation of the resumption bills of
1711 and 1712, Strangways declaring on the first occasion:

qu'il etoit insupportable de voir que pendant que toute la Nation se trouvait
plongeé dans une si grande Misere et accableé non seulement des impôts sans
nombre pour soutenir la guerre mais aussi des Dettes prodigeuses. Ceux à qui le
feu Roy avoit donné des dons, triomphoient et vivoient dans un splendeur et
luxure extraordinaire aux depens de la Couronne et de la Nation, que ces Dons
alloient au de là de ce qu'aucun Roy avoit jamais fait, et qu'il etoit juste de leur
oter ces biens et de les employer pour le bien public.[84]

Admittedly, an attack on the memory of William III was something every
Jacobite would relish, but the 'Country' principles therein should not be
ignored because of that. Their 'Country' principles were as much part of their
Jacobitism as *vice-versa*. Added together these gave a fierce zeal to their
Toryism which made the Jacobites prominent advocates of a thoroughgoing
purge of all Whigs left in the administration after 1710.[85] To the Jacobites an
anti-Whig purge did not so much represent the securing of the Tory party as
the securing of the State and constitution.

The ideological mainspring of Parliamentary Jacobitism was zealous
constitutionalism. Its concomitant was that Jacobites at Westminster were,
virtually *per se*, members of the Country wing of the Tory party. Their
principles represented not just the absorption of the new model Toryism
hammered out in the 1690s, but in many ways the follow-through of its
principles to their logical conclusion. If the Revolution represented the
beginning of so many bad things, was it not reasonable to question the wisdom
of ever having had a Revolution at all? The Parliamentary Jacobites were not
archaic unreconstructed upholders of Divine Right, like the Nonjurors and
Roman Catholics, they were very modern Tories in almost every sense.

It is now possible, with care, to establish a tentative picture of just how the Jacobites at St Germain and Westminster saw their world and their part in it. The most outstanding feature was the belief in a form of historical inevitability. All Jacobites at this time felt themselves to be following the path of rectitude towards a certain reward. In a more mystical sense they saw themselves as the spiritual heirs of the 'Malignants' of the Commonwealth, marching on with nothing but their unflinching loyalty to sustain them, but with no doubts as to their eventual success. In acting out this role they had to have a 'Great Man' to complete the cast: the new Monk, the new deliverer. The amount of effort the Jacobites put into achieving this end suggests that the finding of this saviour was more important than anything else they undertook with a view to restoring James. Thereby they could strike a practical blow for their cause and follow the precedents by which they set so much store. In all this conscious emulation an essential motivating force was the absolute conviction of divine sanction. Through the mediation of his good but timid sister God would restore his servant James and his loyal followers. Ironically, in this the Jacobites resemble no-one so much as the 'Godly Armies' of the Great Civil War, certain that the Lord of Hosts would deliver their enemies into their hands.

The Glorious Revolution and its aftermath were universally regarded as infamous among the Jacobites. But here the Jacobite point of view divides. Whereas to the exiled Court their existence and their victory to come were vindications of the man they regarded as a wronged saint, to the British Jacobites their victory would set right the compounded errors of a process begun by him. As lord North and Grey noted succinctly in his jottings in reply to the Commons Managers' arguments during the Sacheverell impeachment, 'our reputation abroad very good for every thing but our fidelity and obedience'.[86] The new restoration would set this right. The best way of going about this was a subject on which St Germain and the British Jacobites, particularly the Protestants, differed still further. The exiled Court could see nothing better than a French-backed invasion and uprising, which was sure to succeed and entailed no compromises or concessions. Those in Britain became convinced that there was no need for such dangerous measures or distasteful reliance on France, and force of circumstance obliged St Germain to accept this view, though its own wishes remained in the background, to surface whenever there was the faintest hope of fulfilment. Over this issue two opposing 'certainties' clashed and were resolved, but over the religious question no resolution was possible, only gathering acrimony. To the exiled Court it was offensive to be called on to comply with the dictates of a religion it believed was fundamentally flawed, by men whose motives it doubted. To the Protestant Jacobites it was a distasteful necessity that they were obliged to press such an issue, and an affront when they were brusquely rebuffed. The whole episode was characterised by impatience and misunderstanding on the part of St Germain — feelings which also characterised its attitude towards the British political scene: impatience because the leaders at the exiled Court were confident that Parliament would always do as it was instructed, as in the halcyon days of their dimly remembered past, and misunderstanding because they did not understand the changes a Revolution, two wars and innumerable crises had wrought on the world they recalled. The degree to which the exiled Court was out of touch with the Britain of 1710-14 was only ever revealed to old exiles who were allowed to return home, and found themselves in a bewildering new world: 'Monsieur Stafford me mande par sa dernier qu'il se trouve comme dans un nouveau monde. La plupart de ses anciens amis sont morts: nouvelle decoration nouveaux personages. Inclinations, moeurs, maximes, interests, tout est change'.[87]

The Parliamentary Jacobites shared in the beliefs and preconceptions common to the Jacobite movement as a whole, but in a diluted form. Their Jacobitism sprang from a different source than that of their peers: a fixed belief in the 'ancient constitution', which included Indefeasible Hereditary Right in the Royal line. As they saw it, departure from this had wrought terrible havoc on society, Church and State, which could only be retrieved if the 'ancient constitution' was restored in its entirety — by the restoration of the rightful line. Such views naturally put the Jacobites on the Country wing of the Tory party and heightened their party feeling. For men with such an intense commitment to what they saw as the rightful order of the world, there could be no compromise with its enemies. Anyone who threatened what was left of this political order, or opposed its reinvigoration, was fit only to be attacked *à l'outrance*, be he Whig or Court Tory. The Parliamentary Jacobites thus represented an advanced element in the development of the party system. Because they could not conceive of their opponents having any virtues whatsoever, and behaved accordingly, they were acting to drive the Tory party away from any form of political compromise, which meant that a one-party State would be the only adequate means of political management. Above all else the Jacobites were good Tories. By restoring James they would restore the 'ancient constitution' and hence preserve the order in which they fervently believed — an order in which, they were sure, the Tory party would return to its natural dominance.

NOTES

1. Carte 180, f. 1: declaration issued by James from Bar-le-Duc, 29 Aug. 1714 ns.

2. Lockhart, i, 473-5; BL, Add. MSS. 47087 (Sir John Percival's journal), f. 64; H.T. Dickinson, *Liberty and Property* (1977), pp.13-56, note: this chapter follows on from Professor Dickinson's analysis of Tory ideology.

3. See John Lade's comment on the Abjuration Act, cited in: Holmes, *Politics*, p.88; Lockhart, i, 317.

4. Portland, x, 372: [Ogilvie] to [Harley], 26 May 1711; Portland Loan 29/11/2: C[harlwood]. L[awton]. to Oxford (Robert Harley was created earl of Oxford in May 1711), 6 Jan. 1714.

5. Gualterio 31259, f. 51: Nairne to Gualterio, 28 June 1714 ns; Gualterio 31255, f. 12: James to Gualterio, 23 July 1714 ns.

6. For a brief summary of this theory of cyclical progress, see: S. Crehan, 'The Roman Analogy', *Literature and History*, vi (1981), 22-3. I am indebted to Mr. C. Johns for this reference.

7. *Quadriennium Annae Postremum; or the Political state of Great Britain*, ed. A. Boyer (1718-19), vii, 125-69; Bonet 39A, f. 10: 12 Jan. 1714 ns.

8. Portland Loan 29/45J/7/128: 'Extrait d'une lettre de Paris', 9 Nov. [1711] ns.

9. BL, Add. MSS. 14854, f. 54; University Library of North Wales, Baron Hill MS. 6779: 'A Letter from Mr. Lesley to a Member of Parliament', 23 Apr. 1714 ns.

10. Portland, v, 334-6: newsletter, 17 Sept. 1713. See also: Carte 238, ff. 233-5: Middleton to Torcy, 13 July 1712 ns; Hermitage FFF, ff. 259-60: 24 June 1712.

11. Carte 212, f. 35: Middleton to 'Watson', 12 June 1712 ns.

12. *Went Corr.*, pp.340-1: Peter Wentworth to the earl of Strafford (his brother), 3 July 1713; W. Cobbett, *Parliamentary History of England* (1806) vi, 1234.

13. Gualterio 46495, f. 128: 22 July 1714 ns.

14. Macpherson, ii, 365-6: Innes to Middleton, 2 Jan. 1713 ns, ii, 327-31: Buckingham to Middleton, 1 July 1712, may also be referring to this.

15. Fieldhouse, pp.451-2: D'Iberville to Torcy, 21 Mar. 1714 ns; Wickham-Legg, p.506: Gualtier to Torcy, 14 Dec. 1713 ns.

16. Carte 180, ff. 282-4: Middleton to Torcy, Sept. 1711; Macpherson, ii, 333-4: 'S. Johnson' to Middleton, 8 July 1712; Gualterio 31258, ff. 24-5: Stafford to Gualterio, 11 Jan. 1712 ns; AAE 233, f. 16: 'Count' Azzurini to Torcy (extracts), 10-24 July 1711.

17. Gualterio 31256, f. 45: Perth to Gualterio, 29 Feb. 1712 ns.

18. Lockhart, i, 344-5.

19. Carte 212, ff. 28-9: Middleton to St Amand, 31 Mar. 1712 ns; Gualterio 31256, f. 84: Perth to Gualterio, 25 June 1714 ns. See also: Carte 211, f. 180: [lady Middleton] to [Middleton], 30 April 1713 ns; Berwick, *Mémoires*, p.129.

20. Macpherson, ii, 158-9: July 1710. See also: Carte 212, f. 18: Middleton to Menzies, 19 Mar. 1711 ns; f. 36: Nairne to St Amand, 29 June 1712 ns; Stuart, i, 278, 318-19: Berwick to James, 10 Oct. 1713 ns and 27 Apr. 1714 ns.

21. Stuart, i, 307-8: Berwick to James, 13 Mar. 1713 ns; Macpherson, ii, 233: Middleton to Tunstal, 18 Nov. 1711 ns; Carte 212, f. 38: Nairne to St. Amand, 7 Aug. 1712 ns.

22. Carte 212, f. 21; Middleton to Ferguson, 21 Sept. 1711 ns; f. 25: Middleton to Menzies, 17 Feb. 1712 ns; f. 32: Nairne to St Amand, 7 Apr. 1712 ns.

23. *Ibid.*, ff. 50-1: Middleton to St Amand, 9 Mar. 1713 ns.

24. *Ibid.*, ff. 60-1: Nairne to Menzies, 24 Oct. 1713 ns.

25. Stuart, i, 294-5, 299-300; Berwick to James, 4 and 21 Feb. 1714 ns; Salomon, *Geschichte*, pp.335-6: James to Gaultier, 26 Feb. 1714 ns.

26. Stuart, i, 276-7: Berwick to James, 2 and 7 Oct. 1713 ns.

27. *Ibid.*, i, 287-8: Berwick to James, 24 Dec. 1713 ns; AAE 262, ff. 351-4: James to Torcy, 3 Aug. 1714 ns.

28. Stuart, i, 310-11: Berwick to James, 28 Mar. 1714 ns. See also: i, 310: 27 Mar. 1714 ns; AAE 262, f. 188: James to Torcy, 18 June 1714 ns.

29. AAE 230, f. 439: 26 Dec. 1710 ns.

30. Kreienberg 107a, f. 97: 25 Jan. 1712.

31. BL, Add. MSS. 28055 (Godolphin correspondence), f. 440: [?] to the earl Godolphin, 25 June 1712.

32. [Anon, but dedicated to Richard Cresswell M.P., a noted Jacobite], *The Old Wives Tale* (1712), pp.10-20; Gualterio 20311, ff. 180-7: *The D[uke]. of M[arlboroug]h's Vindication* [1712].

33. Lockhart, i, 443.

34. National Library of Scotland, Wodrow Letters, Quarto 7, ep. 82: Thomas Smith M.P. to John Crosse (Robert Wodrow's transcript), 26 Mar. 1713. See also: Bonet 37B, f. 297: 8 June 1711.

35. E. Gregg, 'Was Queen Anne a Jacobite?, *History*, lvii (1972), 358-75, is the best analysis of this subject.

36. Macpherson, ii, 278-9: Mrs Murray to [Middleton], 26 Feb. 1712; AAE 230, f. 318: Gaultier to Torcy, 3 Oct. 1710 ns.

37. Lockhart, i, 481.

38. Carte 180, ff. 256-7: 29 Aug. 1710 ns. See also: Carte 210, f. 408: James to Anne, 28 Mar. 1712 ns; Salomon, *Geschichte*, p.338: James to Anne, 3 Mar. 1714 ns.

39. Carte 210, f. 350: [Middleton] to [James], [Apr.?] 1710; Salomon *Geschichte*, p.346: James to Torcy, 27 July 1714 ns.

40. Gualterio 31259, ff. 25-6: Nairne to Gualterio, 22 Mar. 1714 ns; Gualterio 31256, f. 79: Perth to Gualterio, 1 Apr. 1714 ns.

41. Gualterio 31258, f. 231: Stafford to Gualterio, 11 Dec. 1712 ns.

42. Portland, iv, 629-31: Defoe to Harley, 18 Nov. 1710; Macpherson, ii, 228-33: Tunstal to Middleton, 3 Nov. 1711.

43. G.V. Bennett, *The Tory Crisis in Church and State, 1688-1730* (Oxford, 1975), pp.104-5. There was a tendency, though, among High Tories to regard the Revolution as the beginning of the corruption of the State which must lead to its eventual ruin. This left them ideologically vulnerable to Jacobite propaganda. For an example of its effects, see: G.S. Holmes, 'Gregory King and the Social Structure of Pre-Industrial England', *Transactions of the Royal Historical Society*, xxvii (1977), 41-68.

44. Carte 180, f. 1: proclamation by James, 29 Aug. 1714 ns.

45. Haile, *the Old Chevalier*, p.353.

46. Gualterio 46495, ff. 136-7: Dempster to Gualterio, 5 Aug. 1714 ns.

47. AAE 232, f. 82: French translation of Shippen's speech, 13 Mar. 1711 ns. Another version of this speech can be found in: Scottish Record Office, GD 112/40/7/7/33 (Breadalbane papers): 'Leter from a Gentleman att London to his friend att Edin[bu]r[gh] Concerning Mr. Shippens speech in the House of Commons', Mar. 1711. Lockhart expressed similar sentiments in a conversation with a Hanoverian Tory in 1714: Lockhart, i, 473-6.

48. Wodrow Papers, Folio 35, Item 84. See also: AAE 251, f. 242: D'Iberville to Torcy, 10 Apr. 1714 ns.

49. Baron Hill MS. 6779.

50. Carte 180, f. 1: proclamation by James, 29 Aug. 1714 ns.

51. Salomon, *Geschichte*, pp.331-2: James to Torcy, 16 Apr. 1713 ns; Baschet 200, f. 233: James to Torcy, 12 Oct. 1712 ns; AAE 250, f. 163: James to Torcy, 12 Dec. 1713 ns; 262, ff. 189-90: James to Torcy, 18 June 1714 ns.

52. Carte 180, ff. 255-63: Middleton to Torcy, 29 Aug. 1710 ns; Gualterio 31256, f. 8: Perth to Gualterio, 14 Aug. 1710 ns; Stuart, i, 287-8, 317: Berwick to James, 24 Dec. 1713 ns and 20 Apr. 1714 ns.

53. Carte 180, ff. 286-96.

54. Blair Lett: 14 Dec. 1713 and 19 and 20 Jan. 1714; Dalhousie 14/336/14: Lockhart to Henry Maule, 29 Apr. 1714. For a contrary Nonjurant view, held by a few

hardliners, see: Hertfordshire R.O., Panshanger MSS. D/EP F200, ff. 23-4: the earl of Carnwath to Sir David Hamilton [c. Feb. 1716].

55. AAE 261, ff. 169-70: anon. to D'Iberville, 9 Feb. 1714.

56. Stuart, i, 311-12: Berwick to James, 1 Apr. 1714 ns.

57. Macpherson, ii, 385-6: 18 Feb. 1713 ns.

58. Stuart, i, 251-2, 279-80, 280-1, 306-7: Berwick to James, 20 Nov. 1712 ns, 17 and 25 Oct. 1713 ns and 9 Mar. 1714 ns.

59. Baschet 200, f. 215: Middleton to Torcy, 20 Sept. 1712 ns.

60. Stuart, i, 279-80: Berwick to James, 17 Oct. 1713 ns; Gualterio 31258, f. 198: Stafford to Gualterio, 30 Oct. 1712 ns; Gualterio 46495, ff. 7-8: Dempster to Gualterio, 29 Oct. 1713 ns; Baschet 197, f. 343: Torcy to Berwick, 17 June 1711 ns.

61. Gualterio 31254, f. 443: Queen Mary to Gualterio, 20 Aug. 1714 ns. See also: Salomon, *Geschichte*, p.347: James to Torcy, 25 Aug. 1714 ns.

62. Blair Lett: 9 Nov. 1713. See also: Baschet 201, ff. 107-9: D'Aumont to Louis XIV, 21 Oct. 1713 ns.

63. Lockhart, i, 321-3; Macpherson, ii, 301-2: Netterville to [Middleton], 22 Apr. 1712; ii, 386-7: Ferguson to Middleton, Feb. 1713; ii, 398-400, 412-13: Plunket to Ellis, 22 May and 22 June 1713.

64. Carte 212, f. 38: Middleton to St Amand, 4 Aug. 1712 ns; f. 40: Nairne to Menzies, 1 Sept. 1712 ns; Carte 210, f. 411: open letter by 'John Newnman', 7 Aug. 1712 ns.

65. Macpherson,ii, 384-5: Innes to Middleton, 18 Feb. 1713 ns.

66. Gualterio 20296, f. 13: Perth to Gualterio, 20 Nov. 1712 ns; Blair Lett: 17 Oct. 1710 and 14 Mar. 1711.

67. J. Miller, *James II: a study in Kingship* (1978), pp.151,169,241.

68. Carte 212, f. 45: Nairne to Menzies, 14 Nov. 1712 ns; Stuart, i, 309: Berwick to James, 22 Mar. 1714 ns; Gualterio 31259, f. 30: Nairne to Gualterio, 5 Apr. 1714 ns.

69. Hermitage GGG, ff. 365-6: 13 Oct. 1713. See also: Macpherson, ii, 545-6: Georg von Schütz (Hanoverian Envoy to Britain, 1713-14) to Robethon, 5 Jan. 1714.

70. Carte 212, f. 52: Middleton to St Amand, 6 Apr. 1713 ns.

71. Bodl. MS Rawl. Letters 42 (Rawlinson papers), f. 67: 15 Aug. 1713.

72. Legh MSS: Dr. Roger Kenyon to Peter Legh, 1 and 15 Nov. 1712.

73. Blenheim 61461, f. 138: Maynwaring to the duchess of Marlborough, [July 1711?].

74. Carte 180, ff. 255-63: Middleton to Torcy, 29 Aug. 1710 ns.

75. Gualterio 46494, ff. 238, 246: Caryll to Gualterio, 2 Oct. and 15 Dec. 1710 ns; Gualterio 31258, ff. 113-14: Stafford to Gualterio, 29 June 1712 ns; Gualterio 46495, ff. 5, 81-2: Dempster to Gualterio, 1 Oct. 1713 ns and 25 Mar. 1714 ns.

76. Stuart, i, 272-3: Berwick to James, 18 Aug. 1713 ns; Carte 180, ff. 309-16: Middleton to Torcy, Oct. 1711.

77. Gualterio 46495, ff. 105-6: Dempster to Gualterio, 20 May 1714 ns.

78. Lockhart, i, 21-2, 24.

79. National Library of Wales, Aberystwyth, Ottley MS. 2448 [c. Apr. 1712].

80. Cobbett, *Parl. Hist.*, vi, 932-3.

81. *The Correspondence of Sir James Clavering*, ed. H.T. Dickinson [Surtees Society, Gateshead, 1967], pp.104-6: Anne Clavering to James Clavering, 21 Dec. 1710.

82. Kreienberg 107a, f. 48: 11 Dec. 1711.

83. Cobbett, *Parl. Hist.*, vi, 934. Lockhart showed a similar reverence for the

constitution by his determination to have it respected in Parliamentary speeches; for example see: Lockhart, i, 330.

84. Kreienberg 99, ff. 145-6: 2 Mar. 1711.

85. Portland Loan 29/150/3: Lockhart to Oxford, 27 Jan. 1713; Portland, v, 478-9: Lockhart to Oxford, 30 July [1713].

86. Bodl., MS. North A3 (North and Grey papers), f. 138 [early 1710].

87. Gualterio 46495, ff. 9-10: Dempster to Gualterio, 5 Nov. 1713 ns.

3

'The Church in Danger': the Jacobites and the general election of 1710

Violent contests at general elections were characteristic of the period 1688-1722. Of them all, that of 1710 lays fair claim to being one of the worst. The election was fought along traditional lines: the Tories on the issue of 'the Church in Danger' and the Whigs on the issue of 'Popery and the Pretender'. Each side also tried to create a powerful secondary theme. The Tories hinted that Whig war-profiteering lay behind the failure to make peace in 1709, and promised an investigation and suitable punishment for the culprits. The Whigs tried to work up an invasion scare, but prompt official ridicule and the despatch of a squadron to cruise off the northern French ports soon discredited that.[1] The main Tory slogan was given added credence by the imprint left on the popular memory by both the Whig impeachment of Dr Sacheverell and the Tory protests which had accompanied it. For once, moderate Tory opinion did not doubt that the High-Fliers' loudly proclaimed fears for the security of the Church were justified. With the Court standing neutral or inclining to the Tories, and public opinion roused in their favour by the Sacheverell affair, the Tories managed to inflict a crushing defeat on their rivals at the polls.

As could have been expected from their customary zeal for the Church and its party, the Jacobites were active campaigners for the Tory cause in both England and Scotland. There was, however, a wide divergence between their contribution to the Tory victory in each country. In England and Wales, Jacobites with a Parliamentary interest or ambitions were distributed fairly randomly throughout supporters of the Tory party. In Scotland, the Jacobites had adopted a definitely nationalistic stance during political battles over the passage of the Act of Union. This had brought the Jacobites together as a group in 1707-8, and the Government's arrests of suspected persons in 1708 had hardened this association into what was virtually a separate party. The Nonjurors and Roman Catholics in both England and Scotland discreetly supported their local Tory interest, but where possible put their weight behind a Jacobite candidate.[2]

In England Parliamentary interests in the constituencies were rarely monolithic. The interest of either of the two parties in a given seat was usually made up of a number of individual or family interests acting in alliance. Jacobite interests were likely to be more useful to the Tory party in most situations than calmer, more moderate forms of Toryism because of their greater reliability. Jacobites were extremely unlikely to compromise with the Whig interests under any circumstances, and were therefore liable to constitute the mainstay of the Tory interest where they were strong, or a loyal ally where they were not. This did not mean that they were automatically able to wield greater influence than more moderate Tory interests in the choice of candidates. Enthusiastic as the Jacobites were for the Tory cause, they could still be profoundly embarrassing if allowed to be too outspoken and frighten more moderate Tories into neutrality or the support of Whig candidates.[3] Party zeal predisposed the Jacobite element of the Tory interest in a given seat to accept the nomination of more moderate men than it would necessarily have liked in order to keep the Tory interest united. Because such action inevitably submerged whatever Jacobite interest there was in a given constituency, this is hard to detect precisely. There is indirect evidence, however, where Jacobite candidates were successful. The constituencies which returned them either contained an overwhelmingly preponderant interest acting in their favour, or else they were discreetly reticent about their views relating to the succession.[4] The new Harleyite ministry quickly made it abundantly clear that they did not favour overt displays of Jacobitism even in support of the ministry's own campaign. An example was made of Leslie for writing a violently anti-Whig tract, *the Good Old Cause*, by issuing a warrant for his arrest for high treason. He fled the country and was unable to return until 1711. The Nonjuror George Hickes found in consequence that all his Tory friends were currently shunning him 'for fear of the scandalous imputation of being inclined to pretenderism, which is now a word of greater offence than Atheism, or Deism, or Whiggism, or any other party words which end in that or any other termination'.[5] In essence the Jacobites were put in a cleft stick by their own commitment. Being Jacobites, they could not abide the thought of a Whig succeeding where a Tory might have got in, and were as a result constrained to support whichever candidate local Tory opinion felt was suitable.

Although they were scattered and officially discouraged, it is clear that individual Jacobites throughout England contributed significantly to the Tory electoral success of 1710. Harley had no qualms about using Jacobite interest in returning pro-Government M.P.'s. In June Sir Simon Harcourt was sent to sound out the duke of Beaufort, whom he found 'as well disposed as you can wish him to be, and yet ... not without some apprehensions'. Appointment to the Privy Council and the Lord Lieutenancy of Hampshire soon removed Beaufort's doubts. Thereafter he campaigned energetically to return Tories favourable to the Court wherever he had an interest,[6] in the course of which he was obliged to make local pacts with the Whigs in such constituencies as Petersfield and Monmouth, as well as help return unabashedly pro-Hanoverian Tories like George Pitt for Hampshire. Despite his fabled electoral interest, Beaufort was able to return only one overt Jacobite and three M.P.'s who were probably sympathetic.[7] This is not very impressive, but amply demonstrates the degree to which Jacobite Tories were limited by the need to ensure that, wherever possible, no Whig was returned.

Beaufort was the only Jacobite magnate whose electoral influence extended further than the area surrounding his country seat. Others, such as lord North and Grey and the earls of Scarsdale and Yarmouth, possessed only one among many local Tory interests (except when in office) and so merely threw in their moiety behind the local party's candidate. Otherwise, most Jacobite M.P.'s were returned on a strong personal interest which led the other Tory interests to fall in behind it as the one most likely to succeed. The elections of Thomas Forster in Northumberland, Richard Cresswell in Bridgnorth and Charles Eversfield in Sussex are all examples.

Where a Jacobite interest did manage to seize the candidature, the election campaign was usually fought with singular passion. Other Tory versus Whig contests where Jacobites were not involved were also fought with great fury in 1710, but where a Jacobite was present the likelihood of a bitter struggle was certainly increased. In Bridgnorth, Cresswell made maximum use of Sacheverell's grand progress to inflame Tory opinion in his favour:

> here is a vast bustle at Bridgnorth about the Election for Burgesses for next Parliament. Mr Richard Cresswell everyone thinks will certainly carry it, and most believe that both the old members will be turned out, they have drawn up a Tory address and Mr Cresswell is to carry it up within a short time, Dr Sacheverell is the Idol of the country, and Mr Cresswell designs to carry him to Bridgenorth with as much Pomp and attendance from the Bailiffs and recorder of the Town as he was mett with Bambury Warwick & c.[8]

Sacheverell was greeted with similar demonstrations of acclaim in Worcester, where Sir John Pakington had a strong interest. In spite of Bishop Lloyd's having had the clappers removed from the Church bells to prevent their being rung to greet the procession, pro-Sacheverell demonstrators got into the tower and rang them with hammers. Bonfires were also lit in the streets and the statue of Charles I decked with flowers.[9] In Shropshire the Tory candidates John Kynaston and Robert Lloyd arranged for a body of fifty clergymen, led by Dean Ottley, to ride in procession to the polls to vote for them.[10] In Aberystwyth, Lewis Pryse, John Pugh of Maternfarme, William Powell, William Barlow and other gentlemen drank James's health upon their knees. Jacobite candidates and patrons also made full use of the normal ruses of electioneering. Pryse, who was short of votes, intended to close the poll early on the slightest provocation from the Whigs, and then petition against Sir Thomas Powell, the Whig candidate. Beaufort continuously bombarded Harley with demands for the dismissal of Whig officials and their replacement by 'suitable' Tories in Hampshire and Gloucestershire.[11]

There was some cooperation between Jacobite candidates who had overlapping interests, but no more so than was usual between neighbouring Tory candidates. Cresswell supported Kynaston and Lloyd in the county election, but so did every other Tory standing in Salop. The Jacobites did not differentiate between themselves and other Tories in England in 1710, and were therefore content to support any candidate they could with the right party label. John Kynaston offered to pay half of Robert Lloyd's costs if he would run as his partner in Salop. Thomas Forster had no qualms about offering to support any candidate Harley cared to nominate at Morpeth.[12] Peter Legh returned both his fiery brother Thomas and his Nottinghamite pro-Hanoverian friend, John Ward, for his pocket borough of Newton. Beaufort had no compunction about supporting George Pitt as well as Sir Simeon Stuart in Hampshire, nor in helping his fellow-member of the Board of Brothers, the earl of Barrymore, at Stockbridge. In only one case did a local Jacobite interest refuse to support a pro-Government Tory candidate: in Staffordshire, where lord Ferrers witheld his support and openly abused Harley.[13]

The Jacobite determination to return almost any Tory rather than let a Whig in was not always reciprocated where moderate Tories had an interest in a constituency with a Jacobite candidate. Sir Richard Myddleton curtly refused to appear in support of Cresswell and Whitmore Acton at Bridgenorth.[14] The defection of the Lisburne interest in Carmarthan led to Lewis Pryse's defeat at the poll. It was clearly quite acceptable for a moderate Tory to vote for a Whig candidate if alarmed enough by the Tory candidate's principles, whereas it was almost inconceivable for a Jacobite to do so.

In England and Wales the Jacobites did not yet feel distinct from the Tory party as a whole. They behaved accordingly: as zealous Tories rather than Jacobites. This was greatly to the advantage of the Tory party, as it meant that their efforts were wholeheartedly engaged in ensuring its success. In general the Sacheverell impeachment and the subsequent election united the moderate Tories and the High-Fliers more strongly than anything else since 1702. For a brief but vital period both elements in the party were in accord in believing that the Church was in danger. The Jacobites played the same part in this as the other High-Fliers: they gave the Tory campaign its energy and enthusiasm.

In Scotland the nature of the political situation was completely different. Even outside the Highlands landed magnates still wielded electoral influence of an order almost unknown in England. Political deference was still customary in most of Scotland even among voters with the relatively high level of income required for the franchise. Scotland was an economically backward country too, so that a Scots lord who was poor by English standards could be rich by Scots, and still possessed of considerable importance for an area. A magnate's estates also tended to be fairly concentrated geographically, the prime example being the earl of Sutherland who owned virtually the whole of the area from which he took his title. In the Highlands this considerable potential for electoral influence underwent a manifold increase owing to heritable jurisdictions and the survival of the clan system. However, there were limiting factors. Only a few lords retained estates of any significance. Most were chronically and perennially in debt. A sizeable minority, such as lord Duffus and the earl of Home, were so poor that they had little to distinguish them from their gentry neighbours but the right to vote in the election of Representative Peers, and the legal privileges of peerage. There were also relatively large numbers of Nonjurant and Roman Catholic peers, whose political influence was curtailed by their legal disabilities. In general the Scots political nation was led by its nobility, although there were notable exceptions such as Glasgow, Edinburgh and some of the more economically successful Royal Burghs.

These circumstances favoured the administration, of whatever political complexion. Near-destitute Scots peers could only hope for honourable financial salvation through Government service or charity. The Court made these incentives available only to those who had proved their loyalty in the peers' elections and by returning M.P.'s of whom it approved. Of the two, the election of the sixteen Representative Peers was by far the most important in 1710. Management of the House of Lords always posed a major problem for Tory governments between 1688 and 1714, because of its inbuilt Whig majority. Harley had to keep some Whig peers in his administration for this reason if no other. The Scots peers represented the vital safety margin his Government needed to survive. Without their voting with the Court and the Tories in the Lords, or worse still, if they defected to the Whigs, Harley's ministry faced the prospect of continual harassment or even defeat there. The Scots M.P.'s could have had a similar value to the Court, but in the event the 1710 election was won in England, which meant that their votes were not essential to the Government's survival.

This situation found the Scots peerage broadly divided into three parts. There was a sizeable Episcopal/Jacobite Tory group led by the duke of Hamilton, which because of its anti-Union 'Country' party antecedents still retained some Presbyterians such as the marquis of Annandale ('pour la succession [Hanoverian] contre l'union.'[15]) and lord Saltoun. Opposed to these were the Squadrone peers. In effect these were the Scots Whigs, and they were led by their own Junto: the dukes of Montrose and Roxburgh, the marquess of Tweeddale, and the earls of Marchmont and Rothes. Politically distinct from these two was a substantial Court party. This in turn was subdivided into two parts: those already in the queen's service, and a mass of hopeful place-seekers who usually had links with all three groups but adhered to the Court party in practice in the hope of appointments. Not all of these were merely apolitical, avaricious fortune-hunters. In Scotland, as to a lesser extent in England, there existed the remnants of the old apolitical Court party which shunned all opposition as factious and adhered to the Court irrespective of reward.[16] In 1710 the duke of Queensberry (the Scots Secretary of State) remained well in the background during the political dealing before the election, as he was well aware that he was detested by all parties in Scotland, and involvement in the election might have led to his dismissal as the price of some group's adherence to the Court.[17] This left the organisation of the required electoral alliance in the hands of a group of Harley's associates: the earls of Mar, Kinnoull and Islay, and the duke of Argyll.

Throughout the 1710 elections the Scots Jacobite Tories showed all the characteristics of a contemporary political party. They agitated for political decisions favourable to them through Parliamentary and extra-Parliamentary means. They had an acknowledged leader who negotiated for the benefit of his followers for political as well as material returns. Meetings were held in which proposals of political alliance were discussed and decisions reached upon them. Perhaps most importantly of all, they had their own electoral programme. This was in two parts: one for public consumption, and one mooted quietly among the party faithful. The openly avowed first part consisted of promises to secure redress for the lords carried to London as prisoners in 1708, and to campaign at Westminster for a legal toleration for Episcopalianism. This platform was designed to attract moderate Episcopalian and nationalist interest, which it succeeded in doing.[18] The second part of the programme was not publicised at all: 'The Tories spoke little above board but under hand represented that now or never was the time to do something effectually for the King [James], and by restoring him dissolve the Union'. In areas where the Jacobites could declare their sympathies more freely, as in parts of the Highlands, Defoe was shocked to find this intention openly discussed and acknowledged.[19] This part of the platform served a double purpose not only by giving committed Jacobites an incentive to exert themselves to the utmost, but also in persuading the more uncompromising Nonjurant Episcopalians to take the oaths required to vote. Officially of course, the Jacobites eschewed any ambition to restore James, and Lockhart himself even published a pamphlet ridiculing the idea.[20]

Political negotiations over the Scots elections began early in August, when Harley first realised that he could not avoid having to dissolve Parliament. At first he seems to have hoped that his organisers in Scotland would be able to manage matters so that the Court would only have to take in moderate peers attached to neither party. Harley's reasoning is obvious: it would be embarrassing to be seen to be in alliance with the Scots Jacobites, yet an alliance with the Squadrone would be equally unsatisfactory because their close links with the Whigs made them politically unreliable at Westminster. Accordingly, Hamilton was at first offered only the Lord Lieutenancy of Lancashire and some vague promises (probably of a British peerage) to keep him quiet. Mar soon found that all this had achieved was the arousal of Hamilton's suspicions:

> The Duke of Ha[milton] is very uneasy that the Queen does not send for him, as he says you said she was to do, and the more that you forbad him to go there till then. If you give not him some other place than the Lieutenancy I am afraid he will not play fair with us, and you see by your accounts from Scotland how necessary it is at this time to have him, and it is evident how much your affairs depend on the right returns from Scotland.[21]

Kinnoull and his son, lord Dupplin, had warned Harley how necessary Hamilton was going to be earlier in August, but Harley preferred to listen to Argyll and Islay's assurances that a moderating scheme would work.[22] By mid-September Hamilton was negotiating with the Squadrone, and Kinnoull felt driven to expostulate: 'Whatever may be the measure most proper for advancing the Queen's interest in England I am not capable to judge of, but I am perfectly persuaded that the only measure here in Scotland is to go in entirely to the Tories'.[23] Harley finally bowed to necessity, Hamilton was summoned to the Court, and a working arrangement was patched up between him and his enemy, the duke of Atholl, for them both to support a joint list of peers to be elected. Hamilton ensured that he was a member of the committee, established to choose suitable candidates for the list, and whose other members comprised Argyll, Islay, Mar and Loudon, but that Atholl was not. From this position he was able to bring in six of his followers on the final list of officially approved candidates.[24]

It was by no means a foregone conclusion that the Jacobites in Scotland would support the Court, as was the case in England. Hamilton was well aware that only when Parliament was dissolved would the Jacobites be able to make use of their political strength. To add to the pressure on Harley to do this he had sent a circular letter to his friends in Scotland, asking that they write letters to him applauding the dismissal of Godolphin and advocating a dissolution.[25] A meeting of the leading Jacobites, both peers and commons, was arranged to take place as soon as possible after news of the dissolution arrived. From the tone of the invitations to this conference, it is apparent that the Jacobites were well aware that they held the key to the Government's success or failure in the forthcoming elections:

> By yesterdays post I had a letter from ye D. of Hamilton, desiring me to write to yr Lo[rdshi]p in his name, that as soon as you hear of ye parlmts dissolution, you'd make what hast you can to come to Edinburgh, it being necessar not only for honest men to stand firm to one another, but likewise, that they must concert and prosecute joint measures ... tis' as plain as 2 and 3 makes 5, yt if a certain sett stand together, they can cast ye ballance. Notwithstanding, att Court the language is yt not one of those whom they call Cavaliers [Jacobites], must be admitted in the List of the 16 peers.[26]

In the event, the dissolution did not occur until 26 September, by which time the leading Jacobites had already met. Refusing to be drawn by an attempt by Islay to deal with them piecemeal, they gave Hamilton virtual *carte blanche* to make the most advantageous alliance he could:

> I advised him from them that he should set up for himself and they doubt not but he'll be able to overturn Ambros [the Tories'] designs whom they think as violent for Philip Nortoun [Hanover] as English Rorie [the Whigs] is for Nicolas [Hanover], yet they advise him to dissemble with either of the two that will condescend to admitt manyest of his friends to be chosen for Richard [Parliament] and especially they wish it wer Ambros because seeming to be in with him he could make greatest discoveries.[27]

Hamilton secured the return of six of his own party, and was in a position on the selection committee to help put in two independent Jacobites: Home and lord Balmerino. The Court was most unwilling to accept viscount Kilsyth, who was notorious for his Jacobitism, but Hamilton insisted and carried his point.[28] Even though Hamilton had allied the Jacobites to the Court on advantageous terms, he still consulted St Germain on the subject, enquiring if their plans required him to deal with Whigs or Tories by preference.[29] Middleton replied with an unenthusiastic endorsement of Hamilton's choice:

> As to what relates to Ambrose Baker [Tories] and Nick Brewer [Whigs], let them bake as they brew, however notwithstanding Ambrose coldness on some occasions yet he is of an honest family [Tories], and I had much rather chuse him for my friend, than his antagonists.[30]

Hamilton's alliance assured the Court of success in the peers' election, and in the end the Squadrone gave up the struggle without a contest. Instead, they ostentatiously boycotted the proceedings, and threatened an investigation into corrupt practices by their Whig friends if they still had the majority in the Lords.[31]

In the Commons' elections the Court contented itself with staying neutral for the most part. Mar used his influence in Fife to help return Sir Alexander Areskine, lord Lyon king at arms, and Dupplin favoured the Hon. James Murray against a kinsman of Queensberry's in Perthshire, but these were exceptions.[32] This left some Jacobites with very hard electoral battles to fight. Richard Dongworth found that

> ye Presbyteries of Edinburgh and Dalkeith have given Public Orders to all their members, to use their utmost interest against Mr Lockhart of Carnwath, in ye next election for this shire: and it is said, yt ye Commission of ye Assembly ... has dispers'd their orders thro ye whole country, for their Friends to oppose ye Choice of Prelatic Lds and Commoners.[33]

This did not stop the Jacobites using their interests in favour of the Court's candidates. Having committed themselves to an alliance with the Court, the Jacobites were no less eager than their contemporaries to enjoy the Queen's bounty. Consequently, they were happy to be able to ingratiate themselves with the Court wherever possible by supporting candidates which it favoured. Lord Lyon cheerfully used his interest in Anstruther Easter Burghs in favour of Major General George Hamilton. Hamilton told Lord Glenorchy (Breadalbane's son) to persuade his father to support his enemy, the earl of Caithness's, nominee in Caithness because the Court favoured him. William Keith assured Harley that he was doing his best to return Court M.P.'s wherever he had influence. In Berwickshire Hamilton even supported a Squadrone M.P. at the Court's request.[34] The Court undoubtedly benefited from Jacobite support of many moderate candidates whom they would normally have opposed, or to whom at best they would have given only grudging support. The drawback of Jacobite support for these moderate M.P.'s was that it alarmed moderate Presbyterian political opinion to see such interest used in the Court's favour. Hence the wild rumours of an imminent Jacobite *coup d'état* which Defoe found rife among the Presbyterians, and the assumption that Court-supported M.P.'s were all Tories and/or crypto-

Jacobites. Even George Baillie, the staunchly Squadrone M.P. for Berwickshire, was not immune from such suspicions.[35]

Committed Jacobites took around sixteen of the forty-five Scots Commons seats. This represented a fourfold increase, at least, in the numbers returned, over the 1708 election.[36] It also meant that for the first time a cohesive body of Jacobites was returned to Westminster with an acknowledged political platform of their own. Moreover, their numbers were for the first time sufficient to draw others of similar sympathies to them. It is interesting to note that, since the Jacobites fought this election in the absence of the Court's hostility rather than with its positive help, this proportion of the Commons' representation is probably indicative of the strength of the Jacobite and nationalist interest at that time.

The significance of the Jacobite electoral success in Scotland was profound. Not only did it give the inchoate Jacobitism present in the English representation a nucleus round which to form, it also introduced into Westminster a group of Jacobites with an intrinsic grievance against any English Government. This was only a *potentially* dangerous departure: nationalistic Scots Jacobite Tories would not necessarily cooperate with equally nationalistic English Jacobite Tories. Events and political management had to be the crucial factors in fulfilling that potential.

NOTES

1. G.S. Holmes, *The Trial of Dr. Sacheverell* (1973), pp.242-55; Hermitage DDD, ff. 585 606: 25 Aug. and 29 Sept. 1710 ns; Portland, iv, 584, Dr Friend to Harley, 4 Sept. 1710.

2. R. Sedgwick, *The House of Commons, 1715-54* (1970), i, 295; Buckinghamshire R.O., Claydon House Letters, microfilm M11/54: the earl of Lichfield to viscount Fermanagh, 15 Dec. 1710; Blair Lett: 31 Jan. 1711.

3. As in Carmarthen, where Lewis Pryse's open avowal of James led to the defection of the Lisburne interest: Nat. Lib. of Wales, Penrice and Margam MS. L 695: [?] to Sir Thomas Mansel, 3 Nov. 1710.

4. Viscount Bulkeley was leader of the Anglesey Tories and did not need to conceal his views: Sedgwick, *Commons*, i, 505; nor did Shippen or Thomas Legh, Shippen because his patron had similar views, Legh because of his Nonjuring brother's absolute control of the seat: Szechi, pp.267, 269; George Granville felt it more politic to dissimulate his: Rashleigh MSS. (HPT): Granville to the electors of Cornwall, 29 Sept. 1710.

5. Hermitage DDD, f. 595: 12 Sept. 1710; Bodl. MS Ballard 12, f. 184: Hickes to Dr Arthur Charlett, 23 Dec. 1710.

6. Portland, iv, 545-6: Harcourt to Harley, 21 June 1710; Beaufort MSS. (HPT): Beaufort to John Morgan of Tredegar, 12 Sept. 1710; Beaufort to Henry Whitehead, 14 Sept. 1710; Beaufort to the electors of Bath and Gloucester [Sept. 1710].

7. Szechi, p.270, n.50; p.271, n.2 and n.4; p.272, n.10.

8. Lincoln R.O., Monson 7 book 13 (Newton papers), f. 123: George Scroop to Sir John Newton, 26 June 1710. See also: Holmes, *Sacheverell*, pp.247-8.

9. Portland, iv, 550: Thomas Foley to Harley, 17 July 1710.

10. Ottley MS. 2581: Samuel Baldwyn to lieutenant Ottley, 20 Oct. 1710.

11. P.D.G. Thomas, 'Jacobitism in Wales', *Welsh Hist. Rev.*, i (1963), 284; Penrice and Margam MS. L 695: [?] to Mansel, 3 Nov. 1710; Portland, iv, 599, 611: Beaufort to Harley, 23 Sept. and 9 Oct. 1710.

12. Staffordshire R.O., Bradford Muniments D 1287/10/4A(4B): Roger Owen to Sir John Bridgeman, 4 July 1710; Portland, iv, 598: Thomas Forster to Harley, 22 Sept. 1710.

13. Portland, iv, 608-9: Henry Paget to Harley, 7 Oct. 1710.

14. Nat. Lib. of Wales, Chirk Castle MS. E 985: Myddleton to Acton and Cresswell [Oct. 1710].

15. Holmes, *Politics*, pp.384-5; BL, Stowe MSS. 223, f. 20: list of the Scots peers elected in 1710, with short comments on their political sympathies.

16. Holmes, *Politics*, pp.385-6; see for example the earls of Loudoun and Rosebery.

17. Portland, iv, 622-3: Islay to Harley, 2 Nov. 1710.

18. H.L. Snyder, 'Party Configurations in the Early Eighteenth Century House of Commons', *Bull. Inst. Hist. Res.*, xlv (1972), 39; Lennoxglove, Hamilton MS. 4935: 'Old Donald' to the duke of Hamilton, 11 June [1710]; Christ Church, Oxford, Wake MSS., xvii, 262: Richard Dongworth to Bishop Wake of Lincoln, 10 Aug. 1710.

19. Lockhart, i, 319; Portland, iv, 629-31: Defoe to Harley, 18 Nov. 1710.

20. Lockhart, i, 509-20.

21. Portland, x, 331: Mar to Harley, 21 Aug. 1710.

22. *Ibid.*, iv, 558-9: Dupplin to Harley, 8 Aug. 1710; iv, 566: Kinnoull to Harley, 15 Aug. 1710; iv, 553-4: the earl of Orrery to Harley, 31 July 1710.

23. *Ibid.*, iv, 601-2: Kinnoull to Harley, 27 Sept. 1710; Blair Lett: 20 Sept. 1710.

24. Portland, iv, 601: Kinnoull to Harley, 26 Sept. 1710; x, 349-50: Mar to Harley, 7 Nov. 1710; see appendix 2.

25. GD 112/40/7/4/44: [William Cochrane of] Kilmaronock to the earl of Breadalbane, 29 Aug. 1710.

26. GD 112/40/7/6/23: Lockhart to Breadalbane, 7 Sept. 1710.

27. Blair Lett: 20 Sept. 1710.

28. Portland, x. 348 350-1: Mar to Harley, 2 and 9 Nov. 1710.

29. Blair Lett: 26 Sept. 1710.

30. Carte 212, f. 13: Middleton to Leslie, 23 Oct. 1710 ns.

31. Portland, x, 350-1: Mar to Harley, 9 Nov. 1710; *The Marchmont Papers*, ed. Sir George Rose (1831), pp.377-8: the earl of Marchmont to the duke of Devonshire, 12 Dec. 1710; Wodrow Letters, Quatro 5, ep. 47: Charles Morthland to Wodrow, 2 Dec. 1710.

32. Holmes, *Politics*, p.352; Mar MSS. 15/989/4-5: Sir John Erskine to Sir James Erskine (lord justice clerk), 12 and 29 Sept. 1710; Portland, iv, 564: Dupplin to Harley, 13 Aug. 1710.

33. Wake MSS., xvii, 262: Dongworth to Wake, 10 Aug. 1710. See also: Lockhart, i, 319.

34. Portland, x, 347, 356-7: Mar to Harley, [Oct] and 1 Nov. 1710; x, 340-1: Keith to Harley, 18 Sept. 1710; Mar MSS. 15/1011/1: Lyon to Erskine, 17 Sept. 1710; GD 112/40/7/4/45: lord Glenorchy to Breadalbane (his father), 26 Sept. 1710.

35. Wake MSS., xvii, 269: Dongworth to Wake, 11 Nov. 1710.

36. Lockhart, i, 301; D. Szechi, 'Some Insights on the Scottish Peers and M.P.'s Returned in the 1710 Election', *Scott. Hist. Rev.* lx (1981), 61-75.

4

'Honest countrey-men and dutiful subjects': the Parliamentary session of 1710-11

Though the Jacobites had, to varying extents, been obliged to restrain their enthusiasm during the election campaign, this restraint disappeared when the M.P.'s and peers arrived at Westminster. Once elected, they were constrained only by their consciences and future electoral prospects. The Jacobites constituted no more than a leavening in numerical terms, but their influence was not in proportion to their numbers but their zeal. The dedicated Jacobites formed the vanguard in Country Tory attempts to safeguard the Church and constitution they so valued. In one way this meant that Jacobite schemes and enthusiasm continued to be constrained, in another it gave the Jacobites a disproportionate influence among their fellows. The need to preserve Country Tory unity definitely acted as a brake upon them. On the other hand, backbench groupings have always been moved by their more radical elements, and those of the first Tory party were no exception. The Jacobites formed an articulate body within the Country Tories as a whole, and as such tended to radicalise the Country Tories in directions they favoured.

The mood in which the Country Tories came up to Westminster at the end of November 1710 was very favourable to the Government. Brigadier Hill told Sir William Trumbull: '[They] say they will be discreet, moderate, & governed'.[1] This impression is confirmed by the tone of High Tory correspondence on the subject of the new ministry. William Bromley and Arthur Annesley were frankly unstinting in their praise of Harley's success, and their Jacobite associates were no less admiring:

> Sr I cannot but with gratitude acknowledge your constant friendship to mee But also to the whole kingdoms [sic] In their deliverence from that enchantment they so long lay under, All your friendes heare were for a long time under greate feares, with small hopes till at last the welcome proclamation res[tored] them. And seeing the conjuerer with his juglars are brought downe, All men now hope that England and Englishe men will be fairley dealt by.[2]

All this indicates that at the outset there was a great deal of High Tory goodwill available for utilisation by an adept political manager. What is less obvious is that this goodwill was fragile. The High Tories were prepared to forgive Harley for splitting the party in 1705 now he had so triumphantly installed a Tory ministry, but they were certainly not going to forget it. Failure to make an immediate reality of High Tory dreams of the promised land was

liable to excite barely dormant suspicions. Brigadier Hill sensed this mood
when he remarked to Trumbull: 'our folks at Westminster are very reasonable
yet, & make not ill use of their superiority but I fear they will grow weary of
doing well'. Jaundiced observers like Sir Thomas Cave were already beginning
to take a pessimistic view of the Government's intentions as early as the
beginning of December: 'The ignorant country rejoyceth much, and seemeth
to expect great Alter[ati]ons from your House, by their unanimity in the
Speaker, and by our Confidence yt those, Who wou'd, have not force enough
to obstruct your Good designs'.[3] The greatest threat to this fund of goodwill
came from none other than Harley himself. The events of the summer and
autumn seem to have left him with a dangerously sanguine view of his hold on
the Tory party. This comes out most clearly in a forecast of the nature of both
houses during the next session which he wrote for Queen Anne at the end of
October:

> House of Commons. The majority there is apparent, the Queens servants must
> have directions to be prudent in conducting this majority, & the pleasing the
> clergy, avoiding giving jealousies, & the hopes of places after wil render the
> House easy this session. There is one weak place where the enemy may attack; &
> that is the Affair of the House of Hanover, but that must be left to the Queens
> great wisdome to consider how to prevent it.[4]

Essentially, he did not envisage having to make more than a politic gesture or
two to appease the High Tories' desire for revenge and further safeguards for
the Church. Judging from the boasts of Henry St John (Secretary of State for
the north 1710-13, and for the south 1713-14) to the earl of Orrery that they
would manage the Tory party into moderation, the rest of the ministry
endorsed Harley's attitude.[5] This was taking too much for granted and
undoubtedly helped precipitate the very extremism they wished to avoid.

For the first two months of the session the Commons was relatively calm as
Harley presented grandiose but inconsequential offerings to his backbench
wolves. These consisted of: the Qualification Bill, the Lords' investigation of
Almanza and the Commons' investigation of the Victualling Commission.
Each was calculated to satisfy a long-standing Country Tory grievance,
through which Harley hoped not only to keep his backbenchers quiet, but also
to dissipate their rancour against the former Whig ministry.

Place Bills were a traditional Opposition ploy to sow discord between a
ministry and its Country supporters. The Whigs were quick to utilise it in
1710: 'Its brought in by the Whigs designedly that the Torries may discover
themselves, they being violently for it last year, but the [Court] begin already
to appear otherwayes'.[6] Harley, as head of the administration, could not allow
the Place Bill to pass under any circumstances. At the same time he had to
mute the inevitable Country Tory anger when he had it defeated in the Lords.
The Qualification Bill was a shrewd solution to this problem. It allowed the
ministry to adopt a pose of 'honest' Tory principles, while quietly undermining
the Place Bill. St John was allowed to parade his eloquence in favour of a

measure dear to Tory hearts, while in truth, 'le dessein de la Cour est de faire tomber par là l'autre Bill'.[7] Buoyed as they still were with goodwill towards the Government, the Jacobites were as eager as the other High Tories to support such a Bill. Shippen was prominent in the debate on a motion that the Place Bill should take precedence over other business on 12 December, and told for the noes in the division that defeated it. Lord Lyon had some suspicions about the intentions behind the Qualification Bill, but was reassured as both it and the Place Bill passed their initial stages.[8] Harley's plan only failed due to something he had not taken enough into account: the unusually fierce commitment of the Country Tories in the 1710 Parliament to their principles. As a result, Harley's scheme rebounded upon him, and rather than appeasing the Country Tories, the Qualification Bill merely whetted their appetites. Instead of losing interest in the Place Bill, the Country Tories adopted both measures and backed them with equal enthusiasm. Mungo Graham of Gorthie, M.P. for Kinross-shire until February, noted this happening in mid-December:

> I think I told yr Gr[ace] some time ago that I believed the place Bill had gott such a reception as that I thought we would hear no more of it. However, I was mistaken for some days after it was revived again, and as ye may have observed by the votes, it has gone hand in hand all this while with the qualification bill, which was thought was only brought in to rivall the other and providing it could shift out that, it would be indifferent what became of it... There are severalls who appear very warm for this [Qualification] bill; and I think all that are zealous for the other, approves of both, and say both are necessary.[9]

This zeal remained constant right to the end of both Bills' passage through the Commons.

Just as Parliament began to sit, the Allied war effort in Spain was finally defeated at the twin battles of Brihuega and Villa Viciosa. This immediately revived the old Tory clamour for an investigation of the conduct of the war in Spain, particularly the circumstances surrounding the defeat which had signalled the end of the first, and most successful, period of the Spanish campaign: Almanza. Ever adroit at seizing his opportunities, Harley graciously yielded to this outcry, and set his ministry to preparing an onslaught on the Whigs' war record calculated to satisfy even the fieriest Tory. Bishop Nicolson of Carlisle found the earl of Rochester had been warning Tory peers of 'warm work' when the Almanza investigation began. It was also noticed that the investigation was having special days set aside for it in the Lords, so as to minimise interference with other Government business, and that the Court was visibly standing back and letting the High Tories take the lead.[10] As might have been expected, the Jacobites were in the forefront in delivering the torrent of abuse that showered down on the hapless earl of Galway and his subordinates. Beaufort opened the debate, and thereafter he, Buckingham, lords North and Grey and Ferrers, the earl of Scarsdale and earl Poulet did the bulk of the 'investigation'. The Scots also joined happily in the attack, and as the Whigs rallied towards the end of the investigation, proved crucial in stifling Whig protests at the partiality of the proceedings.[11] At first the Almanza enquiry served Harley's turn admirably:

> La Chambre Basse regarde cette affaire avec beaucoup d'attention et on croit qu'elle n'etre prendra rien avant que les Seigneurs l'ayent terminé. Il est vray que les Communes parlent aussi beaucoup des Malversations du dernier Ministere, mais on ne dit rien de particulier et dans toutes les harangues que Mr Freman, le Nouveau Tresorier de la Marine, Mr Caesar et l'autres font touts les jours on ne marque rien qu'en general qu'ils croyent qu'il y a eu des Malversations et qu'il faut les decouvrir.[12]

But in the long term it too rebounded. The Country Tories gave of their best in the debates and divisions, and were in consequence angry and disappointed to find that all was to be inflicted on their foes was a set of condemnatory resolutions. Smith told Crosse, 'its said the D. of Beaufort was heard say — damn secretary St John it was he yt had put the House of Peers upon these fruitless enquirys'.[13]

Although he hoped to dilute his backbenchers' passions with the Qualification Bill and divert their attention with the Almanza investigation, Harley was well aware that he must give them a sacrifical Whig too. It was an article of faith among Country Tories that the war was so expensive because of embezzling Whig war-profiteers and corrupt placemen. Thomas Ridge, a Whig Victualling Commissioner and M.P. for Poole, fitted both requirements perfectly. Harley personally denounced Ridge in the Commons, where the victim was seized on with delight: 'The Comons have discovered great roguerys amongsts severall that Victualls the Navey theres one Rige of Portsmouth that has cheated severall thousand tons of Beare he's very rich and its hop't they will squeeze him heartily'. Ridge was duly examined and then expelled from the Commons on 15 February, with a recommendation that he should be prosecuted.[14] The Country Tories, having disposed of one malefactor, looked expectantly to Harley for more offerings. He refused to oblige. Harley knew that he could not survive as the head of a one-party ministry, and that he must maintain a moderate stance to keep the Court Whigs cooperative. He therefore decided to call a halt to the proceedings at this point, before a full-scale Tory witch-hunt began. This merely served to shift the Country Tories' anger from the 'malefactors' to their protector:

> Charles Eversfield Esq Kt for the shire of sussex said expresly that unless Mr Harley mad further discoverys (ych if he pleased he could) they must belive, yt a great man in the late ministry (meaning Godolphine) and a great man in this (meaning Harley) wer to direct this house yt they wer to doe in these matters.[15]

These three measures, added to Harley's limitless talent for bland prevarication, probably did slow the erosion of Country Tory goodwill towards his ministry. But such methods could only be counterproductive in the long term. Bonet reached the conclusion that there was little to choose between Harley's ministry and its predecessor in 1710-11:

Les Toris come les Whigs se sont declares pour les Alliances, ils n'ont pas changé les mesures pour parvenir à une Paix solide ; ils ont resolu de vouloir maintenir la Succession dans la ligne Protestante [et] de conserver la Tolerance aux Nonconformistes... En un mot le changement n'est que dans les persones et non dans les choses.[16]

To the Country Tories this gradual revelation came as a profound and lasting disappointment, the effects of which were heightened by the length of time Harley managed to draw it out.

Frustration with Harley's measures in the long term was more than matched by a growing sense of betrayal in the first two months of the session. The Country Tories came to London in December confident that Harley's ministry would undertake at least to clear every Whig possible out of office, impeach Godolphin, Marlborough and the Junto, and rely exclusively on the Tory party in Parliament.

A grand purge of all Whig office-holders was regarded as an essential measure by every Country Tory. Pressure on Harley to do this had begun before he had even decided to dissolve Parliament in the summer, but he had carefully ignored it, and only ejected Whigs who refused to cooperate with the new ministry.[17] Canon Stratford (his son's tutor) hinted at the consequences of not acceding to this demand, in October:

> The Tories here are not a little pleased with the success of the elections and the more because there was no previous change of the lieutenancies and commissions of the peace. That circumstances makes us think our obligation much less to you at Court for the Parliament we hope to have.[18]

The duke of Leeds put it more strongly in December:

> I will take this opportunity to say that if the Queen do not lay hold of the time both openly to encourage some of her friends and as openly to discourage some of her enemies the last error will be worse than the first and past any possibility of remedy for the future.[19]

Harley would not give way, and suffered the inevitable consequence: the dislike of the Country Tories was extended from the Whig placemen to him. One of the early nicknames for the October Club was the 'AntiHarlekins', and one of their early slogans, that they were determined not to be 'Harl'd'. Perceval noted that at the beginning of the year a common Tory toast was 'confusion... to all Harlekites'.[20]

A common Tory electoral promise in 1710 was that there would be a thorough investigation of the Whig ministry's conduct in office. Harley soon made it abundantly clear that he had no intention of doing anything of the kind. He obviously did not consider himself bound by such promises, but many of his backbenchers did:

> The young People in Parliament are very eager to have some Enquiries made into past Managements, and are a little angry with the Slackness of the Ministry upon that Article; they say they have told those who sent them, that the Queen's

calling a new Parliament was to correct and look into former abuses; and if
something of the latter be not done, they know not how to answer it.[21]

Sir Simeon Stuart argued that the fall in the ministry's credit was:

> the consequence of the mismanagements of the former Ministry who had
> exhausted all the funds, and squandred the money away. The only thing that was
> left to this honest parliament, was to inquire into these mismanagements, and
> certify them as far as possible, and punish the offenders to the terror of others.
> That this was the thing the Countrey expected from them, and was indeed the
> thing which was promised to be done, when they sollicited the Elections; and to
> return to the Countrey without doing any such thing, would be ane evidence to
> the Countrey, that they either had been imposed upon when such stories were
> told them, or that the new had succeeded the old in integrity as well as their
> places. That it was true ane honourable gentleman [...Harley] had been pleased
> to let them into a discovery he had made of some abuses in the victualling office,
> which regarded a member of the house..[Ridge].., but that tho that was indeed
> ane abuse as great as fell to the share of a commoner, yet their were certainly
> other abuses which might be made out of some great men in the late Ministry
> wherby it would appear the public had been cheated in millions. And that if that
> honble member [Harley] would not let them in to these secrets likewise: it
> behov'd to conclude that a certain great man of the late ministry had
> compounded matters with another great man in this ministry.[22]

Kilsyth assured Carnegy that 'they'll screw the prerogative as high as they can
& impeach some who in former sessions brought it low'. Bonet had no doubts
at all that the October Club was out to get as many of the former ministry as
possible. Nottingham was quite blunt on the subject when he met the Cabinet
in December, telling them that 'unless we prosecuted them, he should think we
protected them'.[23] Harley could not contemplate such a procedure, even if he
had been sympathetic. His majority in the Lords depended on a handful of
Court Whigs who could not have been relied on if confronted with such a cut-
and-dried party issue. Harley therefore prevaricated, accelerating the Country
Tories' growing disenchantment with him.[24]

All Tories considered their party to be the natural party of Government. It
followed that therefore the idea of a Whig ministry was an abomination. To
the Country Tories there was one form of administration even worse than
that: a mixed ministry. The very idea of cooperating with 'the Faction' was
anathema, only ever to be contemplated under exceptional circumstances, and
then not for long. Hence, the spectacle of Harley and the Court Tories voting
with the Whigs in controverted election cases was most displeasing to the
Country Tories. This came to a head over the Place Bill, which Harley had had
no compunction about opposing from the outset. By early January the
backbenchers' patience with this kind of behaviour was becoming visibly
strained:[25]

> Le Bill pour limiter le Nombre des officiers qui doivent avoir seance dans le
> Parlement passa hier dans la Chambre Basse; Mr Harley et les autres de la Cour
> et une grande partie des Whigs s'y opposerent fortement comme estant une

diminution des Prerogatives de la Couronne,... On a veu dans cette affaire aussi bien que dans la decision de plusieurs Elections contesteés depuis peu de jours, que les veritables Toris continuent toujours à estre fort jaloux de Mr Harley et qu'ils ne le suivent presque en rien.[26]

It increasingly appeared to the Country Tories that 'the present Ministry differed from the last as a Cat in a window from a Cat out of it'. This impression was reinforced, as far as they were concerned, when the Court and the Whigs combined in the Lords to reject the Place Bill with contempt.[27] The Country Tories' reserves of goodwill were finally exhausted at that point. They were in an impasse: their party's acknowledged leader was plainly not going to carry out any of the policies they desired, yet they had no other machinery to act through except that which he controlled. The answer was to form their own organisation: the October Club (which first appeared under the name of the 'Loyal Club' at the end of December).

There was nothing inevitable about the appearance of the October Club. Though Harley's behaviour was bound to incense the Country Tories in the end, it did not necessarily follow that they were capable of organising any kind of counteraction. At the beginning of the session, when grand meetings of more than two hundred Tory M.P.'s were being held to decide on candidates for the chairmanships of important Committees, such as that for Privileges and Elections, the Country Tories had quickly fallen to internal wrangling.[28] No independent backbench group had been formed by the Tories since the days of Harley's Country party in the 1690s, and then the inspiration had been both front bench and Whig. The October Club came into being due to a combination of frustration and anger among the Country Tories, but also out of a determination to do something constructive (in their terms) about their situation and the policies they supported. In large part, this feeling stemmed from the gradual realisation of their intrinsic strength, if only they could coordinate it. The first glimmerings of this appeared in late December:

> I much fear whether this Parl: will either answer those just expectations the People have from it. whether they will come into any effectual enquirys to lay open the late mismanagements, or give us that security to the Church wee have wanted & thought necessary, & now expected. and consequently whether wee shall keep that regular good correspondence wch at this time is absolutely necessary to fix the interest of ye nation upon a right bottom & no less necessary to establish their new Power. if this be not done wee Country Gentlemen must expect as little regard as they have formerly mett with... but tho this is wt I own I cant but fear from some things I have already observ'd, yet I am pretty confident yt [if] None will suffer themselves to be drawn off, tis entirely in their power by keeping firmly & closely united, to make the Ministry in a great measure come in to us, instead of our depending upon them.[29]

St Germain had already indicated that it wanted the Jacobites to do what they could for the cause, and if possible impeach Marlborough, which meant that the Jacobite element among the Country Tories was predisposed to concerting joint action with its fellows. The defeat of the Place Bill, sneeringly dismissed by Poulet for having been brought in by 'the dregs of all ye discontented Parties', provided the final catalyst.[30]

So far the Country Tories have been referred to as a unit. In fact, their solidarity began and ended with their 'Country' sympathies. There were three basic divisions: Jacobites, middle-of-the-road, and Hanoverians. The Jacobites consisted of men like Sir John Pakington and Thomas Strangways, who had always been High Tories, and quietly favoured a restoration on the queen's death. The middle-of-the-road men were Tories like John Hungerford and Sir Robert Davers, who preferred not to think of what was going to happen when Anne died, but were basically unenthusiastic pro-Hanoverians. The Hanoverians were just that: outspokenly pro-Hanoverian M.P.'s like Ralph Freman and Sir Thomas Hanmer, who later favoured active measures to assure the electoral house of their loyalty. From the start even the October Club's usual fifteen speakers and recognised leading men reflected this tripartite division.[31] Attached to the Club, but retaining their own identity, was a group of Scots Jacobite Tories. Individual Scots M.P.'s did join the Club proper, but the Scots Jacobite M.P.'s had their own organisation and an inherent sense of separate identity which kept them distinct as a group.[32] The five-man steering committee which coordinated the activities of the Scots Jacobite M.P.'s usually chose to keep them cooperating closely with the October Club, but did not necessarily need to do so. The October Club was quite a delicate coalition. It had to stick closely to traditionally 'Country' and unexceptionably 'Tory' measures in order to preserve its unity. At the same time, there was inherent tension inside it as the Jacobites tried to orientate the Club's actions to suit their own ends and the Hanoverians opposed them. In the 1710-11 session, however, these rifts only rarely came to the fore, as all the groups within the October Club were agreed on two basic aims. These were: a thorough purge of all Whigs still in office, and an equally thorough investigation of the accounts and activities of the former Whig ministry with a view to impeachment.

'Country' principles were the main unifying factor, so it was these which were stressed at the outset. Sir Thomas Hanmer and Ralph Freman ostentatiously eschewed any thought of taking places. Kreienberg found that 'ils ont disent ils des veritables Anglois, sont content de ce qu'ils ont, ne se soucient pas des charges de la Cour et embrassent les veritables interests de leur Patrie'. Francis Legh told his brother Peter that the main criteria for admission to the Club were a good estate and a past untarnished by office.[33] But problems could still arise over the most impeccably 'Country' measures. The creation of a Commission of Accounts was one of these. No-one in the October Club was opposed to its creation, but there were wide divergences of opinion over who should man it. An attempt by Harley to pack it with his own creatures was easily rebuffed, but a demand by the Scots Jacobites that at least one of their own nationality should sit on the Commission was conceded. Lockhart was the one put forward, and though he was elected with October Club support, the Hanoverian Tories were most reluctant to support him.[34] As simple 'Country' measures were exhausted, a struggle developed over what further measures the Club should adopt. By April this had developed into overt clashes between the two wings of the October Club. In the divisions on the use to which Post Office profits were to be put a Jacobite attempt to defeat a motion put forward by the Court retaining the existing managers in office was beaten off by only one vote, with Peter Shakerly (a Nottinghamite Octoberman) telling for the ayes, and Abraham Blackmore (a Jacobite Octoberman) for the noes. Sir Simeon Stuart and Eversfield opposed Club policy in regard to the way the auditing practices of the previous administration should be condemned. They wanted Godolphin to be specifically named, and when this was refused, divided with the Whigs against the whole package. In May, just as Hanmer was being expelled from the club for being too friendly towards the Court, Whitlock was officially admitted.[35] The Jacobites seem to have been gradually gaining the upper hand in the competition for control of the Club, though as yet a permanent split was avoided. Points on which the two wings clashed were still relatively rare, and the need to stay united to keep up the pressure on Harley to purge his administration of Whigs and prosecute the former ministry kept them together.

Well before the October Club was formed, the Country Tories were acting together to ensure the success of the right sort of candidates in controverted election cases. They began with a flourish, with Shippen and Freman leading the attack on Cowper's actions over the Bewdley Charter. In this matter the Court discreetly backed the Country Tories, probably because it was a foregone conclusion and many moderate Tories also felt strongly on the issue.[36] Having voted the new Bewdley Charter 'void, illegal and destructive', the Country Tories had set the pattern for their behaviour for the rest of the session. Harley's ostentatious attempts to be seen to be fair in election cases accordingly elicited little response, and by the end of December their partiality had become quite scandalous. Mungo Graham was shocked to find even Lord William Powlett's cast-iron case was opposed:

> last night in the Comitte of Elections came on the petition against Lord Wm Paulet we were expecting that torys would be favourable to Lord William and give a proof of their professions of impartiality in this case. It happened that his case was the surest ever came before the house and yet upon the divisions their was 109 against him and 155 for him. The old good inter[est] were all for him but the young ones say they'l throw him out upon the report.[37]

Jacobites were among the first beneficiaries of this partisan feeling. Those Jacobites who petitioned or were petitioned against automatically had the most favourable procedure allotted in each case. Sir Kenneth Mackenzie's petition against Major-General Charles Ross was referred to the Committee of Privileges and Elections, as was Nicholas Carew's against Theophilus Oglethorpe. In contrast, the Hon. James Murray's against John Grier, and Sir John Malcolm's against Mungo Graham, were ordered to the Bar for speedier consideration.[38] The October Club had no qualms about continuing in this tradition of blatant bias. Smith complained bitterly in February that the Scots Jacobites 'never have spared one whigg in yr vote since they came thither: soe yt however these Gentlemen are inclined in our elections, their English friends will alwise be deter[min]ed by them'. Lockhart himself admitted that the Scots Jacobites unjustly had Grier thrown out on petition simply because he was a kinsman of Queensberry's. The most celebrated confrontation of the session between the Country Tories and the Court over a controverted election was brought on by a Jacobite bringing in a manifestly trumped-up charge against lord Halifax's brother and a former Attorney-General, Sir James Montagu, M.P. for Carlisle. Eversfield produced a Colonel Gledhill, who was petitioning against Montagu, with an accusation that Montagu had been given a £1,000 _per annum_ pension with which to buy his return at the election. The only evidence Gledhill had was his own claim to have seen a letter from Bishop Nicolson of Carlisle, mentioning this pension. While the Court vigorously defended Montagu, the October Club (obviously primed and mustered) proceeded to exclude Nicolson when he offered to testify that there was nothing of the sort in the letter, and to vote by 154-151 to give Gledhill three weeks to produce a copy:[39]

> Its to be observed that in this division whig and Court were joyn'd, and Clean October carryed it against both. Mr Harley was in the House all the time, and spoke very warmly for Sr James. The Whigs left the debate to the Court, so it went betwixt them and october.[40]

The Club followed this up by condemning Nicolson for interference in the election when Gledhill reapeared, without a copy of the offending letter. This positively outraged everyone not a member of the October Club, but they were unconcerned.[41] Voting down Whigs, especially Whig Bishops and Court Whigs like Nicolson and Montagu, was obviously something all October-men relished and drew together on. Consequently, there was little to restrain the Jacobites from carrying their party zeal as far as they could.

Much as the October Club espoused 'Country' principles, this did not mean that they were averse in practice to themselves, their kinsmen and friends sharing in whatever offices were spared. Though in general opposed to having too many officials in the Commons, virtually all were willing to allow that some professional administrators did need to sit in Parliament. What they could not accept was that Whigs should be entrusted with these posts. In their eyes this created a fifth column within the Government itself, which in turn threatened the hard-won Tory triumph in Church and State they felt they had achieved in 1710. Sir Arthur Kay was M.P. for Yorkshire and a staunch supporter of the Place Bill:

> this Bill shew'd sufficiently ye respect the house bore to ye Crown by allowing so many exceptions. yt it cou'd be no inconvenience to it, under a good Prince, who having no other view than ye true interest of ye subject, wou'd not stand in need of any corrupt partie in ye house, when he wou'd have ye united hearts of all; nor with a good Ministry, who shou'd act upon right, reason with honour &

integrity, who wou'd not want [need] to be supported. but as so great a number of people might lift their heads up against ye Crown as well as against ye liberties of ye subject, & might support a faction in a Ministry to ye lessening yt power & prerogative of yt Prince, as wee had seen in a late instance, it cou'd never be for [the] true interest of either to have ye House liable to such corruptions and tho tis true it wd not prevent private pensions, yet as ye making that a reason was a tacite confession there might be such, it wd at least take off part of ye inconvenience, by stopping ye current at least of one evill, wch at present flowed upon you in two channels.[42]

Yet he had no compunction about seeking a place for a friend who had supported him in his election. Kay was a Hanoverian Tory, but the Jacobites were no less forward. Weymouth solicited for places both for himself and Sir John Pakington. Pakington later received a secret pension on the Irish establishment, which he unhappily, and unsuccessfully, petitioned to be changed for a 'more public' reward. Lockhart sought places for himself, his kinsmen and his friends. Lord Lyon sought them for George Mackenzie, a member of the October Club, and for his friends in Scotland.[43] The eagerness of the October-men to gain the fruits of office for themselves and their interests caused St John to sneer:

I confess to you..., that it made me melancholy to observe the eagerness with which places were solicited for, and though interest has at all times been the principal spring of action, yet I never saw men so openly claim their hire, or offer themselves to sale.[44]

But this is to misunderstand the motives behind this eagerness for office. It would be foolish to deny the material motivation present, but just as foolish to deny the aim of thereby securing the Tory regime for the foreseeable future.

The repeal of the Protestant Naturalisation Act was a measure on which all Country Tories felt the same. This was initiated by demands for an investigation into who had invited the Palatine refugees over in 1709, and struck a very popular chord outside Parliament: 'We in these parts are well pleasd with ye Parliamts recollecting the managemt and Invitation of ye Palatines'.[45] Tory feeling on the issue ran so high because of their traditional dislike of foreigners, and the suspicion that the influx of refugees and the Naturalisation Act which accompanied them were a Whig ploy for party ends. Few naturalised immigrants would vote Tory due to the party's xenophobia, which meant that they would virtually all be potential Whig voters, hence strengthening the Whig interest in the electorate. A committee was established to look into the question of who had invited the Palatines in December, and it was one of its interim reports that was seized on as an excuse to bring in a Bill repealing the Naturalisation Act in January. It was rumoured that this Bill was a stalking horse for an Occasional Conformity Bill, but memories of the party split of 1704-5 seem to have convinced them to bide their time if this was in fact the case.[46] The Bill passed the Commons easily, only to fall in the Lords. The Court stayed out of the matter, wisely judging it best not to threaten its slender Lords majority by alienating the Court Whigs with a display of party zeal. Court Whigs and Tories accordingly voted as they felt inclined, which left the Whigs with a majority of ten including Mar, Islay and Loudoun. The Jacobites in both Houses were active proponents of the measure, fulfilling their role·as the Country Tories' zealous vanguard: Campion introduced the Bill in the Commons, and North and Grey and Ferrers spoke alongside such traditional Tory stalwarts as the earl of Nottingham, lord Guernsey and the earl of Anglesey in the Lords.[47] The rejection of the Bill irritated the Commons, and they took the first opportunity to get their revenge by passing condemnatory resolutions on the earl of Sunderland:

> That the inviting, and bringing over, into the Kingdom the poor Palatines, of all Religions, at the publick Expence, was an extravagant and unreasonable Charge to the Kingdom, and a scandalous Misapplication of the publick Money, tending to the Encrease and Oppression of the poor of this Kingdom, and of dangerous Consequence to the Constitution in Church and State.[48]

Rumours that Sunderland was to be impeached for his part in the affair followed. But by then the October Club was aware that the Court would not support such a move, and that without Court support an impeachment would be doomed to failure. An address to the queen asking that Sunderland be excluded from her Councils forever was considered by the Club, but when the Court indicated it would not support that either, it was reluctantly dropped.[49]

Frustration with the Harley ministry's refusal to begin investigating its predecessor's conduct was one of the factors which inspired the formation of the October Club. It was therefore a natural development of the Club to take up the matter itself once it was in existence. The only backbench tool with which this could be done was a Commission of Accounts. Harley, whose Country party had first used such a Commission as a means of investigating governments, was well aware of the problems it could cause him. He therefore tried to keep the Commons from debating the National Debt, which would provide the best opening for the proposal of a Commission of Accounts:

> il est pourtant à remarquer que hier jour marqué pour deliberer sur les Moyens de lever le Subside, quelqu'uns de l'Octobre Club proposerent, qu'avant que de passer outre dans cette affaire, on devoit premierement examiner le Rapport touchant les Dettes de la Nation, cequi auroit engagé la Chambre dans un long debat et auroit fait oublier le Subside pour ce jour là, mais la Cour l'empecha adroitement enquoy elle fut soutenüe par les Whigs qui la secondent toujours quand il s'agit du Subside.[50]

Stuart deftly countered by reminding the Country Tories of their promises to their electors, and suggesting that Harley was protecting the Whig ministry by preventing an investigation. Other October Club speakers proposed a Commission of Accounts under the guise of seconding him.[51] The Court and the Whigs vigorously opposed the subsequent Bill setting up the Commission, as both were well aware that it would be looking for evidence with which to impeach Marlborough, Godolphin and the Junto. The Court party did so because many who were part of it in 1710-11 had previously served under Marlborough and Godolphin when they were primarily allied with the Tories between 1702 and 1705 (including Harley and St John). Also, Harley knew that if the Court party was confronted with such a clear-cut party issue as the impeachment of the Whig leaders by the Country Tories, it would probably disintegrate along party lines. This would leave him isolated and at the mercy of the Tory extremists. The Whigs opposed the measure out of sheer survival and a wish to pose as the moderate party in contrast with the wild and bloodthirsty Tories. Predictably enough, the Bill passed the Commons, but by some strange oversight it was not killed in the Lords. This can only have been due to St John's influence. Back in December he had been openly sympathetic to backbench demands for an enquiry into the former ministry's finances. By January he was predicting:

> The House of Commons are entering on the examination of frauds committed in the victualling, they will proceed afterwards to some others, and I make no question, but that the late applauded administration of the Treasury will appear, before this session concludes, to have been the most loose, the most negligent, the most partial that ever any country suffered by.[52]

Harley was stabbed by the Abbé Guiscard on 8 March. From then until the end of April the management of the Commons was in St John's hands. The Commission of Accounts Bill can only have passed the Lords with Court support, which means that St John must have persuaded the Lords' managers, Rochester and Shrewsbury, that the Commons would prove troublesome unless it was allowed to pass.[53] As it turned out, the Commons proved troublesome anyway, and the Commission produced nothing before the end of the session. The committee set up to look into the Imprest Accounts provided the October Club with the ammunition to pass some severe but general resolutions, but these served only to divide them when the Jacobites pressed for Godolphin to be specifically named.[54] The Jacobites were not only in the forefront of getting the Bill through Parliament, as for instance Stuart's introduction of the matter into the Commons, but also in its application. Three of the seven M.P.'s who ultimately sat on the Commission were Jacobites: Lockhart, Shippen and Campion. Other factions within the October Club shared the poll, and resolutely supported the Commission, so it was definitely a joint effort, but the Jacobites' prominence suggests a special commitment.

The measure which came closest to outright Jacobitism in 1710-11 was the Grants Resumption Bill. The intention of the Bill was to resume to the Crown all grants of pensions and lands made since the accession of William III and Mary. This encompassed two elements dear to every Jacobite's heart: it struck at the memory of William III and the Revolution, and at some of the staunchest Whigs. Rumours of such a measure began to circulate late in February, when Allen Bathurst warned Wentworth (whose brother, lord Raby, had such a grant) that something of the kind was in the offing. The measure was actually introduced into the Commons by surprise. Strangways senior launched into a sudden diatribe against the luxury enjoyed by the recipients of these grants while the Crown and people groaned under the burden of war taxation. Shippen seconded him, and a Bill was ordered to redress these grievances.[55] The Bill passed the Commons easily in the absence of Harley (who was stabbed the day before its introduction) despite some desultory Whig opposition. The Court remained warily aloof throughout. It reached the Lords at the beginning of May, just after Harley's recovery and return to office, where it was rejected without a division after the Court had made it abundantly clear that it did not favour the measure. The October Club was incensed, and some elements began making ominous threats of a 'tack' next session: 'The October Club are very angry they have lost this Bill, and swear next year they will bring in one, so that it shan't be in the power of the lords to reject they will make a mony Bill on't'.[56] An additional reason for the Club's anger may well have been the half-hearted reception the Bill received in the Lords from those who usually favoured the Club's measures. It was noticed that many Tory lords absented themselves on the first reading, and even among the Jacobite peers opinion was divided on the issue.[57] There can be no question about the Bill having been a Jacobite-inspired measure. Strangways introduced the issue into the Commons, seconded by Shippen. Those entrusted with the draughting of the Bill comprised Lockhart, Shippen and Strangways. The seven Commissioners elected to carry out the Bill's provisions included Stuart, Eversfield, James Bulteel, John Houston junior and Abraham Blackmore. Because the resumption of Williamite grants had an honourable 'Country' pedigree, going back to the Irish land grants resumption bill of 1700, the more pro-Hanoverian elements of the October Club seem to have been content to support the Bill. A suggestion of how they were persuaded to do so comes from the speech of the Hanoverian Tory M.P. for Stafford, Walter Chetwynd, in support of Strangways on 1 March:

> it coud not but touch every Britishman to see the son of a foreigner outdo all the ancient nobility in riches and fineness, as if he boasted of his robbing the Nation: Portland was the man he meand as is believd, on whom its probable this Commission will be very heavy. He said further that what Grants were made in former Reignes, was in time of peace when the nation was not burden'd with heavy taxes to maintain an expensive war, but the Grants since the Revolution were in the time of war and taxes and more exorbitant than any former...[58]

From this it appears that the pro-Hanoverian elements of the Club were brought into the measure by convincing them they were striking a blow against corrupt foreigners who were lording it over the impoverished natives with their ill-gotten gains. Even so, the attitude of many of the Hanover-inclined Tories appears to have been no more than lukewarm. The Jacobites had to do virtually all the work getting the Bill through in committee and debate, while prominent Hanoverian Tory speakers like Hanmer and Freman appear to have contributed nothing more than their votes. Kay certainly showed no great distress when the Bill was defeated in the Lords, and his attitude was probably typical.[59]

Taxation was never popular with Country members of either political party. The Court usually got it past by the joint expedients of appealing to their backbenchers' patriotism and hurrying it through when they were bored or absent. Opposition to supply bills intended to finance the war would have been a grave matter, and at this stage the Whig Junto did not seriously contemplate it. Thus the only source of such opposition lay among the Country M.P.'s who began to follow their own counsel in this session. It was apparent from quite early on that there was considerable feeling against increases in taxation on basic industrial and comestible items. This was masked at first by the Commons' willingness to vote huge sums in supply when the session opened, and only became apparent as time went on and the Court found itself opposed in the ways and means of obtaining these sums. Harley was first forced to give way over a scheme to make the Malt tax permanent, which it quickly became clear would be rejected:

> feroit trop crier la petite Noblesse qui vivent des Revenus de leurs terres et qui regardent cet impot deja comme trop dur pour Eux, et qu'ils hasardoient mesme de voir rejetter la Proposition dans la Chambre Basse ou les Campagnards sont de beaucoup plus superieurs, semblant avoir mis a coté ce Projêt, et cet impôt sur le Malt a esté donné comme à l'ordinaire pour une année seulement.[60]

A similar plan for taxation of a basic industrial item, coal, was opposed in the Committee of Ways and Means itself:

> wee had a strugle about a duty upon inland coal. but ye inconveniencys appear'd so great, & ye advantage to ye publick so small from ye difficulty of collecting it, & ye multitude of officers it wd require, that ye last appearing impracticable, & ye Ministry coming in to us, for that reason wee carried our point by a Majority of 157 against 61.[61]

Encounters like these made the Government wary of introducing new forms of taxation lest they arouse such particularist opposition again. In itself, the opposition of the M.P.'s from any one region could be ignored and swept aside, but the new Country Tory unity found in the October Club precluded this solution from the beginning of February. Rather than confront this, Harley chose to levy a permanent impost on imports of linen from Ireland and to look for other minor taxes to make permanent and then establish lotteries on. This still left a large gap between Supplies voted and taxation allowed, which the Government seemed at a loss how to fill.[62] Harley's illness after his stabbing by Guiscard compounded the problem. St John tried to push through an increased leather tax, only to meet with a sharp reverse. The October Club summoned up its members early after the Easter recess and managed to defeat the Court and the Whigs combined in a quick raid in committee. Despite St John's attempts to brush it off, this was a serious defeat. He managed to cajole and threaten the Club into allowing a hide tax to pass next day, but he did not dare to risk such a debacle again, so the remaining ways and means bills hung fire until Harley returned.[63] When he did so he was at the peak of his popularity as Prime Minister due to his courage when Guiscard tried to kill him, excited rumours about the South Sea scheme, and probably not a little because of his prolonged absence. In consequence, he had few problems in finishing off the necessary supply bills. By this time the Country Tories were also tired and eager to leave Westminster, which probably helped too.[64] The Jacobite role in all this was totally subsumed in that of the October Club and its antecedents. They were definitely involved in the Government's difficulties, but since it was mostly done in the form of quiet obstruction of the Court's proposals, it is not apparent who led in these matters.

From the outset, the October Club made it quite clear what its intentions were towards the former ministry: '[Ils] vouloient mettre à bas les principales Tetes du dernier Ministere qu'ils croyoient coupables d'extremes malversations'.[65] But by the end of May, with the Commission of Accounts only just beginning its investigations, and the experience with the resolutions against Sunderland showing that it would be impossible to pass addresses to exclude the Whigs from office, the October Club was in a quandary. There were rumours that the 1710 Parliament would be dissolved in the recess, and some sections of the Club felt it was desirable that they should make some kind of public statement to justify themselves should this prove true. Hanmer, who was by now looking distinctly moderate when compared with other Club leaders, advocated generally phrased resolutions against the former Government, as had been done over the Imprest Accounts. These denounced the introduction of the Palatines, the Bewdley Charter and other things generally disliked by the October-men, such as the idea of mixed party government:

> Out of our unfeigned zeal for your Majesty's Honour and Service, and our faithful Affection to the publick Good, we cannot forbear with all Humility and Earnestness to beseech your Majesty, that you would avoid, as the greatest Enemies to your royal Dignity, and to your People's safety, all Persons, who shall endeavour to engage you in such pernicious Measures; and that you would employ in Places of Authority and Trust such only, as have given good testimonies of their Duty to your Majesty, and of their Affection to the true Interest of your Kingdom.[66]

In spite of their hostility and scope these resolutions were unacceptably moderate for many of the Club's members. There had been a schism over the resolutions on the Imprest Accounts for the same reason, and it is probable that Hanmer's expulsion was due to the same elements that had opposed those as too moderate: principally the Jacobites. Other more moderate men detached themselves in his wake. Sir William Wyndham accepted the Mastership of the Buckhounds, Bathurst accepted a peerage at Christmas. As if to symbolise the growing radicalisation of the Club, Whitlock was officially accepted as a member at around the same time as Hanmer left.

One of the areas which Harley contemplated raising new taxation in when faced with the problem of raising extra revenue was that of Scots linen exports. This was a national issue for all the Scots representatives, and one in which the Jacobites in Lords and Commons were quick to take the lead. They based their case on the argument that linen was to Scotland what wool was to England, and that it was already comparatively heavily taxed. The Court refused to accept this argument, and did so in a very offensive manner. Harley alleged (or seemed to) that England had bought all rights to Scotland's economy at the time of the Union, by agreeing to pay the Equivalent. This was supposed to be a refund to Scotland of its portion of taxation to service the English National Debt. Lockhart was quick to seize upon this to make some political capital: 'up rises Carnwath [Lockhart] & said he was very glad to hear that, from so good a hand, for since he knew that we were bought it confirm'd what he ay thought, that we were sold'.[67] Since they could not move the Government on the matter, the Scots representatives turned their attention to gaining some kind of compensation for what seemed to be a foregone conclusion. George Yeaman introduced a Bill to tighten the laws prohibiting the export of flax from Scotland to Ireland. The Whigs promptly adopted the Irish cause, so as to drive as big a wedge as possible into the Tory ranks on a national issue. In the Lords, allied to Ormonde and other Irish peers, they were able to guarantee Irish exports access to the Colonies for a further six years, and effectively to destroy the prohibition of Scots flax exports to Ireland. In the course of the debates on the subject they also took the opportunity to compare Scotland's economic interests unfavourably with any of the English counties. The Scots peers, led by Hamilton and Balmerino, opposed these changes bitterly, with some support from the Court, and were outraged at some of the reflections made on Scotland and its position since the Union. At one point, while telling a division, Balmerino observed to Sunderland that he would as lief beat him with the wand as hold it over his head, but Sunderland's quick withdrawal prevented it going further. The Scots M.P.'s, led by Baillie and Lockhart, managed to delay these two Lords-amended Bills until the recess when they were returned to the Commons, but could not in the end prevent them from becoming law.[68] The whole affair was a minor one in the context of the session, but it did serve to inflame Scots nationalist feeling both inside and outside Parliament. The Whigs had shown that they had nothing but contempt for Scots interests, and the Court had demonstrated little more than indifference. The Scots Jacobite representatives did not need much encouragement to see the entire English political establishment as hostile to Scotland, and the treatment of the Scots linen issue was more than enough.

The Scots Jacobite Tories came to Westminster in 1710 with their own electoral platform to implement. For the immediate future this had two main elements: the compensation of those arrested in 1708, and securing a legal toleration for Episcopalianism. The Scots representatives were most significant in the Lords, where the Government was dependent on them for its working majority. The Whig peers sneered at the Court's need for such support, but the

Scots Jacobites found it equally amusing to mock the earl of Wharton (one of the Whig Junto and a negotiator of the Union) by asking him how he liked the Union now? At the outset the Scots peers intended to act together, the better to safeguard their country's interest.[69] But this initial unity soon proved to be a facade. Hamilton's group of five was, in the main, content to continue following where he led, though his brother Orkney's poverty and innate moderation gradually drew him towards the Court. Of the two independent Jacobite peers, Balmerino's fierce Episcopalian nationalism led him to act in concert with Hamilton, despite his evident dislike of him, whereas Home's near-destitution drew him inexorably to the Court. Atholl briefly tried to steal the Jacobites' clothes over the 1708 prisoners' compensation issue, but when that failed threw in his lot with the Court. Islay and Blantyre were attached to Argyll, and hence consulted nobody's interest but their own. Mar was the leader of the Court party among the Scots peers, who, after these shifts of allegiance, numbered about eight. The Jacobites' efforts to implement their policies, the Court's lack of enthusiasm for them, and the Argyll group's self-seeking left the Scots about evenly split on most issues.[70]

The question of compensation for the prisoners of 1708 was the first of the two Jacobite election promises to be acted on. Atholl took the lead in this, followed by the Hamilton and Argyll groups. This initiative was quickly countered by the Court, who used the queen to destroy it. In an audience with the earl Marischal and Atholl she asked them specifically not to raise the matter in the Lords, as they were proposing to do. Opening moves towards an investigation of who had ordered the arrests in 1708 (aimed at Mar) were also stifled by the Court. Islay blustered about raising the matter anyway, but eventually yielded the point.[71] Atholl conceded defeat and thereafter sided with the Court in the hope of a place. The other plank in the Jacobite election platform had been the legal toleration of Episcopalianism. This issue pared down the Jacobite group and its allies to the committed few. Annandale was a sincere Presbyterian and would not help in such a matter, and the Argyll group seized the opportunity to parade their zeal for the Kirk in order to bolster their interests in Scotland. But in bringing forward the issue the Scots Jacobite peers drew to them two powerful groups in the Lords: the Tory high-fliers both Jacobite and Hanoverian, and the normally Whiggish bench of bishops. This was largely the result of skilful presentation. By portraying the Episcopalians as pious and peaceful followers of the Anglican communion, persecuted by Presbyterian fanatics, the Scots Jacobites out-manoeuvred their opponents from the start. Accusations of Jacobitism by the Whigs and their allies appeared to be simply party political cant, whereas unrepresentative Episcopalian clergy like James Greenshields, who were willing to attest their fidelity to the Revolution settlement, were held up as typical by the Jacobites.

As soon as they arrived at Westminster, Balmerino and Eglinton began to consult with the Tory high-fliers and the bishops on the Greenshields case, and on a suitable toleration. By the time the appeal came to be heard, on 1 March, Jacobite lobbying had already secured the verdict. The Edinburgh magistrates' decision, endorsed by the Lords of Session, to imprison Greenshields and close his church, was reversed. North and Grey, backed by the earl of Abingdon, wanted to go further and declare the whole process illegal, so as to give dispossessed Episcopalian clergy the right to sue their accusers, but this was dropped under pressure from the Court.[72] The Court had opposed the Jacobites over the Greenshields case from the start. Harley hoped to conciliate the moderate Presbyterian interest in Scotland and among the Scots peers in Parliament, most of whom were attached to the Court party. He therefore found the whole affair an embarrassing nuisance. As well as undermining his efforts to win over the moderate Presbyterians, it put the Court in a difficult position with their more zealous Tory supporters among the English peers. The upshot of this was that, though they could not oppose it directly, the Court would have been quite happy to see the appeal fail. The Court therefore tried to sabotage the proceedings by moving an adjournment after Argyll, Islay and Blantyre walked out halfway through. This was defeated by 68-32, twenty bishops voting against it, and thus for the appeal.[73]

The Scots Jacobites triumphantly prepared to follow up this success by bringing in bills to give Episcopalianism legal toleration and restore patronages to their owners from the Kirk synods which had appropriated them. This prompted a wave of hysteria among the Presbyterians at Westminster, and dire warnings of imminent civil war were given to the Government.[74] Harley brought all the influence he had to bear to persuade the Scots Jacobites and their allies to delay these measures, but to no avail:

> Eglinton and [Lockhart of] Carnwath are anxious to have the patronages restored, and some think this would be a greater surprise than a Toleration itself. Yet by all probability, both the Patronages and Toleration will be proposed, but how seasonably time will discover. My Ld Balmarino declard his minde was to have patience and waite till they shoud see how matters was carried in Scotland after the case of Greenshields, and the Arcbishop of York was much of the same opinion and said he did not see any great hazard there was in delaying till November next, however neither would differ from the Generality or Majority of those that appeard friends to the Clergy.[75]

Harley accordingly played his trump card. Rochester and Shrewsbury quietly approached Lockhart and lord Lyon, and from the tone of his letters Balmerino too, and delivered a message from the queen asking that the Scots abandon the project for that session. Lockhart and the others reluctantly agreed, on the express understanding that the Court would support the same measures next year.[76] Harley was then able to calm the Kirk and its supporters with his customary suave mendacity:

> I cannot omit assuring you that the Queen and al who have the honor to have credit with her Majesty are not only resolved to maintain the Union in all its parts, both religious and civil, but there will be no attention given to any proposals which may justly alarme your friends, and particularly as to that affair of the patronages. It was never entertaind and was really an invention suggested to two rash persons with a design to create jealousies but it was never movd nor in the least countenanced or entertaind.[77]

When they came south in 1710 the Scots Jacobites had virtually all been out of office at least since the Union, and some since the Revolution. In consequence, they arrived with an extraordinary hunger for places and the sweets of office. No eighteenth-century politician ever entirely spurned the offer of rewards for himself or his family and friends. The Scots perhaps needed them more than most because of their poorer backgrounds and long exclusion, but their eagerness certainly gave them a bad reputation for greedy self-seeking. In some cases, as with the insatiable Campbell brothers, Argyll and Islay, this was well deserved, but it would be wrong to assume that all the Scots representatives were quite such fortune-hunters. To most, places or favour represented no more than their due for being good Tories — they considered their behaviour even towards the ministry as irrelevant to this. Kilsyth calmly accepted £500 from the Government in 1711, but there is no evidence that because of this he altered his attitude on anything. Balmerino spent a good deal of his time in 1710-11 seeking a place as one of the Lords of Session for his son, but had no qualms whatsoever about opposing the Court over the Greenshields appeal. Lord Lyon accepted a sinecure as third Commissioner of the Signet which did not temper his disposition one jot. Lockhart showed no inclination at all to moderate his behaviour, despite the fact that he was seeking office himself.[78] In the course of this scramble for places the Scots naturally got in each others' way, but this does not seem to have hampered their disposition towards mutual cooperation in their political aims. Hamilton and Balmerino did not get on at all well, and were in competition for the next vacant Lord of Session place, Hamilton for a client and Balmerino for his son, but both cooperated during the Greenshields appeal and the opposition to the linen tax.[79] Their opponents purported to find this rush a disgusting spectacle: 'Here are four Pretenders to be Scottish secretarys, so that some think none of them will be so. D. Ham. Athol. Mar. Isla. They are all so hungry, that I wish every one wou'd take a limb of [the queen], & eat it up'.[80] The effects of satiation of this hunger for office were mixed. With some, like Atholl, the satisfaction of their desires left them malleable and willing to go along with the Court in almost everything. With committed men like Balmerino and Lockhart it simply made no difference: whatever they sought or obtained, they followed their own counsel before and after. Overall, skilful manipulation of this appetite for office by the Court gradually reduced the Jacobite element in the Scots representation to its hard core. In the process, lack of support from their more amenable colleagues may have tempered some of the wilder Jacobite designs. At the same time, as they were unable to find sufficient support and sympathy among their fellow Scots, this may also have acted to push the Scots Jacobites out of their accustomed national insularity into association with other Tories who shared many of their ideas — the English Jacobite Tories.

There can be no doubt that for the ministry the 1710-11 session was a very bad one. In the ebb and flow of party conflict it is easy to lose sight of just how great a departure this session was from the norm. A ministry which represented the greatest change in personnel since the Revolution found itself opposed not only by the party whom it had supplanted, but also by the bulk of its own backbenchers. For the first time since the Revolution an association of Country Tories arose determined to translate its wishes into action and to force its own leaders to behave in a manner of which it approved. Their attacks on Government supply bills had to be restrained twice by the threat of dissolution, which was a two-edged weapon, as although it temporarily checked the October Club's attacks, it slowed the passage of that same supply: 'there being three different parties in the House, they will not agree to dispatch anything of moment, being suspicious that they will be dissolved as soon as that is concluded'. The queen had to intervene repeatedly to check measures liable to wreck her ministry. Six bills had to be killed in the Lords because they could not be stopped in the Commons: l'Hermitage, who had been Dutch resident in London since 1692, had never seen such a tally before. The Court in all its force, led by the 'premier' minister, had been defeated whenever it opposed the wishes of its own backbenchers in controverted election cases. By late February the Court was in awe of its supporters.[81] Throughout this unprecedented furore, recognised Jacobites, encouraged by St Germain, were in the van. Their extremism radicalised and led those who were already party zealots, and by creating fear among the moderate men of the opposite party, struck at the very root of Harley's vaunted plans for a mixed ministry. The Government had survived despite having virtually lost control of the Commons in mid-session, due to the exhaustion and inexperience of the October Club. This could not be relied on next session, when Harley well knew the peace he was negotiating was likely to polarise the political spectrum. Then, he could not afford to be at the mercy of his fanatical backbenchers. Somehow he had to find a means to bind them to his ministry.

NOTES

1. Berkshire R.O., Downshire MSS. D/ED C33: 27 Nov. 1710.

2. Portland Loan 29/371: Sir William Whitlock to Harley, 1 Oct. 1710. See also: Levens MSS. (HPT): Bromley to James Grahme, 1 Sept. 1710; Portland Loan 29/307/5: Annesley to Harley, 10 Aug. 1710.

3. H.T. Dickinson, *Bolingbroke* (1970), pp.77-8; Downshire MSS. D/ED C33: 20 Dec. 1710; Claydon House Letters M11/54: Cave to Fermanagh, 2 Dec. 1710.

4. Public R.O., Chancery Lane, SP 34/13, f. 138: 30 Oct. 1710. See also: Gregg, *Queen Anne*, p.324.

5. *The Letters of St John to Orrery*, pp.148-9: St John to Orrery, 22 Aug. 1710; Dickinson, *Bolingbroke*, p.76.

6. Wodrow Letters, Quarto 5, ep. 50: Morthland to Wodrow, 16 Dec. 1710.

7. Plumb, *Stability*, p.146; Dickinson, *Bolingbroke*, p.78; Kreienberg 99, ff. 23-4: 15 Dec. 1710.

8. *CJ*, xvi, 432: 12 Dec. 1710; Mar MSS. 15/1011/3: Lyon to Erskine [Dec. 1710].

9. Montrose MSS. (HPT): Graham to the duke of Montrose, 21 Dec. 1710.

10. Nic. Diary: 27 Dec. 1710; Hermitage DDD, f. 670: 5 Dec. 1710.

11. Nic. Diary: 2 Jan. 1711; BL, Add. MSS. 47026 (Sir John Perceval's letters), ff. 51-2: Perceval to Colonel Taylor, 9 Jan. 1711; Cobbett, *Parl. Hist.*, vi, 936-97; N. Luttrell, *A Brief Relation of State Affairs* (Oxford, 1847), vi, 689: 8 Feb. 1711. For another view, see: H. Horwitz, *Revolution Politicks* (1968), p.224.

12. Kreienberg 99, f. 55: 9 Jan. 1711.

13. Wodrow Letters, Quarto 5, ep. 82: Smith to Crosse, 6 Feb. 1711.

14. Legh MSS.: [?] to P. Legh, 20 Jan. 1711; Kreienberg 99, ff. 47-9: 5 Jan. 1711.

15. Wodrow Letters, Quarto 5, ep. 82: Smith to Crosse, 6 Feb. 1711. See also: Holmes, *Politics*, p.401.

16. Bonet 37B, f. 297: 8 June 1711 ns.

17. Portland, iv, 551: viscount Weymouth to Harley, 24 July 1710; iv, 611: Beaufort to Harley, 9 Oct. 1710.

18. Portland, vii, 23: Stratford to R. Harley junior, 16 Oct. 1710.

19. *Ibid.*, iv, 642: Leeds to Harley, 7 Dec. 1710.

20. Holmes, *Politics*, pp.379-80; Kreinenberg 99, ff. 115-16: 9 Feb. 1710; Montrose MSS: Graham to Montrose, 6 Feb. 1711; Add. MSS. 47026, f. 68: Percival to Colonel Taylor, 11 May 1711.

21. *The Correspondence of Jonathan Swift*, ed. H. Williams (Oxford, 1963), i, 201: Swift to Archbishop King, 30 Dec. 1710. See also: Dickinson, *Bolingbroke*, p.78.

22. Montrose MSS: Graham to Montrose, 6 Feb. 1711.

23. Blair Lett: 29 Nov. 1710; Bonet 37B, ff. 97-8: 20 Feb. 1711 ns; G. Burnet, *History of My own Time* (Oxford, 1833), vii, 41-2 Dartmouth's note, cited in Horwitz, *Politicks*, p.225.

24. Lockhart, i, 322, 323-4.

25. MS Ballard 31, f. 89: William Bishop to Charlett, 22 Jan. 1711; Kay Diary (HPT): [Dec.] 1710 and 29 Jan. 1711; Plumb, *Stability*, p.151.

26. Kreienberg, ff. 96-7: 30 Jan. 1711.

27. G.S. Holmes, 'The Attack on the Influence of the Crown, 1702-16', *Bull. Inst. Hist. Res.*, xxxix (1966), 61-2; Nic. Diary: 3 Feb. 1711; Gurdon MSS. (HPT): Richard Berney to Thornhagh Gurdon, 3 Jan. 1711, I am indebted to Dr. D. Hayton for this reference.

28. This section and those following to p. 84 are complementary to the analysis of the October Club put forward in: H.T. Dickinson, 'The October Club', *Hunt. Lib. Quarterly*, xxxiii (1969-70), 155-64, though I differ with Professor Dickinson at certain points.

29. *Ibid.*, pp. 158-9.

30. Carte 212, ff. 15, 17: Middleton to Menzies, 18 Dec. 1710 ns and 5 Mar. 1711 ns; Kay Diary, 2 Feb. 1711.

31. Holmes, *Politics*, p.343; *Pol. State*, iii, 117-21.

32. Lockhart, i, 338; Blair Lett: 7 Mar. 1711; Holmes, *Politics*, p.338.

33. Bonet 37B, f. 115: 25 Feb. 1711 ns; Kreienberg 99, ff. 115-16: 9 Feb. 1711; Legh MSS: F. Legh to P. Legh, 20 Feb. [1711].

34. Lockhart, i, 324; Mar MSS. 15/1020/16: Dumbar to Erskine, 17 Mar. 1711.

35. *CJ*, xvi, 602-3: 18 Apr. 1711; Wodrow Letters, Quarto 5, ep. 127: Smith to Crosse, 5 May 1711; Berkshire R.O., Trumbull MSS. LIX, ep. 67: Ralph Bridges to Trumbull, 9 May 1711.

36. Mar MSS. 15/1020/4: Dumbar to Erskine, 19 Dec. 1710; *CJ*, xvi, 439: 19 Dec.

1710; *The Private Diary of Lord Chancellor Cowper*, ed. E.C. Hawtrey (1833), pp.50-1: 19 Dec. 1710.

37. Montrose MSS: Graham to Montrose, 29 Dec. 1710.

38. *CJ*, xvi, 418, 418-19, 421-2: 5 Dec. 1710; Holmes, *Politics*, p.44.

39. Wodrow Letters, Quarto 5, epp. 85, 91, 92: Smith to Crosse, 10, 22 and 24 Feb. 1711; Lockhart, i, 324-5; Kreienberg 99, f. 136: 23 Feb. 1711.

40. Montrose MSS: Graham to Montrose, 22 Feb. 1711.

41. Nic. Diary: 20 Feb. and 14, 18 and 20 Mar. 1711; Wodrow Letters, Quarto 5, ep. 108: Smith to Crosse, 15 Mar. 1711.

42. Kay Diary: 29 Jan. 1711, cited in Holmes, 'Attack', p.62 n.1.

43. Witley-Beaumont MSS. DD/WBC/88: viscount Downe and Kay to Beaumont, 7 Dec. 1710; Portland, iv, 551: Weymouth to Harley, 24 July 1710; iv, 656: Lockhart to Harley, 19 Jan. 1711; v, 462-3: Lyon to Oxford [Sept. ? 1711]; Holmes, *Politics*, pp.122-5 361; Portland Loan 29/371: Lockhart to Harley, 9 Sept. 1710; 29/150/3: Lockhart to Harley, 6 Jan. 1711.

44. *Bol. Corr.*, i, 245-6: St John to Orrery, 12 June 1711.

45. Claydon House Letters M11/54: Cave to Fermanagh, 5 Feb. 1711. For an analysis of the Palatine refugee issue, see: H.T. Dickinson, 'The Poor Palatines and the Parties', *Eng. Hist. Rev.*, lxxxii (1967), 464-85.

46. Hermitage EEE, f. 48: 16 Jan. 1711; Horwitz, *Politicks*, pp.224-8.

47. Nic. Diary: 5 Feb. 1711; Kreienberg 99, f. 66: 16 Jan. 1711.

48. *CJ*, xvi, 595-9: 14 Apr. 1711. See also: Dickinson, 'Poor Palatines', 484.

49. Wodrow Letters, Quarto 5, ep. 123: Crosse to Wodrow, 21 Apr. 1711.

50. Kreienberg 99, f. 120: 13 Feb. 1711.

51. *Ibid.*, f. 131: 20 Feb. 1711.

52. *Bol. Corr.*, i, 58: St John to John Drummond, 5 Jan. 1711.

53. *CJ*, xvi, 588, 618: 10 and 28 Apr. 1711. For Guiscard's attempt on Harley, see: H.T. Dickinson, 'The Attempt to Assassinate Harley, 1711', *History Today*, xv (1965), 788-95.

54. Hermitage EEE, f. 190: 1 May 1711. For another view, see: B.W. Hill, *The Growth of Parliamentary Parties* (1976), p.122.

55. *Went Corr.*, pp.180-1: Wentworth to Raby, 20 Feb. 1711; Kreienberg 99, ff. 145-6: 2 Mar. 1711; Hermitage EEE, ff. 103-5: 2 Mar. 1711.

56. Kreienberg 99, f. 219: 4 May 1711; *Went Corr.*, pp.195-6: Wentworth to Raby, 4 May 1711.

57. Dalhousie 14/352/8: Balmerino to Maule, 1 May [1711]; Kay Diary: 3 May 1711.

58. Mar MSS. 15/1020/13: Dumbar to Erskine, 1 Mar. 1711.

59. GD 112/40/7/7/33: 'Leter from... London... Concerning Mr. Shippen's speech'; *CJ*, xvi, 528-30, 605-8: 1 Mar. and 20 Apr. 1711; Kay Diary: 3 May 1711.

60. Kreienberg 99, f. 70: 19 Jan. 1711.

61. Kay Diary: 26 Jan. 1711. See also: Staffordshire R.O., Dartmouth MSS. D(W) 1778/III/156: speech written by Kay against duties on land-borne coal [Jan. 1711]; Kreienberg 99, ff. 95-6: 30 Jan. 1711.

62. Kreienberg 99, f. 85-8, 115-16, 174-5: 26 Jan., 9 Feb. and 23 Mar. 1711; Hill, *Growth*, p.131.

63. *Bol. Corr.*, i, 131: St. John to Marlborough, 27 Mar. 1711; Dickinson, *Bolingbroke*, pp.82-3; Kay Diary: 26 Mar. 1711; Kreienberg 99, ff. 182-3: 27 Mar. 1711.

64. Kreienberg 99, ff. 194-5, 212-13: 10 and 27 Apr. 1711.

65. Bonet 37B, f. 173: 30 Mar. 1711; *Journal to Stella*, ed. H. Williams (Oxford, 1958), i, 194-5: Feb. 1711.

66. *CJ*, xvi, 684-5: 31 May 1711. See also: Kreienberg 99, f. 251: 25 May 1711; Holmes, *Politics*, pp.48-9.

67. Dalhousie 14/352/3: Balmerino to Maule, 30 Jan. [1711].

68. *CJ*, xvi, 583-4, 665, 673: 7 Apr., 15 and 19 May 1711; Lockhart, i, 328-32; Dalhousie 14/352/10: Balmerino to Maule, 2 June [1711]; Mar MSS. 15/1024/11: Mar to Erskine, 23 June 1711.

69. Kreienberg 99, f. 61: 12 Jan. 1711; Dalhousie 14/352/2: Balmerino to Maule, 16 Jan. [1711].

70. Blair Lett: 7 Mar. 1711.

71. Dalhousie 14/352/2: Balmerino to Maule, 16 Jan. [1711]; GD 112/7/8/11-12: Breadalbane to Atholl, 2 Jan. and 3 Feb. 1711; Wodrow Letters, Quarto 5, ep. 78: Morthland to Wodrow, 6 Feb. 1711.

72. Nic. Diary: 15 Feb. 1711; Dalhousie 14/352/2: Balmerino to Maule, 16 Jan. [1711]; MSS. North A3, f. 125: North and Grey to Buckingham (draught), June [1711]; Lockhart, i, 348; Wodrow Letters, Quarto 5, ep. 97: Smith to Crosse, 10 Mar. 1711.

73. Portland, x, 352-3: Mar to Harley, 24 Dec. 1710; Wodrow Letters, Quarto 5, ep. 100: Smith to Crosse, 3 Mar. 1711.

74. Hermitage EEE, ff. 110-12: 6 Mar. 1711; Wodrow Letters, Quarto 5, ep. 96: Morthland to Wodrow, 6 Mar. 1711.

75. Mar MSS. 15/1020/14: Dumbar to Erskine, 6 Mar. 1711.

76. Lockhart, i, 339-40, 348; Dalhousie 14/352/5-6: Balmerino to Maule, 8 Mar. and 3 Apr. [1711]; HMC, *Mar and Kellie MSS.*, p.488: Mar to Erskine, 15 Mar. 1711.

77. HMC, *Laing MSS.*, ii, 161: Harley to William Carstares (moderator of the general assembly of the Kirk), 8 May 1711. See also: Wodrow Letters, Quarto 5, ep. 116: Smith to Crosse, 29 Mar. 1711.

78. Portland, iv, 645-6: Islay to Harley, 14 Dec. 1710; v, 96: Balmerino to Oxford, 2 Oct. 1711; x, 324: Mar to Oxford, 29 Oct. 1714; Portland Loan 29/150/3: Lockhart to Harley, 6 Jan. 1711.

79. Dalhousie 14/352/9: Balmerino to Maule, 19 May [1711]; Portland, v,96: Balmerino to Oxford, 2 Oct. 1711.

80. Blenheim 61461, f. 141: Maynwaring to Sarah Marlborough [8 July 1711].

81. Kreienberg 99, f. 136: 23 Feb. 1711; *Went Corr.*, pp.189-90: Wentworth to Raby, 27 Mar. 1711; Hermitage EEE, ff. 186, 224: 24 Apr. and 5 June 1711; HMC, *Buccleuch MSS*, iii, 250-1: 'P.L.' to [John?] Molesworth [c. Apr. 1711]; Holmes, *Politics*, p.342.

5

'Creatures and Slaves to the Ministry': the session of 1711-12

The principal problem facing the ministry at the beginning of the 1711-12 session was that of securing Parliamentary approval of the peace preliminaries with France. Other disruptive issues also remained unresolved from the previous session, compounding the Government's problems, as the frustrations of the previous year had not left the October Club and its associates with a favourable view of Oxford's ministry or its intentions. Speaker William Bromley confided his apprehensions on this score to Oxford in late November:

> I am under no apprehension that the enemies to peace can give any trouble in the House of Commons,... I more fear uneasiness of another kind there, gentlemen being very desirous to answer the expectations of those that sent them thither, and to act as becomes a House of Commons chosen by a spirit raised from an opinion of great corruption in the late administration, that it would be now detected and punished, and that something would be done to secure our constitution in church and state against the vile principles and practices that had been countenanced to the endangering of both.[1]

Bromley saw it as the ministry's role to lead in effecting these changes by ridding itself of the Whigs left in office and legislating safeguards certain to exclude them for the foreseeable future. Bromley's analysis of the problem was an accurate one.[2] Oxford had to deflect the October Club from seizing upon the preliminaries to destroy him out of despair and anger, and at the same time win them over to provide the backing necessary for his peace policy.

Throughout the summer of 1711 the Jacobites nursed their grievances in the country, and prepared for a full-scale confrontation with the ministry in the next session. Menzies told St Germain that '[Oxford] shall be drove off the exchange [Parliament] unless he pay his debts'. Into this gathering storm the exiled Court dropped a bombshell. About 8 November a formal directive arrived: 'If Phipps [the peace] comes on his trial this term, you should engage all your friends to do him what service they can'.[3] The implications of this order were obvious: the Government was to be supported on the one issue which the Jacobites could expect to turn to maximum advantage in extracting concessions. There was an immediate protest against such a limitation of their room to manoeuvre. Hamilton begged James 'not to interpose but to leave his friends to manage their party for him, & express'd himself with great vehemence and discontent when ye Kg repeated & insisted on his orders'.[4] Hamilton was unable to resist St Germain on the matter because of the automatic deference accorded to any order coming from the exiled Court. Even though he was the acknowledged leader of the Scots Jacobites, Hamilton was helpless against the call of duty on his followers. The earl of Kincardine reflected this in a letter about the tactics proposed for the next session:

> After talking of that affair with him [Hamilton], I earnestly entreated him to be cautious in giving ear to any advyses or propositions from any of the two partys above, and more especially because, there had been severall dayly hints and surmises that both those partys were laying themselves out to catch their opportunitys of engadging our friends either seperatly or by wholesale: and that it was impossible for us here to judge by our selves what was proper for us to doe in that point: that therefore it was absolutely necessary for us to deferr our selves entirely in that and all other resolutions of moment to our friends above, and I desyred him to write to them that wee were resolved to doe so.[5]

St Germain remained unmoved by Hamilton's pleas, and not only repeated the original order, but further required the Jacobites to ingratiate themselves with the British Court so as to learn its intentions.[6]

The upshot of this order was to boost the ministry's influence in Parliament for that session. In late November Maynwaring gleefully told the earl of Coningsby: 'Parliament is again prorogued...: there is a mutiny in the troops, & the leader will have much ado to succeed in his great undertaking'. By mid-February, having weathered the 'No Peace Without Spain' crisis of December to January, St John could contentedly describe the Commons as 'perfectly secure', and the Government was winning votes in the Lords by a crushing majority. Some changes of personnel had been effected in late December and early January, supplementing those made in the summer of 1711, but these had not satisfied the backbench Tories.[7] As Bromley observed to Oxford:

> there wants no inclination in the members of this House of Commons to come into everything that may support you and render your Ministry easy and glorious; there only wants a confidence which will unavoidably increase, the longer the making those thorough changes are delayed...[8]

Somehow the attitude of the Country Tories had been altered from one of profound distrust to one of at least tacit cooperation, and in many cases enthusiastic support. The Government's espousal of a peace policy undoubtedly won a good deal of favour among the war-weary Country Tories, but support over other matters did not necessarily follow from this. The October Club certainly moderated its tone during the session, indeed, to such an extent that many contemporaries could only attribute such a *volte-face* to flagrant corruption:

> [Oxford] travailloit à ranger cette Clubb sous ses Etendarts; on croyoit... au commencement de cette seance, qu'il n'y reussiroit pas, mais l'evenement a fait voir le contraire, et on a veu, que luy et Mr St Jean les ont gouverné pendant tout cet hiver comme ils ont voulû; On ne scait pas bien, comment cela s'est passe,

mais on croit communement, que cette revolution doit estre principalement
imputée aux Vertus singulieres de la baguette du Grand Tresorier.[9]

Neither the peace policy nor the presumed buying-off of prominent backbench
critics (which should be taken as a constant for most eighteenth-century
administrations anyway) can entirely explain the Club's sudden change of
heart. The enforced subdual of the Jacobites who had radicalised the Country
Tory coalition in 1710-11 offers a further dimension which helps to explain this
phenomenon. It is certain that the Jacobites' own feelings about the ministry
did not alter significantly. In early December Beaufort was angrily refusing to
come to London, on the grounds that Oxford had consistently refused to
gratify him and other Country Tories in their requests for patronage with
which to reward the faithful. Smith noticed that North and Grey and several
Scots peers were unhappy about the preliminaries. Even the courtier
Buckingham was observed to have reservations on the subject.[10] By March
these same men were supporting the ministry loyally, yet if anything their
suspicions of Oxford had deepened:

> Those [Tories] he knows look another way [Jacobites], he finds ways to lessen
> and discourage, and whatever they have is what he cannot avoid. He would not
> have a clamorous complaint, so manages it with dexterity. Your relations
> [Parliamentary Jacobites] see it, but cannot help themselves; for on the other side
> Mr Willie [Whigs] would ruin them worse: so that... they are forced to hold the
> candle to the devil, at present, and after a little time he will defy them to hurt
> him, when the great decision is over.[11]

Oxford's Government therefore gained the advantage of direct Jacobite
support for its peace policies whenever these were considered in Parliament,
and the indirect bonus of a more restrained October Club, despite the
inclinations of many of the individuals concerned. In numerical terms this was
a far from inconsiderable gain, but in qualitative terms a far greater one.

The Jacobites might be induced to restrain themselves by St Germain, but
their associates in the October Club felt no such pressure. The Jacobites had
added the leaven to Country Tory discontent in 1710-11, but their fellows had
quite enough zeal to keep up some of the October Club's reforming impetus.
The peace policy sweetened their temper towards the ministry, but it did not
remove Country Tory commitment to the policies the October Club had been
formed to impose on it. Nor could the Jacobites be taken completely for
granted: if angered by the Government, they were likely to forget all about
their orders from St Germain. Country Tory support for the Oxford ministry
in this session was still conditional on their policy wishes being humoured. As
long as the Court allowed certain measures dear to the Country Tories through
Parliament, and carried out acceptably Tory policies itself, they were prepared
to support it, but not otherwise. After having spent a very satisfying period
examining and censuring the Allies over shortfalls in their quota of
contributions to the war, the October Club was most unwilling to vote further
supply for the war. Led by their Jacobite wing, they procrastinated
obstinately:

Messieurs de la Cabale d'Octobre se recrierent extremement par la bouche de Chevalier Simeon Stuart et du Sieur Eversfield contre ce Projet; ils avouerent, que la saison estoit assés avancée pour qu'on dût songer au subside... soutinrent encore leur raisonnement, en exposant, qu'il n'y avoit que deux jours que la Chambre avoit pris avec les Concurrence des Ministres des Resolutions très vigoreuses là dessus, et qu'elle travailloit mesme actuellement en consequence de ces Resolutions à une Remontrance à la Reyne pour la prier de ne payer des subsides ni de fournir des Trouppes au de la de sa juste proportion.[12]

When the ministry found it necessary to introduce an increased leather tax, it raised such an outcry from the Country Tories that the Court prudently adjourned the measure, and then slipped it through in easy stages. Even then the October Club was content to let the Ministry get a mauling from the Opposition[13] in the debate, despite voting for the measure themselves:

the Leather Tax has enrag'd many, who pretend an Absolute Promise to be exempted from that Duty: And notice having been taken to several Octobermen, how tamely they sate still, when the ministers were rudely handled; they have answerd that they were very glad to hear those Persons abus'd, who had so long abus'd them.[14]

The Court also had to accept a rebuff when Sir Henry Belasyse accepted a Commissionership for the inspection of garrisons in British ports, and was promptly voted to have thereby vacated his seat in the Commons. St John was probably not exaggerating overmuch when he warned the French that evasion of their treaty obligations would turn the Country Tories against the Government.[15]

Within these limits, the October Club and its associates' loyalty to the ministry was assured. This was a tremendous asset gained for the Government. In effect it secured the Court in the Commons in all but the most exceptional cases. The neutralisation of the Jacobites catalysed the process. In the Lords St Germain's support would not have been so important, given the pro-Court inclinations of most Jacobite peers, had it not been for the Government's problems with the Scots peers and the loss of control of the Lords in December 1711.[16] The exiled Court made it clear that it wished the Scots Jacobite peers to support the ministry: 'I bid him desire ye Scots peers from yr K. to joyn together in every thing to go along wth Psse An. and Harlay and to forward the peace', and in the end they did so.[17] Other Jacobite lords were simply encouraged to follow their own inclinations and support a ministry of whose policies they at last approved. North and Grey thus became the proposer of a wrecking amendment to the annual Place Bill. He and the marquis of Carmarthen (Leeds's son) provided a furious counterblast for the Court after the 'No Peace without Spain' amendment had been passed on 7 December. The Opposition's attack on the peace terms in June was routed after Ferrers proposed a counter-address lauding them.[18] Outside Parliament too, Jacobite peers, M.P.'s and sympathisers proved useful to the ministry. Fiercely worded addresses were drummed up at convenient moments, and the Jacobites' interest was used to lobby recalcitrant peers and important individuals.[19] Securing the Commons was the single most useful gain, because it could always be used to check Whig moves in the Lords where the Court's control was always less certain. Using it, the ministry was able to crush several highly inflammatory Opposition addresses introduced in coordination with similar moves in the Lords. A motion to consider the Queen's latest speech on the progress of the negotiations was converted into one expressing total confidence in the Government: 'this House will effectually stand by and support her Majesty in all things recommended to them in her Majesty's most gracious Speech from the throne'. Another, to have the British plenipotentiaries seek guarantees for the Protestant succession from the Allies, was treated in the same fashion, and the proposed address against the restraining orders was overwhelmingly rejected.[20] In more mundane matters the support of the Country Tories in the Commons proved valuable too. With it, the Court was enabled to rush the land tax through before Christmas 1711. St John was able to use the Jacobites not only to savage the Allies' interference in British politics, but also to conceal the Government's own moves in the Commons, as in the case of the Barrier Treaty debates. And when the Court's own men came under attack the October Club showed more inclination to support them. Thus, an attempt to have a creditors' petition against St John's henchman Arthur Moore, M.P. for Grimsby, declared 'frivolous and vexatious' received the Club's backing.[21] Altogether, through the support of St Germain and its own more visible commitment to Toryism, as well as a certain amount of prudent compromise, the Oxford ministry was able to regain the domination of the Tory party that it had lost in 1710-11.

The October Club was a fragile Country-orientated coalition because its members had so few other areas on which they could all agree. Support for the Court on a consistent basis was the antithesis of Country principles, so the Club's wholehearted alignment with the ministry was bound to create internal stress. Virtually the entire October Club was willing to support the Government on the general issue of peace negotiations, but many were unhappy at the type of peace the preliminaries seemed to be indicating would be made. Nottingham felt obliged to make his famous move into opposition on the issue. The Hanoverian Tory wing of the Club was not inclined to go so far, but it was a difference of degree only. As the shape of the peace being made became gradually clearer, the Hanoverian Tories came more or less to support it (though with considerable reservations at several points), but they did not see why they should become a mere adjunct to the Court over other matters because of it. Their reservations over the peace being negotiated, combined with their continued determination to uphold 'Country' Tory policies, put them in conflict with the Jacobites, who had been ordered to support the Court, and the middle-of-the-road October-men who were delighted at the prospect of any peace at all, and viewed the ministry with favour simply because it was negotiating one. In response, the Hanoverian Tories began to draw apart from the rest of the October Club. Beginning with individual defections over the issue of peace without Spain, such as John Aislabie and

Lord Daniel Finch, this drift increased during the Barrier treaty debates, until by March they had become a discernible dissident group within the Club. 'All well-inclined are enraged at Harley's proceedings, and that part of the Commons they call the October Club of forty.' The trigger for their separation was the election of St John as president for one of the Club's meetings by the other two groups.[22]

The March Club was intended to reaffirm its members' commitment to solidly Country Tory principles, hence the appellation 'Primative October men'. It numbered between thirty-five and fifty M.P.'s and also had some adherents in the Lords, such as the earl of Jersey. Of its Commons membership, an unusually high proportion were felt to be wealthy for Country Tories, as in the cases of the Pitt clan and of Charles Cholmondeley. If this was so, it could explain the insistence in the Club rules on an absolute refusal of all Court places and pensions, as wealth obviously diminished the need for such perquisites. From the outset the new Club strove to demonstrate its pro-Hanoverian sympathies wherever it could. Prominent October Club Jacobites were specifically excluded on the grounds that they were the tools of the Court. Sir Simeon Stuart was debarred on this count, as was Eversfield and the entire Commission of Accounts. Toasts which laid an ostentatious emphasis on the Hanoverian succession were adopted at March Club meetings, and the slogan 'A good peace or a good war' was taken up.[23] In accord with this emphasis in their public statements, the Club supported measures which were felt to support the Protestant interest and facilitate the continuance of the war until a good peace was secured. Thus the March Club supported the Lords' insertion of an amendment into a Bill to prevent the creation of fraudulent votes which allowed Quakers to affirm rather than swear to the authenticity of their votes. Without this clause the Quakers would effectively have been disenfranchised, so the October Club Jacobites had been leading a campaign to prevent any such saving amendment since February, in the hope of striking a blow at the Whigs' Nonconformist allies. The March Club's support preserved the Lords' amendment.[24] The Club also supported the leather tax and the untacking of the Grants Resumption Bill on the grounds that not to allow these measures would impede the war effort.[25] In the process they also made it abundantly clear that they would not tolerate the Court making a *separate* peace, criticising St John in Parliament when he suggested that the nation was too exhausted to carry on the war:

> Ce raisonnement fut relevé d'une maniere assés forte par le Sieur Lawson et quelques autres du Clubb de Mars lesquels donnoient à entendre, que ces sortes de discours ne contribueroient gueres à obtenir une bonne Paix, que le Royaume n'etoit pas encore si fort epuisé que de faire une mauvaise Paix ou une Paix separée comme le bruit s'en repandoit à l'indignation de touts les honnêtes gens; ils ajoutoient, que la Chambre etoit prête d'entrer en tout ce qui pourroit avancer l'affaire du Subside.[26]

For all this elaborate display of Hanoverian-cum-Protestant sympathies, the underlying thrust of March Club principles was solidly Country Tory. They were happy to humiliate the October Club and the Court by voting down the Committee of Privileges and Elections' decision that the creditors' petition against Moore was 'frivolous and vexatious'. But when it came to matters of Tory principle they were steadfast in their support of the 'right' side. They backed the Court and the October Club in their indirect censure of the Dutch Estates-General for replying to proposals from the ministry in the pages of the *Daily Courant*. They also combined with the October Club to reject a Bill, brought in by the Whigs, which would have given the Quakers a *statutory* right to affirm rather than swear in all cases. This was a transparent attempt to exploit Country Tory divisions over the Quaker clause in the Fraudulent Votes Bill, and was treated as such. In the debates on the restraining orders and the peace terms they had no hesitation in backing the ministry.[27] The March Club represented another fissure in the ranks of the Tory party, but it was not necessarily one which the Opposition could use to bring down the ministry. The Club had its differences with the Court and its October predecessor, but they at least were Tories. By the end of May the Opposition had come to the bitter conclusion that they 'n'avoient rien a esperer du Clubb de Mars'.

This session saw the gradual eclipse of the Scots Jacobite peers' earlier organisation. They returned to Westminster with their policies and identity still basically intact. Hamilton was busy at the end of November summoning up his friends and allies, and letting Oxford know in no uncertain terms that he had only himself to blame for any tardiness:

> if her Majesty's service necessarily requires their attendance... you should take the effectual measures of bringing them here in time; for I can assure you that hitherto it has not been done and I would by no means have her Majesty's interest suffer and your Lordship disappointed. Therefore it is absolutely necessary that you lose no time to give those Lords satisfaction; for the continuation of the others in the posts who opposed her Majesty's measures last year makes them very slow at present... if you don't come to facts immediately, depend upon it, you need not reckon upon their assistance.[28]

Hamilton's strident tone may in part have stemmed from elements among his own group who wished him to bargain for better terms now the Court was in difficulties. John Hamilton urged, 'your Grace and your friends should now make your aggreament with ye Court for I don't beleive such ane opportunity for getting good termes will fall out in haist'.[29] In the event Hamilton does not appear to have demanded fresh concessions from the Court. His orders from St Germain were quite explicit on what they expected his conduct to be, and he clearly did not intend to jeopardise his position as leader of the Scots Jacobite peers or to risk the gains he had already made. Both his position as leader of a group of Scots peers usually attached to the Court interest, and the Brandon patent which he had extracted from the ministry for himself, marked him out as a target for the Opposition. He duly suffered the inevitable consequences of this when the Opposition wrested control of the Lords from the Government on 7 December.[30]

The Hamilton affair and its aftermath left Hamilton in the invidious position of trying to lead a Parliamentary group when he himself no longer had access to the Lords. None of the remaining Scots Jacobite peers had sufficient stature to succeed him, and this left the group to drift into the ambit of Mar's Scots Court group. By the end of the session they were virtually a permanent attachment to this interest. It was inevitable that, lacking their own leader in Parliament, they should look to the Court for guidance, and St Germain's repeated directives to support the ministry facilitated the process. Mar also tried to ingratiate himself with the Jacobite Court so as to command their support. To achieve this he cultivated a rather stupid unofficial Jacobite correspondent, whom he encouraged to believe that he secretly favoured a restoration. She obligingly wrote encomia about him to the exiled Court:

> All your friends and correspondents may do that piece of right, to own it: he of all the Scots has the best interest with Q. Anne and E. Oxford; and also he is believed by the English as a good and great lawyer [Minister] and a man of much goodness and honour.[31]

St Germain was cautious about accepting Mar's proffered friendship, on the advice of Maule and others, but it did not seem to realise, or demur if it did, Mar's attachment of the Scots Jacobite peers to the Court group. At the end of the session Lockhart found the Scots peers were so enervated by their dependence on the Court for leadership, and their hopes of reward, that there was nothing he could do to rouse them to action.[32]

Hamilton seems to have been unable or unwilling to halt this process, of which he must have been aware. After the breakdown of the Scots peers' boycott he turned his attention entirely towards gaining some sort of compensation from the Court for his disappointment over the Brandon patent. As a result, from January onwards his name was linked to every major post then vacant or rumoured to be about to be so. Hamilton used all the interest he had to this end, even asking the Jacobite Court quietly to pressurise the French Court to ask for him to be sent as Ambassador once peace was made.[33] In the end his continued influence outside Parliament among the Scots peerage secured him his desire. The earl Marischal died early in the summer, and the prospect of an alliance between Hamilton and Argyll to return a replacement of their choice against the Court greatly alarmed Mar:

> if Duke Hamilton be not some way provided for at this time, and soon too, I see plainly he will join with these two [Campbell] brothers in this affair and everything else, and if they do they will go fair to carry who they have a mind to; and that will lay such a foundation for the next election, or anything that is to be done there in relation to the peers, that it will be very difficult to get anything done but what they please.[34]

Mar was right to be concerned over this possibility: his long sojourn in the wings had already moved Hamilton to try to persuade St Germain to reconsider their attitude to the ministry. He appears to have been surprised to find that the Jacobite Court had no more idea of Oxford's plans and intentions than he did, and that they were taking the ministry's goodwill on trust. He was moved by this, and probably by his own self-interest, to try to obtain a personal messenger to go to St Germain and warn them from him that Oxford was playing no-one's game but his own. His first choice fell upon the Catholic priest, James Carnegy, who was a trusted correspondent of long standing with the exiled Court. Carnegy was, however, very loth to bear such bad tidings, arguing that it 'perhaps is not true, and if it be true I doubt not but Sir John [James] may have it from other hands'. Hamilton seems to have considered sending Lockhart instead, but then abandoned the idea.[35] His concern may have been genuine, but Oxford's offer to him in mid-June of the offices of Master of the Ordnance and Ambassador Extraordinary to France certainly silenced his doubts, and he loyally backed the earl of Findlater, the Court's candidate, in the election. At the election Hamilton did make some attempt to work up a joint remonstrance over the Brandon patent (on the grounds that the Lords' decision was a breach of the Union), but this petered out.[36] His behaviour during this election, allied to his blatant self-seeking in the preceding months, had built up a certain amount of dissatisfaction among the Scots Jacobites, as Carnegy did not hesitate to inform him:

> I wrott to him with much freedom... that his misterious way of doing bussienes had lost him much with Mark [Jacobites] who I doubt not has given Sir John [James] account of him, and if he do not some thing for his own vindication now when providence furnishes him with an opportunity of so doing he'll be lost at all hands.[37]

Hamilton was in the process of doing something to retrieve his reputation when he was killed by lord Mohun in their notorious duel.

Hamilton died still leader of the Scots Jacobite interest, though by then it had fallen into lassitude at least in the Lords.[38] Mar had succeeded in attaching the Jacobite group there to the Court on a more or less permanent basis, and had taken over the role of their patron and manager. It was Mar who successfully pressed for the election of the earl of Linlithgow, another Jacobite, to replace Hamilton, at the end of 1712. Lassitude should not be taken to signify demoralisation, however. The Scots Jacobite peers remained attached to their anti-Union pro-Jacobite views.[39] All that was lacking to revitalise them was an issue on which Mar's pro-Court management was felt to be unsatisfactory.

The Jacobites' enforced attachment to the Court on St Germain's orders had never been very popular among the warmer of the Jacobite Court's adherents, particularly in the Commons. By the end of May Hamilton was not the only Jacobite leader who was beginning to suspect the ministry of deceit. Lockhart too 'began very much to suspect the integrity of the Ministry; at least I was of opinion that ther was or woud be soon ane absolute necessity of holding a rod over their backs and forcing them to mind what was their duty and interest'. The preconditions for translating this feeling into action had been established earlier in the year. In January the Scots Jacobites led a movement among the Scots M.P's to support the peers by a simultaneous boycott of the Commons as well as the Lords. Lockhart and Lyon required, however, that the peers agree that this would not be terminated except by a joint and democratic decision, which it appears that the peers would not agree to. At the end of February the Scots Jacobite M.P's headed a united Scots deputation to protest to Oxford about proposals to restrict Scots access to Dutch markets to one port. In April Netterville reported a scheme afoot among the Jacobite M.P.'s to produce Plunket's revelations of the Whig plot of early 1712 in the Commons, before they were forestalled by Oxford producing them in Cabinet instead. Finally, in early May the Jacobite M.P.'s were outraged to find that the ministry had carefully reinserted all the clauses in favour of the Hanoverian succession into the new Barrier treaty. St Germain promptly told Menzies: 'The Jacobites to be advertised to go along with him [Oxford] in every thing'.[40] But matters had gone too far for there not to be an attempt to evade the spirit of this order — at the very least.

The Scots Jacobite M.P.'s had been loosely organised by their own secret steering committee since 1711. This constituted a good nucleus round which to form an independent Jacobite group of both nations, but only in the House where the ministry had most room to manoeuvre: the Commons. There, the Government could always hope to find Whig support if the extreme Tories pressed it too hard. The Lords presented far greater tactical opportunities to put pressure on the Court, and hence the best hope of forcing concessions. After consulting his English friends, Lockhart tried to move the Scots Jacobite peers to action:

> many of the English gentlemen came to have the same thoughts and heartily wishd that the Scots Peers, who had the ballance in their hands in the House of Lords, would be somewhat free with the Earl of Oxford,... and I spake to severall of them, but with no success so much did they depend on and resign themselves to the Ministry, on account of what they either then received or expected in time by preferments.[41]

Denied aid or a lead from his fellow Scots, Lockhart turned towards his fellow Jacobites of both nations, and a separately organised Jacobite Tory group began to emerge in the Commons:

> I did then cast about among the Commons, and finding them well enuff disposed to enter into measures for obliging the Ministry to do what was expected with respect to the King and other matters of moment, wee began to form a party for that purpose and concert measures to be prosecuted.[42]

The outline of the measures proposed was sent to St Germain for approval at some time in June or July. The principal component was a straightforward attack on the legal basis of the Hanoverian succession:

> Les amis du Roy d'Angleterre demandent qu'il soit tres humblement representé a sa Majesté que ceux qui sont bien intentionnés pour Elle ont dessein de presenter à la prochaine sceance du Parlement un Bil ou projet d'Acte pour revoquer le present Act d'etablissement de la succession à la Couronne sous le titre de Bil

pour donner pouvoir à la Reyne de nommer son Successeur par Testament pourveu qu'elle le nomme de la ligne Royalle, & Protestant.[43]

They apologised for the necessity of putting in such a religious clause, but, in accord with the exiled Court's concurrent religious feuding, also asked that James should hear the Protestant theological case right away, though they promised to let the matter be if he remained unconvinced. The Jacobite Court was still interested in the political initiative at this time, and had been tantalised by claims about what the united Jacobite interest in Parliament could achieve earlier in the session.[44] Middleton therefore showed a cautious interest:

> it will be a great step gain'd to have Harpers [Hanover's] decree revers'd and the nomination left in Aylmer [Queen Anne]; for tho Plessington [James] will never comply with the limitation above mention'd, yet when a rich a numerous family are turn'd out of doors, and the house left empty, it will be much easier to get possession of it.[45]

In the end St Germain's determination to keep up a friendly front towards Oxford got the better of it, and Lockhart was ordered to desist — much to his disgust:

> Mr John Meinzies... came and shewd me a letter to him from the Earl of Midleton, signifying that it was the King's pleasure that all his freinds shoud join in supporting the Ministry and give them no uneasiness; requiring him to communicate the same to me and severall others. I told Mr Meinzies that it was my duty to obey but I was very sorry for this occasion of shewing my regard to the King's commands, being now more than ever jealous [suspicious] of the Ministry, at least of the Lord Oxford;... this message to the Kings freinds did put a stop to the bustle which they designd to have made and which I dare say woud have been some use to the King's affairs, by obliging the Lord Oxford sooner to declaire what he aimd at.[46]

The Jacobite equivalent of the pro-Hanoverian March Club was avoided then, only due to the direct intervention of the exiled Court against it. The sentiments which had given rise to it still remained, and were only liable to harden as the Jacobite M.P.s' discontent with Oxford grew, so that in effect the emergence of an independent Jacobite group was merely deferred, not prevented.

In the light of the developments mapped out above, it is now appropriate to consider the effects of Oxford's alliance with the October Club and the High Tories in general on the conduct of his administration and policies. All political bargains have a positive and negative side for those concerned. What must now be assessed is who benefited most, and with what repercussions this was accompanied.

Oxford certainly did not intend to give anything up to the Country Tories when he met Parliament in December 1711. He seems to have been confident that the Country Tories' desperate desire for peace would overcome their growing disillusion with his ministry. This was a serious misjudgement of quite how unpopular his Government had become on the back-benches. Though very few lords were refusing to support the preliminaries at all (only Nottingham and the earl of Pembroke), far more serious was the widespread reluctance, particularly among the High Tory and Scots peers, to rush to London to save his ministry from the gathering Whig storm.[47] When this broke on the first day of the session, the ministry found itself dangerously isolated and with an ominous wavering in its own ranks. Ferrers led for the Court in the Lords, but otherwise the Government had to fight its own battle with Nottingham and the Junto, with only half-hearted support from North and Grey, Anglesey and lord Guernsey, mainly on procedural points. Buckingham's silence during the debate, except for one interjection upholding Nottingham's right to make an amendment to the address of thanks, is symptomatic of the general attitude.[48] In the Commons, Eversfield was the only leader of the October Club to speak in the debate, and what he had to say was not calculated to bolster the ministry's confidence:

> En effet on à remarqué, que l'Octobre Clubb n'a pas parle un seul mot pendant tout le debat, a la reserve du Sieur Eversfield un des Principeaux, qui dit a la fin des disputes sur la Clause, que par deference pour ce que la Reyne avoit declaré dans son Discours, il ne voteroit pas pour cette Clause, mais qu'il ne vouloit pas qu'on entendit par là, qu'il consentoit à une mauvaise Paix, et qu'il ne voyoit pas comment l'omission de cette Clause pourroit mettre un Ministre à couvert, qui aviseroit la Reyne de faire une Paix prejudiciable au Royaume. On dit que ce Complement n'embarrasse pas moins les Ministres que le mauvais succés qu'ils ont eu dans la Chambre Haute.[49]

Oxford clearly found the experience very sobering. Though he tried to blame his defeat on the tardiness of the Scots, bribery by Marlborough and the treachery of the Court Whigs,[50] he was nothing if not a realist when it came to ensuring that the Court was not to be isolated again:

> This proceeding will oblige the Queen, without reserve, to use the gentlemen of England, and those who are for her prerogative, it will draw marks of displeasure upon those who have barefaced set up a standard against her, and proffered to advise things which they know the States will never come into.[51]

Over the next few weeks Oxford and his lieutenants worked energetically to bring the Country Tories into the ministry's interest. Marlborough and the duke of Somerset were dismissed, and the Court refrained from obstructing measures dear to the Country Tories, such as the presentation of the Commission of Accounts report against Marlborough and the Naturalisation Act Repeal Bill. Though Nottingham's old following showed signs of moving into Opposition after him, the ministry steadily tied in the rest of the Tory party by hints at the 'secret articles' of the peace, half-promises of impeachments of Marlborough, Godolphin and the Junto, and full promises of a thoroughgoing Tory regime in Church and State — as soon as the peace was concluded.[52] The Opposition was not signally checked until Oxford brought in his 'dozen' of newly created peers, but that was only the *coup de grâce*. The background work which brought in the Country Tories was what really secured his position. In the process notably Jacobite peers such as Beaufort, Yarmouth and Scarsdale, North and Grey, Carmarthen and Ferrers were brought into prominence in the Lords, while the Court worked on establishing a rapport with the October Club in the Commons.[53]

One Whig measure which proved a considerable obstacle to Oxford's plans to attach the Country Tories to his ministry was the rejection of the Brandon patent by the Lords. There had been signs earlier in the year that the elevation of Hamilton to a British peerage would precipitate a joint display of xenophobia by the English Whigs and Tories. Cynical manipulation by the Junto of their fears of being swamped by the 'mercenary' Scots produced a substantial rift in the Tories' ranks, and allowed Hamilton to be excluded on the basis of a truly Jesuitical interpretation of the Union.[54] Altogether, this was a very shrewd move on the part of the Opposition. Not only did they deny the ministry the ability to use Scotland as a reservoir of needy, and hence cooperative, peers, but also they drove a wedge into the ministry's ranks on a national issue. The resulting division and ill-feeling might induce the Scots to defect to the Opposition or boycott the Lords as part of their own quarrel with the Court, either of which would substantially weaken the ministry's position in that House.[55] The anti-Union group round Hamilton naturally played a central role in the crisis, though itself internally divided on the best course of action. Hamilton was primarily interested in having his patent recognised by some means. He was therefore willing to consider compromise hereditisation schemes whereby twenty-five or more Scots peers would have received hereditary Lords' seats and the rest would have been eligible to stand for election to the Commons. Such tinkering with the detested Union, rather than its outright demolition, was anathema to some of his friends. Balmerino and Annandale advocated far more extreme measures, and began their own boycott of the Lords from around 26 January. Both men were insisting that the peers alone could not alter the Union, and that any change required the convening and consent of the Scots Estates. This was patently a device intended to get the Union dissolved by an irate Scots assembly, but their vocal denunciations of any attempts to alter the Union unilaterally made such an expedient difficult to approach politically.[56] Nor did Balmerino deny that this was his aim:

> they say I would have the Estates to be call'd and I might as well propose a dissol'n of the Union — I say I shall propose yt whenever they please, but it is not my fault yt nothing can alter any Article in our contract, but the party's who made it.[57]

As it became clear that the ministry was unwilling to make a generous settlement, or to risk its English Country Tory support in an attempt to reverse the Brandon decision, the attitude of Hamilton and the other anti-Unionists hardened. By the end of January Hamilton was denying that he had ever favoured a hereditisation scheme, and his group became the prime movers of the plan to boycott the Lords.[58] Their zeal shamed all the Representative Peers into going into the plan initially, as Mar admitted to Swift, for fear of being branded traitors at home, but the boycott quickly crumbled due to the need to watch over the passage of the Episcopalian Toleration Bill. It was finally wound up at the end of February, though not before it had given the ministry some unpleasant moments, such as when they had to yield to an Opposition demand for an address requesting the queen not to negotiate with the French until they recognised her title.[59] The Scots Jacobite peers were themselves put in a very difficult situation by the boycott, although they had advocated it. Measures dear to every Country Tory were passing through Parliament at this time, which put men like Eglinton in an agonising dilemma: 'he says if we please he shall absent but if he be present by god he will never let the Whigs gain a vote of the tories if he cane help it'. Another directive from St Germain solved the problem and rescued the ministry by ordering the Scots Jacobite peers to return and support it in the Lords. The Government was duly relieved and thankful, as Mar signified to Mrs Murray: 'it was mighty well taken that the King had sent an intimation to his friends to go again to parliament, and join with the Court'.[60]

The first test of Oxford's new association with the Country Tories came over the Occasional Conformity Bill, passage of which had been a long cherished ambition of theirs. Nottingham, the originator of the 'Tack' of 1704, made Whig support for this measure his price for joining them in 1711, in the hope that his introduction of it would 'reconcile me to my old-friends, & make 'em asham'd of their ridiculous jealousies & may I hope bring 'em to think better of my opinion abt ye Peace'. In fact he was late in the field. The October Club and other prominent Country Tories had already decided to try and bring in such a measure. Their leaders had approached Oxford on the matter, who had procrastinated magnificently, giving them a half-promise of support from the Court in the Lords (the most difficult part of the Bill's passage) 'when the time is right', in return for a pledge to support the peace preliminaries in Parliament.[61] Hanmer and other, more moderate, Country Tory leaders seem to have been satisfied with this, but the Jacobites were not:

> some who have a true zeal for it [the Church], were captivated by these strange politicks both for peace & ye unseasonableness at present of such a Bill, especially Sr Tho: Hanmer, others viz Sr Sim: Stuart Mr Eversfield & c resolv'd however to bring in ye Bill tho' they defer'd it for some weeks, in hopes yt ye time might come wn their friends at least might think it seasonable, tho' ye Great Man shou'd not, for they little expected it from him.[62]

Nottingham duly approached them and offered what Oxford could not at that time: unimpeded passage through the Lords for the Bill. They seized upon it, and the brief alliance rushed the Bill through both Houses with 'not one word said against it'. Aware of his delicate position with respect to the Bill, and that the Country Tories would be watching him for the slightest sign of opposition to it, Oxford made no attempt to block the Bill directly, even though it struck at the heart of his policy of winning over the Dissenters. He did try, though, to have the proposed penalties left at the discretion of the administration. Oxford apparently presented this as a means by which to bind the Dissenters to the Tory interest, but the manoeuvre was foiled by Nottingham and Anglesey, who lobbied the Commons against allowing this loophole to be built into the Bill,[63] arguing 'yt ye Dissenters must have all depended on the Ministry for fear as ye Tory's now do for hopes & so a party had been formed of the worst of both parties, under the Governmt of the Ministry, wch is the scheme yt was lately call'd Moderation'. The October Club recognised the threat and put statutory penalties into the Bill. Stratford enthusiastically predicted that 'the Bill will make the October [Club] easy for this session', but this was over-sanguine.[64] Oxford had sacrificed his Dissenting interest to the necessity of winning over the Country Tories, and the October Club probably had a warmer view of him as a result. It can, however, be put in no more tangible terms than that. All Oxford can be seen to have gained was a slight mellowing of the Country Tories' hostility towards him. Nottingham gained even less. Because they had been in the process of bringing in their own Occasional Conformity Bill themselves, the October Club felt no particular gratitude towards him and continued to rail at him as a 'Deserter.'

When Marlborough returned at the end of the 1711 campaign, the ministry had already decided it would be his last. His subsequent alignment with the Opposition over the preliminaries determined Oxford to discredit him thoroughly, and if possible to drive him into exile.[65] The Country Tories were in possession of the best weapon with which to achieve this: the Commission of Accounts report against Marlborough. This was a weighty but tendentious piece which the October Club planned to introduce at the beginning of the session. By not opposing this, as would normally have been their wont, the ministry brought off a dual coup. Wholehearted support of the resolutions against Marlborough pleased their backbenchers, and at the same time discredited him as a public figure.[66] It served not only as an issue on which the Court and the Country Tories could unite, but as one which kept the October Club together for a while longer. All elements in the Club were fully represented in the denunciations, divisions and votes against Marlborough, but the Court particularly allowed the Jacobites to have their head, which gave them the opportunity for some unbridled extremism. If anything, the ministry helped them whip the rest of the Country Tories on, by publishing the Commission's report on Marlborough *verbatim* in the Commons Journals after the House had voted that they should not be published for the public.[67] Lockhart and Shippen actually presented the case against Marlborough. Shippen, Stuart, Pakington, Ross and Eversfield were among the most notable speakers against him in the debates.[68] The ministry was quite happy to conclude the affair once Marlborough's public reputation had been blasted forever. Their allies wished to carry it further. Following a suggestion made in the debates by Pakington:

le Sieur Campion proposa à la Chambre Basse que veu qu'elle avoit declare les 2½ p. Cent retenûs par le Duc de Marlborough sur la paye des Trouppes Etrangeres, Deniers publics, il etoit juste de l'obliger à la Restitution de cet argent, et qu'il demandoit permission de porter un Bill pour cet effêt, et il fut secondé par les Chevaliers Stuart et Dolben et le Sieur Eversfield;... comme aucun de sa [Queen Anne's] Cour ne disoit rien, l'affaire tomba bientôt; On croit que les Ministres estoient d'autant moins disposés à entrer dans ce dessein, que l'affaire seroit portée de cette maniere devant la Chambre Haute, à l'examen de la quelle il n'y a pas d'apparence, qu'on la veuille exposer.[69]

The Court moved to appease this desire for retribution shortly afterwards, by submitting the case to the Attorney-General for recovery of the money by litigation.[70]

The Commission of Accounts' report struck not only at Marlborough, but also at Robert Walpole, Secretary at War in the previous ministry, and Adam de Cardonnel, the duke's secretary. Oxford had tried to enlist Walpole for his own ministry when he first came into office in 1710, and Cardonnel was of no significance politically. Hence, it is not likely that the Government particularly wanted to hound these two out of politics. In effect, the Court sacrificed them both to keep its backbenchers happy. Both were prime targets for the Country Tories, Walpole having been a Whig placeman and subsequently one of the Junto's leaders in the Commons, and Cardonnel as a Court Whig placeman and servant of Marlborough's. The Country Tories fell on them with as much relish as they had done on Ridge in 1711, while the Court gave tacit support despite its alleged disgust at the partiality displayed by its allies. This was an issue which brought all elements of the Country Tories together, and Strangways, Eversfield, Stuart and Lockhart cheerfully cooperated with Hanmer, Grahme, Warburton and Cholmondeley throughout.[71] The expulsions of Walpole and Cardonnel from the Commons illustrate the price Oxford's ministry had to pay to gain its ends. He wanted to have Marlborough disgraced. To do so he had to allow more measures of the same kind, and with as little justification, against targets that might have been better left alone from his point of view. In the case of Marlborough and the question of the repayment of his perquisites it had also threatened to get out of control, and could have ended in a full-scale clash between Lords and Commons.

One measure which the ministry had to undertake in order to prepare the way for direct negotiations on the secret terms they had already agreed with the French was the repudiation of the Barrier treaty. This was not only the means by which a pro-British peace could be justified, but also a convenient way to set aside the Lords' amendment to the address earlier in the session:

> as soon as the Queen has declared herself, the Comons will call for the several Treatys to observe what should and what has been done and desire a better warr or a Peace wch they will trust to the Queen, and by asking the Lords concurrence will therby retrieve the question lost in the Lords House about what is a safe and honourable peace...[72]

To achieve this end, the Court simply showed the October Club where to look, and unleashed them.[73] Apart from a handful, such as the Pitts and Cholmondeley, who were later to form the nucleus of the March Club, the October-men were delighted to be allowed to tear up a treaty with the loathed Dutch, and proceeded to do so with zest. As with the attack on Marlborough, a useful byproduct of this was that it also disposed them better towards the Government. Netterville found the Jacobite M.P.'s outraged at the contents of the treaty, and content to destroy it merely to give Britain increased room for manoeuvre at Utrecht. Philip Parker flatly stated to Percival that it was an obstacle to peace and therefore must be disposed of. Hanmer wrote a set of condemnatory resolutions on the Barrier treaty for the Commons, and Eversfield, Lockhart, Stuart and Shippen were notable advocates of their endorsement.[74] The October Club insisted on having their customary Whig scapegoat, which did not please the ministry, but which it tacitly allowed. Viscount Townshend and his fellow negotiators were duly voted 'Enemies to the Queen and Kingdom'. The Court had achieved its ends by this time, but found that the passions aroused among the backbenchers were not so easily damped down as initially fired. In the Committee of Supply, the October Club proved obstinately difficult about voting supply to pay the Palatine auxiliary troops, arguing 'that they might be consistant with themselves who had voted the day before they had paid more than their quotas for several years'.[75] The Court persuaded them to relent, but the incident typifies the problems of using the Country Tories in alliance with the Government's supporters. They had their own standards of integrity and consistency which were not the same as those of the basically amoral, politically professional, Court and the devoted 'Harlekins'.

Nowhere is the value of the October Club and its associates' support better demonstrated than in the debates on the restraining orders. These were orders sent by St John to Ormonde (with Cabinet approval) directing him not to become involved in any battles or sieges with any of the troops under his command. When Prince Eugene informed the Opposition leaders of these orders they immediately planned an all-out attack on the Government, and were confidently predicting they would put Oxford in the Tower by the end of the debate. All possible pressure was brought to bear on the Court Whig peers to bring them over during the inevitable divisions, and other Whig peers were summoned up from the country. The Tories meanwhile appeared to be in a state of confusion, unsure whether to believe the reports of the orders which had been published in the Dutch newsletters, and alarmed at the prospect that they might be.[76] Instead of proving a catastrophe for the ministry, however, it proved one for the Opposition. In the Lords Oxford first succeeded in confusing the issue by lying briskly about the exact content of Ormonde's orders. Poulet then sidetracked the debate by a tirade about the motivation behind Marlborough's great victories, during which he was so rude to Marlborough that the duke later challenged him to a duel. The ministry then won the division by a crushing majority. In the Commons it was even more of a debacle for the Opposition. St John needed to do little while Campion,

Eversfield and John Manley savaged their opponents. Inevitably, they got carried away and at one point threatened to send William Pulteney (a Junto Wing leader in the Commons) to the Tower for reflecting on the ministry.[77] By the end of the debate the Opposition were laid so low that they could not even muster a riposte to a ministerial resolution praising its own conduct:

> this House hath an entire Confidence in her Majesty's most gracious Promise to communicate to her Parliament the Terms of peace before the same shall be concluded: And that they will support her Majesty in obtaining an honourable and safe Peace against all such persons, either at Home or Abroad who have endeavoured, or shall endeavour to obstruct the same.[78]

The price Oxford had to pay to get this exculpatory resolution through — promising to lay the peace terms before Parliament before they were ratified — may seem small, but it epitomises Oxford's relationship with his backbenchers. He had a dynamic association with them: the ministry had to feed the Country Tories lest they devour it. Oxford could not have survived this crisis if he had not had the support of the Country Tories. His problem was that he was not acting as their leader but as an untrusted ally, so that every measure of support had its price or else had to be something that the Country Tories wanted to do anyway. Oxford's progress from one crisis to another stemmed from his inability to do this, keep the Court Whig peers with the ministry and satisfy Anne's requirement that moderate men of all parties remain in office, all at the same time.

One measure which Oxford certainly did not want brought in in 1712 was the Scots Episcopalian Toleration Bill. He had only managed to prevent its introduction in 1711 by persuading the queen to intervene personally with the offer of Court support in 1712 if it was delayed for one session. The Scots Jacobites had agreed only with reluctance then, and Oxford did not dare to oppose them openly in 1711-12 as a result, lest he make the queen out to be a liar and precipitate a full-scale confrontation with them and their English sympathisers. He did his best to procrastinate the Bill into oblivion by having clients like Greenshields lobby the Scots Jacobites about the 'unseasonableness' of the time, and getting Anne to have a 'politick gout' which delayed the introduction for a week. These tactics had some success. Balmerino was persuaded that it would be better not introduced, but once this had been done in the Commons he gave it his full backing. The bishops seem to have been less unanimous in their support for the Bill than they had been in the prevous year.[79] Altogether these amounted to little more than pinpricks, and did not seriously impede the Bill's progress. Oxford realised this, and reluctantly gave way, limiting his opposition to it to expressions of sympathy with the Kirk's delegation in London to lobby against the measure.

The Bill's passage through the Commons was totally under Jacobite auspices, with those who were members of the October Club joining in to help the Scots. Despite opposition at every stage the measure went through the Commons without even having an abjuration clause added. Lockhart achieved this by first of all threatening to extend any abjuration clause inserted to include the Solemn League and Covenant, and then by making a pact with Islay and William Carstares that they would only oppose the whole measure and not try to put in a wrecking amendment like an abjuration clause acceptable to the Kirk.[80] Even so, the Bill came up for its third reading in the Commons with a requirement that all clergymen to receive the benefit of the Toleration must pray expressly for Anne and the Hanoverians. This divided the Scots Jacobites, and some opposed the Bill as a result, while a larger number, including Lockhart, abstained.[81] In the Lords, despite the Jacobites still being able to count on the support of most of the bishops and even of Opposition Tories like Nottingham, they could not prevent the Presbyterians reneging on their bargain and inserting an abjuration clause acceptable to the Kirk.[82] At this point the Jacobites considered letting the Bill fall, as there was no possibility of removing the abjuration clause once it was put in. Moreover, the Episcopalian clergy were appalled at the prospect of a statutory Toleration from which they were excluded by an unacceptable abjuration oath. This would have left them even more at the mercy of the Kirk Courts:

> yn C[arnwath, i.e. Lockhart], L. Lyon &c heard of ye amendmts they cursd & blasphemd. ye Bp of Edinburgh has sent a letter to ye Bp of London, Balmarino, Carnwath begging ym for Gods sake to stope ye passing of yt Bill for it woud ruine their interest here [Scotland]...[83]

Instead, the Scots Jacobites made a shrewdly vindictive riposte by amending the wording of the abjuration clause into a form which was as unacceptable to the Presbyterians as to the Episcopalians. They did this without taking the usual step of first having a conference with the Lords, and it was rumoured that the Court would seize on that to join the Whigs and throw out the Bill. However, Oxford did not choose to risk the opprobrium, and despite the pleas of the Kirk delegation it passed in that form, Lockhart and the Scots Jacobites having primed their Lords sympathisers in advance.[84] The net effect was to improve the situation of the Episcopal clergy in Scotland by giving them the opportunity for legal retaliation against Presbyterian nonjurants if Episcopalian nonjurants were persecuted. In practice it enforced an armed truce on both sides.

The Scots Jacobites had two other measures which they viewed as essential for the security of Episcopalianism in Scotland: the restoration of patronages to lay owners from the Kirk synods which had appropriated them, and the resumption of confiscated Episcopalian ecclesiastical property. The restoration of patronages was the next to be taken up. The passage took much the same form as that of the Toleration Bill. Oxford did his covert best to stifle the measure. The Scots and English Jacobites pushed it through the Commons nonetheless, though an abjuration clause was inserted. It then passed the Lords easily, despite growing disenchantment among the bishops with the Scots Episcopalians, and the pleas and petitions of the Kirk delegation. A separate Bishops' Rents Bill was not brought in this session owing to lack of time, but a clause was inserted into the Grants Resumption Bill of 1712 empowering the Commission established in it to consider these as well.[85]

As far as Oxford was concerned, the net result of these measures was the complete discrediting of his attempts to convince the Scots Presbyterians of his goodwill and attachment to the Union and Hanoverian succession. As Smith darkly hinted to Crosse:

> If some Gentlemen ym we may presume not to be friends to ye Revolution, are become necessary to support a min[ist]ry, and yt nothing is to be refused they insist upon, one may venture to say we are in danger of lossing those Blessings ych are secured to us upon yt foot. This I leave you to judge from the following passage ych I Believe to be trou. Some gentlemen of our country Representing to a great man nou in power [Oxford], how great ane infraction of ye Union the patronage bill was. he assured them it was contrary to his Inclination yet yn he came to vote... in his legislative capacity he divided for it.[86]

In a more practical sense this discontent showed itself in riots in Edinburgh and Leith which were as much anti-Union and anti-abjuration as they were pro-Jacobite. Hard-core Presbyterians refused to accept the oath at all and seceded from the Kirk to hold Cameronian assemblies in the west of Scotland.[87] Only about half of the rest of the Presbyterian Ministers were prepared to take the oath, and those with a preamble which was not strictly legal. The Episcopal clergy had few difficulties with the abjuration oath — a tiny minority took it 'with a mental reservation', the rest refused it point blank. Nor were they easily persuaded even to present an address of thanks to the queen for the amelioration of their condition.[88] Oxford had been obliged to trade a certain amount of moderate Presbyterian trust and support, in return for little more than continued Episcopalian disdain.

The Grants Resumption Bill of 1712 was a much more moderate measure than that of 1711. Instead of an immediate resumption of all William III's grants, it merely set up a Commission to investigate them. It was rumoured that this was not even with a view to complete confiscation, but only with the intention of extracting fees equal to several years' revenues from the holders.[89] The reason for this uncharacteristic moderation in a fundamentally Jacobite-inspired measure is not readily apparent. It may have been that the Jacobites who brought it in had decided to approach their objective in a more circuitous manner, the better to achieve their ends. Alternatively, Oxford may have let it be known that the Court would support a more moderate measure in the Lords, so inducing its sponsors to lower their sights. The October Club and its Jacobite fellows were certainly incensed at Oxford's opposition to the tack of the Bill to a Lottery Bill:

> ils s'echaufferent aprés d'autant plus, quand ils virent, que les Ministres les desavouoient si hautement, et le Sieur Shippen, les Chevaliers Stuart et Barker s'expliquoient tres fortement là dessus; Ce dernier prit sur tout feu et ressentit si fort le procedé d'un certain Grand Lord..., qu'il disoit mille duretée, en l'attaquent particulierement par l'endroit sensible de manque de probité et d'integrité; il fit clairement entendre, que c'etoit ce grand Lord qui avoit donné

lieu à cette affaire de la Combination, que sans cela on n'y auroit peut-être pas songé, et qu'il ne voyoit pas, comment on pourroit se fier à l'avenir à ce qu'il diroit; it parloit du grand desir qu'il avoit de gouverner la Chambre comme il luy plairoit, voulant dit-il que toute le monde passe et repasse le baton la fantasie luy en prend.[90]

As far as the Bill's backers were concerned, though, they may not even have considered it as a tack. Possibly following the precedent of the 1699 tack of the clause instituting Commissioners to investigate the Irish forfeitures, they argued that the Commission was one aimed at funding the supply, and that therefore it was perfectly acceptable to pass it as part of a money Bill.[91]

There can be no doubt that the Bill was as Jacobite in origin as the one passed by the Commons in 1711. Lockhart, Strangways, Shippen, Campion, Charles Aldworth and lord Ferrers were all active proponents of the measure. The remaining pro-Hanoverian elements of the October Club were far from averse to it, however, and Sir William Barker (whose speech is quoted above) and Weymouth worked energetically for it too.[92] The Court seems to have kept its distance until the Bill was tacked to a Lottery Bill at the Committee stage. This took the Court's men in the Commons by surprise apparently, as many Court Tories seem to have been unsure which way to vote (possibly because of intimations that the Court tacitly favoured the untacked measure). Oxford quickly rallied his forces, bought the March Club's support and put the maximum pressure he could on the October Club to drop the tack. They stubbornly fought the matter to the end, but the Court succeeded in separating the Bills on 6 May with an *ad hoc* combination of the Court, the Whigs and the March Club.[93] Oxford had to promise Court support for the untacked Bill in the Lords in order to achieve this, and circumstances obliged him to honour this promise. In particular, the October Club delayed supply Bills then going through the Commons to make sure he kept his word.[94] In the Lords Oxford duly exerted himself as far as he could. He was, however, confronted with the fundamental problem that Tories as well as Whigs possessed grants given by William III, and while some, like Leeds, were willing to let the Commission examine them, most, like Strafford, were not. The upshot of this was that significant numbers of otherwise stalwart Tories, such as lord Arran, the duke of Northumberland and the earl of Rochester, divided with the Whigs, while others such as Argyll, Strafford and lord Windsor made sure that they were absent at crucial moments. The Bill was finally rejected on a tied division of seventy-eight votes a side. The high number of votes cast is indicative of the effort the Whigs put into defeating this Bill, even persuading Opposition Tories like Nottingham to appear against it by the end.[95]

While the Grants Resumption Bill was going through the Lords, the October Club and the Jacobites were having their own trial of strength in the Commons with the March Club, over who was to fill the seven Commissionerships established by the Bill. By this time there was a good deal of animosity between the Clubs, the October in particular being very resentful over the part played by the March in the untacking of the Resumption Bill. Despite this hostility, the Whigs were well aware that any attempt by them to contest these Commissionerships would probably result in the Clubs combining against them, so they contented themselves with backing the March Club list (very likely alongside the Court):

> Comme les deux Clubbs d'Octobre et de Mars tentoient dans cette affaire leurs forces en quelque maniere, on y a fait d'autant plus d'attention, que la Cour a soutenu au possible Messieurs d'Octobre, et que les Whigs ont opiné pour Ceux de Mars; Ces derniers y ont remporté la victoire, quoy qu'elle ne fut pas complête, car de ces sept..., il n'y a deux scavoir le Sieur Murray et le Sieur Bulteel qui soyent de l'Octobre Clubb, les autres cinq estant touts de celuy de Mars.[96]

This defeat did not put the October Club in a good disposition for news of the defeat of the Resumption Bill in the Lords. Had they expected it, there could have been a fresh, harsher, Bill proposed, and with it an inevitable clash with the Lords:

> I found the Herd of those that were for the Bill, very mutinous; & I was ask'd, whether in our Court,... I ever knew a question of that consequence lost for want of one vote: I answerd, never: as I shall do, to all such questions, whatever I may think of [Oxford's] true zeal to have carry'd it. Mr Campion at last stood up, & in a very disorderly manner, took notice of the speech of Ld. Not[tingham]. & allmost repeated it; adding that he hoped the House wou'd have in their imediate thoughts the *resumption* itself, & think no more of *Enquirys*: especially since that noble lord had declar'd he wou'd be as much for the resumption as any Person, & onely disliked the last Bill, because it left room for partiality & Favour. But all this was no more than an empty sally, & went off without being seconded.[97]

As it fell out, the October Club contented itself with letting the Court get abused over the leather tax, no doubt having decided on reflection that even Oxford could not calculate a Lords' division as finely as that. There were other repercussions to the defeat of the Resumption Bill, however. During the Lords' debates on the Bill the Argyll group of Scots peers had first abstained and then defected to the Opposition. The Opposition leaders took this as a sign of incipient disenchantment with the ministry, and were soon trying to coax Argyll back into the fold. They did not succeed, but the perceptible wavering in the ranks of the Government's supporters during the passage of the Bill probably did a great deal to encourage the Opposition to attempt their onslaught about the restraining orders nine days later.[98] Jacobite extremism during this episode had, then, succeeded in delaying supply, put great stress on the fragile ministerial majority in the Lords and encouraged an Opposition attack that could have ended with Oxford being put in the Tower. Obviously an alliance with Country Tories like these was only practical in the long term for a manager who was able to run with his backbenchers rather than behind them.

Oxford had succeeded in tying the Country Tories to his ministry by a combination of measures, including: the use of St Germain's influence; discreet concessions to the Country Tories on points dear to them (such as the

Occasional Conformity Bill); judicious bribery; and manipulation of the hold any politician seen to be negotiating peace was liable to have over the war-weary backbenchers by this time. This alliance had served his needs well during what could have been a very dangerous session, despite several crises when the Country Tories took advantage of his reliance on them. The basic flaw in this was that Oxford had made the issue of the peace the cornerstone of the alliance and hence of his management of the Commons. All the other Country Tory demands, such as a thorough purge of the administration, the impeachment of Marlborough, Godolphin and the Junto, and so on, remained unfulfilled. Oxford kept the Country Tories cooperative by promising them all that they desired — as soon as the peace was completed. In 1712 that was reasonably distant, but all he was doing in effect was to build up a massive reserve of expectation among his backbenchers of all shades of opinion, for which they were going to demand satisfaction the moment peace was made.

NOTES

1. Portland, v. 116: 25 Nov. 1711.

2. MS Ballard 21, f. 95: William Lancaster to Charlett, 8 Nov. 1711; Panshanger MSS. D/EP F 228, f. 87: Sarah Marlborough to lady Cowper, 23 June 1711.

3. Carte 212, f. 20: Middleton to Menzies, 6 Sept. 1711 ns; Macpherson, ii, 233: Middleton to Menzies, 8 Nov. 1711 ns.

4. Carte 231, f. 55a: anecdote told to Carte by Mr Symmer, 3 Mar. 1724; AAE 242, f. 224: [Balmerino?] to Torcy, 14 Dec. 1711.

5. Dalhousie 14/321/18: [Kincardine] to Maule, 25 Sept [1711].

6. Macpherson, ii, 234: Nairne to Menzies, 19 Nov. 1711 ns; Carte 212, f. 22: Nairne to Menzies, 29 Nov. 1711 ns.

7. Add. MSS. 57861, f. 170: Maynwaring to Coningsby, 27 Nov. 1711; *Bol. Corr.*, ii, 178-9: St John to Strafford, 16 Feb. 1712; *Swift Corr.*, i, 294: Swift to King, 29 Mar. 1712.

8. Portland, v, 167-8: 29 Apr. 1712.

9. Kreienberg 107a, ff. 150-1: 28 Mar. 1712. See also: Holmes, *Politics*, pp.75-8; Dickinson, *Bolingbroke*, pp.93-4.

10. Gregg, *Queen Anne*, pp.336-7; Beaufort MSS: Beaufort to John Manley, 7 Nov. 1711; Wodrow Letters, Quarto 6, ep. 28: Smith to Crosse, 29 Nov. 1711; Trumbull Add. MSS. 136/1: Dr. Burrows to Trumbull, 5 Nov. 1711.

11. Macpherson, ii, 269-71: Netterville to Middleton, 12 Feb. 1712.

12. Kreienberg 107a, ff. 122-3: 22 Feb. 1712. See also: Holmes, *Politics*, pp.343-4.

13. The Tory earl of Nottingham defected to the Whigs in December 1711 over the issue of peace without Spain, and was followed by a trickle of other Tories thereafter. To describe this anti-ministerial coalition more accurately, I shall henceforth refer to it as the 'Opposition'.

14. Blenheim 61461, f. 153: Maynwaring to Sarah Marlborough, [23 May 1712]. See also: Kreienberg 107a, f. 167: 7 Mar. 1712.

15. *Bol Corr.*, iii, 123-4: Bolingbroke to Prior, 29 Sept. 1712; *CJ*, xvii, 91: 15 Feb. 1712.

16. G.S. Holmes, 'The Commons' Division on "No Peace Without Spain" ', *Bull. Inst. Hist. Res.*, xxxiii (1960), 22.

17. Carte 212, f. 29: Nairne to Menzies, 3 Apr. 1712 ns.

18. Add. MSS. 47026, f. 116: Edward Southwell to Percival, 4 Mar. 1712; MS Ballard 21, f. 176: William Delaune to Charlett, 9 Dec. 1711; Kreienberg 107a, ff. 256-61: 10 June 1712.

19. Baron Hill MS. 6766: loyal address [early 1712]; Portland Loan 29/372: the earl of Seaforth to Oxford, 13 Sept. 1712; Blair Castle, Box 45 Bundle 9, ep. 194: Balmerino to Atholl, 1 Dec. 1711.

20. *CJ*, xvii, 77, 271: 12 Feb. and 17 June 1712; Add. MSS. 47026, f. 125: Southwell to Percival, 29 May 1712; Hill, *Growth*, p.136.

21. Hermitage FFF, ff. 3-5: 18 Dec. 1711; Kreienberg 107a, ff. 157–61: 8 Apr. 1712; *Bol. Corr.*, ii, 172-3: St John to Bothmer, 2 Feb. 1712; *CJ*, xvii, 168: 2 Apr. 1712.

22. Macpherson, ii, 295-7: Netterville to Middleton, 18 Mar. 1712; Dickinson, 'October Club', pp.167-8.

23. *Went. Corr.*, pp.283–4: Wentworth to Strafford, 8 Apr. 1712; Kreienberg 107a, ff. 142–3: 1 Apr. 1712.

24. *CJ*, xvii, 74, 170, 223: 9 Feb., 4 Apr. and 14 May 1712; BL, Add. MSS. 22220 (Strafford papers), f. 29: lord Berkeley of Stratton to Strafford, 6 May 1712.

25. *CJ*, xvii, 212, 238: 6 and 22 May 1712; Hermitage FFF, f. 183: 6 May 1712.

26. Kreienberg 107a, f. 165: 11 Apr. 1712. See also: Wodrow Letters, Quarto 6, ep. 104: Crosse to Wodrow, 19 Apr. 1712.

27. *Went. Corr.*, pp.283–4: Wentworth to Strafford, 8 Apr. 1712; Lockhart, i, 367; Dickinson, *Bolingbroke*, pp.95-6; *CJ*, xvii, 257: 6 June 1712; Kreienberg 107a, ff. 163-6, 185-8, 256: 11 and 15 Apr. and 10 June 1712.

28. Portland, v, 109-10: Hamilton to Oxford, 13 Nov. 1711. See also: v, 107: Hamilton to Oxford, 9 Nov. 1711.

29. Hamilton MS. 5760: J. Hamilton to Hamilton, 29 Nov. 1711; A. McInnes, *Robert Harley, Puritan Politician* (1970), pp.139-40.

30. See pp. 105-6.

31. Macpherson, ii, 307-8: Mrs. Murray to Middleton, 9 May 1712.

32. Blair Lett: 17 Mar. 1711; Lockhart, i, 368-9.

33. *Went. Corr.*, pp. 256-7: Wentworth to Strafford, 22 Jan. 1712; Add. MSS. 22220, f. 18: Berkeley to Strafford, 5 Mar. 112; Macpherson, ii, 324-5; Hamilton to Middleton, 19 June 1712.

34. Portland, x, 270: Mar to Oxford, 3 June 1712.

35. Blair Lett: 3 and 14 June 1712; Lockhart, i, 401-10.

36. Gaultier 139, f. 104; Gaultier to Torcy, 24 June 1712 ns; Portland, v, 199: Findlater to Oxford, 8 July 1712; v, 210-11: Kinnoull to Oxford, 14 Aug. 1712.

37. Blair Lett.: 16 Aug. 1712. See also: 1 Nov. 1712.

38. Dalhousie 14/245/20: lady Nairne to the countess of Panmure, 2 Dec. 1712.

39. Portland, x, 284-6: Mar to Oxford, 15 Dec. 1712 and 13 Jan. 1713; v, 182-3: Balmerino to Mar, 11 June 1712; Portland Loan 29/150/1: Linlithgow to Oxford, 5 July 1712.

40. Lockhart, i, 368; Dalhousie 14/352/15: Balmerino to Maule, 31 Jan. [1712]; Portland, x, 464: Scots M.P.s to Oxford, 28 Feb. 1712; Macpherson, ii, 301-2, 313-15: Netterville to Middleton, 22 Apr. and 12 May 1712; Carte 212, f. 33: Nairne to Menzies, 26 May 1712 ns.

41. Lockhart, i, 368.

42. Idem.

43. AAE 242, f. 137; St Germain memo on proposal for Torcy, [June/July] 1712.

44. *Ibid.*, f. 224: [Balmerino?] to Torcy, 14 Dec. 1711.

45. Carte 212, f. 38: Middleton to St Amand, 4 Aug. 1712 ns.

46. Lockhart, i, 369.

47. *Went. Corr.*, p.216: Wentworth to Strafford, 30 Nov. 1711; Beaufort MSS: Beaufort to Manley, 7 Nov. 1711; Dartmouth MSS. D(W) 1778 I ii/287: Oxford to Dartmouth, 16 Nov. 1711; Horwitz, *Politicks*, p.230.

48. *Went. Corr.*, p.220: Wentworth to Strafford, 7 Dec. 1711; Trumbull Add. MSS. 136/3: Bridges to Trumbull, 7 Dec. 1711; Hermitage EEE, f. 389: 11 Dec. 1711.

49. Kreienberg 107a, ff. 46-8: 11 Dec. 1711. See also: Kay Diary; 7 Dec. 1711. For another view, see: Dickinson, *Bolingbroke*, p.90.

50. BL, Add. MSS. 22222 (Strafford papers), ff. 188-9: Poulet to Strafford, 20 Dec. 1711; *Journal to Stella*, ii, 432-6: 7 and 11 Dec. 1711; AAE 233, f. 258: Gaultier to Torcy, 22 Dec. 1711 ns.

51. *Bol. Corr.*, ii, 49-50: Oxford to Strafford [8 Dec. 1711].

52. Portland, v, 133: Bromley to Oxford, 30 Dec. 1711; Hermitage FFF, ff. 15-16: 28 Dec. 1711; Kreienberg 107a, ff. 73-5: 4 Jan. 1712; Trumbull Add. MSS. 136/3: Bridges to Trumbull, 7 Jan., 1712; Lockhart, i, 323, 400-1. For another view, see: Dickinson, *Bolingbroke*, p.91.

53. Portland Loan 29/10 ii/16: Oxford's memos of persons to be consulted [Dec. 1711].

54. The account of the Brandon patent case and its aftermath put forward hereafter is complementary to that in: G.S. Holmes, 'The Hamilton Affair of 1711-12: A Crisis in Anglo-Scottish Relations', *Eng. Hist Rev.*, lxxvii (1962), 257-82, though I differ with Professor Holmes on some points.

55. Trumbull Add. MSS. 136/3: Bridges to Trumbull, 18 Jan. 1712; Northamptonshire R.O., Finch-Hatton MSS. FH 281, ff. 13-14: Nottingham to lady Nottingham, 20 Feb. 1712; Hermitage FFF, f. 395: 14 Dec. 1711.

56. Dalhousie 14/352/13-15: Balmerino to Maule, 24, 26 and 31 Jan. [1712]; Portland, v, 138; Hamilton to Oxford, 16 Jan. 1712; v, 141; Balmerino to Oxford, 29 Jan. 1712.

57. Dalhousie 14/352/15: Balmerino to Maule, 31 Jan. [1712].

58. *Went. Corr.*, pp.256-7, 260: Wentworth to Strafford, 22 and 25 Jan. 1712; HMC, *Mar and Kellie MSS.*, pp.493-5: Mar to Erskine, 17 Jan. 1712; Wodrow Letters, Quarto 6, ep. 56: Smith to Crosse, 22 Jan. 1712; Dalhousie 14/352/15: Balmerino to Maule, 31 Jan. [1712].

59. *Journal to Stella*, i, 479: 2 Feb. 1712; Kreienberg 107a, f. 109: 19 Feb. 1712; McInnes, *Harley*, p.144.

60. Dalhousie 14/352/12 15: Balmerino to Maule, 15 and 31 Jan. [1712]; Wodrow Letters, Quarto 6, ep. 67: Crosse to Wodrow, 16 Feb. 1712; Macpherson, ii, 292-3: Mrs. Murray to Middleton (Ellis's extracts), 14 Mar. 1712.

61. Finch-Hatton MSS. FH 281, f. 5: Nottingham to lady Nottingham, 16 Dec. 1711; Kreienberg 107a, f. 44: 4 Dec. 1711. For another view, see: Hill, *Growth*, p.134.

62. Finch-Hatton MSS., FH 281, f. 6: Nottingham to lady Nottingham, 26 Dec. 1711.

63. HMC. *Polwarth MSS.*, i, 3: Baillie to Polwarth, 20 Dec. 1711; Wodrow Letters, Quarto 6, ep. 40: Smith to Crosse, 25 Dec. 1711; Horwitz, *Politicks*, p.233.

64. Finch-Hatton MSS., FH 281, ff. 7-8: Nottingham to lady Nottingham, 26 Dec. 1711; Portland, vii, 82: Stratford to lord Harley, 18 Dec. 1711; Horwitz, *Politicks*, p.235.

65. Gregg, *Queen Anne*, p.345; Lockhart, i, 375-6.

66. *Bol. Corr.*, ii, 165-6: St John to Strafford, 18 Jan. 1712; Portland, v, 139; Bromley to Oxford, 21 Jan. 1712; Kreienberg 107a, f. 97: 25 Jan. 1712.

67. Wodrow Letters, Quarto 6, ep. 58: Smith to Crosse, 26 Jan. 1712; Trumbull Add. MSS. 136/3: Bridges to Trumbull, 25 Jan. 1712; *CJ*, xvii, 15-18, 23-4, 37-8: 21 and 22 Dec. 1711 and 24 Jan. 1712; Lockhart, i, 353-6; Kreienberg 107a, ff. 61-2: 25 Dec. 1711.

68. *CJ*, xvii, 37-8; 24 Jan. 1712; Trumbull Add. MSS. 136/3: Bridges to Trumbull, 25 Jan. 1712; Hermitage FFF, ff. 36-7; 25 Jan. 1712.

69. Kreienberg 107a, f. 132: 29 Feb. 1712.

70. *Went. Corr.*, pp.283-4: Wentworth to Strafford, 8 Apr. 1712.

71. *Ibid.*, pp.253-6: Wentworth to Strafford, 18 Jan. 1712; Luttrell, *Brief Relation*, vi, 716; *CJ*, xvii, 28-9, 97, 128: 17 Jan., 19 Feb. and 6 Mar. 1712; Plumb, *Sir Robert Walpole* (1956), i, 165, 178-81.

72. Add. MSS. 22222, f. 189: Poulet to Strafford, 20 Dec. 1711.

73. *Went. Corr.*, pp.266-9: Wentworth to Strafford, 15 and 19 Feb. 1712; Hermitage YYY (Dutch secret reports), f. 283: 16 Feb. 1712.

74. Holmes, *Politics*, pp.69-70; Macpherson, ii, 269-71, 279-82: Netterville to Middleton, 12 Feb. and 'February' 1712; Add. MSS. 47026, f. 110: Parker to Percival, 31 Jan. 1712; *CJ*, xvii, 51-4, 69-70, 92, 122-3: 29 Jan., 5 and 16 Feb. and 1 Mar. 1712.

75. Add. MSS. 22220, f. 8: Berkeley to Strafford, 29 Jan. 1712; *CJ*, xvii, 92: 16 Feb. 1712; *Went. Corr.*, pp. 269-70: Wentworth to Strafford, 22 Feb. 1712.

76. Claydon House Letters M11/54: Cave to Fermanagh, 29 May 1712; *Journal to Stella*, ii, 535-6: 31 May 1712; Kreienberg 107a, ff. 235-8: 27 May 1712; Gregg, *Queen Anne*, pp.356-7. For another view, see: Hill, *Growth*, p.137.

77. Add. MSS. 47026, f. 125: Southwell to Percival, 29 May 1712; Kreienberg 107a, ff. 240-5: 30 May 1712. For another view, see: Dickinson, *Bolingbroke*, p.98.

78. *CJ*, xvii, 246: 29 May 1712.

79. Wodrow Letters, Quarto 6, ep. 57: Erskine to Wodrow, 31 Jan. 1712; Portland, x, 379: Greenshields to Oxford, 28 Jan. 1712; *Went. Corr.*, pp.251-2: Wentworth to Strafford, 15 Jan. 1712; Dalhousie 14/352/15: Balmerino to Maule, 31 Jan. [1712]; Trumbull Add. MSS. 136/3: Bridges to Trumbull, 3 Mar. 1712.

80. *CJ*, xvii, 33, 35, 53-4: 21, 23 and 29 Jan. 1712; Wodrow Letters, Quarto 6, ep. 57: Erskine to Wodrow, 31 Jan. 1712; ep. 61: J. Loudon to Wodrow, 9 Feb. 1712; Lockhart, i, 379-80.

81. *CJ*, xvii, 69, 73: 5 and 7 Feb. 1712; Wodrow Letters, Quarto 6, ep. 65: division list for the Scots M.P.s on the Toleration Bill, 7 Feb. 1712. I am indebted to Mr. C. Jones for a copy of this list.

82. Nic. Diary; 31 Jan. and 8, 10, 12, 13 and 15 Feb. 1712; Horwitz, *Politicks*, p.236; Wodrow Letters, Quarto 6, epp. 68, 70: Smith to Crosse, 9 and 15 Feb. 1712.

83. Wodrow Letters, Quarto 6, ep. 74: [?] to Wodrow, 26 Feb. 1712.

84. Lockhart, i, 380-5; Trumbull Add. MSS. 136/3: Bridges to Trumbull, 25 Feb. 1712; *CJ*, xvii, 103-4: 21 Feb. 1712; Wodrow Letters, Quarto 6, ep. 72: Smith to Crosse, 19 Feb. 1712.

85. *CJ*, xvii, 135-6, 143, 159, 165-6, 169-70, 174, 218: 13, 20 and 28 Mar., 1, 3 and 7 Apr. and 10 May 1712; Trumbull Add. MSS 136/3: Bridges to Trumbull, 15 Apr. 1712;

Kreienberg 107a, f. 228: 14 Mar. 1712; Wodrow Letters, Quarto 6, ep. 83: Col. Erskine to Wodrow, 14 Mar. 1712.

86. Wodrow Letters, Quarto 6, ep. 104; Smith to Crosse, 25 Apr. 1712.

87. *Ibid.*, ep. 79: Col. Erskine to Wodrow, 8 Mar. 1712; Carte 238, ff. 233-5: Middleton to Torcy, 13 July 1712 ns; Gualterio 31257, f. 32: Middleton to Gualterio, 6 Mar. 1712 ns; Hermitage FFF, f. 334: 2 Sept. 1712.

88. Trumbull Add. MSS. 136/3: Bridges to Trumbull, 21 Nov. 1712; Portland, v, 230-1: Andrew Cunningham to Oxford, 3 Oct. 1712; Dalhousie 14/348/2: Lyon to Maule, 2 Apr. 1713; B. Lenman, *The Jacobite Risings in Britain* (1980), p.103.

89. Hermitage FFF, f. 132: 25 Mar. 1712.

90. Kreienberg 107a, ff. 217-18: 9 May 1712.

91. Kreienberg 107a, ff. 201-5: 25 Apr. and 6 May 1712; Lockhart, i, 366.

92. *CJ*, xvii, 148, 164, 194, 212: 22 and 31 Mar., 21 Apr. and 6 May 1712; Portland Loan 29/143/8: Edward Harley to Oxford [3 May 1712, n.b. I have put this date on the letter from internal evidence].

93. Trumbull Add. MSS. 134: Thomas Bateman to Trumbull, 5 May 1712; Portland, v, 167-8: Bromley to Oxford, 29 Apr. 1712; *Journal to Stella*, ii, 532: 10 May 1712; Kreienberg 107a, ff. 208, 217-18: 29 Apr. and 9 May 1712.

94. Trumbull Addit. MSS. 136/3: Bridges to Trumbull, 14 [May] 1712; *CJ*, xvii, 229, 231-2: 17 and 20 May 1712.

95. Kreienberg 107a, ff. 227-34, 231: 20 and 23 May 1712; Trumbull Add. MSS. 136/3: Bridges to Trumbull, 21 May 1712; Macpherson, ii, 352-3: Strafford to the Electress Sophia, 26 May 1712.

96. Kreienberg 107a, ff. 225-6: 16 May 1712.

97. Blenheim 61461, f. 149: Maynwaring to Sarah Marlborough [20 May 1712].

98. Blenheim 61461, f. 153: Maynwaring to Sarah Marlborough [23 May 1712]; *CJ*, xvii, 238: 22 May 1712.

6

'All opposition and discouragement': the session of 1713

In many ways the expectations with which the Country Tories returned to Westminster in 1713 were very akin to those with which they had come up in December 1710. They viewed the coming peace with relief and pleasure, but looked for it to be associated with that long-promised purge of all Whigs from Government service which they had been promised as soon as peace was made. Bolingbroke (St John was created viscount Bolingbroke in July 1712) was doing no more than stating their general opinion when, later on in the year, he exhorted Oxford to 'Separate in the name of God, the chaff from the wheat, and consider who you have left to employ'.[1] This keen sense of anticipation was, moreover, heightened by the number of prorogations the ministry had been obliged to make as the peace negotiations dragged on. Parliament was first prorogued in November 1712. It did not meet until 9 April 1713. In the interim the Country Tories' hunger for peace whetted those suspicions of Oxford, which were by now deeply ingrained. The Jacobites, as ever, tended to take this feeling to extremes:

> He makes himself many enemies, and secures but a few friends; for those that are in Mr Jenkins [James's] interest, abominate the trimming way he takes and he will not be able to go on much longer, without giving some other demonstration than he yet has ... When Mr Medlicote [Parliament] comes there will be another storm raised against him.[2]

Their irritation with him was common, however, to most of the Country Tories.[3] The situation was further exacerbated by Oxford's need to have as many of them as he could in London from the beginning of February, ready to receive the peace as soon as it was finished so that the session might be completed as soon as possible. To achieve this, he made extensive use of his skills as a manager to persuade the leading Country Tories to get their friends up early in the year, and then to keep them there. As time went on, these gentlemen were duly embarrassed by the non-appearance of either the peace or the session, and exposed to the complaints and annoyance of their fellows. This did not increase their goodwill towards the ministry and intrinsically undermined its alliance with them.[4] By the beginning of the session the Country Tories were so irritable and impatient with the Government that the merest hint of a rumour that Oxford was negotiating with the Whigs provoked absolute fury among them.[5]

The means which Oxford used to inveigle the Country Tories into cooperating with his ministry for one more session were desperately short-term. He was confronted, as in December 1711, with hostility among the backbench Tories. It had not yet reached the same level of acrimony as at that time, but the possibility was there. This time he was not at all dilatory in moving against it. In essence, he turned the Country Tories' longing for peace and the Toryisation of the administration against them once more. Oxford first induced the leaders of the Country Tories to come to London, bringing their friends, by promising to redress their grievances:

> I hope the Affairs of yr Family wil permit your speedy returne to Towne, where your presence is necessary; I beg you wil hasten up al yr friends both Lords & commons; and that you wil come fully instructed about justices of the Peace & al other matters requisite for the repose of yr country. I have spoke to Lord Keeper upon the subject of the letter you honord me wth wch I was then hindred from Answering by a bad feavor, you wil find every thing wil be adjusted to your mind.[6]

Once they were there, he fell back on his limitless talent for procrastination to stave off their demands for the performance of what he had promised. Smith pungently described his technique in a letter home in March, by which time Oxford had made ample use of it:

> He is one who receives all sorts of men, in the very spirit of ye party he knows ym to be of. to ye Jacobite he is such to ye Dissenter he is one of ym &c. he is very dextrouse in making you believ you shall have yt you seek of him. tho if you relye upon him its a 100d to one if you are not disappointed, yt is to say he deceives you wt as good a grace as any body can doe.[7]

This was a workable means of keeping people quiet for a short time, but patently incapable of deceiving anyone for a long period. As Georg von Schütz (Hanoverian Envoy to London, 1713-14) put it: 'He promises the same thing to five different persons, which, at least, will procure him four enemies for one friend'.[8] Nevertheless, this use of what remained of Oxford's credibility served his turn before it depleted his stock. St Germain swallowed his excuses about the peace having not yet been sufficiently well established, and ordered its adherents to continue supporting the Court. It also obligingly suppressed a fresh scheme mooted among the Jacobite M.P.'s to reveal Plunket's discoveries about the Whig plot of 1712 to Parliament, and tried to soothe the Scots Jacobites' anger over various occurrences in Parliament from April onwards.[9] Many of the Country Tories seem to have adopted a reserved attitude towards the ministry, but nonetheless bided their time — which was sufficient for Oxford's purposes. The October Club alone seems to have been less inclined to take Oxford at his word again, and tried to induce Bolingbroke to move against him with its support. Bolingbroke cautiously but politely refused for the time being, while urging the October Club's deputation to bear with and stick by the ministry. This was accepted, in the confident expectation that in the natural course of events Oxford and Bolingbroke must soon fall out, at which time the Club could put its weight behind the younger man. A few, particularly among the Jacobite element, still wanted to exert direct pressure on the Government, but they seem to have been overruled.[10]

The association of the October Club with the ministry during the 1713 session continued to be no more than a working agreement between suspicious partners. The Club duly supported the usual Court measures against Opposition attacks. A joint March Club-Opposition attempt to interfere with the schedule laid down for passing the ways and means was repulsed. An Opposition motion to adjourn for consideration after the terms of the peace of Utrecht were presented to Parliament was defeated. The supply required was passed quickly and efficiently.[11] Yet none of this brought the Court and the Country Tories closer together. When Wyndham carelessly asserted that the Opposition were attacking the French Commercial Treaty because they knew its success spelt their downfall, Aldworth took great exception and let the ministry know in no uncertain terms that the Country Tories did not consider the Opposition in any way adequately threatened by it:

> il fut contredit par le Sr Aldworth ... lequel dit, qu'il croyoit plutôt que la faction etoit Croissante et que si on n'employoit pas des remedes bientôt d'une maniere efficace elle seroit fort dangereuse qu'on voyoit malheureusement que cette faction, n'estoit pas encore ruinée, puis qu'elle avoit eté capable de seduire tant de Gens et produire tant de Petitions contre le traitte le plus avantageux qu'on eut jamais veu.[12]

In a more practical vein, the October Club continued to back its own policies and inclinations even when these clashed with the Court's desires. Their stubborn battle to disenfranchise the Quakers by removing their right of affirming rather than swearing to the authenticity of their votes went on, only to be defeated once again by an *ad hoc* coalition of the ministry, the Opposition and the March Club. They did not hesitate to demand to see the Navy's accounts for the duration of the war, or to show their dissatisfaction over the repeated prorogations of Parliament by criticising the Government for thereby allowing the supplies allocated to it to expire, hence increasing its debts.[13] The October Club also took the lead in extending the Malt Tax to Scotland in order to oblige the Scots to aid in its total repeal in the next Parliament, directly against the Court's wishes. Indeed, it was only imposed on Scotland against the combined efforts of the ministry and the Scots by the determination of the October Club: 'The Whiggs & Octr Clubb being for charging Scotland wth the Malt-Tax & ye Scots & ye Court agst it, ... these last were outnumbred'. When the Court tried to prevent a merchant witness named Torriano from criticising the Commercial Treaty, on the grounds that he was referring to articles ten and eleven rather than eight and nine, then under consideration, they had to retreat precipitately due to the outrage their erstwhile allies felt no compunction about showing.[14] The clearest indication of the increasing fragility of their alliance was the ministry's reluctance to put any strain on it. Bolingbroke frankly informed Argyll in the previous November that the ministry did not intend to antagonise the backbenchers by fresh demands for money, and all other requests for extraordinary funding were met with the same reluctance. The Court also maintained a discreet silence when Pakington, Whitlock and William Newland secured an invitation for Sacheverell to preach to the Commons on Restoration day.[15]

Oxford purchased an extension to his alliance with the Country Tories by making a great many promises. He maintained it during the session by continual circumspection in his dealings with them. This could only be the last gasp of his accustomed tool of management: deceit. Unless something more was forthcoming, Oxford could not expect their support next session. As it was, it was probably only the short length of the 1713 session (just over three months) that saved him from an eruption of backbench frustration that year.

The continuation of their association with a ministry now notorious for its mendacity towards them increasingly rankled with many of the middle-of-the-road Hanoverian Tories who remained in the October Club. The previous year's Hanoverian breakaway, the March Club, became steadily more disruptive in response to the same phenomenon. It still cooperated happily with its old friends among the Tory backbenchers on clear-cut issues of Country Tory principle, such as the condemnation of Wharton for corruption while lord lieutenant of Ireland and in general support for the peace. But their growing distrust of the ministry led them to align themselves more and more with the Opposition, so that by June Defoe's description of them as 'very Whimsicalls indeed' was amply justified.[16] Those basically pro-Hanoverian Tories who remained in the October Club began to have doubts about the ministry's capacity for negotiating a good peace early in 1713, as a result of the prolonged deferment of Parliament. Though the treaty presented to Parliament removed most of their worries, the feeling of discontent that had been aroused did not have time to fade before the end of session.[17] The attack on the Commercial Treaty was a demonstration of that discontent and their growing frustration at Oxford's refusal to rid the administration of Whigs. Consequently, the chief motive for their action on 18 June was not the nature of the peace, but Oxford's refusal to redress their grievance:

> The loyal party have complained, many times, of his not altering the greatest part of the Whig lieutenancy, and almost all the justices of the peace in the kingdom, and all the employments, officers, and collectors of the customs, excise, etc. These he has promised 20 times to remove; but never has done any thing in it. So now, they say, in general they will force him to act like an honest man, though there is not a word to be trusted to what he ever said; so that if there is not a clean house of all Whigs, before next parliament, it will go hard with him.[18]

This is borne out by the behaviour of Hanmer and Anglesey, the leaders of the raid on 18 June, during the rest of the session. Hanmer was not very pleased with the Government when he was in France in January and February. This stemmed from a fundamental divergence of interests. Their primary concern was the survival of the ministry, his was the triumph of the Tory party. Hanmer felt that, whatever the Government did, the Tory party must stay united and in power. Only a full Toryisation of the administration and a determinedly pro-Hanoverian foreign policy could guarantee this. Thus, when he led the raid which killed off the Commercial Treaty Bill, he did so on carefully chosen grounds that would not offend even the supporters of the Bill, merely criticising its format and suggesting it should be deferred to the next Parliament. This allowed him to put pressure on the ministry while cushioning the impact of the 'Whimsicals" action on those Tories who espoused the treaty. It further provided him and his friends with a convenient loophole by which they could approve of a similar measure next session.[19] He signified that this was his intention shortly after the defeat of the Bill on 18 June, by proposing and carrying an address for the renegotiation of the Treaty of Commerce. Oxford proceeded to make some offers to Hanmer and Anglesey, but not on a scale sufficient to satisfy them. Hanmer, at least, would not consent to be bought off individually, and left London in anger when Oxford tried to do so.[20] The only post he eventually agreed to accept was the one conferring the least obligation towards the ministry: the Speakership of the Commons. Though he and Anglesey had only organised the attack on the Commercial Treaty as a warning shot, they maintained the links they had formed with Opposition and dissident Tories in case Oxford should yet again prove untrue.[21]

The Hanoverian Tories were in the process of taking up a policy of wholly independent action with regard to the ministry in 1713. This was born out of continued Country Tory frustration with the domestic policies of the Government, allied to unease at its bad relations with the incoming dynasty. Oxford did not seem to understand what was occurring, and only made a reflexive response by attempting to buy off their leaders. These leaders were concerned with more than personal advantage (at least in the case of Hanmer), so this can only have deepened their alienation from the ministry. It certainly did not retard the development of the independent Hanoverian Tory pressure group which was well on the way to completion by the end of the session.

The Jacobites were prevented from following the same path as the Hanoverian Tories only by St Germain's refusal to countenance it, and by the profound internal turmoil to which the Jacobite organisation was subject during the first half of 1713. They had never been very happy about giving unqualified support to the Oxford ministry, and his behaviour in early 1713 served only to deepen their distrust in him. At the same time, the Parliamentary Jacobites were becoming increasingly dissatisfied with the chief administrators of the Jacobite organisation at the exiled Court, whom they blamed for James's refusal to convert. An extra complication was added by the development of considerable mutual antagonism between the English and Scots Jacobites at Westminster. In combination these internal problems and disagreements left the Jacobites impotent for most of the session, though they continued to remain prominent as individuals. However they were not immune to the developments that were forcing the coalescence of the

Hanoverian Tory pressure group, and when their own squabbling died down they too began to evolve in the same direction.

St Germain carefully restated its instructions for the Jacobites' conduct in February:

> You are ... desir'd to tell them to recommend to all their friends to associate with Hickman [Oxford] and Company and go along with them in all their measures according to the directions given last year to Morley [Parliamentary Jacobites], and particularly caution his relations in Proby's family [Parliament] to move nothing of La: Jean's [James's] concerns in that company unless it be in conjunction with How [Oxford] and his factors, who will be sure to obstruct any thing of that kind that comes not originally from themselves, and such a disapointment would be irreparable.[22]

This produced another angry denunciation of Middleton as a traitor by the Scots, closely followed by the threat of a refusal to work with him any longer. The Jacobite Court tried to calm them down, but found itself obstructed by a Court intrigue hatched by Melfort to displace Middleton and replace him with either himself or Perth. While the Court was occupied dissociating itself from Melfort's conspiracy, the Scots Jacobites fell out with their English counterparts over the Malt Tax.[23] The Scots Jacobites took the lead in urging their fellow nationals to join with the Opposition, and had no qualms about attacking some of the English Jacobites' most cherished projects, such as the campaign to disenfranchise the Quakers. The English Jacobites retaliated by supporting the ministry on the Union issue, so a group of Scots M.P.'s led by Lockhart began harrying the Government in the Commons. This bruising contest clearly had to be brought to an end. The Jacobite Court accordingly reiterated and explained its orders once more, specifically called Lockhart to order, and had him and his friends supporting the Court for the remainder of the session.[24] Disenchantment with the ministry was by then becoming too profound to be constrained for much longer by the exiled Court's directives. Yarmouth and Leeds were plotting to desert the Government at some suitable inconvenient moment in late June. North and Grey was trying to work up support around the same time for the removal of the treason provisions from an Act the Jacobites disliked.[25] Nothing came of these moves, but they indicate how close the Jacobites already were to undertaking independent action despite St Germain.

The idea of forming their own Parliamentary pressure group re-emerged in response to this tension between what they wanted to do to the ministry, and what the Jacobite Court wanted them to do. Again, what was proposed was an attack on the legal basis of the Hanoverian succession, though in a more circumspect manner than in the previous year:

> this Lord [Fingall] ... desires, yt My Ld Midleton will be pleased to send him his instructions, what the King would have moved in Parliament this next session, for several of the House, yt will be chosen again, doe desire him to know, what the King would have them doe, & they will doe it; Sir John Pakington has

promised to be the leading man, & the rest promise to second it, & I know severall that say they will, Sir Wm Whitlock says he will, who is a leading man: If the King approves of it, they will call for the Box, where ye names of those are, whom Prss Sophia sent to be commissioned to have ye Governmt in their hands, till she coud come after the death of Prss Anne ... And then the Parliamt, if the Box be produced; will declare against ye choice, as men yt are against ye Constitution, & will take ye occasion to prove yt there are numbers of Papists in imployments in that state, & yt they have built them a Church, & then prove all ye disrespectful things wch that court has done against Prss Anne & the present ministry, & by degrees fall on ye succession.[26]

The Jacobite Court returned its usual response, ordering them to support the ministry. However, the proposal and the obvious dislike which the Jacobites at Westminster were by now showing towards the Oxford ministry must have struck a chord, because in November the exiled Court, itself increasingly exasperated with Oxford by then, was clearly beginning to favour some kind of independent demonstration by the Jacobites: 'Equivocal appearances may impose for a while, but if no reall effects appear in a competent time Joseph [James] and Juxon [Jacobites in Parliament] must take their measures another way'.[27] An independent Jacobite grouping was on the verge of appearing in Parliament.

One of the special peculiarities of the 1713 session was unusually strong tension between the Houses. The Lords as a body had not been too happy about the creation of Oxford's 'dozen' in 1712. Consequently, rumours of a fresh mass creation before Parliament opened made the Lords more sensitive than usual over the question of their privileges. This feeling did not diminish in the course of the session because of sheer lack of time for it to die down. Certain measures emanating from the Commons also served to maintain, if not intensify, this strain. One of these was Lockhart's Bill against the creation of bogus votes in Commons elections in Scotland, which struck at the electoral influence of many Scots peers. The Bill accordingly found little favour with the Representative Peers, whose annoyance was heightened when the English majority in the Lords cheerfully imposed it on them. The annual Bill renewing the Commission of Accounts was received with more hostility than usual, Buckingham and North and Grey openly opposing it.[28] Both the Opposition and the ministry were aware of this tension and that it could be exploited to create a clash between the Lords and Commons. An opportunity for the Opposition to do this arose after a ministerial blunder over the Civil List Bill. When it made the formal request for supply which customarily indicated that a money Bill was about to be introduced, the Government neglected to ask the Lords as well as the Commons. Since the Lords traditionally did not introduce or alter money Bills, this was no more than a formality, and the transgression should have earned little more than some sharp comment. But on this occasion the Opposition seized their opportunity, and the duke of Bolton moved for consideration of whether this constituted an infringement of the Lords' privileges. Oxford adroitly evaded the thrust by counterproposing an investigation of all the Lords' privileges, and in the meantime he had the Civil List Bill amalgamated with a Bill covering a loan from the Bank of England for which permission had been requested in both houses. Properly speaking, this was a tack, but since it was of two money Bills which the Lords customarily did not touch anyway, they grudgingly let it pass. This did not, however, put them in a receptive frame of mind to receive the Tobacco Drawback Bill shortly afterwards. This was the usual means by which amendments, extensions and explanations to existing legislation were passed. Consequently, it was always a ragbag of various measures, which in this case included a clause extending the powers of the Commission of Accounts to allow it to investigate the Army's debts. This was too much for many of the High Tory peers to stomach. The Opposition denounced the Bill as a mass of tacks, and were overwhelmed by the rush of Tory support they received. Halifax had not thought of going further than arranging a conference with the Commons on the matter, well aware that such a procedure so late in the session would result in the Bill falling of its own accord. Buckingham, North and Grey and the usually self-effacing earl of Orkney demanded its categorical rejection — and secured it easily. The Court wisely chose not to intervene.[29] It was too late for the matter to lead to a clash between Lords and Commons, but the episode well illustrates the underlying volatility of the Lords during this session.

These developments formed the background to what proved to be, despite its brevity, an unusually fraught session. Backbench hostility towards the ministry steadily increased as Oxford's procrastination became more and more blatant. This forced him to adopt a very circumspect attitude towards the activities of the various Country Tory groups, lest they turn on him. With each of the crises which beset Parliament during the session, Oxford's control of the situation became visibly weaker and the Country Tories' patience with his eternal evasions steadily more threadbare. The pattern for the session was one of progressively deteriorating relations between the backbenchers and the ministry. All that saved Oxford was the lack of any recognised alternative to him in the Tory party and the Country Tories' own squabbling.

The first major trial of strength between the ministry and the Opposition in 1713, following a pattern similar to that of December 1711, was at the opening of Parliament. The Opposition hoped by this to maximise their superior party organisation and defeat the ministry early in the session, before all of its supporters could arrive. The issue chosen was once again that of peace, which meant that, by contrast with 1711, the resulting debate was a fairly straightforward party clash. In the Commons it pared down the Opposition ranks to hardcore Whigs and the handful of Tories who had gone over with Nottingham in December 1711. The Country Tories solidly backed the Government, and as a result the Opposition could scarcely initiate a debate, let alone a serious attack. Lord William Powlett was the only speaker against the address of thanks, and when Stanhope tried to amend it to point out that the Commons were not yet aware on what terms peace had been made, the Opposition was crushingly defeated.[30] In the Lords the Jacobite element in the ministry's support was of more value, as Nottingham had managed to persuade his brother, lord Guernsey, Archbishop Sharp of York and Bishop Dawes of Chester to defect. Beaufort led for the Government and, despite a vigorous rejoinder from Halifax, the ministry won the eventual division by thirty-two votes.[31] This was an extremely propitious start to the session — it was also a feat of astute political management rather than genuine strength. Learning from his humiliation in 1711, Oxford had used all the tools available to crack what seemed to be a formidable Opposition offensive in the making. Fresh promises of the redress of their grievances brought Country Tories of all shades of opinion in to attend the first day of the session.[32] The queen was enlisted to closet doubtful supporters among the old Nottinghamite High Tories and the Court Whigs. Her speech was carefully constructed so as to preclude an Opposition attack on the Government for having strained Britain's relations with Hanover and the Allies in the course of making the peace. By asserting that there was 'perfect friendship' between her ministry and Hanover, she left the Opposition with no alternative but to swallow it or to suggest that she was lying. Halifax ultimately flinched from doing that, yielding the day to the Government.[33] For all the magnitude of this victory for Oxford, it remained a hollow one. Oxford expended the last of his political credit among the Country Tories to secure the address he required. His displacement of the earl of Cholmondeley and Sir Richard Temple (both Court Whigs) shortly before the opening of Parliament no doubt pleased the Country Tories, but it also dissipated what little remained of the Court Whigs' faith in his sincerity or the practicality of his 'moderating' scheme. All that kept them with his ministry henceforth was their respect for the queen. She had been brought further forward on the political stage than she usually cared to be, in order to lie sturdily in Oxford's cause. The upshot of all this was that the real backing for Oxford had been reduced to its essentials: the Court and Treasury party, which was apolitical and at the queen's disposal anyway, his personal friends and relations in both houses (the old 'Harlekins'), and the queen's goodwill.[34] The first of these was dependent on the last, so Oxford in truth had little more to sustain him from now on than her appreciation of his managerial skills. The queen was a powerful friend, but, by the nature of her office as well as her character, an inconstant one. She was a hard-headed pragmatist in her own right, and if the political situation ever slipped out of Oxford's control again (which was becoming more likely as his credit waned), she was quite likely to cast him off.

The support Oxford had received from the Country Tories in the opening debates had been bought at a price he could not pay in offices and patronage. As a result he could not obstruct the Country Tories if they chose to push through some of their own measures, lest they turn on him. The first of these was a reduction in the rate of the Land Tax. The Country Tories had been quietly mooting a united attempt to achieve this since the beginning of the year, with or without the ministry's agreement. The Land Tax was the most burdensome of all the war taxes as far as the country gentry were concerned, so cutting it not only appealed to their fellows at Westminster, but was also a sound electoral ploy for the forthcoming election.[35] Whitlock led the raid for the October Club in the Committee on Supply on 22 April. The Court was taken unawares and overwhelmed by a united Country Tory assault delightedly backed by the Opposition:

> La chambre des communes delibera Mercredy sur le subside et quelqu'un du party de la cour proposa de mettre des taxes, mais ne s'expliquant pas, un autre [Whitlock] dit qu'il declarast ce que c'estoit, que pour luy il ne vouloit pas faire de proposition et qu'il demandoit seulement si c'estoit 2 shillins par livre sur le revenu des terres qu'on voudroit proposer et alors le general Stanhope se leva et dit, qu'il seroit volontiers pour cette taxe et la propose et il fut suivy tant des toris que des whigs et dans cette union et le nombre en fut si grand qu'il ne fut pas question d'envenir a une division et la resolution en fut prise et on y fit ajouter que non seulement cette tax n'excedroit pas 2 shillins, mais que meme on n'en pourroit pas mettre d'avantage et il n'y eut que ceux qui etoient attachés a la cour qui s'y opposerent inclinant pour laisser la liberte d'en mettre d'avantage s'il estoit jugé a propos, quelqu'un de ceux la ayant dit que devant que de prendre cette resolution, il faudroit voir si la banque voudroit se charger de faire circuler pour un million de billets de l'echiquier mais cette raison ne fut pas goutre ayant esté repliqué qu'ils n'oseroient retourner dans leur provinces s'ils consentoient a mettre plus de 2 shillins.[36]

The Court, which had been preparing to put forward a three shilling land tax which would have been worth nearly half a million more in revenue, was in such confusion after this that the Opposition was able to induce the united Country Tories to support an amendment specifically forbidding alteration of the two shilling limit at a later stage.[37] There were rumours that the whole episode was arranged by the Court in return for an increased Malt Tax, but it is more likely that these were merely noises designed to reconcile the Country Tories to a three shilling Land Tax. The ministry did rally in time to fight off a secondary attack on the Land Tax by the Scots Jacobites. They proposed to divide the Burghs' proportion of the tax in Scotland equally between them all, much to the advantage of the Shires and the greater Burghs. This would have diminished the electoral influence of the Government in some of the Burghs, and was accordingly opposed.[38] The Jacobites' role in this affair was as ever to take the lead and drive on as far as the matter would bear it. It is interesting to note how they were by now prepared consciously to evade the spirit of St Germain's directives in order to extract something they desired from the Court.

The second part of the price the ministry was forced to pay for the October Club's support during the session was an equalisation of the Malt Tax throughout Britain. This has usually been seen as a concomitant of the Country Tories' cutting the rate of the Land Tax. In fact it was a long-term piece of chauvinist planning by the English Country Tories of both the October and March Clubs. They were determined to rid themselves of this tax, which figured second in their demonology only to the Land Tax or a general excise, and they hoped to force the 'mercenary' Scots, whom they largely regarded as the tools of the ministry, to aid them in its complete abolition next year. To do this they linked the Malt Tax with the Land Tax in their arguments, suggesting that more must be raised by the Malt Tax to offset the reduction in the Land Tax. An increase was unlikely due to the tax's unpopularity, and the only possible extension was to Scotland. This not only allowed them to justify their reduction of the Land Tax, but also furthered their long-range plan and was satisfyingly Anglocentric. A measure so nationalistic and impeccably Country Tory had no problem in gaining enthusiastic English Jacobite support. Aldworth, Pakington and Blackmore accordingly became its prominent advocates, alongside their erstwhile rivals from the March Club, Gilfrid Lawson, Cholmondeley and Chetwynd.[39]

If it was an impeccably nationalist issue for the English Jacobites, it was very much more so for the Scots Jacobites. The Malt Tax crisis was in many ways an absolute gift to them. It presented proof sufficient to convince most Scots, at least for a time, of what the Jacobites had always passionately believed: that the Union was bound to be detrimental to Scotland as the weaker partner. In both Lords and Commons it was the Scots Jacobites who fought the measure most bitterly, gaining a moral initiative which allowed them to lead their fellow countrymen on to more extreme measures when the opportunity arose. As non-ministerial Tories, they were also the readiest of the Scots on that side to consider joining the Opposition. The Squadrone M.P.'s had been with the Whigs since 1707 anyway, and the Court Tories were loth to risk their places, which left the Scots Jacobites as the most volatile element in the Scots representation. They seem to have believed too that new circumstances exempted them from obeying their last instructions from St Germain, probably in the belief that the exiled Court would condone their action when it heard of the situation, or that it would not be averse to their manipulating the issue to dissolve the Union.[40]

The three principal organisers of the Scots to resist the extension of the Malt Tax were, in the Lords, Argyll and Balmerino, and in the Commons, Lockhart. It was Lockhart who first broached the idea of a joint Tory-Squadrone and Lords-Commons campaign of opposition to any extension of the tax in April, before Parliament had even met. He and the Scots Jacobite steering group took the initiative in demanding the ministry's support against the extension of the Malt Tax to Scotland, which was grudgingly conceded after they made it clear that they would consider the passage of the extension as a breach of the Union, for which they would hold the Government responsible. In the Commons it was again Lockhart who first joined the Jacobites with the Squadrone group led by Baillie to take joint measures against the Malt Tax Bill.[41] The Scots used every tactic they could to delay or kill the Bill. A fraudulent counterproposal of two months' cess was offered in lieu of the tax, though they were well aware that this would not yield an equivalent sum. An attempt was made alongside some Country Whigs to tack the Place Bill of 1713 to the Malt Tax, in the confident expectation that the

Lords would then reject it. With some Whig and Court support they managed, on the chairman's vote in Committee, to reduce the duty to be paid in Scotland to three pence a bushel, only to have the English Country Tories doggedly recommit the resoluton and force the duty up to six pence again. Wrecking amendments were skilfully inserted, only to be as carefully removed in later readings. Finally, Baillie tried to have the tax commence only from the date that the peace with France was ratified, but that too was rejected. By the end of its passage through the Commons on 22 May, the Scots had forced close divisions on the Bill at every reading except the last when they were left with only the Court in support. They had also fought it through every stage in Committee twice.[42] By the end of its passage Lockhart and the Jacobites were consistently aligning themselves with the Opposition in attacks on October Club and ministerial measures, on the grounds that they had been betrayed by them both:

> Mr Speaker desired I would tell you he hopes to see you in the House as soon as possible. Our North Britains have taken a whim one and all to desert and are resolved to vote conscientiously with the Whigs who good men have as conscienciously promised to vote with them for dissolving the Union. It would make you spew to hear what fawning doings there is between 'em.[43]

Oxford's reputation for duplicity was responsible for this, as the Scots believed he could have stopped the Bill if he had wished, and that therefore the apparent support by the Court for their resistance was no more than a sham.

In the Lords the Jacobite Scots peers and their outrage at the Malt Tax were instrumental in concerting a united opposition, due to Balmerino's efforts to achieve a common front with the other Representative Peers in the early stages of the crisis. But once this had been achieved, they lapsed into little more than an auxiliary role in the actual battle against the Malt Tax. By 1713 the remnants of Hamilton's nationalist-cum-Jacobite group had been almost entirely subsumed in Mar's Court group. Two issues on which his leadership was not credible were: an attack on the ministry, or one on the Union, and it was precisely these two elements which constituted the thrust of the opposition to the Malt Tax Bill by the time it reached the Lords. This allowed Argyll, who had been showing steadily increasing signs of discontent since 1712, to seize the initiative and gain the adherence of the Jacobites by taking an aggressive stance on both points. He did so with some success, shaming the Court group into following his own group and the Jacobites into an anti-Union position, though Mar and other Courtiers continued to try and block any plan which would have committed them to opposing the ministry. Having gained an ascendancy over all the Representative Peers, he was able to use his connections with the Opposition to arrange for mutual support: the Scots to help the Opposition against the French Commercial Treaty and on other matters, in return for aid against the Malt Tax.[44] This aid was used to oppose the Malt Tax Bill at every stage of its passage through the Lords, though in a perverse way some of the Jacobites were beginning to appreciate the good the

Bill might do for their cause. As Kilsyth put it when speaking to a clause at a critical moment in the Committee stage: 'My Lords I do approve this Motion because it is most reasonable and would free us of a great burden, and yet it is wt regrate I do it becaus the laying on this Tax will tend to the dissolution of the Union'. Their association with the Opposition did act as a brake on the Jacobites' extremism, which otherwise would have had free rein on such an issue. One case of this occurred when Sunderland prevented Balmerino from putting an amendment to the Bill – a tactic which, had it succeeded, would have led to the instant dismissal of the Bill by the Commons, who traditionally refused to accept any Lords' amendments to money Bills. Another, when Nottingham and the Junto insisted on watering down a protest that Balmerino and other Jacobites intended to have read into the Lords' records. With the support of the Opposition, the Scots were able to run the ministry close on several votes. Defeat would almost certainly have dangerously weakened the Government's control of Parliament, so it too exerted itself to the utmost to ward off such an eventuality. It was helped in this by the wavering of the Opposition Tories and some of the Court Whigs whom the Junto had persuaded to support it. The Opposition Tories were presumably unhappy at opposing a measure so obviously to England's advantage, and the Court Whigs at opposing the supply for the queen's Government. Whatever the reason, it was only due to the timely defection to the Court of the duke of Kent and lords Carteret and Herbert and the simultaneous abstention of Guernsey and the bishop of St Asaph that the ministry was able to get the Bill through its third reading by 73: 66. In the debates on the issue the Jacobites on both sides played only a supportive role, North and Grey and Leeds backing Oxford and Bolingbroke, and Balmerino and Eglinton backing Argyll, Nottingham and the Junto. The final passage of the Bill left the Jacobites in something of a dilemma, as they had no great wish to help the Opposition carry through the measures it was proposing, yet they owed it a considerable debt. St Germain's reiterated orders rescued them from this embarrassing situation, though relations with the ministry remained cool.[45]

The passage of the Malt Tax in the Commons led straight on to the attempt to repeal the Act of Union in the Lords. The bitterness felt by the Scots representatives over the conduct of their English counterparts in pushing the Malt Tax through against their wishes was ripe for exploitation by the Jacobites, who duly capitalised on it to work up an attack on the Union. Lockhart was its instigator, first putting the idea to a select meeting of about a dozen Jacobite and Court Tory M.P.'s at the beginning of May. As the passage of the Malt Tax became increasingly likely, he quietly gathered further support for this plan, notably among the Squadrone M.P.'s. Balmerino backed him to the hilt in the Lords. Despite Oxford threatening him and some of his supporters with the Tower for proposing such a scheme, Lockhart remained resolute and, when the tax passed the Commons, was able to engineer a united front with the other M.P.'s to negotiate jointly with the Representative Peers for a united campaign to repeal the Union.[46] He arranged this meeting, and after the peers had been induced to cooperate with the M.P.'s on the basis of joint democratically decided consultation, it was agreed to introduce a Bill dissolving the Union in the Lords while the M.P.'s harried the ministry in the Commons. Only an uncomfortable combination of the foremost Whigs and Court Tories dared to oppose Lockhart, and they were silenced by the overwhelming consensus he had built up in his favour among the rest of the Scots representation. This group, composed of Mar, Findlater, John Pringle and Baillie, covertly continued to try and obstruct the attack on the Union, but they had lost the initiative completely at this stage to Lockhart, Balmerino, Argyll and Islay. The Campbell brothers were by now well on the way to stealing the Jacobites' clothes over the Union issue, though the irony of hearing them 'roar & exclaim bloodily' against the Union they had helped to create was not lost on Lockhart at least. Lockhart carefully maintained the unanimity of the Scots' representation by ostentatiously taking a moderate stance on the question of settling the succession to the Scottish throne if the attempt to break the Union was successful. To this end he even suppressed some of the more radical Jacobite proposals, such as one put forward by General Charles Ross and Colonel Douglas for a joint boycott of both Parliament and the forthcoming elections, which would have been tantamount to open incitement to rebellion, if the dissolution attempt failed.[47] Argyll gained the leadership of the Scots over this issue after he had sought, and secured, aid from the Opposition on a compromise basis: although they would not consider supporting an attack on the Union right away, they would consider it provided certain guarantees were forthcoming with regard to the Protestant succession and other matters. Findlater, who, despite himself, had agreed under pressure from his fellow Scots actually to introduce the Bill to dissolve the Union, and Mar, were against this delay, preferring a head-on attack on the central issue immediately. They hoped that by concentrating the debate on specific grievances and then leading the Scots into a direct defeat on the main issue, they could open the way for the Government simply to redress the Scots' grievances piecemeal when they were demoralised after their failure. In the actual debate on 1 June, after the Scots had stated their case and the ministry replied to it, the Court wanted immediate consideration of the proposal to bring in a Bill repealing the Union, abetted by Mar and Findlater from the Scots' side. The Opposition, who wanted to spin the affair out as long as possible to ensure that the Scots stayed with them, shrewdly tried to avoid a straight trial of strength and moved to adjourn consideration in lieu of proposals regarding the safeguarding of the Protestant succession in an independent Scotland. Argyll managed to persuade the rest of the Scots peers to go along with this, dragging Mar and Findlater with them. In the event, the Government managed to defeat the motion to adjourn in a division on the previous question by four votes on a count of proxies, and then dispatched the proposal to bring in a Bill to repeal the Union immediately afterwards without a division.[48] As Mar and Oxford had intended, this took the heart out of the campaign and restored the initiative to the managers. Next day Lockhart and

Alexander Murray, a Squadrone M.P., were voted down at a joint meeting of the Scots representatives, when they proposed that the peers should continue harassing the ministry in the Lords while the M.P.'s did likewise in the Commons.[49] Lockhart refused at first to give up the battle, and led a small group of Jacobites in a series of pinprick attacks in the Commons until called to order by the Jacobite Court. St Germain politely sympathised with the Scots Jacobites' feelings, but questioned

> whether Snows [Scotland's] joyning with such a knave as Williamson [Whigs] to endeavour to do himself justice may not be his own as well as his friend Johns [James's] ruin and the remedy worse than the disease is what Juxon [Parliamentary Jacobites] upon the place is best judge of and should be very wary in, taking care in this critical juncture not to countenance or foment any rash undertaking wch may exasperate to no purpose Charles Hickman [the queen and Oxford] Cowley and partners [the Church i.e. the Tories], with whom measures ought to be kept in being as you know widow Jean's [James's] positive directions, reiterated to Juxon to joyn his interest with Hickman's Company upon all occasions in opposition to Williamson, etc. It is expected therefore that Will Morly [Parliamentary Jacobites] will bestirr himself as he ought in this matter and stick to his directions with a prudent view still to the main and essential point of sustaining widow Jean's interest in opposition to Laurence [Hanover].[50]

Lockhart and his friends duly obeyed this directive, leaving Argyll and Islay as the only permanent recruits for the Opposition out of the affair (lord Blantyre being mortally ill at this time). In Scotland, a scheme adopted by the Scots representation to salve their consciences before they wound up the affair, to work up a host of petitions against the Union for use in the next Parliament, was quietly killed off by the ministry and the Squadrone.[51]

The net effect of the Malt Tax crisis, including the attack on the Union, was minimal. Oxford realised that violent opposition to its collection was likely, and duly allowed considerable leniency as regards its payment. This removed the sting from the Jacobite campaign to rouse public opinion in Scotland against the Union in sufficient force to oblige the ministry to let the country go, once the initial storm had been weathered in Parliament.[52] What the episode did bring out very clearly was the disparity which now existed between the strength and coherence of the Scots Jacobites in the Lords and those in the Commons. Though Jacobites had been the mainstay of both the opposition to the Malt Tax and the harrassing campaign in the Commons, in the Lords they had become merely adjuncts attached to whoever took the most anti-Union line. Though Balmerino and Eglinton spoke on several occasions against the Union and Malt Tax, it was very much as auxiliaries to Argyll, Mar, Nottingham and the Junto. Balmerino was prominent in organising the Scots' opposition in the early stages, but willingly deferred to Argyll and was soon eclipsed by him. Oxford's ability to undermine the campaign from within was plainly enhanced by the leaderlessness of the Scots Jacobite peers, who were by then accustomed to following the ministry's directions implicitly. By Mar's manipulation of their uncertainty and disappointment in the aftermath of the failure on 1 June, they were gradually brought back into the ministerial fold. Hence, by mid-June Oxford felt sure enough of Mar's management and St Germain's admonitions to count on all of the Jacobite peers save Balmerino in his forecast of the voting in the Lords on the Commercial Treaty.[53] Except on absolutely clear-cut nationalist or Jacobite issues, the Scots Jacobite peers' separate identity had obviously decayed completely by this time.

One incipient crisis created by the furore over the Malt Tax and the Union was the possibility of an attempt by the Opposition to invite over a member of the electoral family. The queen would have been incensed by such a move, and any ministry which failed to prevent it would incur her severest displeasure at the very least. It was therefore a masterly stroke if it could be brought off. Rumours of such a plan, based on an address by one of the Houses of Parliament (probably the Lords, where the Opposition was relatively strong) were circulating well before Parliament opened.[54] These were well founded in fact, as is demonstrated by a letter written by Sunderland in April:

> Since it is so difficult for the Elector to contribute to the expence of the ensuing elections, all friends agree to make another proposal to him, which is of greater consequence, and which appears to them to be absolutely necessary. It is to send over the Electoral Prince.[55]

The Opposition was well aware that under normal circumstances they would never be able to pass such an address, so they hoped that the elector would send his son uninvited. George wisely refused to contemplate such an act, which led to an impasse until the Malt Tax crisis. The Opposition leaders seized the opportunity to press the Scots for aid in passing such an invitation, in return for their help against the Union and Malt Tax, and threatened to support the ministry on both issues unless the Scots agreed. This was one of the reasons why the Opposition wanted to adjourn the Union debate rather than vote on it straight away;[56] they hoped to persuade the Scots to help them in the interval:

> the designe, of the delay, proposed by ye Whiggs, was to see if we would join them, for calling over Han[ove]r Instanter, & ruining this ministrie, Ych when spock to us, illa, & most of our peers, would not goe in to yt, and said, They would nott be the stepping stone for bringing over Han—r for yt end, and after be kikt over stairs. Upon ych they deserted us when the resolve came in & the Courtt carried it wtout a division.[57]

Clearly, calling over a Hanoverian prince was too much for the Scots Court Tories to contemplate, and likewise for the Jacobites, though a few really determined anti-Unionists, such as Balmerino, may have been willing to support such a move. The Argyll group plainly could not take it up alone, and so refused along with the rest. Soon afterwards the Opposition reluctantly dropped the idea for the rest of the year. This was probably the single most serious threat to Oxford's ministry during the 1713 session. In early June he was only narrowly managing to push the Malt Tax through by a handful of votes against the Scots-Opposition alliance. Oxford was able to achieve even that only because of the qualms of some Opposition Tories and Court Whigs, and in the process could not fail to stoke the passions which had first placed the Scots in the Opposition camp. Though the Jacobites were disorientated without the Court's leadership, which in time worked in Oxford's favour, one vital reason for their returning to support the Court at that time in early June was the renewed exhortations they received from St Germain. Without the exiled Court's intervention, or worse, if the Jacobite Court had urged the Scots Jacobite peers against him (as they had done in their 1710-11 instructions for the Commons), Oxford could have found himself facing a much more intractable situation, and possibly even an address calling on the queen to invite the electoral prince over from Hanover.

The translation into law of those articles of the French Commercial Treaty requiring legal sanction was certain to be contested, given that 1713 was an election year. Since the peace itself was generally popular, the Opposition had to find some defect in the terms themselves in order to challenge the ministry's head start as far as the goodwill of the electorate was concerned. The mass of the Country Tories did not wish to endanger their, or their friends', electoral prospects either, so they were equally cautious about endorsing something which was not certain to please the electors. In accord with this reserve the October Club and its associates gave firm but cautious support to the precursor to the Bill inplementing articles eight and nine of the Commercial Treaty (by repealing former legislation so as to allow France 'most favoured nation' status), the Bill suspending the duties on French wine. The March Club took a far more belligerent attitude, having already written off the treaty as a craven betrayal of Britain's commercial interests, and threw itself into a campaign of outright opposition. It also felt some distaste for a measure improving Britain's relations with France, but far more evident is a suspicion that the implementation of the treaty would adversely affect certain economic interest groups whose influence could well prove crucial in the elections. Once the Wine Duty Suspension Bill had been dropped and the Commercial Treaty Bill was introduced, the growing chorus of opposition from the mercantile lobby began to concern many of the more moderate Hanoverian Tories who remained with the October Club. A slow drift by them onto the Opposition side in divisions on the Bill soon followed.[58] They appear to have had few doubts about the virtues of a French Commercial Treaty in principle, but growing fears of its unseasonableness:

> when a Treaty of so vast Consequence was so ill digested & so dubiously express'd as to want so many explanations to prevent French Cavils & their putting their own constructions on it to our disadvantage: when part of those Exports remain'd still actually prohibited, & so high a duty still left upon some part of our Woollen Manufacture, as in ye circumstances of their Improvemts amounted to a prohibition in effect of allmost all ye species of it: when wee run a very great hasard of loosing our Portugal trade & weakning that to

Hamborough: it was thought advisable to deferr it to another session of Parl.
before wee took their duties off.[59]

After the queen's death many claimed they were voting in favour of the
Hanoverian succession by opposing the Bill, but this looks suspiciously like
political hindsight. The only achnowledged 'secret' motive at the time was
their wish to make the ministry aware of their power to check it if they chose,
and their dwindling patience with the Government's failure to completely
purge its administration of Whigs. When the Bill was finally defeated at the
end of the Committee stage, on a question of whether to engross or not, 38%
of the Opposition vote of 194 was composed of Country Tories. Of these, 19%
were probably members of the March Club, and 19% went over with
Hanmer.[60] Hanmer definitely did not take over more than forty with him at the
final stage, and throughout the last debate on the Commercial Treaty Bill he
and his friends kept a markedly low profile, contributing little to the debate
except reservations about the beneficial results expected of the Bill.
Consequently, of the eighteen speakers at that stage only two — Kay and
Hanmer—came from Hanmer's following, compared to four— Cholmondeley,
Aislabie, Paul Docminique and Francis Annesley — from the March Club and
twelve from the rest of the Opposition.[61] Moreover, once the Bill was defeated,
Hanmer's group returned to their comrades with some alacrity.[62]

The Jacobites' part in the passage, and eventual failure of the French
Commercial Treaty Bill was, to say the least, confused. The English Jacobites,
along with the bulk of their moderately Hanoverian Tory fellows, supported
the Bill fairly unequivocally, as might have been expected from their orders
and their automatic sympathy with anything disliked by the Hanoverians and
Allies. This did not denote blind obedience to the will of the ministry, as
Moore found out when he tried to restrict debate on the treaty to the whole
rather than individual articles, faced a massive defeat on the point and had to
retract precipitately. But in general the English Jacobites provided solid and
useful backing for the ministry on the issue, including six of the seventeen
speakers in favour of the Bill in its final stage: Whitlock, Sir Alexander
Cumming, Campion, Eversfield, Aldworth and James Murray.[63] The Scots
Jacobites' position on the Commercial Treaty was dictated entirely by tactical
considerations. They supported the Wine Duty Suspension Bill without any
hesitation, but by the time the Bill implementing articles eight and nine of the
French Commercial Treaty was introduced, they were in the middle of the
Malt Tax crisis in which the Jacobites were leading the way in demonstrating
the Scots' ability to wreck Government legislation: 'because ye court were ye
persons who keepd ye Scots under ye Union and woud do so till ye end of ye
world whilst they gained by it & yrfore it was fitt to let ym see what wee durst
do'. Consequently, almost all the Scots opposed the first reading of the Bill. By
the time of the second reading on 4 June, however, the attack on the Union had
failed and a continuing policy of harassing the ministry in Lords and
Commons had been voted down by a meeting of Scots Parliamentarians.[64]
Lockhart and a group of his friends refused to accept this: 'there were a good

number who expresst their resentment of the usage they had mett with, and by joining with the Whigs and discontented Tories, on some occasions carried several votes, to the no small dissatisfaction of the Ministry'. Apart from Lockhart and his clique, all the Scots returned to their traditional or directed alignments. The Squadrone M.P.'s returned to the Opposition, the Court Tories and many of the Jacobites to the ministry, leaving only Lockhart's group of hardline Jacobites pursuing an independent course. In accord with their inclinations, they deliberately abstained at the last moment during the second reading of the Commercial Treaty Bill. Before the Committee stage, however, messages specifically ordering Lockhart and his friends back into the ministerial fold arrived from St Germain, one via Straton and the other via Menzies to ensure that they were received and understood. These ended the Scots Jacobite Parliamentary rebellion, and they were all present and voting for the Government on 18 June.[65]

It is difficult to assess exactly what the effects of the Jacobites' attitude, especially the violent shifts of the Scots, could have had on the passage and eventual defeat of the Commercial Treaty Bill. It is possible that the harassing campaign of early June may have encouraged Hanmer and his friends to believe that the Bill was more unpopular among Tory M.P.'s than was actually the case. Concomitantly, the end of the harassing campaign may have encouraged the Court to grow lax in watching over the Bill as the obvious threat to it had vanished. In effect, Hanmer and his friends' discontent may have gone unnoticed as its increase was masked by the cessation of harassment by the Scots. It was certainly a common complaint among the Bill's supporters after its defeat that the ministry had been careless about ensuring its passage.[66] Other than these possible repercussions, the Jacobites had nothing to show either for their support or their opposition to the Commercial Treaty. Their lack of unity and a common position allowed no significant contribution to either side, other than sheer numbers, in sharp contrast to the decisive impact of the temporarily united Hanoverian Tories. The Jacobite reaction to their poor showing can only be surmised, but it is possible that their consciousness of their impotence may have reinforced the renewed idea of forming an independent Jacobite group which emerged at the end of the session.

The fact that 1713 was an election year dominated the activities of all parties during the 1713 session. The most blatant manifestation of this by the Tories was over the Land Tax, but as the end of the session approached the Opposition still had to score some telling and unalloyed electoral point on their own behalf. As the self-appointed guardians of the Protestant interest, they had already decided at the beginning of the year that the best gambit to emphasise this role would be an address against James. On the grounds that an Opposition scheme spoilt was a point gained for the ministry, Oxford was felt to be certain to try to steal their thunder if he got the chance. Consequently, the Opposition bided its time until late in the session, despite having received Hanover's blessing for the plan in January. When it was finally introduced, it was done as a carefully planned raid, with the Hanoverian Tories, represented by Anglesey, in support. Bolton took advantage of the prevailing tension between the two Houses to move for a consideration of the Lords' privileges. When the Lords met on 30 June, instead of debating this, Wharton suddenly moved for an address requesting the queen to secure James's expulsion from Lorraine, and was seconded by Sunderland. Oxford adroitly side-stepped the thrust by blandly concurring with the sentiments expressed, while insinuating that it was unnecessary as measures to secure James's expulsion were already under way. The Jacobites seem to have been totally disconcerted, North and Grey alone finding the courage to reply. He blustered about how unnecessary it was, as France (a friendly power) lay between Britain and Lorraine, but the only backing he received was from a dissident Whig, the earl of Peterborough.[67] When a motion to agree with the Lords' address was introduced by Stanhope in the Commons, both the ministry and the Jacobites were better prepared. Edward Harley first seconded Stanhope, and then tried to take over his motion by some dubious procedural tactics. Whitlock delivered a veiled threat on behalf of the Jacobites:

> [il] parla de la meme maniere que Ld North and Grey avoit fait le jour precedent, hormis que le Che'er ajoutait qu'on devoit se souvenir que lorsque le Protecteur Cromwell s'etoit mis dans la teste d'insister aupres des princes au dehors, de ne pas souffrir le Roy Charles dans leurs Etats le retablssement Glorieux de ce Prince s'etoit en suivi peu de mois apres.[68]

This was the best the Jacobites could do while the treason laws remained unaltered and an election was in the offing. To have spoken out more directly would have resulted in the offender being sent to the Tower, and to have forced a division without a debate would not only have meant certain defeat, but also inclusion in a blacklist for use in the elections. Netterville tried to pass it off as having been allowed through by the Jacobites 'with a sneer and a laugh', but that was merely bravado to cover their undoubted anger and embarrassment. Oxford tried to make the best of it by portentously quoting Whitlock's words whenever he was reproached by a disconsolate Jacobite. This impressed no one except the Opposition, and his ministry's equivocation on this issue provided the final push needed for another attempt to launch an independent Jacobite Parliamentary group. All in all this was a shrewd blow by the Opposition. Not only did it compromise the Government with a section of its Country Tory support, but by their inclusion of Anglesey in the planning of the venture the Opposition also drove a wedge between the ministry and the group of Hanoverian Tory dissidents steadily coalesing around him and Hanmer.[69]

At the end of the 1713 session Oxford's ministry was in serious difficulties. In the Cabinet, Bolingbroke, viscount Harcourt, lord Trevor and Shrewsbury were plotting to 'put a Junto' on Oxford, a scheme which he only just managed to foil by making maximum use of his influence with the queen in order to reshuffle the Cabinet to his advantage.[70] By the end of September he had seriously damaged his standing with her too, by asking for his son to be made duke of Newcastle.[71] In Parliament Oxford faced a full-scale backbench revolt along the lines of that of 1711, but with extra complications that made it incomparably harder to deal with. In 1711 the Country Tories had formed a united, if hostile, body, which could be negotiated with and/or appeased as such. Now there were in effect two inimical groups among them: the Hanoverian Tories and the Jacobites. An attempt to placate one was certain to offend the other, and to compound the problem further, the moderately Hanoverian Tories who still formed a substantial section of the Country Tories wanted no part of either. Among the Country Tories as a whole his credibility was at its last gasp. All of his promises to them had been revealed to be false. There had been no purge when the peace came, no Tory millennium, only yet more procrastination. None of the backbench groups trusted him, and each was suspicious of his future intentions. A 'thorough' Tory scheme might yet have saved the day, but Oxford could not contemplate that if he wished to remain premier Minister. This confluence of crises meant that Oxford was henceforth living on his wits. From 1713, his only hope of survival, at least for a while, was to try and manipulate the backbench groups' divergent aims, hostility to each other, and long-cherished dream of a Tory regime in Church and State, to keep them out of the Opposition camp and supporting his ministry. Reduced to its essentials, his problem was to keep these hostile groups cooperating, thus maintaining his ministry, while they were as hostile and as suspicious of him as they were of each other and the Whigs.

NOTES

1.   Portland, v, 311–12: Bolingbroke to Oxford, 27 July 1713; v, 295–6: Grahme to Oxford, 13 June 1713: Lockhart, i, 411–12. G.S. Holmes and C. Jones, 'Trade, the Scots and the Parliamentary Crisis of 1713'. *Parliamentary History*, i (1982) 47–78, has appeared since I wrote this book and offers an alternative interpretation to that put forward here.

2.   Macpherson, ii, 369–71: Netterville to Middleton, arrived 19 Jan. 1713 ns.

3.   Add. MSS. 22220, f. 35: Berkeley to Strafford, 27 Jan. 1713; *Journal to Stella*, ii, 613, 621, 625: 3, 16 and 22 Feb. 1713; Hermitage GGG, f. 114: 31 Mar. 1713.

4.   *Went. Corr.*, pp. 322–3: Wentworth to Strafford, 3 Mar. 1713; Portland Loan 29/10 ii./14: list of Scots M.P.'s and peers, and English bishops to be summoned for the session, 7 Feb. 1713.

5.   *Went. Corr.*, pp. 324–5: Wentworth to Strafford, 20 Mar. 1713; Bennett, *Tory Crisis*, p. 163.

6.   Portland Loan 29/150/3: Oxford to Lockhart, 9 Feb. 1713.

7.   Wodrow Letters, Quarto 7, ep. 80: Smith to Crosse, Mar. 1713.

8.   Macpherson, ii, 503, 505: Schütz to Robethon, 22 and 29 Sept. 1713.

9.   Stuart, i, 264: Berwick to James, 12 May 1713 ns; Macpherson, ii, 400–1: Ellis to Plunket, 9 Apr. 1713 ns; ii, 387–94: Plunket to Ellis (Ellis's extracts), 9–27 Feb. 1713; Carte 212, f. 53/55: Nairne to Menzies, 27 Apr. 1713 ns.

10. Lockhart, i, 412–13; Portland Loan 29/10 ii./14: list of doubtful supporters, 26 Feb. 1713.

11. *CJ*, xvii, 298, 344, 410: 21 Apr., 9 May and 9 June 1713; Kreienberg 113a, ff. 66–7: 1 May 1713.

12. Kreienberg 113a, ff. 138–9: 12 June 1713.

13. Add. MSS. 47027, f. 29: viscount Castlecomer to Percival, 28 Apr. 1713; *CJ*, xvii, 385, 426: 29 May and 16 June 1713; Hermitage GGG, ff. 139–41: 21 Apr. 1713.

14. *Went. Corr.*, 336–7: Wentworth to Strafford, 26 May 1713; Trumbull Add. MSS. 136/3: Bridges to Trumbull, 1 June 1713; *Parl. Hist.*, vi, 1222: 10 June 1713.

15. *Bol. Corr.*, iii, 181: Bolingbroke to Argyll, 19 Nov. 1712; iv, 79–80: Bolingbroke to Strafford, 28 Apr. 1713; Kreienberg 113a, f. 71: 5 May 1713; Holmes, *Sacheverell*, pp. 262–3.

16. *CJ*, xvii, 298, 308, 356, 458: 21 Apr., 1 and 16 May and 8 July 1713; MS Ballard 31, f. 109: Bishop to Charlett, 14 July 1713; [Defoe], *A Letter from a Member of the House of Commons to his Friend in the Country Relating to the Bill of Commerce* (1713), pp. 24–5.

17. Bennett, *Tory Crisis*, pp. 164–5; Kreienberg 113a ff. 5–6, 16–17: 6 and 27 Jan. 1713.

18. Macpherson, ii, 419–20: Ralph Wingate to Ellis, 23 June 1713. See also: Baschet 201, f. 60: D'Aumont to Louis XIV, 5 July 1713 ns. For another view, see: Dickinson, *Bolingbroke*, p. 108.

19. Macpherson, ii, 369: Innes to Middleton, 9 Jan. 1713 ns; Lockhart, i, 426–9; *Bol. Corr.*, iv, 164–6: Bolingbroke to Strafford, 20 June 1713; MS Ballard 31, f. 104: Bishop to Charlett, 20 June 1713. For another view, see: Hill, *Growth*, pp. 139–40.

20. Dalhousie 14/338/7: Lyon to Maule, [23 June 1713]; Holmes, *Politics*, p. 279; *Hanmer Corr.*, pp. 143–5: Oxford to Hanmer, 8 and 30 July 1713; pp. 145–6: Bromley to Hanmer, 30 July 1713; p. 147: Ormonde to Hanmer, 1 Aug. 1713.

21. Macpherson, ii, 511–12: Schütz to Robethon, 7 Nov. 1713; ii, 495–7: L'Hermitage to Robethon, 18 June and 4 July 1713; Portland Loan 29/310: Bromley to Oxford, 4 Sept. 1713.

22. Carte 212, f. 49: Middleton to Menzies, 13 Feb. 1713 ns. For another view, see: Gregg, *Queen Anne*, p. 367.

23. Carte 212, f. 48: Nairne to Straton, 25 Jan. 1713 ns; f. 53: Nairne to Straton, 27 Apr. 1713 ns. Lockhart, i. 417 437.

24. Dalhousie 14/352/18 22: Balmerino to Maule, 28 May and 6 June [1713]; Holmes and Jones, 'Crisis', appendix pp. 68–70; Carte 212, f. 56: Nairne to Straton, 8 June 1713 ns; Nairne to Menzies, 22 June 1713 ns.

25. Portland Loan 29/135/2: Ferguson to Oxford, 22 June 1713; Portland, v, 297–8: the duchess of Buckingham to Oxford [received 22 June 1713].

26. Carte 211,f.140: Netterville to Middleton, 7 Aug. 1713.

27. Carte 212, ff. 59–62: Nairne to Menzies, 19 Sept., 8 and 24 Oct. and 25 Nov. 1713 ns.

28. Add. MSS. 22220, f. 54: Berkeley to Strafford, 27 Feb. 1713; Add. MSS. 47027, f. 16: Southwell to Percival, 31 Mar. 1713; Lockhart, i, 437–9; Trumbull Add. MSS. 136/3: Bridges to Trumbull, 8 May 1713.

29. *Went. Corr.*, pp. 340, 343: Wentworth to Strafford, 30 June and 14 July 1713; Kreienberg 113a, ff. 169–70: 14 July 1713; Burnet, *History*, vii, 174.

30. Holmes, *Politics*, pp. 220–1, 236–7, 239, 245, 305; Wodrow Letters, Quarto 7, epp. 84, 87: Smith to Crosse, 9 and 11 Apr. 1713; *CJ*, xvii, 281: 10 Apr. 1713.

31.   Horwitz, *Politicks*, p. 238; Hermitage GGG, ff. 124-6: 10 Apr. 1713; *Went. Corr.*, pp. 328-9: Berkeley to Strafford, 10 Apr. 1713.

32.   Dartmouth MSS. D(W) 1778/I ii./364: Oxford to Dartmouth, 8 Mar. 1713. Kreienberg 113a, ff. 35-7: 3 Mar. 1713.

33.   Kreienberg 113a, f. 38: 10 Mar. 1713; *Parl. Hist.*, vi, 1172: 9 Apr. 1713; Gregg, *Queen Anne*, p. 366.

34.   Holmes, *Politics*, pp. 264-5, 356, 401-2.

35.   Add. MSS. 22220, f. 36: Berkeley to Strafford, 27 Jan. 1713; Claydon House Letters M11/55: Cave to Fermanagh, 23 Apr. 1713.

36.   Hermitage GGG, ff. 144-5: 24 Apr. 1713. See also: Kreienberg 113a, ff. 58-9: 24 Apr. 1713.

37.   Kreienberg 113a, f. 59: 24 Apr. 1713; Hermitage GGG, ff 149-50: 28 Apr. 1713.

38.   Trumbull Add. MSS, 136/3: Bridges to Trumbull, 21 Apr. 1713; *CJ*, xvii, 305: 29 Apr. 1713; Mar MSS. 15/1099/3: Alexander Reid to Erskine, 7 May 1713.

39.   *Went Corr.*, pp. 336-7: Wentworth to Strafford, 26 May 1713; MS North A3, f. 199: notes for a speech to rebut the Scots' arguments, [June 1713]; *CJ*, xvii, 354, 359, 373, 377: 15, 19, 21 and 22 May 1713; Grey-Neville MSS. F 23/2: Aldworth to Northumberland, 20 May 1713.

40.   Lockhart, i, 413-17; Holmes, *Politics*, p. 243; *Marchmont Papers*, p. 7: Baillie to Marchmont, 30 Apr. 1713; *CJ*, xvii, 359, 373, 377: 19, 21 and 22 May 1713.

41.   GD 248/561/49/15: John Lorimer to [William Lorimer], 7 Apr. 1713; Loudoun MSS. (HPT): Lockhart to Loudoun 7 Apr. 1713; Kreienberg 113a, f. 111: 22 May 1713; *Marchmont Papers*, pp. 7-8: Baillie to Marchmont, 30 Apr. 1713.

42.   GD 248/566/87/23: Lockhart to Findlater [May 1713]; Holmes, *Politics*, p. 135; Marchmont Papers, pp. 8-12: Baillie to Marchmont, 12, 16, 21 and 23 May 1713; HMC, *Laing MSS.*, ii, 167-8 [newsletter from London], 26 May 1713.

43.   Isham MSS. (HPT): Sir George Beaumont M.P. to Sir Justinian Isham M.P., 30 May 1713. See also Lockhart, i, 413-17.

44.   Dalhousie 14/352/20 22 24: Balmerino to Maule, 4, 6 and 9 June [1713].

45.   Dalhousie 14/352/20-1, 22, 24, 26: Balmerino to Maule, 4, 6, 9 and 23 June 1713; Kreienberg 113a, ff. 131-6: 9 June 1713, n.b. on 5 June, when the votes cast were 76: 74 in favour of the Malt Tax, Oxford secured his majority by bribing the Whig earl of Warrington to defect, Holmes, *Politics*, p. 397; Scots R.O. GD 18/3150/3 (Clerk of Penicuik MSS.): John Pringle to Erskine, 6 June 1713; GD 248/561/48/47: J. Lorimer to [W. Lorimer], 30 June 1713.

46.   Lockhart, i, 417-26; *Marchmont Papers*, pp. 11-12: Baillie to Marchmont, 23 May 1713; HMC, *Laing MSS.* ii, 168-71: newsletter from London, 26 May 1713; Dalhousie 14/352/16: Balmerino to Maule, 12 May 1713.

47.   *Marchmont Papers*, p. 13: Baillie to Marchmont, 26 May 1713; Nat. Lib. of Scotland, Newhailes papers 7228/1: [Lockhart] to Dalrymple, 28 May [1713]; Lockhart, i, 429-2; Dalhousie 14/352/17: Balmerino to Maule, 26 May 1713. Professor Holmes and I differ on the question of Ross's Jacobitism: Holmes, *Politics*, p. 289.

48.   Add. MSS. 47027, ff. 37-8: G. Berkeley to Percival, 2 June 1713; Lockhart, i, 432-7; Dalhousie 14/352/18-19 26: Balmerino to Maule, 28 May and 2 and 23 June [1713].

49.   *Hamilton Diary*, p. 55; 4 June 1713; Holmes, *Politics*, p. 339; Dalhousie 14/352/19: Balmerino to Maule, 2 June 1713; 14/364/1: Alexander Murray to Maule, 2 June 1713; Lockhart, i, 436-7.

50.   Carte 212, f. 56: Nairne to Menzies, 22 June 1713 ns.

51. Lockhart, i, 436-7; Dalhousie 14/352/19-20, 26: Balmerino to Maule, 2, 4 and 23 June [1713]; Blair Castle MSS., Box 45 Bundle 11, ep. 23: Breadalbane to Atholl, 7 June 1713.

52. Hermitage GGG, f. 244: 26 June 1713; Dalhousie 14/352/25-6: Balmerino to Maule, 16 and 23 June [1713].

53. Portland Loan 29/10 i./3: forecast of Lords vote on the Commercial Treaty [June 1713].

54. Macpherson, ii, 387-94: Plunket to Ellis (Ellis's extracts), 9-27 Feb. 1713; Portland, v, 267: Bromley to Oxford, 18 Feb. 1713.

55. Macpherson, ii, 481-2: Sunderland to Bothmer, 6 Apr. 1713. See also: *Cowper Diary*, p. 56: 28 Mar. 1713.

56. Add. MSS. 47027, ff. 37-8: G. Berkeley to Percival, 2 June 1713; Blair Castle MSS., Box 45 Bundle 11, ep. 25: John Flemyng to Atholl, 8 June 1713.

57. Blair Castle MSS., Box 45 Bundle 11, ep. 24: John Douglas to Atholl, 8 June 1713.

58. Kreienberg 113a, ff. 71, 72-4, 74-5, 76-106, 126-8: 5, 8, 12 and 15 May and 5 June 1713; *CJ*, xvii, 310, 314, 315, 353-4, 386, 402, 410: 2, 4, 6, 14 and 30 May and 4 and 9 June 1713; *Bol. Corr.*, iv, 60, 138: Bolingbroke to Shrewsbury, 19 Apr. and 29 May 1713.

59. Dartmouth MSS. D(W) 1778/III/156: Kay to Dun [June 1713]. See also: *Parl. Hist.*, vi, 1223: [18] June 1713.

60. These calculations are based on Defoe's list of 'very Whimsicals indeed', which, following Professor G.S. Holmes *(Brit. Pol.,* p. 280 and note 127 same page), I take to consist mainly of the March Club: [Defoe], *Letter*, pp. 25-42.

61. *A Collection of White and Black Lists* (1715), p. 26; MS Ballard 31, f. 104: Bishop to Charlett, 20 June 1713.

62. Dalhousie 14/338/7: Lyon to Maule [23 June 1713]; Kreienberg 113a, ff. 149-51: 26 June 1713; Hermitage GGG, ff. 243-4: 22 June 1713.

63. Carte 231, f. 36a: anecdote told to Carte by Lansdowne, 23 Apr. 1724; Isham MS. 2791: Sir Gilbert Dolben to Isham, 2 June 1713; *White and Black Lists*, p. 26; *Went. Corr.*, pp. 334-6: Wentworth to Strafford, 15 May 1713.

64. Kreienberg 113a, f. 125: 2 June 1713; GD 18/3150/3: Pringle to Erskine, 6 June 1713; Newhailes papers 7228/1: [Lockhart] to Dalrymple, 28 May [1713].

65. Lockhart, i, 437; Jones and Holmes, 'Crisis', pp. 68-70.

66. *Went. Corr.*, p. 338: Wentworth to Strafford, 23 June 1713; *Swift Corr.*, i, 375: Swift to Charles Ford, 9 July 1713; Portland, v, 299-300: Bolingbroke to Oxford [June 1713].

67. Macpherson, ii, 468-9: Robethon to Grote, 27 Jan. 1713; ii, 483: Sunderland to Bothmer, 10 Apr. 1713; Holmes, *Politics*, pp. 306-7; Gregg, *Queen Anne*, p. 368; Kreienberg 113a, ff. 155-7: 30 June 1713.

68. Kreienberg 113a, ff. 158-9: 3 July 1713.

69. Macpherson, ii, 424-7: Netterville to Middleton, 30 July 1713; Kreienberg 113a, ff. 155, 159: 30 June and 3 July 1713.

70. Gregg, *Queen Anne*, pp. 370-1; Bennett, *Tory Crisis*, pp. 172-3.

71. Gregg, *Queen Anne*, p. 373.

7

'Popery and the Pretender': the Jacobites and the election of 1713

In England and Wales the election of 1713 was an unusual one for the period 1689-1722. It was essentially a three-cornered contest the like of which had not been seen since the Court Tory campaign against the High Tories in 1705. The three participants were: the dissident (Hanoverian or Opposition) Tories; the ministry and its Country Tory allies; and the Whigs. 'Contest' is in one sense a misnomer, because the dissident and ministerial Tories only rarely actually opposed each other, lest in the process the Whigs managed to steal a march and supplant a divided Tory interest. It is perhaps more accurate to regard them as in competition within the Tory party and its constituency interests for the candidature of a given seat rather than fielding rival candidates at the actual poll — in the majority of cases. In practice, this meant that a dissident Tory interest could usually expect an undivided Tory vote provided it was the strongest. If a dissident Tory candidate chose to stand against a ministerial Tory where the Whigs were not fielding a man of their own, he could count on Whig support. This was not, however, reciprocal or overriding. A Whig could not expect help from the dissident Tories, and if there was only a dissident Tory candidate standing against a Whig, the contest would be as fierce as could have been expected in normal times (as, for instance, with the earl of Barrymore's contesting of Stockbridge). The upshot of this was that of all the groups with which to be identified, dissident Tory was electorally the most advantageous. Not only did it collect anti-ministerial votes in all cases, it also drew to it the ministerial vote where it was contesting the seat with a Whig interest or the Whig vote if it was contesting the seat with a ministerialist Tory interest.[1] This was of course considerably altered by local electoral pacts, feuds and the presence of an overwhelming interest fixed in one group. Even the Nottinghamite Tories must be separated from their Whig Opposition partners when considering this election. Though they were almost inseparable in Parliament, that was very much a marriage of convenience. Outside Westminster the Nottinghamites, and even more the March Club and other Hanoverian Tories, were very much High Church country gentlemen.[2] Except on grounds of strict electoral necessity, High Churchmanship and Revolution principles remained basically incompatible. Dissident and ministerial Tories differed on many things, but they were internal rivals, each seeking to control the Tory party — in the final analysis the Whigs were the enemies of all. The

Jacobite candidates featured as ministerialist Tories, and were correspondingly at an electoral disadvantage compared with their Hanoverian opponents.

Since their biggest electoral success of the reign had come in the wake of a real Jacobite scare, in 1708, the Whigs did their best to work up a fake one as a substitute in 1713. In January, one of Oxford's old 'Country party' friends, John Toland, informed him that the Junto were beginning a campaign of tendentious rumours in an attempt to prove Oxford was a secret Jacobite:

> Not that the abdicated ministers are capable of believing anything so gross themselves; but they hope you'll be afraid of disobliging or irritating some, as to give handle enough for misrepresenting your intentions with much plausibleness. They are at present most industrious on the subject of the Scots advocates, and confidently report that you opposed in Council Lord Shrewsbury's motion of making them a severe example, even naming those who sided with each of you. Then to give this insinuation the greater force, they make people remark, that not one man has been punished for the invasion; that Lord Middleton's sons were discharged in triumph; that we are so long without a minister at Hanover, and that my Lord Griffin's attainder is to be reversed.[3]

This whispering campaign next moved on to providing incidents of 'proof', as with the entirely fabricated story of how a 'Mr. Lewis', having been mistaken for the earl of Dartmouth's secretary (Dartmouth was Secretary of State for the South) by the earl of Sussex and his Irish-born French father-in-law, Brigadier Skelton, was astounded to receive from them the compliments and thanks of James and Melfort for all his aid. The fact that Melfort had not been allowed near the Jacobite Court since before 1702 seems to have bothered no-one. From there it was an easy step to trying to manufacture alarmist petitions and declarations. The Whig circuit judges duly furthered this by solemnly warning the Commissions of the Peace to keep themselves in readiness for surprise attacks by the Jacobites and Papists. The Whig bishops tried to persuade renownedly Tory stalwarts like the archbishop of York to join them in expressing concern over the decline in the Protestant interest in general and hence the Hanoverian interest in particular. Concern was ostentatiously voiced over the numbers of *émigré* officers returning to Britain, and it was rumoured that Berwick was to follow shortly.[4] All this succeeded in creating many misgivings in the uncertain atmosphere engendered by the continued prorogation of Parliament. The queen's personal intervention, coupled to the actual peace terms, and the meeting of Parliament dispelled most of this careful fabrication. Only lower down in the social scale did it take root. When the election came round, the common people in Buckinghamshire were still afraid that James and a Popish army were about to arrive at any time. By then the Whigs were trying to expand their electoral platform from 'Popery and the Pretender' to claim the glory for defeating the Commercial Treaty, and even trying to steal the Tories' clothes by posing as the true protectors of the Church. But the defeat of the Commercial Treaty was patently a joint endeavour with the dissident Tories, and the latter claim convinced no-one. Both smack of a degree of desperation in the Whig camp to find a popular platform that they did not have to share with the dissident Tories.[5]

Tories of all kinds based their campaign on having achieved peace since 1710. The dissident Tories went beyond this to assert their Country principles and fidelity to the Protestant succession, which they had spent two years insinuating the Government was lax about safeguarding.

This was the best platform anyone could stand on in 1713, and they correspondingly did well. The Jacobites in England and Wales remained as interspersed in interests and representation throughout the body of the Tory party as they had been in 1710. They still did not consider themselves as having a separate identity outside the Tory party, so there were still no recognised leaders outside St Germain, and there was only *ad hoc* co-ordination of no greater significance than any other similar arrangements to be found between Tories with overlapping interests. The Jacobite Court this time left its adherents in no doubt as to whom it favoured in the election:

> You are ... desired to tell all your friends not only those of the College [Catholics] but all others of Juxon's family [Jacobites] whom you can trust that Jeremy [James] desires and expects from them that they'l spare no pains, and lose no time to employ all the influence they have upon Everard [elections] either by themselves or by relations or by acquaintances to perswad that gentleman to be firm to Cowley [Tories] and to unite with Charles Lawyers [ministry] and be directed by them in all that matter now in hand, that Hickman [Oxford] may see yt Juxon [James] is his friend [and] desires no better than to joyn stocks with him and trust his interest in his hands.[6]

Oxford was also to be quietly informed of the exiled Court's efforts on behalf of him and his ministry. The Jacobites would have undoubtedly supported their local Tory interest anyway, but Oxford's Government had been a sore disappointment and St Germain's exhortations were probably needed to rekindle their enthusiasm. Lichfield was certainly most obliging in helping viscount Fermanagh and John Fleetwood in Buckinghamshire, and lord Arundel contributed what he could to supplement the Beaufort interest in Salisbury.[7] Beaufort himself was absolutely tireless in trying to return Tories in constituencies from Wales to the Isle of Wight, with conspicuous success. He even managed to fight off Robert Pitt close by the Pitt family's electoral strongholds in the south-west, in Salisbury.[8] Lord Lansdowne proudly boasted that never before had an electoral manager been able to secure forty of the forty-four Cornish seats for the ministry, and that despite protracted delays in the requisite patronage because of Oxford's tergiversations. North and Grey succeeded in returning an M.P. of his own sympathies for Portsmouth on the Court interest.[9] Although this increase in Jacobite influence appears to be a dramatic change from 1710, the qualitative difference was nil. It remained the case that while a few more Jacobite M.P.'s were being returned, this was simply a function of more Tory M.P.'s being returned in general. Of a given number of Tory M.P.'s, some would have Jacobite sympathies, therefore if the number of Tory M.P.'s increased, so did the absolute number of Jacobites in Parliament. Although more Jacobites were now in positions of power and influence, they did not alter this ratio because they still did not consider themselves outside the Tory party. Because of this they were still striving to secure the election of 'honest' Country Tories, and as long as the candidate was not too aggressively pro-Hanoverian, as in the case of Robert Pitt, any man with Country Tory principles would do. Personal friendships mattered more than Jacobite principles in this context. Thus Peter Legh was quite content to continue returning his Nottinghamite High Tory friend, John Ward, while that gentleman's Finch associates were attempting to install the Hanoverian Tory earl of Barrymore at Wigan, to the detriment of the staunchly Jacobite George Kenyon. Conversely, the Jacobites did not expect to be, nor were they, distinguished from other Tory candidates by their fellow Tories in most cases, so nothing was thought of Bolingbroke helping to return Cresswell at Wooton Basset, or Beaufort asking lord Windsor for his interest for Sir Charles Kemys in Monmouthshire.[10] Because they were not at liberty to oppose the local choice of Tory candidate, even had they wished to do so (which few did), the Jacobites' influence in the 1713 election in England and Wales is once again irretrievably masked. All that can be said of it was that it remained generally distributed throughout the Tory interest in the political nation, and appears to have contributed at least its share to the party's success in 1713.

In 1710 the Harley ministry knew it had to have a clean sweep in the Scots Representative Peers elections in order to survive. A good deal of the ministry's efforts had therefore gone towards securing a good result there, with the attendant effect that once they were in alliance the Jacobites and the Court had done well in the Commons elections as a mutually supporting unit (though the ministry's support for the Jacobites was mainly confined to friendly neutrality). Because of their visible association with the new ministry, both partners had also had no qualms about making liberal promises of patronage which they were confident the Government would honour. In fact, between 1710 and 1713 precious little attention was paid to Scotland by the ministry, despite the pleas of the Scots M.P.'s for the promised patronage to consolidate what they had won. The Squadrone used this neglect to recoup and extend its electoral influence, almost entirely in the area of the Commons' elections. This was the easiest area for them to re-establish themselves, as the Scots peerage had more fundamental political divisions, and moreover had more to sustain its loyalty by being the recipient of whatever dribbles of patronage reached Scotland. Hamilton's death left the anti-Unionist peers almost permanently attached to the Court both at Westminster and in Scotland, and with this alliance frozen in support of it the ministry was assured of victory in any election of Representative Peers. This created a division between the Jacobite M.P.'s and the peers. The M.P.'s knew that careful retrenchment by the Squadrone, allied to the alarm created among moderate Presbyterian voters (who traditionally followed the Court's lead) by the measures that passed Parliament relating to Scotland between 1710 and 1713, was steadily undermining their electoral interests. The Jacobite peers had relatively little interest in Commons elections, apart from noted boroughmongers like

Hamilton, and saw no reason to pester the ministry for Commons patronage while their own position among the Representative Peers was secured by their alliance to it.[11] Without Hamilton's guidance the Jacobite peers were too caught up in pursuing their own concerns to act cooperatively on behalf of the M.P.'s, which was what would have been required to stir the ministry to action. Hence, the M.P.'s were left to shift for themselves.

Their only chance of retrieving the situation was to persuade the Government to give them copious patronage to distribute and to be seen to be the cause of the downfall of the Whigs who still staffed the Scots administration:

> The Tories in Scotland were in hopes to have been otherwise dealt with, and though their zeal carried them on at the last elections to interest themselves and carry a representation in both houses, which, I think, hath served the Queen very faithfully, the same will not continue, nay I am afraid will be found to be much cooled already by reason of the many disappointments and little encouragement they have met with, for if I be not much mistaken in the accounts I had and observations I made when I was lately in Scotland, there will be more difficulty than is imagined, or perhaps represented to your Lordship in making of right returns of either Peers or Commoners to the next Parliament, it being generally complained of, that those persons who did, and still continue to, oppose the Queen's measures are continued in offices of power and profit, that any few alterations that have been made are in favour of those who joined heartily with, or at best but trimmed during the last ministry, and such as did stand it out then, and have served the Queen since, have not interest to obtain the smallest favour either to themselves or their friends.[12]

In the meantime, the Squadrone had begun a vigorous election campaign before Parliament had even sat in 1713, and as early as May, Atholl was alarmed enough to write to London pleading that any two of Mar, Kinnoull or Balmerino be sent to help maintain the Court's interest. Rumours that Papist hordes were about to descend from the Highlands and kill all good Presbyterians were rife throughout Scotland, while Oxford was said to be about to defect to the Whigs as soon as the peace was completed. Such propaganda looks remarkably crude to the twentieth-century eye, but given the poor communications in most of Scotland, even compared with the rest of Britain, and the low level of political sophistication, such fabrications could still wreak great damage to the ministry's interest if unchecked. And the only thing that could check them conclusively would be the very purge to which the Government was so averse. The *coup de grâce* to the ministry's interest in the Commons elections in Scotland was administered when the Campbell interest defected to the Squadrone. Argyll and Islay had been growing steadily more restive ever since Oxford had first frozen the third Secretaryship of State which Islay so coveted, and then given it to his rival, Mar. Islay was visibly reforging the brothers' links with the Squadrone by May, and the process was completed in the wake of the Malt Tax crisis. Official retribution was held off, partly by Oxford's equivocation, possibly in the hope that the brothers would return once they had displayed their independence, and partly by Islay's impassioned (and insincere) denials of any collusion with the Squadrone.[13]

As far as the platforms espoused by the parties in Scotland were concerned, the 1713 election saw a very strange reversal of roles. The Malt Tax crisis had aroused considerable popular hostility towards the Union. The anti-Unionist, predominantly Jacobite, party would have been the group most likely to seize on this for electoral purposes under normal circumstances. However, because they had reluctantly, but consistently, gone along with St Germain's directive to support the ministry since 1711, they were linked in the public mind with the ministry and its policies. Also, the moderate Presbyterian vote which had given the Court the victory in the 1710 election by supporting candidates favoured by the Government had been alienated by 1713 by the Linen Act, the Hamilton affair, the Toleration Act and the Patronages Act. Finally, they had been roused to belated anti-Unionism by the Malt Tax crisis. Squadrone propaganda about the ministry's intentions in making peace and the threat to the Protestant succession completed their separation from the Government. The result was the loss to the Court of a widespread and vital section of its support. These moderate Presbyterians could not turn to the Jacobites because of their fears for the Kirk, yet they were at least temporarily in an anti-Union mood. The Squadrone neatly captured their support, in alliance with Argyll and Islay, by adopting an anti-Union, anti-ministerial, but pro-Hanoverian, position:[14]

> In managing the elections, the Whigs have recourse to their old topics of Popery and the Pretender, and the security of the Kirk, but these being bugbears they insist very much on the fatal consequences of the peace, the designed bad effects of the bill for commerce, and the necessity for having the Union dissolved, and though they themselves were the tools of bringing it about, they will not allow that any set of men besides themselves are for dissolving of it ... the Whigs have this advantage, that they are an united party, act by concert, and are supported by the best advice and the greatest encouragement of their great men, whereas the Tories are without a head, and every one does that which is right in his own eyes, and have not that weight which they might justly claim, by reason that so many who enjoy offices under her Majesty still appear against them.[15]

Oxford seems not to have realised what inroads the Squadrone-Campbell alliance was making into the Court's interest until Mar delivered the direst possible warning:

> If you do not now contrive some relief as to the Malt tax in Scotland and some redress for that of the peerage, it will not be in the power of man to prevent addresses from all in Scotland who are able to hold a pen against the Union by the meeting of next Parliament; and, if you do not very soon think of some things with regard to the elections there, in all probability such returns will be made as will not be much to your liking and I am afraid will tend more to your disquiet than perhaps you are aware of.[16]

This roused Oxford to action on the Malt Tax issue, but came too late to have much effect on the course of the Commons elections. Official denials of support for Islay and the Campbell interest were hurriedly despatched to Scotland, which served to prevent Islay being elected as one of the Representative Peers but could not alter the strength of their interest in the constituencies in time. Argyll remained 'in' as Commander-in-Chief of the forces in Scotland, and he did not hesitate to use all the influence attached to the office to return Campbell clients and Squadrone candidates.[17]

In the meantime the Jacobites had begun to rally the vestiges of their former organisation in Scotland to counter the Campbell-Squadrone alliance. The mainstay of this move was an attempt to distance themselves from the ministry and its policies, and Breadalbane told Atholl in June, in the aftermath of the failure of the attack on the Union, that the Jacobite peers had consulted and decided to return only hardline anti-Unionists in the Representative Peers' elections.[18] This movement towards a new consensus and solidarity among the Jacobite peers was halted by a fresh directive from the Jacobite Court, effectively committing them to Mar's care in support of the ministry in the elections:

> It being now the time that this business is in agitation I am order'd to reiterate the same directions to you in wch I do not doubt but you'l use all your endeavours with Cary [Lockhart], King and others of that kidney of your acquaintance that they may by themselves and by all others whom they can in any way influence, contribute to satisfy Mr. Cant [the ministry] that all Joseph's [James's] friends of Stirling's family [Scotland] are in his interest, it is hoped they may turn to both Jos: and Stirl.'s accts at least as far as we can judge in the darkness we are in, therefore I hope you'l be active in this matter and let Mr. Martel [Mar] hear from you upon receipt of this.[19]

The peers loyally did as they were told, though there were ominous rumbles at one point when Mar and Findlater seemed to be trying to have a list of sixteen peers returned on which there were not enough 'honest' (i.e. Jacobite) peers. This had been settled by the time the election took place, and, as in 1710, the combined Court and nationalist/Jacobite vote swept all before it. In fact, the outcome was so predictable even before the election was held that Islay could not even persuade his Squadrone associates to make an attempt at getting him elected. Instead, as in 1710, they ostentatiously boycotted the whole event.[20] The Commons had a much harder time of it altogether. The sheer preponderance of the Squadrone and Campbell interests when combined forced the Jacobites back on their safer seats, with consequent squabbling over who was going to be the candidate. The duchess of Hamilton's choice of a moderate Presbyterian, William Hamilton, to stand for Lanark Burghs as part of an electoral pact allowing Houston's and Sir James Hamilton's return for the shires of Linlithgow and Lanark, was vigorously opposed by the former Lanark Burghs Hamilton nominee, Colonel George Douglas. Picqued, he transferred the interest he had built up to a local Squadrone supporter, Sir James Carmichael, who was as a result able to renege on the pact and defeat William Hamilton at Lanark Burghs. The pact having been broken, Argyll was also able to put his weight behind the opposition to Houston in Linlithgowshire, where Houston was accordingly defeated (though he regained the seat on petition). In Elgin Burghs the Hon. James Murray, having been displaced from Dumfriesshire, promptly activated his interest there in his own favour rather than that of the Court, as he had done in 1710. This enabled him to defeat and replace Findlater's client Alexander Reid, the sitting M.P. In the duke of Atholl's family, a quarrel broke out when his brother, the sitting M.P. for the family's traditional seat of Perthshire, refused to surrender it to his nephew and defeated him in a contest. Lockhart was fortunate to escape with an uncontested election, but even that veteran anti-Unionist felt obliged to parade his opposition to the Union, so much had association with the ministry tarnished his reputation.[21]

The results of the Scots elections of 1713 were a mixed blessing for both sides. The Squadrone-Campbell alliance won a thumping victory in the Commons elections but were utterly vanquished in the elections for Representative Peers. Given the landslide Tory victory in England and Wales, it might seem the ministry had the best part of the exchange. The Representative Peers were certainly vital if it was to maintain itself in the Lords, but the Commons was the more important of the two Houses and the ministry's grip on it was loosened by this result. Because of the scale of the Tory victory in England and Wales, many new M.P.'s still burning with something of the old pro-Sacheverellite fervour had been returned, along with significant numbers of Hanoverian Tories favoured by the circumstances of the election in general. Both of these groups and the Government's increasingly restive Jacobite associates needed to be placated, at the same time as the number of docile Scots Court Tories available to support the ministry was drastically cut. Of the forty-five Scots M.P.'s returned in 1713, about twenty-nine were brought in by the Opposition. Of the sixteen Tories returned, about ten were Jacobites rather than ministerial Tories.[22] The net effect was to intensify the problem of conflicting expectations among militantly restive groups of backbenchers with which the Government was confronted, while at the same time reducing its room for manoeuvre.

NOTES

1. *Went. Corr.*, pp.353-4: Wentworth to Strafford, 13 Sept. 1713; Kreienberg 113a, ff. 176-7: 18 Aug. 1713; Fox-Strangeways MSS. (HPT): William Waterman to Sir Charles Fox, 13 Nov. 1713; Portland Loan 29/153/7: Poulet to Oxford [Sept. 1713]; v, 342-4: A. Carleton to Oxford, 1 Oct. 1713; vii, 139: Stratford to lord Harley, 11 June 1713; Claydon House Letters, M11/55: Elizabeth Fermanagh to Fermanagh, 11 May 1713.

2. Jervoise MSS. (HPT): Harris to Thomas Jervoise, 30 Oct. 1713; Erle MSS. (HPT): James Craggs to Lieutenant-General Thomas Erle, 21 Sept. 1713; Horwitz, *Politicks*, p. 240; Nat. Lib of Wales, Bettisfield MS. 32: Hanmer to Mr Hanmer, 13 Nov. 1714.

L

3. Portland, v, 258-60: [Jan. 1713].

4. *Went. Corr.*, pp.315-16: Berkeley to Strafford, 27 Jan. 1713; Hermitage GGG, f. 107: 20 Mar. 1713; Bonet 38C, f. 35: 20 Mar. 1713; Add. MSS. 47027, f. 12: G. Berkeley to Percival, 14 Mar. 1713; Gregg, *Queen Anne*, p.353.

5. Claydon House Letters, M11/55: John Bingby to Fermanagh, 4 Aug. 1713; Macpherson, ii, 439-40: Plunket to Ellis, 7 Oct. 1713 ns; *Went. Corr.*, p.351: Wentworth to Strafford, 8 Sept. 1713. For another view, see: Hill, *Growth*, p.140.

6. Carte 212, ff. 59-60: Nairne to Menzies, 19 Sept. 1713 ns.

7. Claydon House Letters, M11/55: Lichfield to Fermanagh, 28 May 1713; Beaufort MSS: Beaufort to Arundel, 15 Aug. 1713; MS Ballard 15, f. 107: Joseph Johnson to Charlett, 5 Sept. 1713; Hermitage GGG, ff. 365-6, 368: 13 and 16 Oct. 1713.

8. Beaufort MSS: to Charles Cox, 8 Aug. 1713; to Shrewsbury and Oxford, 15 Aug. 1713; to Kent, 10 Nov. 1712; to George Pitt, 20 Aug. 1713; to Oxford, 14 July 1713; Portland, v, 325: Beaufort to Oxford, 29 Aug. 1713.

9. Portland Loan 29/308/2: North and Grey to Oxford, 26 June 1713; Portland, v, 312, 315, 322, 330-1: Lansdowne to Oxford, 28 July, 2 and 19 Aug. and 11 Sept. 1713.

10. Holmes, *Politics*, p.90; Portland Loan 29/143/4: E. Harley to Oxford, 26 Sept. 1713; Horwitz, *Politicks*, p.240; Kenyon MSS. DDKe/98/15: Dr Kenyon to Anne Kenyon, 6 Aug. 1713; Beaufort MSS: Beaufort to Clayton Milbourne, 15 Aug. 1713.

11. Portland, v, 238: Lyon to Oxford, 20 Oct. 1712; x, 285-6: Mar to Oxford, 15 Dec. 1712 and 13 Jan. 1713; v, 313-14: Dupplin to Oxford, July 1713; Portland Loan 29/451 ii./19: Lockhart to Oxford, 21 Mar. 1713. There was also a strong sense of post-Union disillusionment arising from events since 1707, Lenman, *Jacobite Rebellions*, pp.96-106.

12. Portland, v, 252-3: Lockhart to Oxford, 28 Dec. 1712.

13. Portland, v, 291: Atholl to Oxford, 12 May 1713; v, 266-7: Defoe to Oxford, 14 Feb. 1713; v. 327: Islay to Oxford, 5 Sept. 1713; *Swift Corr.*, i, 388: Swift to King, 28 Mar. 1713.

14. Portland, v, 303-4: Kinnoull to Oxford, 2 July 1713; x, 297: Carstares to Oxford, 9 July 1713; Hamilton MS. 8806: [?] to the duchess of Hamilton [Dec. 1714].

15. Portland, v, 478-9: Lockhart to Oxford, 30 July [1713].

16. *Ibid.*, x, 296: Mar to Oxford, 12 June 1713.

17. Dalhousie 14/352/26: Balmerino to Maule, 23 June [1713]; Portland, v, 345: Findlater to Oxford, 8 Oct. 1713; Panshanger MSS. D/EP F54, ff. 3,5,8-9: Islay to Cowper, 25 and 31 Aug. and 1 Oct. 1713.

18. Blair Castle MSS., Box 45 Bundle 11, ep. 30: Breadalbane to Atholl, 13 June 1713; GD 248/561/49/28 41: the earl of Galloway to Findlater, 29 Sept. and 14 Oct. 1713.

19. Carte 212, f. 60: Nairne to Straton, 19 Sept. 1713 ns.

20. Portland, x, 298-9: Ogilvie to Oxford, July 1713; x, 303-4: Mar to Oxford, 6 and 8 Oct. 1713; Gregg, *Queen Anne*, p.369; GD 112/45/1: marked list of the Scots peerage, showing those ineligible to vote (41), Squadrone (29) and the combined Court and Jacobite group (85) [c.Oct. 1713].

21. Portland Loan 29/133/9: duchess of Hamilton to Oxford, 21 Sept. 1713; GD 150/3461/7 12: Douglas to Morton, 20 Mar and 23 Sept. 1713; 248/561/49/36: Murray to Findlater. 28 Sept. 1713; *CJ*, xvii, 486: 5 Mar. 1714; GD 18/3149/1: Lockhart to Clerk, 31 Mar. 1713.

22. Carte 212, ff. 60-1: Nairne to Menzies, 24 Oct. 1713 ns; *CJ*, i, 179-81; Gregg, *Queen Anne*, p.369; Macpherson, ii, 558-61: Polwarth to Robethon, 9 Feb. 1714.

8

'The King's service most at heart': the session of 1714

The session of 1714 was politically the most Byzantine of any encompassed by the period of Harley's ministry. The queen's illness over Christmas brought the question of the succession to the fore in a way that all the Opposition's polemics since 1711 had failed to do. With the queen visibly ailing, the new Parliament's attention was riveted on the succession, and it pervaded every question of note which was debated. The impending crisis gave, too, added urgency to the gathering campaign to purge the administration of Whigs. Bolingbroke, who was supported by the bulk of the Tory party in this aim, obviously had to move quickly if he was to carry the plan into practice. At the same time, both the Hanoverian and Jacobite Country Tories were determined to ensure that the succession question was resolved in the way they desired. To complicate the situation further, the one thing that all the Country Tories could agree on was their distrust of Oxford's intentions:

> All in generall of whatsoever Party were discontented with my Ld High Treasurer's obscurity, there not being a man in England who was thought to know his designs or presum'd to know them...what for these fears [of danger to the Protestant succession], disappointments in matter of Interest and debts of the Crown, there was scarce a man satisfyd at this time, not one who would take up the Lrd Trea'rs deffence.[1]

Compounding all these conflicting problems, ambitions and interests was the emergence of an overt power struggle at the highest level in the Tory party: Bolingbroke's bid to displace Oxford was now set to come out into the open. Their battle at court has often been studied, but without securing primacy in Parliament no victory there could be secure or final.[2] Hence, a major section of this chapter will be devoted to examining the two rivals' battle for supremacy in Parliament, bringing out the role of the backbench groups. The complexity of the situation demands this broader approach to the session, as without an appreciation of the general political situation and the activities of their Hanoverian rivals, an analysis of the Jacobites' role in these events would be unbalanced and hence much of their activity unintelligible.

The Hanoverian Tory group which formed up around Hanmer in the Commons and Anglesey in the Lords at the beginning of the 1714 session was a new departure. The group which Hanmer had led in the previous year had been formed on an *ad hoc* basis from the March Club and the moderately pro-Hanoverian elements of the October Club. For most of them the attack on the French Commercial Treaty was the swan-song of their old associations, and in the aftermath the group broke up into individual connexions, the March Club apparently disappearing in the process. Some went into permanent opposition, many lapsed into independent backbench Toryism, but about forty 'Hanoverian' Tories gathered around Hanmer in early 1714. The old Nottinghamite group was now virtually permanently in the Opposition camp alongside a few individual defectors like Aislabie and Chetwynd.[3] As these now formed a fixed part of the Opposition's strength, they were effectively excluded from influencing the policies of the ministry or the politics of the Tory party, and this was what Hanmer and Anglesey aimed at above all else.

The Hanoverian Tory split for most of the time amounted in practice to little more than ostentatious aloofness from the ministry and its policies. They remained determinedly Country Tory throughout, and hence felt little love for the predominantly Whig Opposition: 'The Whigg Party were stronger than any one Party of the Tories taken singly, but there was that perfect hatred to the whigs that all the Torys united in a considerable matter against them'. These feelings were heartily reciprocated by the Whig rank and file.[4] In controverted election cases the Hanoverian Tories always supported the Tory candidates, the only exception being if they suspected them of Jacobitism, as in the cases of John Lade's petitions for Southwark and Benedict Calvert's for Harwich. They adamantly refused to oppose any address of thanks proposed by the ministry for the peace obtained by the queen and her Government — which obliged the Opposition, to their chagrin, to allow such an address to pass *nem. con.* rather than pique their prospective allies.[5] Where the honour of the Tory party was concerned, they also had no compunction about silencing its Opposition detractors. The Hanoverian Tories co-operated willingly with the ministry in its attack on Richard Steele for his offensively Whiggish pamphlets, and showed little sympathy with his cause then or later.[6] Like the March Club before them, the Hanoverian Tories were very self-conscious about their need to demonstrate just how pure their Country Toryism was. From this came their ostentatious support for such unimpeachably Tory measures as the annual Place bill, the Schism Bill and the Court-inspired amendments to the proclamation against James formulated by the Opposition.[7] Co-operation with the Opposition was something the Hanoverian Tories viewed as a distasteful necessity, and when they did agree to it it was on the strict understanding that if the ministry fell, a joint Hanoverian Tory-Nottinghamite one would replace it. Nor would they accept the Opposition charge that the ministry had irrevocably committed itself to the Jacobite cause. Schütz told Baron Bothmer in March that 'Hanmer assures me, that our acts are in no danger during this session, and he will not allow that the ministry are against us [Hanover], nor for the Prince of Wales'.[8] When the Hanoverian Tories did take part in an Opposition attack on the Government, they tended to take a reserved position, as was the case over the state of the nation debate on whether the succession was in danger, when they simply argued that because the ministry had not disproved the Opposition's charges there must be something in them. Even then, Kay moved the previous question rather than face the issue head on, and when the Opposition tried to reopen the debate when the resolution was reported, the Hanoverian Tories wanted no part of it.[9] Strictly speaking, they did not constitute part of the Opposition during this session. Instead, the Hanoverian Tories took the part of independent Country Tory watch-dogs on the ministry's behaviour, checking it when it strayed from what they considered to be the right path. Their prime motive for maintaining this position was the positive aversion in their ranks to co-operating with the Opposition, for this thinned their numbers if they did so for any length of time.[10] The only exception to this was where the Jacobites were concerned. In such cases the Hanoverian Tories cheerfully accepted any amount of Opposition aid, as when they opposed the October Club's list of candidates for the Commission of Accounts.[11]

The Hanoverian Tories wished to extract three concessions from the Government by the threat of their allying with the Opposition. The first was that a member of the electoral family should be invited over to Britain, the second was that the administration should be thoroughly Toryised and the third, which developed only as their distrust of him increased, was that Oxford be dismissed.

They wanted a Hanoverian prince to come to Britain for two main reasons. A member of the incoming dynasty in residence and ready to assume the reins of power in the event of Anne's death was the best possible guarantee against a Jacobite *coup d'état* in the interregnum between then and the arrival of her successor in Britain. Such a situation would also allow the Tory party the opportunity to ingratiate themselves with the incoming dynasty and to establish an interest at the Hanoverian Court.[12] They were aware of the queen's antipathy to such a suggestion from memories of a painful humiliation on the same subject in 1705, and hence baulked at the idea of trying to address the queen for a formal invitation to one of the electoral house. Instead, the Hanoverian Tories hoped that if the duke of Cambridge (the future George II) arrived of his own accord, Anne would accept the *fait accompli*. Hanmer and Anglesey were correspondingly delighted when Schütz asked for Cambridge's Parliamentary writ and announced that he was on his way over. The queen's clear distress at the prospect appears to have touched them, however, and by the end of May they were suggesting that Cambridge should delay for a year.[13] The Hanoverian Tory leaders plainly saw this as only a respite while they won Anne over to their views, and it undoubtedly figured prominently in their demands when negotiating with Oxford and Bolingbroke.

The oft-delayed Toryisation of the administration by the ministry had become a major grievance to the Country Tories by 1714. In this the Hanoverian Tories were merely reflecting the feelings of their fellow backbenchers when they made it one of their principal demands. Their resentment at the situation was heightened just before the session began by the crisis in the Irish Parliament. Anglesey, who had considerable estates and influence in Ireland, arrived in London full of righteous Tory spleen, looking for disclosures from the ministry which would allow impeachment proceedings against the Irish Whig leaders.[14] Oxford hoped that Court support for Hanmer's election as Speaker and a few cosmetic removals of offending Whigs would placate the Hanoverian Tories, but these failed so to do. When Oxford tried to ease the Government's financial difficulties in Ireland caused by the enforcedly premature prorogation of the Irish Parliament — by revoking the drawback on tobacco re-exported from England to Ireland, to protect the future yield of the Irish revenue, it was the Hanoverian Tories who blocked it. By dividing with the Opposition they managed to tie the votes in the Supply Committee, and Hanmer then defeated it with his casting vote. Hope of redress for this grievance was a major element in Bolingbroke's attraction for the Country Tories, as he did not have a consistent record of prevarication on the issue to cast doubt on his promises, unlike Oxford.[15]

The removal of Oxford from his post did not become a central plank of the Hanoverian Tories' platform until the session had begun. When confronted with demands for purges by them before Parliament opened, he had as usual procrastinated and promised them action shortly. By 1714, however, the Country Tories, and in particular the Hanoverian Tories, would wait no longer. Apparently no extensive changes were being undertaken, and they finally lost all patience with him.[16] In the formal agreement made between the Hanoverian Tories and the Opposition as a prelude to joint action against the ministry, Oxford's removal became a central plank of their association:

> 1. To live in friendship with the Whigs, and to concert with them what must be done to secure the protestant succession, and oppose the Pretender.
> 2. Not to support lord Oxford, but to assist one another in depriving him of his employment.
> 3. Not to allow the Treasury to be in the hands of one man; but to put it in commission; that our friends [the Opposition] leave them to choose, for that purpose, as they may judge proper; all acknowledging that it was as necessary as it was prudent, to have in the Queen's council two or three persons who would be for the protestant succession, and in opposition to the Queen's ministers.[17]

Though intermittent negotiations between Oxford and the Hanoverian Tories never ceased entirely, the Hanoverian Tories stuck to this aim throughout the months that followed — and this orientated them in such a way as to draw them automatically towards Bolingbroke rather than his rival.[18]

The Hanoverian Tory rebellion of 1714 had definite objectives, just as the October Club had had in 1711. It was not simply factious. As in 1711, the elements of their policy were of an impeccably Country Tory pedigree, albeit with a pro-Hanoverian bias. The only new development was their regarding Oxford as the source of all obstruction and their consequent determination to be rid of him. Essentially, the Hanoverian Tories were 1714's equivalent of the Hanoverian Tory elements of the October Club in rebellion once again. Oxford had promised them a thoroughgoing Tory regime when the peace was concluded — their renewed activity was the Country Tory response to his mendacity.

All that remained of the October Club 1714 was a predominantly Jacobite rump. The former, basically pro-Hanoverian majority had either transferred themselves, via the March Club, to the Hanoverian Tories or Opposition, or reverted to being independent backbenchers. There had been no substantive change in the Jacobites' aims since 1712: they wanted the repeal of the Act of Succession and the institution of a Tory regime in Church and State. St Germain's orders had not changed either. Throughout the autumn of 1713 the Jacobites were directed to continue supporting the ministry in the next session. But annoyance with Oxford's 'negotiations' did produce one important change, just before the session began: 'I told him... that he must recommend to all his friends and acquaintances at M. Puysieux [Parliament] to oppose stoutly M. Horne [Hanover] without mentioning M. Raucourt [James], whose affaire will goe well, if the other once be cast'. The Jacobite Court eagerly, and the Parliamentary Jacobites more suspiciously, then awaited some Government action in their favour. When none materialised, Lockhart and Pakington, representing the more radical elements among the Jacobites, promptly advocated independent action to achieve their ends while continuing to support the ministry as long as it did not interfere with them.[19] The other Jacobites were not convinced of the wisdom of this, and preferred to wait on Bolingbroke's long hoped-for success in his struggle with Oxford, in the confident expectation that he would restore James. Much to their disgust, Lockhart and his allies were obliged to shelve the plan as a result. Nothing better illustrates the dire consequences of the lack of Jacobite leadership in Britain than this irresolution, which was reflected in all areas of Jacobite activity at this time.[20] Despite this false start and their chronic leadership problems, the exigencies of politics and the session's preoccupations inexorably reinforced their sense of unity and common identity. Jacobitism was under severe attack during 1714, and this increasingly obliged its adherents to drop their differences and make common cause against their opponents.

The Scots Jacobites led the way towards a more militant policy in the course of several more nationalistic moves. The Scots Jacobite peers initiated this process before Parliament was even opened, albeit on apolitical grounds. Virtually all the Representative Peers returned in 1713 were placemen then or shortly thereafter, on whom the Government relied for its majority in the Lords. Their places and pensions, so eagerly sought to begin with, were by 1714 their principal source of frustration. Oxford was willing enough to distribute largesse at moments of crisis, but very loth to pay the Representative Peers' wages in the normal course of events. In late January the Scots Jacobite peers inspired what was tantamount to a strike by the members of the Scots Board of Trade and several other peers. They refused to travel to London unless their wages and arrears were paid. Aware that his own credit was nil, Oxford forced Mar to promise payment as soon as they arrived, while desperately searching for Whig courtiers or poor lords whom he could win over.[21] The unhappy Mar meanwhile had to face irate Scots Jacobite peers demanding the promised payment:

> it makes them think themselves ill treated and more out of humour (and I cannot say but justly) than if they had never been made to expect it, so this must of consequence make us lose all credit not only with them but every body there who knows their story, and that will be no secret.[22]

Oxford and Mar eventually managed to coax most of them into coming south before the opening of Parliament, though Northesk, Eglinton and Breadalbane still held out. As Mar had predicted, this episode created considerable ill-feeling among the Representative Peers, and it ultimately required substantial payments by Oxford to keep them there.[23] Even then, they still felt no compunction about carrying through their election pledges to continue opposing the Malt Tax. A raid by them during the second reading of the Bill was thwarted only by Harcourt stalling for time, while the neighbouring taverns and coffee-houses were frantically scoured for pro-ministerial peers. Enough were found and the Bill was saved, but it was a grim situation for the ministry to be caught in.[24]

The Scots Jacobite M.P.'s began the session with a split in their ranks occasioned by the refusal of the majority of the Scots' steering group to fall in with Lockhart and Pakington's call for independent action. This rift was healed only gradually in the course of several co-operative endeavours during the session. Lockhart was chosen to present a joint demand from the Scots Jacobites to the ministry, requiring that they dismiss the Scots lord advocate after he had made a rabidly Whiggish speech. A Scots Ecclesiastical Revenues Resumption Bill was introduced by Lockhart, Murray, Carnegy and Campion. The furore this caused in Scotland led the ministry to invoke their ultimate sanction: Anne threatened to veto the Bill if it passed. This forced the Jacobites to change the Bill for one merely setting up a Commission to investigate the value, and uses made, of former ecclesiastical rents. A Scots Militia Bill was proposed, which Lockhart alone of the Scots Jacobites opposed, arguing that laws passed by one ministry to disarm Whig clans could be turned against Jacobite clans by another.[25] All these ventures served to restore the confidence and unity which the Scots Jacobites had lost at the beginning of the session. By June they were able to inspire a united raid by all the Scots M.P.'s on the Stamp Duty bill, which had offended the Scots by a provision for drawbacks to be paid on taxed soap used for washing English wool but not Scots linen:

> the stamp duty bill was recommitted by 154 to 101 votes ych is a very great blow to the Court, all our members wer for recommiting it ych is the 1st time they were at one in any vote this parliat, being very much incensed at the English for voting the soap imployed in their woolen manufactory free, and not soap imployed in our linnen ych was very partiall in the English.[26]

The Government replied by reintroducing the clauses the Scots had recommitted and then slowly pushing them through in the teeth of their opposition. This slowed the Stamp Duty Bill's passage considerably, so that it was still in the Committee stage in late June.

Concerted English and Scots Jacobite activity during March and April was limited to mutual support in the hearing of controverted election petitions. Despite dogged opposition from the Hanoverian Tories they were quite successful, and lost only two prospective recruits: John Lade and General George Hamilton (who was a very mild Jacobite if at all).[27] The Jacobites owed their success to the false position into which they usually manoeuvred the Hanoverian Tories. Because they were voting against prospective M.P.'s they suspected of Jacobitism, the Hanoverian Tories had to support their opponents in the petition, who, naturally enough, were usually Whigs. The independent Country Tories shied away from this, except where the candidate's Jacobitism was glaring, as in the case of Benedict Calvert, who was a *very* recent convert from Catholicism. Hence, the Jacobites tended to have weight of numbers on their side.[28] Otherwise, the Jacobites contented themselves with supporting the ministry against the Opposition's offensive.

The Jacobite radicals had not abandoned their plans for independent action despite their initial rebuff, and at the end of April Pakington and Whitlock suggested to the October Club that they attack the succession through an investigation of the list of regents kept in Schütz's 'black box':

> Le dernier article touchant la succession fut debattu il y a huit jours dans l'assemblée de la Cabale d'Octobre, ou 50 à 60 persones de ce parti se recontrant le Chevalier Packinton, soutenu du S. Whitlock representerent le desagrement qu'il y avoit pour eux de ne savoir quels Regens la Maison de Hannovre aura nome pour agir en son nom dans l'interregne, et la juste apprehension s'etre gouvernés par les whigs, leurs rivaux; qu'il leur convenoit de prendre des mesures en Parlemt pour se tirer de cette incertitude. Cette proposition n'ayant été goutée d'aucun de l'assembée, quoyque tous violents Torres, ces Messrs ne s'ouvrirent pas davantage, et ils ont laisse tomber cette affaire...[29]

Although this suggestion, first made to St Germain in 1713, was not adopted, political developments gradually encouraged the Jacobites to take a more aggressive line. In the debate on arrears owing to Hanoverian troops in British pay since 1712, they did so for the first time, nearly taking over the debate for their own ends and outstripping all present in their extremism. Around the same time Ormonde and North and Grey represented a forlorn hope of Jacobite peers, including twelve Scots, in symbolically voting for the Catholic heir against a Protestant claimant in an appeal before the Lords. Faced with a Hanoverian Tory list of approved candidates for the Commission of Accounts, the October Club fielded its own list, and after diligent canvassing had won the support of the independent Country Tories suspicious of any list backed by the Whigs, carried the election. During the struggle to bring in John Lade on petition after a second controverted Southwark election, the October Club managed to set a precedent disallowing Quaker votes. This was something they had been trying to achieve since 1712 and marked a signal success which can only have encouraged them to press their own initiative.[30] These events engendered an atmosphere of confidence and solidarity among the Jacobites, only for them to receive a rude shock when the Cabinet, which they believed favoured them, issued a proclamation against James on 21 June with a reward of £5,000 for his apprehension.

The Jacobites were outraged by this *dénouement*, and their anger was quickly exploited by the Jacobite radicals to lead them to action:

> I can assure you this measure has allarumed a great many people, & the Ox [Pakington] & some of us are upon considerations how to behave & have some thoughts that Ox & spyder [Lockhart] shoud propose to water [Parliament] yt Table [Cambridge] be desired to come to Fidler [Britain]. They think such a step & seconded by a certain set of men, will let Frog [Queen Anne] & orange [Bolingbroke] see they resent such odd proceedings, & 2dly yt if ye proposals be agreed to, it will bring matters to some clear light or another, ych they think better than to be alwise thus in the mist & ruind & betray by degrees.[31]

This plan was evidently abandoned as too risky, and an attack on the supply was agreed instead. The Stamp Duty Bill, already delayed by the Scots, was still in the Committee stage. It was the last Supply Bill still passing the Commons, but owing to general difficulty in getting supply through that session, the ministry could not afford simply to abandon it. The Jacobites first attacked it on 30 June, loading it with extra requirements to delay it. On 2 July, when resolutions draughted by the Bill's Committee were presented to the Commons, spurious amendments were proposed and debated to delay it further. Towards the end of the day as the House thinned, a snap division succeeded in defeating a proposed increase in the Buckram Cloth Tax.[32] Bolingbroke was under pressure in the Lords at this time, on account of the Spanish Commercial Treaty investigation. He was desperate to finish the session before anything damning was revealed, and so he promised the Jacobites whatever was necessary to buy them off:

> 'Tis true indeed that his Lordship did not particularly name the King's restauration, yet he expresst himself after such a manner, and gave such hints and innuendos, that it was obvious he intended I shoud understand what was the great thing he design'd and aim'd at. And he concluded his discourse by beseeching me to speak to these other gentlemen, with whom I was in concert to dispatch the supplies that so Parliament might be prorogued, till which nothing of consequence cou'd be done.[33]

The Jacobites eagerly accepted this 'promise', and the Stamp Duty Bill received an unopposed third reading.[34]

The final weeks of the 1714 session completed the metamorphosis of the Parliamentary Jacobites into an independent pressure group of some significance. This represented the apogee of the political initiative adopted by the Jacobite organisation in 1710 — notwithstanding the patent falsehood of Bolingbroke's promises. They had reached the point when they were on a par with the Hanoverian Tories in cohesion and direction, though not in leadership. St Germain also entered the political fray after years of fearful reticence, ordering the Jacobite courtiers to use their influence to help Bolingbroke in his struggle with Oxford. Ironically, this apparent success only just preceded Queen Anne's death and the collapse of all hopes of a restoration through political means. A military solution to the problem was immediately accepted as the only appropriate one in both Britain and Lorraine.[35]

Superficially, Oxford and Bolingbroke began the year relatively equal in terms of political strength. Oxford began the session much higher in the queen's favour than his rival. Bolingbroke, on the other hand, was popular with the Country Tories, whereas Oxford had no credit outside the Court and Treasury party and the Harlekins. Even the Opposition loathed him, though they were beginning to realise that Bolingbroke was a far greater threat. Bolingbroke's main line of attack was to destroy the queen's confidence in Oxford's managerial skill. If he could achieve that, nothing would remain to Oxford except the Harlekins, and his fall would become inevitable. The dissident Tory groups greatly complicated the political situation. Other than in the closing stages of the session, the Whigs' superior party organisation gave the Opposition between 100 and 150 votes in the Commons. Given the Country Tories' propensity for drifting home when they got bored or the weather improved, the ministry could muster between 200 and 250. Hence, if about fifty Tories began to divide with the Opposition, the ministry would be walking along a thin edge between success and failure every time, and would be extremely vulnerable to sudden raids. Thus both the Hanoverian and Jacobite Tories had to be kept out of the Opposition camp. Yet this was nearly impossible, as each wanted specific concessions certain to alienate the other. At the outset, the Hanoverian Tories assumed greater political significance because they were organised and ready, with a recognisable leadership, while the Jacobites were only a potential threat. By the close, the Jacobites had been matured from an inchoate mass into an organised body by the events of the session. By then, they were equivalent to the Hanoverian Tories in the threat they posed to the ministry. In the Lords the ministry's situation was even more delicate. Oxford boasted of a majority of eighteen peers in February.[36] Anglesey's squadron of around five was therefore significant, and enforced caution and careful management on the ministry in the Lords. The Jacobites had the numbers to be more troublesome, though nothing came of this. Still, it would have been unwise to assume that they would remain with the Government whatever its actions, so their sensibilities also had to be considered.

Oxford and Bolingbroke had completely divergent ambitions. Oxford's was the simpler: he wanted to survive as prime minister as long as the queen lived, and if possible after the Hanoverian succession. Bolingbroke wanted far more: he wanted to establish an unbreakable Tory hold on the institutions of Church and State with himself as the indispensable director. Fundamental to Bolingbroke's plan was the assumption that the electoral family would succeed the queen. He demonstrated this practically, all promises to St Germain notwithstanding, as soon as he felt he could manage without Jacobite support. Lansdowne found messengers waiting to leave for Hanover on Bolingbroke's behalf when he visited Kensington between 27 and 30 July. Queen Anne was surreptitiously arranging for a member of the Hanoverian house to visit her, just before her death. Hanoverian Tories figured prominently in the various Cabinet reshuffles rumoured in the aftermath of Oxford's fall. Conversely, prominent Jacobites looked like getting short shrift, Buckingham, Poulet, Ormonde and Lansdowne to be displaced at the very least. Bolingbroke always insisted that he had not intended anything detrimental to the Hanoverian interest at that time, and certainly did nothing to impede the succession, despite plenty of opportunity, when the queen died. To instance his flight to join James as proof of his secret Jacobitism is to practise hindsight. He was panicked in 1715 by ominous preparations for a gory Whig revenge and fled in sheer desperation.[37] The political circumstances of summer 1714 and spring 1715 were worlds apart.

Bolingbroke's aim was the establishment of a 'thorough' Tory regime. He set out to achieve this in two clear stages. The first was the reunification of the Tory party behind the ministry:

> this proposition is certain, that if the members of the Church of England, lay aside their little piques and resentments, and cement closely together they will be too powerful a body to be ill treated.[38]

Once achieved, this alliance of Country Tories and ministry was to be consolidated by a political purge throughout the administration, with the resulting vacancies being distributed on the basis of political loyalty and as required by local Tory interests. At the upper levels the new order would have been secured by a ruthless displacement of all Harleyites: Oxford and Dartmouth as well as the Jacobites already mentioned. The Court and Treasury places held by lesser Harleyites, such as Auditors Harley and Foley, would have been cleared too. The nature and extent of the intended changes are indicated by the remodelling of the Board of Trade shortly before the queen's death, and by the scale of the patronage network to have been established by the Scots Militia Bill.[39] The second stage was to make the Tory regime as near irremovable as possible. Bolingbroke hinted at how he intended to do this to D'Iberville in February:

> s'il convient que la Princesse ou le Duc d'Hannover soient les maistres de nommer des gens inconnus pour etre associés a la regence apres la mort de la Reyne, et tout de suite ils proposerent de faire un acte par lequel le Duc d'Hannover ne pourra se servi d'aucun etranger, ny dans ses conseils ny mesme dans sa maison, qu'il ne pourra donner aucun employs dans les cours étrangeres a d'autres qu'a nés dans les trois Royaumes, qu'il ne pourra sortir d'Angleterre sans la permission du Parlement, qu'il ne pourra entretenir aucunes troupes, mesme nationales de ses propres revenus, soit patrimoniaux, soit vennus de ses Estats d'Allemagne, ou de la liste civile qu'il n'employera aucuns étrangers sans exception ny dans les trouppes nationales, ny dans la marine, que la Grande Bretagne ne poura etre impliquée dans aucune guerre pour les interests

particuliers de sa maison ou de ses Estats à Allemagne, ny pour ceux de l'Empire, qu'il ne luy sera mesme pas permis d'y inviter le Parlement, qu'il declarera les noms de ceux qu'il a résolu d'associer a la regence.[40]

This would have had to be supplemented by a moratorium on any dismissals from office for a fixed period after the Hanoverian succession. Altogether, this was a most unpalatable mixture to expect the electoral family to swallow. Two measures were therefore planned to sweeten it and disarm the inevitable Opposition charge that it was all a Jacobite plot: the restoration of Marlborough to the Captain-Generalship and British involvement in the Great Northern War. Marlborough's return to command of the Army would have removed the sting from Opposition claims that the Army was unreliable as regards the Protestant succession. Since they had lauded his martial ability and fidelity to the Hanoverians for years, his return to the office in which they had argued the nation required him would have hoist them with their own petard. Marlborough's reinstatement would also have given Hanover a token of the new ministry's determination to uphold the Hanoverian succession.[41] Hanover entered the Northern war in 1713 by occupying the Swedish possessions of Bremen and Verden. Britain had been moving steadily, if reluctantly, into conflict with Sweden since 1709 owing to depredations by Swedish privateers. Only a week before the queen died, a naval squadron was ordered to convoy British ships to and from the Baltic.[42] George I used the same situation in 1717-19 to involve Britain in the war on Hanover's behalf. Bolingbroke could easily have given 'helpful' instructions to the squadron, ending Swedish command of the Baltic. Given the elector's concern for the welfare and aggrandisement of Hanover,[43] this would have been a tempting offer and must have improved relations with the incoming dynasty.

Bolingbroke aimed at achieving the Tory millennium through the political situation of 1714. This would have left the Tories with the administration and the Church as their exclusive preserve, while Marlborough's command of the Army would have guaranteed equal or Whig-biased access to preferment (depending on his own political advantage). Central to the whole scheme was a rapprochement between the electoral family and the Tory party so as to ensure the continuation of the Tory regime beyond the Hanoverian succession. Shaky as this scheme may appear to modern historians, it attracted the Bolingbroke faction. They hoped to establish a Tory State and win Hanover's acceptance of it, thus guaranteeing its future and their own. What mattered was that they believed it could be done, not whether or not it was actually possible.

Both Oxford and Bolingbroke were active well before Parliament opened as they sought support for the expected confrontation. Each concentrated on winning over the dissident Tory groups by offering to satisfy their demands. Oxford's approach was based on going over the heads of the Parliamentarians to whatever source of external authority they accepted: Hanover for the Hanoverian Tories, St Germain for the Jacobites. Bolingbroke based his on winning over the dissident groups by negotiating with their leaders or prominent men in Parliament. These differences in approach were not absolute, and sometimes both men tried the alternative method. Oxford's was motivated by an appreciation of how much the backbenchers distrusted him, which aversion made it futile to try and win them over in London. By eliciting support from those they respected overseas, he stood a greater chance of making them co-operate with the ministry than by trying to buy their aid with his now valueless promises. Bolingbroke's method was forced on him by Oxford's advantage of position as prime minister. He was debarred from making approaches over the heads of the Parliamentarians as this would have been grossly exceeding his office — an error which Oxford could have exploited to demand his dismissal. This meant he had to make the most of his position as the militant alternative to Oxford, outflanking him on grounds of party principle by greater extremism.

Both men had equal access to the source of the Jacobites' orders, so each wooed the Jacobite Court in an attempt to win over its adherents at Westminster. The rivals separately offered the same inducement: *eventual* restoration in return for James's conversion to Anglicanism and other 'minor' concessions. The intention in each case was to convince the exiled Court that the politician concerned was an 'honest' man. Thus each man demanded hard concessions from St Germain, but offered nothing substantial himself. The gambit did not work in either case, though it served to prevent direct support for either one of the rivals as St Germain, bemused, sought refuge in neutrality. While not a gain, this at least meant that the opponent did not have the backing of the exiled Stuarts. Sporadic attempts to break this down in favour of one of them continued for the duration of the session.[44] Oxford at one point considered doing something practical to bring St Germain over, by paying Queen Mary's dowry, but Bolingbroke's confederate, Harcourt, foiled him by refusing to put the great seal to any authorisation for such payments. Bolingbroke, meanwhile, bypassed St Germain to play off the Parliamentary Jacobites' Toryism against their Jacobitism. By insinuating among them that once his Tory regime was established, after Oxford had been ousted, he would move to restore James, he not only stifled the Jacobite radicals' plan for independent action, but converted most of the Jacobites at Westminister into active sympathisers.[45]

Oxford made his most determined effort diplomatically in an attempt to win Hanoverian support. Again, aware that his own credit was negligible, he made full use of other people's. The queen and Bromley provided the front for this initiative, in which he offered anything he felt had any credibility: diplomatic support for Hanover in Germany; payment of the Hanoverian arrears; even a half-promise that the ministry would invite over Cambridge.[46] All this was undertaken in the hope of pressurising the Hanoverian Tories into staying aligned with Oxford and the ministry, and of softening the Opposition's attitude towards him. Oxford did try to reinsure against failure at Hanover by negotiations with the Hanoverian Tory leaders, but they demanded more concessions than Oxford would give, reducing the discussions to an exchange of insincerities. He ended by just trusting to their basic party loyalty and the hope that the Irish crisis would alienate them from the Opposition sufficiently to keep them attached to him and his ministry. As Gaultier reported to Torcy: 'nous croyons presentement que les affaires d'Irlande les reuniront a Nous'. Bolingbroke did not have access to Hanover for negotiations, so he concentrated on winning over the Hanoverian Tory leadership. He failed to gain their open support, but impressed them with his militancy — a good start when dealing with Country Tories after four years of Oxford's procrastination.[47]

Bolingbroke spent early March demonstrating his capacity as a political manager. Oxford, whose neglect of the backbenchers stemmed more from an appreciation of the futility of his wooing them than from idleness, could do little while his rival usurped his prime function. This culminated in a signal success for Bolingbroke mid-month, when he persuaded the Cabinet to endorse his proposal for a purge of pro-Opposition Army officers.[48] He then displayed his formidable eloquence backing Oxford's proposal to introduce a Bill barring the introduction of foreign troops into Britain on any pretext. This was intended to discourage the Opposition's attempts to inveigle Hanover into trying a repeat of 1688, and this it succeeded in doing. However, it also gave Oxford the opportunity to make a devastating riposte after the debate, by threatening to resign.[49] This totally disconcerted Bolingbroke's supporters, who still shrank from the thought of driving Oxford out of office and planned only to 'put a Junto' on him to remove his managerial capacity. Bolingbroke had, doubtless, no illusions about removing Oxford completely, but he obviously had not brought his friends round to that position yet.[50] Panic about the fate of the ministry without Oxford leading it was transmitted, with his careful assistance, to the queen, who received dire warnings of the imminent triumph of the Whigs if he was allowed to go. This galvanised her into publicly refusing to accept his resignation at a Cabinet meeting on 24 March. Bolingbroke tried to maintain the Cabinet's decision to purge the Army and other institutions, but could find no support, Oxford having put him in the position where insisting on this was to go against the queen's choice of minister by trying to make him do what he implied he would rather resign than do. Persistence would only have brought calls for his own dismissal, so Bolingbroke gave up and retired to lick his wounds.[51] This was a clever piece of political footwork by Oxford. Unable to fight his enemy on the backbenches due to his lack of credibility, he transferred the combat to an arena where he was stronger and routed his foes by manoeuvring the queen into making a public statement of her support for him. This was fine as far as it went. Bolingbroke was defeated, not destroyed, and would recover. Moreover, the threat of resignation was too dangerous to use again. Anne was never fond of being dragged onto the political stage, and undoubtedly did not relish being manoeuvred into supporting Oxford by the implicit threat that he would throw her back to the Whigs if she refused. Nor would Bolingbroke's friends be so disconcerted by a threat of resignation again. It was now clearly a fight to the finish, and alignment with Bolingbroke henceforth signified a determination to have Oxford out.

Oxford's supporters hoped for some respite after this coup, which they urged him to use to consolidate his position with the queen. But he had little time for that before the Opposition's offensive created another crisis: Schütz's request for Cambridge's Parliamentary writ of summons. Oxford was partially to blame for this because he had implied that the ministry would be happy to see Cambridge in Britain if they could arrange it themselves.[52] As prime minister, Oxford had to bear the blame too when the request was considered in Cabinet before the irate Anne, and also had the miserable duty of upholding the Hanoverian demand. Unless he did so, he could not hope to establish an interest with Hanover, but by doing so, on whatever grounds, he displeased the queen. Oxford also had to send a spate of assurances and promises of imminent action to St Gemain for fear lest they give way to their frustration and launch a military adventure in response to the news. Even his backing the Hanoverian case was negated by the queen's insistence that it should be he who prevented Hanover using the writ he had obtained.[53] All this was a golden opportunity for Bolingbroke to improve his standing with the queen, and he exploited it to the full. In Cabinet he opposed Oxford's legally correct assertion that the writ could not be refused. Outside the Cabinet Bolingbroke cheerfully boasted of his efforts to make the ministry stand up to the Opposition, while promulgating rumours that Oxford had engineered the whole business to curry favour with the electoral family.[54] By relentless exploitation of Oxford's vulnerability, Bolingbroke more than recovered the ground he had lost in March from this one incident alone.

Oxford's position deteriorated in general throughout April notwithstanding the fracas over the Cambridge writ. He continued to try to win over both the Hanoverian Tories and prominent men in the Opposition, without any success.[55] Bolingbroke was meanwhile in the favourable position of having his proposals vindicated by the extremism of the Opposition attack on the ministry. This enabled him to gain credit from every development. Opposition factiousness not only highlighted his own case, but also the usefulness of his more zealous adherents, such as North and Grey, Leeds and the earl of Clarendon. While Oxford was forced to ask the queen to do his canvassing for him, Bolingbroke played the honest broker, introducing the Hanoverian Tories to Queen Anne to explain their case, and openly sympathising with their grievances. When they voted against the ministry, Bolingbroke was free ostentatiously to urge that they be purged — by Oxford. After eloquently applauding his rival's justification of the Government's subsidising of the clans, he was able to abort a proposal to vote a resolution of thanks specifically directed to Oxford. In the aftermath of the close vote in the Lords on whether the succession was in danger, he was able to humiliate Oxford at a Cabinet meeting by raising the issue of the purges Oxford had been charged with carrying out and had not completed. Queen Anne formally reprimanded Oxford and Ormonde volunteered to act as his guarantor for their future implementation.[56] Significantly, Oxford did not threaten to resign again, indicating how far his position had deteriorated since March.

To extricate himself from his increasingly precarious situation, Oxford needed to create a new alignment to back him from the groups then operating at Westminster. Characteristically, he tried to work up an alliance of Harleyites, Hanoverian Tories and some moderate Opposition Whigs. These were to be united on a common policy of securing the Hanoverian succession. Unfortunately for Oxford, neither the Hanoverian Tories nor the moderate Whigs showed any inclination to trust him without a concrete demonstration of his sincerity. He chose to give them this on an issue calculated to please Hanover too: the payment of the arrears of Hanover's military subsidy.[57] This was, however, an issue which all sections of the Tory party, other than the Hanoverian Tories and Harleyites, were certain to oppose him on. Memories of the Auxiliary troops' 'desertion' of Ormonde's Flanders army in 1712 still rankled, and Bolingbroke's friends only had to give the lead, supported by prominent non-aligned Country Tories like Bromley, for the Tory backbenchers, delightedly headed by the Jacobites, to block the proposal in the Supply Committee to pay the arrears by adjourning the question indefinitely. This left Oxford badly compromised with the Jacobites and other Country Tories, and estranged from his erstwhile allies, as both the Hanoverian Tories and the Opposition suspected him of duplicity in the affair. Despite desperate attempts to pose as the embattled guardian of the succession in the aftermath, he was as a result more isolated than before. Bolingbroke emerged from the affair with his hold on the Tory party (except the Hanoverians and Harleyites) strengthened. The Jacobites soon convinced themselves that his conduct was evidence of his Jacobitism. The other Country Tories were impressed by his determination to uphold the integrity of the party regardless of the Opposition's jibes.[58]

Bolingbroke was now situated to try to drive his rival out of any semblance of control of the Tory party. With the Jacobites and other Country Tories now wholeheartedly backing him, he needed only to win the Hanoverian Tories over to replace Oxford, de facto, as the ministry's Parliamentary leader. To achieve this he needed to polarise the parties along traditional lines. His instrument for doing this was the Schism Bill. The Hanoverian Tories were very conscious of the need to restate their Toryism after dallying with the Opposition in April and early May, and made full use of the opportunity to parade their principles by taking a leading role in the Bill's passage. Indeed, the rallying call of an attack on the Dissenters, and hence the Whig interest, was so strong that only a handful of diehard renegades and Nottinghamites remained with the Opposition against the Bill.[59] Oxford could not oppose the Bill openly, as its passage would reveal that he had lost control of Parliament, as well as going against the queen's wishes. If, however, he did not oppose it somehow he would completely alienate the Whigs, who were by now his only hope of staying in power, and whose price had been steadily climbing since the Hanoverian arrears debacle. Oxford compromised by voting for it himself, but

M

having his followers divide with the Whigs. This mollified them a little, but also effectively severed his remaining ties with the Tory party in the eyes of the backbenchers. The queen was also turning from him despite his constant criticism of Bolingbroke and his plans whenever he saw her. Oxford's clumsy attempts to ingratiate himself with Hanover and the Whigs by claiming he had really wanted the electoral Prince to come over cannot have endeared him to her, and he had patently failed to foster better relations with Hanover as she desired. The first indication of her dwindling patience came at the end of May when she cut through Oxford's procrastination about sending a fresh envoy to Hanover by despatching Bolingbroke's friend Clarendon. Oxford did not want a new envoy sent to Hanover lest he return with more unpleasant demands, so it was obvious he would try to delay Clarendon's departure. The queen circumvented this by ordering that his expenses be paid out of the privy purse.[60]

Bolingbroke had only won the Hanoverian Tories' guarded support for one specific piece of legislation. To convert this into a firm attachment, he had to capitalise on their goodwill, generated through mutual co-operation in passing the Schism Bill, by convincing them of his commitment to the Hanoverian succession. After a short hiatus while he retrieved the Stamp Duty Bill after the Scots had recommited its resolutions (which he carried off so well that suspicions were voiced that he had set up the whole affair to display his skill as a political manager), and aware that the Country Tories were growing weary of the session, Bolingbroke decided on a dramatic gesture to prove his reliability. He persuaded the queen to issue the proclamation against James formulated by the Lords in April. The Hanoverian Tories were delighted, and promptly added £100,000 to the reward offered by the queen from the Civil List by a vote in the Commons. The unenthusiastic Hanoverian Tories were surprised but not unhappy with the proclamation. The Jacobites were furious.[61] Bolingbroke knew that there could be trouble from this quarter due to his part in the proclamation's issue and hastened to obscure his role by spreading rumours that he had been forced to do it to pre-empt Oxford, who had been planning it all session. Oxford did his best to steal the glory by posing as the originator of the proposal to the Whigs, but simultaneously told the Jacobites that he had not only opposed it in Cabinet, but also would try to prevent its publication. Nothing better exemplifies Oxford's fall from grace with the Jacobites than their response to this overture: they ignored it. They were determined to revenge themselves on Bolingbroke, but not out of any attachment to Oxford. Pressed by the Jacobites' attack on the vital Stamp Duty Bill in the lower, and the Lords' investigation of the Spanish Commercial Treaty in the upper, House, Bolingbroke traded on his good reputation among the Country Tories to lie his way out of trouble with truly Harleian aplomb.[62] With the Jacobites back under control, Bolingbroke had finally achieved what he had set out to do at Westminster. Bolingbroke rather than Oxford was now the acknowledged leader of the reunited Tory party.

Having struck an attitude of militant Hanoverianism over the proclamation,

Bolingbroke now tried to establish a consistent reputation for it by backing swingeing measures against unauthorised recruitment of British subjects for foreign armies, capitalising on the alarm generated by the discovery of French officers recruiting in England and Ireland. Oxford meanwhile prepared one last desperate thrust with which to unseat his opponent.[63] This consisted of feeding the Opposition with information and witnesses from his own following, such as Robert Monkton, so that they could uncover Bolingbroke and Moore's alleged corruption during negotiations on the Spanish Commercial Treaty. Initially, this plan worked brilliantly. The Opposition worked steadily closer to Bolingbroke, who was saved from questioning at one point only by the queen's refusal to divulge the names of the ministers who had advised her to sign part of the treaty. By 3 July Bolingbroke was so alarmed about his probable fate that he wrote to Oxford begging to be reconciled. Oxford ignored the plea, only for Bolingbroke to make a sudden recovery in the last few days of the session. By the close, he had managed to convert himself from a corrupt minister into a Tory martyr backed by all sections of the party except the Harleyites.[64] Oxford's plan also misfired by angering the queen with some of the addresses voted by the Harleyites and Opposition. She returned steadily curter replies, culminating in one so tart that Anglesey wanted to address for the name of the minister who had draughted it. Officially, the author was Oxford, as Anglesey must have known, but he, Shrewsbury and Bolingbroke all advised against this response, so the sentiments were definitely the queen's. The Opposition leaders were displeased by Oxford's failure to prevent Anne proroguing Parliament before they had succeeded in pinning Bolingbroke down, and this effectively terminated their alliance with him. Oxford fought on doggedly after the prorogation, but could not prevent Bolingbroke winning over the courtiers, such as Shrewsbury, while retaining his grip on the Tory party. With these and the queen in his favour, Bolingbroke was proof against all Oxford could do and merely had to await the arrival of Marlborough to complete his plans. When this became imminent, Oxford was curtly dismissed by Anne while Bolingbroke dined with Opposition military officers to gauge the Army's probable attitude to the forthcoming changes.[65]

Bolingbroke won his battle with Oxford by judicious use of his unsullied credibility and the general appeal of his policies among the Country Tories. He used this attraction to end the Hanoverian Tory schism, break the Opposition offensive and carry the war to them through the Schism Bill. All these were achievements Oxford could not match. The Tory backbenchers' patience with moderate men and measures had expired in 1711. All that had kept them in check until 1714 was their desire for peace, which Oxford could guarantee. Otherwise, the only policy Oxford had to offer them was one of total inactivity covered by an everlasting fund of promises that were never honoured. By 1714 his pusillanimity was rewarded when the party slipped from his control, apparently doomed to irreversible fregmentation — in effect, destroyed by Oxford's 'moderating' schemes. Bolingbroke had the broad appeal necessary to reunite it, and so became the only one of the two who could offer Anne the option of keeping out the Whigs and securing her chosen ministry.

Having established the course of the struggle between Oxford and Bolingbroke at Westminster, and the part played in it by the Jacobites and Hanoverian Tories, it is now appropriate to examine the part they played in the various crises of the session. This will establish their influence on these crises and how these in turn dictated the course of the struggle between the two rivals and hence the future of the Tory party.

The Steele debate was a classic party clash along traditional lines. The Whigs fought to delay action on the issue, while trying to widen the scope of the debate to allow as broad an attack as possible on the ministry. Clearly, the wider-ranging the debate, the more chance they had of exacerbating the divisions in the Tories' ranks. For its part, the Government tried to keep the argument focused on whether Steele's writings were seditious or not.[66] Their success can be measured by the fact that the Whigs only managed to draw to them a few Nottinghamites and long-lost renegade Tories. What concerned the Country Tories was that Steele, as Barker put it, 'brings her Majty into contempt as having broke her word with her Parl.' Consequently, both Hanoverian and Jacobite Tories were prominent speakers against Steele and co-operated fully in securing his expulsion. To both groups the issue went no further than the need to vindicate the queen's good sense in installing a Tory ministry and making an example of Steele to discourage other Whig polemicists from abusing ministerial achievements of which the Country Tories approved.[67] Measures they had endorsed were not to be calumniated by Whig hacks, but this did not mean that they were defending the ministry itself. It was from this fact rather than from the handful of Tories dividing with them that the Opposition's leaders took comfort after their defeat.

For the opposed Country Tory groups, the debate on whether the succession was in danger was an opportunity to try and drive the ministry closer to their viewpoint. The Hanoverian Tories tried by a threatened alignment with the Opposition, the Jacobites by zealously upholding the Government's cause while pushing its position in the direction they desired. The Hanoverian Tories in the Lords took a bellicose stance against the ministry. Anglesey stated no particular reason why he felt the succession to be in danger, other than that many peers seemed to think it was, but went on to suggest this was the result of a dishonourable peace very different from what had been promised. In the Commons, Hanmer and his friends took a far more cautious attitude:

> the Speaker spoke against it and severall others of our friends and voted accordingly, wch they woud not have done if the Division had been upon the main Question, no instances were given by them of the succession being in danger, but because there was a pretender and he not removed from Lorraine.[68]

The occasion for this difference in approach lay partly in Anglesey's disposition. He was a man who took a violent stand on every issue and for or against every ministry. He was also pushed into taking a more hostile attitude than perhaps originally intended, by North and Grey's deliberate insistence on voting directly on whether the succession was in danger. His speech caused something of a sensation, as well as giving Bolingbroke the opportunity to speak 'like an Angell' defending the ministry, while slyly parading his endeavours to force James out of Lorraine.[69] The Jacobite speakers for the ministry in the debates were numerous: North and Grey and Ferrers in the Lords, Bulteel, Eversfield, Shippen, Campion, Lockhart and Whitlock in the Commons. North and Grey pushed the Lords' debate to extremes by insisting on the final vote being on the question of whether the succession was in danger, instead of an adjournment motion as Oxford intended. Having forced the Hanoverian Tories into an uncomfortably militant position, North and Grey, abetted by Leeds, amended the Lords' reply to the queen's answer to the address on the succession not being in danger so as to imply that public concern on the matter had been concocted by the Opposition. This provoked a long debate and was only passed by a narrow margin.[70] In the Commons the Jacobites tried to widen the scope of the argument to suggest that if the succession was in danger the Hanoverians deserved it, and if not, that the Hanoverian Tories were traitors to the party to forget Hanover's behaviour over the peace so soon. Eversfield fiercely attacked the conduct of the Allies during the war. Lockhart exposed Squadrone preparations for an uprising in Scotland, with the obvious inference that they had been made with Hanoverian connivance. Shippen came close to an outright statement of the Jacobite case by ostensibly criticising Nottingham for allegedly asserting that no law could bar proximity of blood, thus implying the illegality of debarring James from the throne at all.[71] Between them the two opposed groups did not move the ministry in either direction: they merely counterbalanced. What they did succeed in doing was to precipitate a fresh crisis of confidence in the Government, which could only work in Bolingbroke's favour.

At the end of the Lords' debate on the succession Bolton suddenly proposed an address requesting that a reward be put on the Pretender's head for the presentation of his body dead-or-alive to the authorities. This caught the ministry and the Jacobites unawares, despite a similar resolution passed by the Irish Whigs the previous year, and signs of the same thought occurring to the Opposition in March. The only resistance was a few desultory calls for adjournment which the Opposition ignored, passing the motion *nem. con.*[72] Neither the ministry nor the Hanoverian Tories were averse to such a proclamation in principle, though they regarded the wording with distaste. The only serious opponents were the Jacobites and, unexpectedly, the queen. She seems to have disliked the wording intensely, and ordered the ministry to amend it, even adding her personal authority to keep the Hanoverian Tories neutral. Consequently, when the resolution was reconsidered the Jacobites were guardedly seconded by the Court in a successful attempt to remove the dead-or-alive provision, and made the proclamation's issue at her Majesty's pleasure. North and Grey and Buckingham led the attempt, which they grounded on the wording being an offence to all civilised nations, and this was confirmed on legal grounds by Trevor.[73] The Jacobites also made what capital they could out of the situation in propaganda terms:

> il y avoit un vieux seigneur Ecossois qui avoit plus de 80 anns [Breadalbane] qui a dit dans la chambre des Peres que ce Pretendent faisoit bien du bruit et il vouloit scavoir qui il estoit, et turnant vers le Duc de Bucquingham...; il dit voyla un seigneur qui a ce qu'on dit estoit dans la chambre de la Reine pendant son travaille d'Enfant qu'il nous disse qu'il a veu. Le Duc dit messeigneurs il est vray que j'estoit alors dans la chambre j'ay veu naitre le Prince en question et cela est si vray que les particularites de ce que je veu d'un enfant nouveaux né furent tells que la Modestie m'empecher de les tous dire. Mais je suis encor sure qu'il n'y avoit point d'imposture sur cette occasion.[74]

The matter was then forgotten until Bolingbroke induced the queen to order the proclamation issued on 21 June. The Jacobites could do little but protest in impotent fury against demeaning the queen's gesture by capping her offer of £5,000 with an additional £100,000, as the Hanoverian Tories and Opposition were advocating. Moderately pro-Hanoverian Tories also found this excessive, as indicated by Bromley's criticism of the size of the reward, but the Jacobites were too unsure of them to risk a division.[75] The course of the proclamation issue epitomises the vulnerability of the Jacobites to such ploys. There was little they could do to change or reject an anti-Jacobite resolution once it had been introduced. They were only able to amend it in April because the queen disliked the wording, otherwise the result would have been the same then as it was in June: angry but impotent Jacobites confronted by tacit acceptance of the measure by the rest of the Country Tories. The affair also shows how Bolingbroke could have forced pro-Hanoverian legislation past the Jacobites had his scheme come to fruition.

Schütz's request for Cambridge's Parliamentary writ was the final stage of an Opposition campaign lasting over a year. The Opposition leaders hoped that Cambridge's arrival would trigger the permanent defection of enough dissident Tories to bring down the ministry. In such an event they expected that the queen would accept the *fait accompli* and appoint a mixed administration including them.[76] This was a strategic political error of the first order. Anne was absolutely determined not to have a successor in residence while she lived, and never forgave Nottingham for a similar attempt in 1705. Her attitude had hardened in the intervening years. Although she seems to have considered allowing a visit by one of the electoral family just before she died, that was as a political expedient at her initiative and on her terms. In all probability she would have rejected out of hand any Parliamentary proposal of this kind. The Hanoverian Tories were reticent about forcing the issue in Parliament for exactly that reason, though they patently hoped that if Cambridge arrived uninvited Anne would accept his presence and dismiss Oxford, leaving them to head an uncompromisingly Hanoverian Tory ministry. All this centred on one assumption: Anne would accept Cambridge once he was in Britain. When she made it clear she would not, their determination fell away, although they continued to pay lip-service to the Opposition's pleas that Cambridge be sent over.[77] It was popularly assumed that Cambridge's arrival would be the death-knell of the Jacobites' hopes, and therefore a Jacobite rising was certain to greet him. In fact the Jacobites were almost completely unprepared militarily, and were in reality helpless observers of the crisis created by Schütz's request.[78] The effect of this episode on the nature of British politics was profound. Thereafter the Opposition could hope for nothing from the queen. Their delight at Schütz's request and their barely concealed plotting had finally alienated her completely.[79] This meant that thenceforth the Tory party's internal politics were all that really mattered. Jacobites or Hanoverian Tories might use the Opposition as a buttress from which to harass the ministry, but as an alternative to a Tory Government the Opposition might as well have ceased to exist.

The question of the Hanoverian arrears was a contentious one in the Tory party. Most of the Country Tories were disinclined to pay them as a suitable punishment for George's withdrawal of his troops serving under Ormonde in 1712 after the restraining orders were revealed. The Jacobites were opposed in principle. The Hanoverian Tories agreed with withholding the Auxiliaries' arrears in general, but thought that Hanover should be specifically excepted. The Harleyites wished to pay them to bolster their leader's position in Hanover and Westminster. Bolingbroke's friends wanted to thwart Oxford and make interest with the Country Tories. When the matter was debated in the Supply Committee, the Harleyites, Hanoverian Tories and Opposition united in trying to pass a resolution ordering payment of the arrears, asserting that 'popery, slavery, and arbitrary power were at the very doors'. The Jacobites promptly seized the initiative with a fiery speech by Campion attacking Hanover.[80] Others followed, culminating with Whitlock, who was so outspoken as to be called to the Bar to explain his words:

> If he [the Elector] had any regard or love for Brittain, it woud appear as much now, when such occasions offer'd, as afterwards; and if he now preferr'd his German interest and dominions to the interest and honour of Brittain, he'd do the same when he was king and had it more in his power to do them good offices at Brittain's expence. He [Whitlock] concluded that King William's extravagance to his Dutch favourites had cast him a fair copy, and least he shou'd come to the crown, *which he hop't he should never do*, it was necessary to check him in the bud.[81]

Whitlock jesuitically explained his words as having meant that the queen was only middle-aged and might outlive the elector. Bolingbroke's friends then closed the debate with an adjournment motion before the Jacobites put upon all opponents of paying the arrears the reputation of being disaffected.[82] The same pattern repeated itself in June over a request for supply for the Army's debts. Campion immediately proposed that this should be considered only if a clause excluding payment of the arrears from the money voted was added. Auditors Harley and Foley seized on this portentously to remind the M.P.'s of their oaths of abjuration, thereby implying that opposition to such a proposal was tantamount to open Jacobitism. Wyndham managed to retrieve the situation (which was beginning to look as if it might end in a Jacobite defeat at the hands of all the other groups united behind the Harleyites) by declaring that the queen had told him to assure the Commons that none of the supply would be used to pay the arrears. Predictably, the Jacobites felt they had scored a great victory and that Bolingbroke was now irretrievably committed to their cause. Bolingbroke actually went to great pains to stress that obedience to the queen's wishes had been his paramount motive in preventing payment of the arrears, so as to placate the Hanoverian Tories for having crossed them in the matter.[83]

The Schism Bill was a piece of political engineering from its inception. It set out to rally all sections of the Tory party together to pass it, and by a successful mutual endeavour bond them together again. It was introduced by Bolingbroke's friend Wyndham, though it was rumoured that he only narrowly pre-empted Hanmer and Anglesey, who were anxious to parade their continued attachment to Tory principles. The intention of reforging party unity through the Bill was signalled from the start by the choice of the Committee charged with preparing the Bill, on which every non-Harleyite section of party opinion was represented. Whitlock, Campion and Aldworth represented the Jacobites, Cholmondeley, Kay and viscount Downe the Hanoverian Tories, Dixie Windsor and Heneage Finch the Opposition Tories. The consensus between these groups was based on the traditional Tory belief that Dissent was as much a threat to the Church as Catholicism. This precluded the Whigs forcing the amendment of the Bill by extending it to include Catholics.[84] The attraction for the Tories of a Bill designed to extirpate the 'Nurserys for Rebellion' (the Dissenting Academies) was indeed so great that the Whigs managed to split them in the Commons only once, on the question of an amendment allowing the teaching of reading and writing by Dissenting schoolmistresses. All the other Whig sallies were brushed aside.[85] Notice was also served of future measures against Dissent, by ominous talk of softening the Bill if the Dissenters would agree to their own disenfranchisement. Bromley and Wyndham were expressing the general feeling of the Country Tories in making this 'offer', and Bolingbroke clearly intended to keep the party united next session by further persecution of Nonconformity.[86] In the Lords a similar pattern emerged. Bolingbroke, Buckingham, North and Grey, Anglesey and Abingdon steadily pushed the Bill through against determined Harleyite and Whig opposition. The Harleyite vote there was proportionately more important, however, so that several critical amendments were passed, despite the queen's open support for the unaltered Bill.[87] Anglesey retaliated by introducing his own amendment extending the Bill to include Ireland. This rallied the Tory peers for the final push, and the Bill was passed in this form despite the protests of Shrewsbury, the Harleyites and many Bishops. The eventual result of this running battle was a very much watered-down version of the original measure, but it had served its purpose. Bolingbroke's reputation as the scourge of the Dissenters was second to none, and the party as a whole henceforth looked to him for leadership. Oxford had been revealed as an impotent half-Whig out of touch with his backbenchers.[88]

Bolingbroke's successes in reuniting the party and usurping the leadership were nearly overturned shortly after the Schism Bill's passage by Oxford's counter-attack over the Spanish Commercial Treaty. The South Sea Company had been expressing unease about certain articles of the treaty since March, particularly several explanatory clauses. The Opposition tried to take these up, but could not exploit suspicions of misconduct attached to them for lack of evidence. In June witnesses of this alleged misconduct suddenly started appearing to testify against Moore before the Company's board. The Commons took the matter up, but when the queen gave up her share of the Assiento (the monopoly of supplying slaves to Spanish America) profits, one of the Company's main grievances, they seemed inclined to drop the matter.[89] The Lords thereupon abruptly began an investigation of their own and, with Harleyite support, the Opposition was first able to address for the names of the ministers who had advised Anne to sign the explanatory articles and then vote for the renegotiation of the treaty *nem. con.*[90] Oxford was by now visibly feeding the Opposition with directions as to where to press his rival, and Bolingbroke was panicking:

> My papers are in order, and the several points shall be stated to the Lords of the Council as their meetings give me opportunity of doing; but I submit to your Lordship whether you will not think that some of them should be previously considered by you, and ripened, and digested by your direction, as I have always desired they should be. I am ready to take any method you prescribe. I have neither power nor capacity to act alone in matters of this importance, and if I had both, I know too well the order and subordination which is essential to government, to attempt any such thing.[91]

Bolingbroke was saved only by a last-minute rally led by Anglesey and Shrewsbury and inspired by the queen, who had shown by her refusal to divulge his name where her sympathies lay. After he made his peace with the Jacobites over the proclamation, they too came to his defence, North and Grey being prominent as usual. Backed by this combination, Bolingbroke made a stand and softened or defeated several Opposition addresses directed against him. Moore then proved that one of the witnesses against him was lying, allowing Bolingbroke finally to escape with the air more of an aggrieved innocent than a fugitive criminal. Anglesey's quick use of the queen's reply to an address asking her to give up any remaining share she still possessed in the Assiento profits turned the tables on Oxford, as, technically, he was responsible for the insult Anglesey claimed the Lords had received.[92] Bolingbroke was rescued by the Hanoverian Tories and the queen in the first instance, but could not have escaped without Jacobite acquiescence. If they had remained aloof in the Lords, as it seems they did when the investigation began, and had continued their harassing campaign in the Commons,

Bolingbroke would have been crushed between the Harleyites and Opposition in the Lords and the Jacobites in the Commons.[93]

The session of 1714 had all the prospects of being a watershed for the Jacobites. With the decline of St Germain's confidence in British politicians there followed greater freedom of action for its adherents in the British Parliament. The events of the session, particularly the power struggle between Oxford and Bolingbroke, directed the emerging Jacobite group's interest and thinned its ranks, but also provided it with ideological rallying points. By the time Parliament recessed these had created a recognisable, separate, interest group in the Tory party. In many ways the new Jacobite group in the Commons was a product of the same forces and frustrations which had produced the Hanoverian Tories. It lacked leadership, and was constrained rather than encouraged by its leaders at St Germain. There remained also that natural reluctance to expose themselves typical of the adherents of proscribed causes. Nonetheless its future significance was assured. With the Opposition henceforth doomed to the political wilderness as long as Anne lived, ideological interest groups within the Tory party were bound to be of disproportionate political influence from then on. The Hanoverian Tories represented the complete success of such a pressure group. Though Oxford and Bolingbroke had both attempted to manipulate them for their own ends, they had resisted them, and in the end only fully committed themselves to Bolingbroke when he had satisfied them about his future intentions. The Jacobites had just barely reached the same stage when the session drew to a close.

NOTES

1. Add. MSS. 47087, ff. 61-2: 2 Mar. 1714. See also: Gregg, *Queen Anne*, pp.369,379-80. For other interpretations of the events of this session, see: Eveline Cruickshanks, 'The Tories and the Succession in the 1714 Parliament', *Bull. Inst. Hist. Res.*, xlvi, (1973), 176-85; G.S. Holmes, 'Harley, St John and the Death of the Tory Party', in *Britain After the Glorious Revolution, 1689-1714* (1969), pp.216-35; Dickinson, *Bolingbroke*, pp.114-33; Gregg, *Queen Anne*, pp.377-92.

2. Holmes, *Politics*, p.216.

3. Sedgewick, *Commons*, i, 162-81: list of Tory and Whig M.P.s returned in 1713, noting those who were 'Whimsical' [c. Aug. 1714]; *Parl. Hist.*, vi, 1282-3: list of those voting against the expulsion of Richard Steele M.P.. For another view, see: Holmes, *Politics*, p.283.

4. Add. MSS. 47087, f. 62: 2 Mar. 1714; Wodrow Letters, Quarto 8, ep. 21: Smith to Crosse, 15 Feb. 1714. For another view, see: Holmes, *Politics*, p.94.

5. *CJ*, xvii, 583,618,641,643,685: 21 Apr., 6 and 25 May and 15 June 1714; Wodrow Letters, Quarto 8, ep. 53: Smith to Crosse, 25 Mar. 1714; Hermitage HHH, ff. 106,192-5,198-200: 9 Mar. and 20 and 23 Apr. 1714.

6. *CJ*, xvii, 498: 15 Mar. 1714; *Hanmer Corr.*, pp.159-60: Hanmer to Steele, 20 Mar. 1714; *Parl. Hist.*, vi, 1282-3: list of those voting against Steele's expulsion.

7. *CJ*, xvii, 631,640,663: 12, 24 and 27 May 1714; Holmes, 'Attack', pp.64-5; Macpherson, ii, 590: Schütz to Bothmer, 9 Apr. 1714; Hermitage HHH, ff. 113,232,262-3: 12 Mar., 25 May and 15 June 1714.

8. Macpherson, ii, 574-5,586: Schütz to Bothmer, 26 Feb. and 30 Mar. 1714; *Pol. State*, vii, 261: 19 Mar. 1714.

9. *Parl. Hist.*, vi, 1335-6,1347: 5 and 15 Apr. 1714; Blackett Diary (HPT): 15 Apr. 1714; Hermitage HHH, ff. 187-8: 16 Apr. 1714.

10. Macpherson, ii, 546-7: Schütz to Robethon, 12 Jan. 1714; Portland Loan 29/138/3: Hanmer to Oxford, 23 Apr., 24 May and 12 July 1714; Holmes, *Politics*, pp.135,283; Panshanger MSS. D/EP F 132, f. 10. For another view, see: Horwitz, *Politicks*, pp.242-3.

11. Dalhousie 14/336/11: Lockhart to Maule, 8 June 1714; Wodrow Letters, Quarto 8, ep. 94: Smith to Crosse, 26 June 1714.

12. Portland, vii, 181: Stratford to lord Harley, 16 Feb. 1714; Macpherson, ii, 549-50: Schütz to Robethon, 19 Jan. 1714; *Hanmer Corr.*, pp.163-4: Hanmer to the Electress Sophia [1714].

13. Macpherson, ii, 592-3: Schütz to Bothmer, 13 Apr. 1714; ii, 577-8: Schütz to Robethon, 21 Mar. 1714; ii, 571-2,623: Kreienberg to Bothmer, 23 Feb. and 25 May 1714; Add. MSS. 31159, f. 144: Bromley to Strafford, 30 Apr. 1714.

14. D. Hayton, 'The Crisis in Ireland and the Disintegration of Queen Anne's last Ministry', *Irish Historical Studies*, xxii (1981), 193-215; Portland, v 403: Bromley to Oxford, 21 Mar. 1714.

15. Gaultier 121, f. 37: 7 Jan. 1714; A.N. Newman, 'Proceedings in the House of Commons, March-June 1714', *Bull. Inst. Hist. Res.*, xxxiv (1961, henceforth: Knatchbull Diary), 214-15: 11 and 19 Apr. 1714; Bonet 39A, f. 102: 20 Apr. 1714.

16. Add. MSS. 47087, ff. 61-3: 2 and 23 Mar. 1714; Macpherson, ii, 577-8: Schütz to Robethon, 21 Mar. 1714; AAE 255, f. 87: D'Iberville to Torcy, 19 Apr. 1714 ns.

17. Macpherson, ii, 587-8: Schütz to Bothmer, 2 Apr. 1714.

18. AAE 255, ff. 86-7: D'Iberville to Torcy, 19 Apr. 1714 ns; *Swift Corr.*, ii, 77: Ford to Swift, 22 July 1714.

19. Stuart, i, 299-300: Berwick to James, 21 Feb. 1714 ns; Gualterio 46495, f. 34: Dempster to Gualterio, 21 Jan. 1714 ns; Gualterio 31259, f. 19: Nairne to Gualterio, 1 Mar. 1714 ns. Lockhart, i, 441-2.

20. Dalhousie 14/336/19: Lockhart to Maule, 7 Mar. 1714; Lockhart, i, 442-3; Stuart, i, 304-5: Berwick to James, 1 Mar. 1714 ns; Blair Lett: 25 Feb. and 9 Mar. 1714.

21. Portland, x, 307-9: Mar to Oxford, 6 and 22 Jan. 1714; GD 248/561/50/26: Findlater to Deskford, 9 Feb. 1714; Portland Loan 29/151: lord Maynard to Oxford, 26 Feb. 1714; Macpherson, ii, 574-5: Schütz to Bothmer, 26 Feb. 1714.

22. Portland, x, 310-11: Mar to Oxford, 3 Feb. 1714.

23. Blair Castle MSS., Box 45 Bundle 11, epp. 66-7, 97: J. Douglas to Atholl, 20 and 25 Feb. and 25 May 1714; Portland Loan 29/10 i./11: memo on the peers' strike, 20 Feb. 1714; Nott. Univ. Portland MSS: Balmerino to Oxford, 28 [Feb.] 1714.

24. GD 30/1562: Houston to Thomas Shearp, 8 May 1714; Dickinson, *Bolingbroke*, p.125. For another view, see: Holmes, *Politics*, p.397.

25. Lockhart, i, 447-52,457,459,559-61; *CJ*, xvii, 637-8,671,711-12,716: 22 May, 7 and 30 June and 3 July 1714; Dalhousie 14/336/12-13: Lockhart to Maule, 25 May and 8 June 1714.

26. Wodrow Letters, Quarto 8, ep. 92: Crosse to Wodrow, 18 June 1714. The implication that this was a *Scots* rather than *Jacobite* affair is further supported by:

Went. Corr., pp.387-8: Wentworth to Strafford, 14 June 1714; Dalhousie 14/336/12: Lockhart to Maule, 8 June 1714; Knatchbull Diary, p.217: 12 June 1714. In this I differ with professor Holmes, *Politics*, p.279 note 122.

27. *CJ*, xvii, 483,514,541,603,687,710-11,716: 4 and 19 Mar., 6 and 29 Apr., 16 and 29 June and 3 July 1714.

28. Claydon House Letters M11/55: Fermanagh to Verney, 27 May 1714; Knatchbull Diary, p.214: 6 Apr. 1714; Dalhousie 14/336/17: Lockhart to Maule [Apr. 1714].

29. Bonet 39A, f. 113: 7 May 1714.

30. Macpherson, ii, 613-14: Galke to Robethon, 7 May 1714; Dalhousie 14/336/10: Lockhart to Maule, 19 June 1714; Wodrow Letters, Quarto 8, ep. 94: Crosse to Wodrow, 26 June 1714; *Pol. State*, vii, 466-7, 553-5: 25 May and 25 June 1714.

31. Dalhousie 14/336/8: Lockhart to Maule, 26 June 1714.

32. Lockhart, i, 472-3; *CJ*, xvii, 711-12, 714-15: 30 June and 2 July 1714; Baschet 202, f. 204: D'Iberville to Louis XIV, 3 May 1714 ns.

33. Lockhart, i, 477.

34. *Ibid.*, i, 478; *CJ*, xvii, 717-18: 5 July 1714.

35. *Mémoires de Berwick*, pp.132-3; Baschet 203, ff. 256,258: D'Iberville to Louis XIV, 12, 23 and 24 Aug. 1714 ns. For another view, see: Holmes, *Politics*, pp.279,337; Gregg, *Queen Anne*, pp.388-9.

36. Holmes, *Politics*, pp.247,249-51; Gregg, *Queen Anne*, p.380.

37. Dickinson, *Bolingbroke*, p.117; Bennett, *Tory Crisis*, p.175; Carte 231, f. 50: Lansdowne's anecdote told to Carte, 30 May 1726; Gregg, 'Was Queen Anne a Jacobite?', p.374; *Swift Corr.*, ii, 51,65-6: Ford to Swift, 6 and 17 July 1714. For another view, see: Hill, *Growth*, p.143.

38. *Bol. Corr.*, iv, 498: Bolingbroke to Phipps, 13 Apr. 1714. See also: iv, 440: to Anglesey, 25 Jan. 1714.

39. Knatchbull Diary, pp.213,214: 4 and 11 Apr. 1714; HMC, *Kenyon MSS.*, p.456: R. Kenyon to G. Kenyon, 29 July 1714; *Swift Corr.*, ii, 51,77,78-9: Ford to Swift, 6, 22 and 24 July 1714; *Pol. State*, vii, 613: 26 July 1714; Lockhart, i, 452-7.

40. Baschet 202, ff. 167-8: D'Iberville to Louis XIV, 4 Mar. 1714 ns. By 1714 the intention of making the new dynasty captive was intrinsic to Toryism: Plumb, *Stability*, p.151.

41. Bonet 38C, ff. 115-16: 18 Aug. 1713; Gregg, 'Marlborough', pp.614-16.

42. J.J. Murray, *George I, the Baltic and the Whig Split* (1969), pp.49-53,75,80,86; *Pol. State*, vii, 613: 26 July 1714.

43. R.M. Hatton, *George I* (1978), pp.78-104 *passim*.

44. Stuart, i, 304-5,307-8,309,314-15,320-1: Berwick to James, 1, 13 and 23 Mar., 8 Apr. and 6 May 1714 ns. See the next chapter for a more detailed analysis of these moves.

45. *Calendar of Treasury Books* (1969), xxvii, 163: Lowndes to Northey, 3 Mar. 1714; Stuart, i, 317: Henry Eyre to Berwick, 21 Apr. 1714; Lockhart, i, 441-2.

46. Add. MSS. 40621, ff. 163-4: T. Harley's instructions, Jan. 1714; ff. 165,167: Anne to Sophia, 9 Jan. 1714; f. 170: Bromley to T. Harley, 11 Feb. 1714; Macpherson, ii, 542,544-5,550: Schütz to Robethon, 25 Dec. 1713 and 1 and 22 Jan. 1714; ii, 564-7: Kreienberg to Robethon, 16 Feb. 1714; Gregg, *Queen Anne*, p.383.

47. Bennett, *Tory Crisis*, pp.166-7,174; Macpherson, ii, 548-9: Schütz to Robethon, 15 Jan. 1714; ii, 564: Schütz to Bothmer, 16 Feb. 1714; Wodrow Letters, Quarto 8, ep. 20: Morthland to Wodrow, 13 Feb. 1714; Gaultier 139, ff. 195-7: Gaultier to Torcy [March 1714]; *Bol. Corr.*, iv, 440: Bolingbroke to Anglesey, 25 Jan. 1714.

48. *Bol. Corr.*, iv, 436: Bolingbroke to the queen, 20 Jan. 1714; iv, 475: Bolingbroke to Prior, 16 Feb. 1714; Holmes, *Politics*, p.28.

49. Hermitage HHH, ff. 126-8: 19 Mar. 1714; Add. MSS. 40621, f. 178: Oxford to T. Harley, 14 Mar. 1714; Portland v, 396: William Breton to Strafford, 10 Mar. 1714 ns; Portland Loan 29/138/5: Oxford to Harcourt, 17 Mar. 1714.

50. Portland, v, 400: Harcourt to Oxford, 17 Mar. 1714; v, 403: lord Masham to Oxford, 22 Mar. 1714; Portland Loan 29/159/9: Trevor to Oxford, 21 Mar. 1714; Gregg, *Queen Anne*, p.379.

51. Macpherson, ii, 585: Schütz to Bothmer, 26 Mar. 1714; *Bol. Corr.*, iv, 492,510: Bolingbroke to Strafford, 23 Mar. and 23 Apr. 1714; Portland, v, 404: Bolingbroke to Oxford, 27 Mar. 1714.

52. Portland, v, 404-5: Lewis to T. Harley, 29 Mar. 1714; v, 405: E. Harley to Oxford, 29 Mar. 1714.

53. Add. MSS. 40621, ff. 210-14: Oxford to T. Harley, 13 Apr. 1714; ff. 193-4: Oxford to Cambridge, Sophia and the Elector, 16 Apr. 1714; Stuart, i, 320,326: Berwick to James, 2 May and 5 June 1714 ns; Gregg, *Queen Anne*, p.381.

54. *Bol. Corr.*, iv, 522: Bolingbroke to Strafford, 27 Apr. 1714; Trumbull Add. MSS. 134: Bateman to Trumbull, 21 May 1714.

55. Portland Loan 29/159/4: Weymouth to Oxford, 23 Mar. 1714; 29/151/7: Halifax to Oxford, 21 Apr. 1714; Panshanger MSS. D/EP F 60, f. 37: Oxford to Cowper, 30 Mar. 1714; Add. MSS. 47087, ff. 70-1: 3 May 1714.

56. *Pol. State*, vii, 319,334-8: 9 and 16 Apr. 1714; Baschet 202, ff. 198-9; D'Iberville to Louis XIV, 26 Apr. 1714 ns; Bonet 39A, f. 88: 2 Apr. 1714; Knatchbull Diary, p.213: 4 Apr. 1714; Portland, v, 425: Bolingbroke to Oxford [21 Apr. 1714]; Gualterio 31256, f. 81: Perth to Gualterio, 14 May 1714 ns.

57. McInnes, *Harley*, p.165; Add. MSS. 40621, ff. 210-14: Oxford to T. Harley, 13 Apr. 1714; Gaultier 122, f. 301: Gaultier to Torcy, 21 May 1714 ns; Portland Loan 29/159/13: Jersey to Oxford, May 1714; Holmes, *Politics*, p.393.

58. Baschet 203, f. 217: D'Iberville to Louis XIV, 27 May 1714 ns; *Hanmer Corr.*, pp.168-9: Oxford to Hanmer, 13 May 1714; Lockhart, i, 468-70.

59. Hermitage HHH, ff. 238-9: 1 June 1714; *Went. Corr.*, p.383: Berkeley to Strafford, 25 May 1714; Gregg, *Queen Anne*, p.386; Bennett, *Tory Crisis*, pp.176-9.

60. Macpherson, ii, 626-7: Marlborough to Robethon, 7 June 1714; Portland Loan 29/10 i./6-9: memos of points to be brought up in interviews with the queen, 8 June to 4 July 1714; *Hamilton Diary*, p.62: 15 June 1714; E. Gregg, *Queen Anne*, pp.385-6; Dickinson, *Bolingbroke*, p.124.

61. Dickinson, *Bolingbroke*, p.125; *Bol. Corr.*, iv. 538: Bolingbroke to Shrewsbury, 20 May 1714; Dalhousie 14/336/8: Lockhart to Maule, 26 June 1714; Gregg, *Queen Anne*, pp.386-7.

62. Gaultier 122, ff. 46,49-50,54: Gaultier to Torcy, 2, 6 and 9 July 1714 ns; Macpherson, ii, 631-2: Kreienberg to Robethon, 25 June 1714; Dalhousie 14/336/7: Lockhart to Maule, 29 June 1714; Lockhart, i, 471-3, 476-8.

63. *Went. Corr.*, pp.391-4: newsletter to Strafford, 25 June 1714; pp.394-5: Wentworth to Strafford, 29 June 1714; Gregg, *Queen Anne*, p.387.

64. Gregg, *Queen Anne*, p.387; Hill, *Growth*, p.145; *Bol. Corr.*, iv, 562: Bolingbroke to Strafford, 14 July 1714; *Pol. State*, vii, 564-5,568,573,615,624-5: 2, 6, 9 and 27 July 1714; Portland, v, 454-5: Bolingbroke to Oxford, 3 [July] 1714 (I have redated this letter to July on the basis of internal evidence and: Portland Loan 29/10 i./6: 4 July 1714); *Went. Corr.*, pp.401-2: Wentworth to Strafford, July 1714.

65. Portland Loan 29/7/5: draught royal reply with exculpatory note by Oxford, 9 July 1714; Baschet 203, f. 245: D'Iberville to Louis XIV, 23 July 1714 ns; *Swift Corr.*, ii, 89: Lewis to Swift, 29 July 1714; Gaultier 122, f. 66: Gaultier to Torcy, 9 Aug. 1714 ns; Macpherson, ii, 630: Galke to Robethon, 18 June 1714.

66. *Pol. State*, vii, 241-4: 11, 13 and 15 Mar. 1714.

67. Plumb, *Walpole*, i, 190-1; Blackett Diary: 18 Mar. 1714; *CJ*, xvii, 498,514: 15 and 18 Mar. 1714. For another view, see: Hill, *Growth*, p.143.

68. Add. MSS. 31159, f. 114: Bromley to Strafford, 16 Apr. 1714.

69. Add. MSS. 47087, ff. 64-5: 8 Apr. 1714; Add. MSS. 22221, f. 107: Bathurst to Strafford, 5 Apr. 1714; Hermitage HHH, ff. 165-9, 186-7: 6 and 16 Apr. 1714.

70. *Went. Corr.*, pp.369-72: newsletter to Strafford, 20 Apr. 1714; Blackett Diary: 15 Apr. 1714; Dalhousie 14/336/18: Lockhart to Maule, 6 Apr. 1714.

71. Lockhart, i, 561-4; Blackett Diary: 15 Apr. 1714; Holmes, *Politics*, p.298.

72. Gualterio 46495, f. 34: Dempster to Gualterio, 21 Jan. 1714 ns; *Pol. State*, vii, 243-4,308-9: 15 Mar. and 2 Apr. 1714; *Went. Corr.*, pp.362-4: Bathurst to Strafford, 6 Apr. 1714.

73. Macpherson, ii, 590: Schütz to Robethon, 9 Apr. 1714; Baschet 202, ff. 191-4: D'Iberville to Louis XIV, 22 Apr. 1714 ns; *Parl. Hist.*, vi, 1338: 8 Apr. 1714; Gregg, *Queen Anne*, p.380.

74. Gualterio 31256, f. 80: Perth to Gualterio, 14 May 1714 ns.

75. *Went. Corr.*, pp.391-4: newsletter to Strafford, 25 June 1714; Kenyon MSS. DDKe/6/55: notes for a speech [1714].

76. *Pol. State*, vii, 322: 12 Apr. 1714; Horwitz, *Politicks*, p.241; Macpherson, ii, 575-7: Kreienberg to Robethon, 2 Mar. 1714.

77. Gregg, *Queen Anne*, pp.209-13,377-8,381-5,390-1; Add. MSS. 47087, ff. 73-4: 1 June 1714; Macpherson, ii, 612: Kreienberg to Robethon, 8 May 1714 ns.

78. Wodrow Letters, Quarto 8, ep. 68: Smith to Crosse, 17 Apr. 1714; above, pp.155-6.

79. Holmes, *Politics*, p.188.

80. Portland, v, 419: Oxford to T. Harley, 13 Apr. 1714; v, 434: Lewis to T. Harley, 4 May 1714; Wodrow Letters, Quarto 8, ep. 83: Erskine to Wodrow, 19 May 1714.

81. Lockhart, i, 469 (my italics).

82. Lockhart, i, 469-70; *Went. Corr.*, pp.384-5: Bathurst to Strafford, 28 May 1714.

83. Wodrow Letters, Quarto 8, ep. 89: 'B.G.M.' to Wodrow, 12 June 1714; *Bol. Corr.*, iv, 528: Bolingbroke to Strafford, 18 May 1714; Portland, vii, 185-6: Stratford to lord Harley, 3 June 1714.

84. Add. MSS. 47087, f. 74: 1 June 1714; *CJ*, xvii, 631: 12 May 1714; Wodrow Letters, Quarto 8, ep. 82: Smith to Crosse, 19 May 1714; Bonet 39A, ff. 117-18: 14 May 1714; *Parl. Hist.*, vi, 1349-51.

85. Knatchbull Diary, p.215: 27 May 1714; Worcestershire R.O., BA 4567 (ii.) 1: Pakington's speech on the Church in danger [1705]; *CJ*, xvii, 636,640,644,660,698: 21, 24 and 27 May and 1 and 23 June 1714; Hermitage HHH, ff. 221-2,240-2,237-9: 14 and 28 May and 1 June 1714.

86. Holmes, *Politics*, pp.103-4; Hermitage HHH, ff. 284-7: 25 June 1714; Baschet 203, ff. 227-30,231-3: D'Iberville to Louis XIV, 17, 23 and 25 June 1714 ns.

87. Add. MSS. 47087, f. 75: 11 June 1714; *Went. Corr.*, pp.385-6: newsletter to Strafford, 1 June 1714; Pol. State, vii, 517-19, 529: 9 and 23 June 1714; Portland, vii, 188: Stratford to Mr Hill, 12 June 1714; Hermitage HHH, ff. 245-7: 4 June 1714.

88. Hermitage HHH, ff. 255-7,261-3: 11 and 15 June 1714; MS Ballard 18, f. 63: Carte

to Charlett, 16 July 1714. For another view, see: Hill, *Growth*, p.144.

89. Hermitage HHH, ff. 93-4,95-6,268-71,274-5: 26 Feb., 2 Mar. and 18 and 22 June 1714; Knatchbull Diary, p.212: 17 Mar. 1714; Blackett Diary: 22 Apr. 1714. The Assiento was an official monopoly of the slave trade to Spanish America.

90. Hermitage HHH, ff. 282-3,288-9,292-5; 29 June and 2 and 6 July 1714.

91. Portland, v, 454-5: Bolingbroke to Oxford, 3 [July] 1714. See above, n.62.

92. *Swift Corr.*, ii, 51-2, 58-9: Ford to Swift, 6 and 10 July 1714; Baschet 203, ff. 242-4: D'Iberville to Louis XIV, 19 July 1714 ns; *Went Corr.*, pp.396-400: Wentworth to Strafford, 9 July 1714; Add. MSS. 47087, f. 79: 10 July 1714.

93. *Pol. State*, vii, 572-7: 9 July 1714; Lockhart, i, 564-9.

9

'Very full of nothing': the Harley ministry's negotiations with the Jacobites, 1710-14

Having established the political circumstances out of which Parliamentary Jacobitism arose, it is now appropriate to consider the effects this had on the leadership of the Tory party. The development of Parliamentary Jacobitism as a force in the Tory party inevitably led to the party's managers attempting to manipulate it for their own ends. Initial, hesitant, contacts for one purpose soon expanded under the pressure of events at Westminster into a full-scale attempt to harness the influence of the exiled Stuarts for the benefit of the Government. By tracing the development of their relationship and analysing the forms it took, and correlating this with events at Westminster, the real significance of these contacts can be gauged. The role of the French Court must also be considered, as it constituted the medium for this process and at times exerted a decisive influence on it.

Harley's primary concern when he initiated contact with the Jacobites was to limit his exposure to the minimum necessary to convince the French Court of his goodwill. By doing so he hoped to convince the French that Jacobite plans for an invasion and insurrection (always dependent on French support), which were certain to fragment the ministry if they occurred, were basically unnecessary. He was not even particularly interested at the outset in winning over the Jacobite Court. Without the French the Jacobites were impotent (at that time), so that it was the French Court at whom he aimed his declarations. These were correspondingly dramatic:

> Scavez vous bien que Mde Prothose [Queen Anne] a des sentimens fort tendres pour Mr de Montgoulin [James] et qu'elle le regarde comme son propre Enfant et que Mr R [the earl of Jersey] m'a assuré que tout ce qu'elle faisoit presentement n'etoit en partie que pour l'amour de luy et que messieurs Morand [Shrewsbury], Vivant [Buckingham] et Van-der-berg [Harley] ne travaillent que pour et dans la veüe de luy rendre ce qu'il luy a esté oté autrefois et luy faire bon les marchandises qu'on luy a confisqués.[1]

Harley then conducted a sustained delaying action through his agent in the early stages of the negotiations, the earl of Jersey, to prevent St Germain knowing anything more than that the ministry was friendly. Berwick was the first Jacobite to be informed, and he was expressly forbidden to let James know. Meanwhile the French were regaled with hints of Jacobite master plans at Cabinet level and a stream of assurances of the ministry's fond regard for

James, coupled to a distinct reluctance to discuss either with Gaultier, their link to the French Court.[2] After prolonged French intercession on James's behalf, Harley was tempted into allowing him to be informed in order to prevent a summer visit to the French Atlantic maritime provinces which James was planning. Harley knew that the Whigs would seize on this to work up an invasion scare and sought to use his Jacobite connection to forestall them. By May, too, Harley was probably aware of the Jacobite Court's encouragement of the October Club Jacobites in their attacks on the ministry. The establishment of a good reputation at St Germain therefore became useful politically in Parliament and outside it in Britain, moving Harley to expand his contacts with St Germain in order to achieve it.

Though Oxford had now revealed himself, warnings that James should do nothing on his own initiative now became a constant theme of Oxford's messages to him.[3] This was at first concealed by rigidly insisting that no-one other than Berwick at the Jacobite Court must know of the negotiations, and that nothing could be done before the peace was settled.[4] In practical terms, compliance with these strictures meant that James could do nothing on his own behalf. The French were too concerned that the peace negotiations succeed to risk any venture that might upset them, and this left the Jacobites totally neutralised diplomatically and militarily. By 1714 the demand for quiescence on James's part still remained the central element in Oxford's proposals to James, though the ultimate absurdity in this approach was not argued by him but by Bolingbroke:

> si le Duc d'Hanover etoit sur le trosne,...Ce Prince d'un esprit mediocre n'auroit aucun Ministre au Conseiller qui ne fust Anglois, et avec une autoritée limitée par les loix tres dures qui sont deja faites, et auxquelles on en ajouteroit encore d'autres. Cela suppose, ou il voudra retablir les prerogatives de la Royaute, à quoy les Whigs s'opposeroient et seroient les premiers à le chasser, ou il foudroit qu'il souffrist a l'exemple de Guillaume toutes les nouvelles atteintes qu'on y donneroit, auquel cas on acheveroit de sapper l'autorité royale continuellement degradée par eux sous Guillaume et sous le règne present avant le Ministere d'aujourd'huy. Ce ne seroit plus qu'une vraye anarchie qui ne seroit pas durable, et les Torris ..., mesme une partie des Wighs se reuniroient aux bien intentionnes pour le rappel du Roy legitime, qui seroit en droit par sa naissance de demander la retablissement des choses en l'estat qu'elles etoient sous le Roy son père, a quoy tous se porteroient d'eux mesmes apres en avoir connu la nécessité par expérience.[5]

James refused to believe this, which is hardly surprising. Right up to the moment the new dynasty arrived in Britain the Ministers continued to try and lull the Jacobite Court into inaction. Oxford tried to convince James that, even if Cambridge arrived, an uprising would be unnecessary, while Bolingbroke inveigled Ormonde and Ross into endorsing his arguments against a Jacobite rebellion after Anne died.[6]

The ministry's desire to win control of, or support from, the Parliamentary Jacobites sprang from its experiences at Westminster in 1711 and 1712. Jersey first broached the subject in May 1711 when the Government's troubles with the October Club were at their height, by hinting at the desirability of the ministry's having complete control of St Germain's adherents:

> L'on me dit que Vanderberg [Harley], Prothose [the queen] et Rolland [Jersey] ont dessein de prendre desormais soin de la conduite et des affaires de Montgoulin [James]: s'ils veullent s'en charger comment pourroit on les en empecher, laisser les donc faire, ce sera autant de debarrasé pour vous; comme vous estes de ses amis, faites luy seulement entendre qu'il est de son interest de se soumettre entierement et toutes choses a leurs volontes et de ne rien faire qui puisse leur deplaire ny les chagriner.[7]

The Jacobite Court responded by directing its unwilling supporters to obey the Government in all matters relating to the peace and, as its hopes of the ministry increased, eventually everything else. This, with occasional interventions by St Germain to see that this position was maintained, satisfied the ministry until 1713. By then Oxford was suffering from such a dearth of means to ensure continued Country Tory support for the Government that he was driven to try and expand his Jacobite connection to improve its position:

> On supplie V.M.te de faire en sort que ceux dont j'ay l'honneur de luy envoyer les nomer agissent en tout pour la Cour. Les Cat[oliqu]es en procurant des Elections favourables dans leurs Terres, les autres en ajoutant a ce service leurs suffrages dans la Chambre Haute.[8]

James promptly ordered the Jacobites to back the ministry in the elections and at Westminster. This emboldened Oxford to make a bid for complete control of the Jacobites in Parliament. In 1714 he tried to persuade James that he should order Nonjuring peers like the earls of Winchelsea and Lichfield to take the oaths, and that henceforth they and the Scots Jacobite representatives should obey Oxford while James refrained from further communication.[9] James baulked at this and Oxford had to fall back on his own resources.

As the Jacobites were well aware, France was near collapse and desperate for peace by 1711. Accordingly, they yielded gracefully to French pressure to leave France, though St Germain naturally tried to extract as many concessions as possible from the British and French Governments for doing so.[10] James was delayed in leaving for Lorraine by the need to get money from the French and passports and safeconducts from the Emperor. During this time Oxford decided that he would prefer James further away from Britain. This may have been his own decision or it may have been inspired by forewarning of Opposition plans to use James's proximity to Britain to embarrass the Government. Whatever his motivation, in 1713 he began to urge James to leave Lorraine for a more distant haven:

> Les amys de Montgoulin [James] trouvent qu'il est absolument necessaire pour le bien et l'avancement de ce Prince, et ils m'ordonnent de vous mander qu'il sera plus pres de Londres quand il sera a Berne que s'il restoit à St Germain et qu'il leur sera plus facile de travailler pour luy parceque son sejour en ce pays la pendant

quelque tems dissipera tous les soupcons que ses Enemys ont icy de luy et de ses amis &&&.[11]

This pressure steadily mounted for the rest of the year, and Oxford soon revealed that he really did not care where James went as long as it was further from Britain than Lorraine. Treves, Coblenz and Venice were the most favoured of his recommended choices.[12] The Jacobite Court prevaricated in response to these directives, abetted by the sympathetic Torcy. Oxford was obliged by this to develop his Jacobite connection a stage further, so as to persuade James to leave Lorraine voluntarily. He tried to do this by an old diplomatic trick: the adding of totally unacceptable demands to ones which had hitherto been acceptable but unpalatable. A demand that James announce his conversion to Anglicanism was now included in a package of advice of which the real intent was that he should remove himself from Lorraine.[13] This produced exactly the desired effect on the French Court, Torcy advising James that though:

> Le voyage chez Sturton [Switzerland] est un point desagreable il faut cependant considerer qu'on ne propose rien de permanent, mais seulement un sejour assez court et liberte de retourner chez M. de Laumarie [Lorraine] lorsque M. de Puisieux [Parliament] sera party. C'est une satisfaction pour M. Tillemont [Tories] et quoy faire saire Walker [Whigs] a la verite l'eloignement est double pour un certain temps mais il n'est pas encore fort considerable. Et comme M. Rose [Louis XIV] tient un agent chez M. Sturton il sera plus facile encore de donner sans soubcon des avis a M. de Raucourt [James]. Enfin Belley et Talon [Berwick and Torcy] croyent que cette promenade ne scauroit au moins prenduire de mauvais effects et que le refus absolu de suivre les conseils des amis dans un point qui ne paroit bien essential, pourroit estre dangereux.[14]

The Jacobite Court reluctantly made some enquiries about other refuges, notably in Bavaria, in accord with this advice. Oxford tried to hurry them by alleging that Leopold of Lorraine was spying on the Jacobites for the Emperor. By then they distrusted Oxford too much to credit such assertions, but preparations for departure were under way at the time of the queen's death, though James was still dragging his feet by insisting on payment of Queen Mary's dowry and adequate safeconducts before he left.[15]

Closely associated with Oxford's determination to move James from Lorraine was a desire to please the house of Hanover. His removal would silence the Opposition on that point, as well as gratify the electoral family. Hanover had been working since early 1713 to increase the distance between James and Britain, but with no success. Oxford calculated on ingratiating himself with Hanover through achieving this where they could not. The promise that he would do so figured prominently in Thomas Harley's instructions for his trip to Hanover in 1714: 'The Pretender...Is to go from Bar le Ducke [though the] Adress makes ye place [to which he is to go] difficult to find'. Oxford also promised Schütz that James would be leaving Lorraine shortly, just after he made his proposals to James.[16] What he had not taken into account was that James's patience with his endless procrastination was near exhaustion, and his proposals only served to deplete what remained:

> J'y renonce à ma religion (sans, dit-on, aucune vue humaine, quelle plus visible fausseté), le plus grand obstacle à mon retablissement, et puis je renonce à mes droits, à moins qu'il ne plaise au peuple de m'y appeler; J'y déclare que je n'aurais jamais l'intention de me rendre maitre de l'Ecosse et que j'aime mieux errer par le monde que d'inquiéter les Anglais. Tant de duplicité, de deshonneurs, et de bassesses seraient-ils le moyen de me faire appeller, et si Olléron [Oxford] me propose sérieusement ces infamies, n'ai-je pas lieu de craindre, que c'est un panneau inévitable? En les refusant je lui donne un prétexte de rompre avec moi, en les acceptant je me rends même indigne de vivre, encore plus de regner et le juste objet du mepris de chaque honnête homme; car conscience à part, qui voudrait se fier à moi si je changeais de religion par un motif si grossier de l'intérêt et d'avantage temporel?[17]

Oxford was in no danger of James's accepting his 'terms'. James had been under constant pressure to convert from within the Jacobite movement ever since he came of age. He had always courteously refused, and showed no signs of changing his mind — as Oxford was well aware. In the autumn of 1713 the Jacobite Court had been alarmed by a report that Oxford had suggested to a Jacobite sympathiser that James must convert, and anxiously enquired about his views on the subject. Oxford let it be known that he laid down no such stipulation, but the incident shows that he knew in advance both James's attitude and that the controversy about the need for James's conversion was still raging among the Jacobites. He continued to try and press James into converting after his initial rebuff because he stood to gain so much if by some miracle James acceded.[18] This was founded on an assessment of the probable reaction of the political nation if James did convert. James asserted that no-one would believe he was sincere, and that it would merely serve to blast his reputation. To judge by the popular reaction to strong rumours that he had done so, he was absolutely correct. All a conversion would have achieved would have been to reinforce existing prejudices. Jacobites would have lauded it, Hanoverian Tories and Opposition condemned it and the middle-of-the-road Tories unenthusiastically stuck with the devil they knew. It would certainly not have altered the queen's attitude towards him. Anne was an anti-Catholic bigot, and the likelihood of her being so awestruck by a piece of blatant temporising like James's conversion as to overturn the Hanoverian succession established to protect the Church she loved was virtually nil.[19] The only person who could have gained from James's conversion was Oxford. A conversion would have created a political crisis in Britain which would have given him an excellent opportunity to pose as the unflinchingly loyal guardian of the *Hanoverian* succession, as well as making any attempt to oust him seem factional and unwise while the nation was confronted with such danger. The electoral family might also have been more amenable to his requests and suggestions out of anxiety for their inheritance. By 1714 nothing could offer so good a prospect of retrieving Oxford's flagging fortunes for the remainder of the queen's life and after the arrival of the new dynasty as a hasty and clearly insincere conversion by James.

Oxford's negotiations with the Jacobites were caught in a cycle of progressive inflation. In order to get the French to drop any invasion plans he had to declare he secretly favoured James. To prevent James giving the Whigs the opportunity to create an invasion scare he had to allow him to learn of his 'goodwill'. Finally, to try and remove James from Lorraine he had to concoct a whole pack of bogus proposals — all to maintain the facade of friendship while he tried to bend James to his will. Bargaining with the Jacobites had to have the appearance of an exchange of political goods, which meant that the more Oxford needed to use his Jacobite connection, the more proofs of his 'fidelity' he had to provide.

Oxford wanted various things from the Jacobites but wished to give them nothing substantial in return. Therefore the development of his relations with St Germain took on a pattern imposed by his need to find, at each stage, a pretext by which he was 'regretfully' unable to do anything for the exiles. He was constantly seeking an excuse for inactivity on their behalf while still continuing to represent himself convincingly as the Jacobite Court's best hope. Thus they would be induced to try and keep his goodwill by following his advice and using their influence in his favour, while he did nothing for them because of whatever obstruction he was currently using as a pretext.

During the first stage, 1710 to 1713, Oxford demanded inaction on St Germain's part, coupled to submission to his wishes with regard to leaving France. At the same time he informed Gaultier that he could do nothing about restoring James until the peace was completed.[20] Once it had been completed, Oxford prevaricated for a time about the need to consolidate it, but that was obviously too feeble to last and the Jacobite Court was showing signs of impatience. Oxford consequently moved to a seemingly irreconcilable controversy already convulsing the Jacobite movement: Middleton's continued tenure of office. Oxford transformed the diffidence the ministry had displayed about Middleton knowing of the negotiations into an absolute personal aversion. Though never forthrightly stated, it was now made clear that as long as Middleton remained near James the Government 'regretfully' could do nothing, because he was a security risk. As Middleton himself once put it: 'The way to prevent a bargain is to spread jealousys amongst the partys, and the most effectual means for that is to represent them as Blabbes'. This pretext lasted until November 1713, when James dismissed Middleton.[21] Oxford's package of proposals — the most dramatic being the demand that James convert — came next. Apart from its political basis, this demand had a particular significance for future relations between Oxford and St Germain: it represented the perfect pretext for inaction. James would not convert, therefore Oxford could do nothing — indefinitely.[22]

Oxford had in fact miscalculated: by 1714 James was so consumed with impatience that Oxford's proposals merely served to incense him. At the outset the Jacobite leaders had viewed the Harley ministry with hope, an attitude which predisposed them to accept Oxford's vague promise of assistance when it came, albeit that nothing better was available. This initial enthusiasm first became strained in autumn 1712. Nothing had been received from Oxford but vague promises and peremptory demands, so when Anne fell ill James seriously contemplated flinging himself on the mercy of Ormonde and the Army in a desperate bid to secure the throne. Torcy and Berwick calmed him down, but the circumstances that had given rise to this pitch of frustration remained, ensuring that the situation would recur.[23] In January 1713 James dismissed Richard Hamilton, a friend of Gaultier's, for intriguing against Middleton and as a demonstration of his continued confidence in his Secretary of State. When Gaultier shortly afterwards implied that Middleton's dismissal was the *sine qua non* of further negotiations, James angrily refused to accede, arguing that he could not dismiss him without cause and without a suitable replacement. James stuck to this position until the French Court added its weight to the lobby calling for Middleton's dismissal.[24] Having finally given in, however, James felt entitled to an immediate response for Oxford. When only more exhortations to travel arrived, attached to advice to 'imite la conduite du Roy Charles Second' (with all that that implied in Jacobite circles), James began to take note of the antipathy towards Oxford felt by most British Jacobites, particularly those in Parliament. An ultimatum to Oxford followed shortly afterwards:

> Il y a me dit Mr Raucourt [James] pres de 3 ans que j'entends parler du dessein que mon oncle Mr Olleron [Oxford], avait, de menager un accomodement entre mon Pere [Queen Anne] et moi, et du desir qu'Albert [Anne] même avait que cela fut concu. J'ai fidelement gardé le secret, j'ai tout fait ce qu'on m'a demandé, j'ai écrit des lettres pleines de tendresse, j'ai meme defendu à mes avocats [British Jacobites] de poursuivre mon procès; tant je recherchais la paix et l'union dans ma famille...Mais ajouta-t-il que dois-je penser après tant de demarches de mon côté et pas un de leur, quand je vois mon Père à la veille du trépas sans m'avoir par lui-même, ni par mon oncle, assure du désir d'accomodement, sans avoir repandu à mes lettres, ni même songé a révoquer son testament par lequel il laisse tout à mon cousin Horne [Hanover] à mon préjudice. Mes avocats me pressent sans cesse de renouveller mon procès...J'ai pris mon parti de le renouveller, si dans 2 mois on ne me donne des assurances et fasse voir des effets qui me puissent convaincre de la sincerité de mon Pere et mon oncle à cet égard.[25]

Oxford promptly clarified what he had been insinuating as part of his proposals, meeting James's ultimatum and serving his own political needs in the one move. Though James began to accommodate Oxford on his political demands (notably by beginning to look for a haven other than Lorraine), he was so angered by Oxford's demand that he convert that from March, when he formally rejected it, James was on a hair-trigger, ready to race to Britain at any sign of the arrival of Cambridge or of Anne's health deteriorating. He began to revise this policy to one of continued political initiative only as Oxford visibly began to fail against Bolingbroke, and as the woeful state of military unpreparedness among the British Jacobites became clearer. The French

Court's assurance that they would give military support to any Jacobite revolt endorsed by Bolingbroke completed the process, so that James was caught off balance when Anne died, unsure of what to do.[26]

Like so much of the edifice of political management Oxford built up from 1710, his ability to direct St Germain collapsed in 1714. His dramatic call on James to convert, intended to satisfy James's demand for action on the part of the ministry, stall the process once again and drive the Jacobite Court into making concessions to offset its obstinacy, rebounded completely on Oxford. All it did was translate their pent-up frustrations over the course of the negotiations until then into outright anger that he should pick 'une querelle Allemande' when events were clearly moving towards a crisis.

The French Court's role in Oxford's relations with St Germain was crucial. All serious Jacobite contacts with him were conducted under French auspices and supervision, and the exiled Court instinctively looked to the French for advice and direction as its protector and mentor. This sympathy and trust was heartily reciprocated by the French Court. Louis XIV was genuinely concerned for the welfare of the exiled Stuarts, and his warmth was reflected by his ministers. From this stemmed French support for James's refusal to convert, and their unwillingness to help Oxford drive him out of Lorraine.[27] More positively, Torcy and Gaultier spent a great deal of time and effort unsuccessfully trying to extract payment of Queen Mary's dower from both Oxford and Bolingbroke.[28] The most significant manifestation of French concern for the Jacobite cause was the provision of James with the means of invading Britain. Though the French Government would not risk overt involvement, it secretly prepared two ships at Le Havre, ready to carry James to Britain at very short notice, possibly with some officers from the Irish regiments in support. James was warned that to make use of them he must get there as fast as possible, avoiding Paris, so that the French Court would not be obliged to take official notice of him.[29] It was because he disregarded this stricture, not because of any unwillingness to help him, that the French Government rebuffed James's approaches after Anne's death in August, and returned him to Lorraine.

Despite their sympathy for James, circumstances obliged the French Court to act as Oxford's abettor in his manipulation of St. Germain. France was absolutely desperate for peace in 1710. When Gaultier first approached him that autumn, asking if he wished to participate in secret peace negotiations, Torcy feelingly recalled: 'To ask his majesty's minister at that time, whether he chused to have peace, was the same thing as to ask a person lingering under a dangerous malady, whether he chused to recover'.[30] This brought out the flaw in the Jacobites' reliance on France: French national interest now steadily diverged from that of the Jacobites, and with ruthless realism the French Court was willing to allow the Jacobites to be used by the British Government for whatever ends it chose, so long as peace was achieved. The French Court therefore encouraged James to go along with whatever Oxford desired of him and the Jacobites in general. In late 1712 Torcy enjoined James to keep his followers well in check and to hand over the names of his Whig correspondents to Bolingbroke as requested, so as not to disrupt the peace negotiations. When Oxford pressed James to exchange Lorraine for Germany, Torcy backed him. After James refused to convert in 1714, it was Torcy who advised him to give way on the 'peripheral' demands made by Oxford.[31] France needed peace, so for all their concern for James's cause, Louis XIV and his ministers put the national interest first. Thus when peace was established and Oxford revealed to have been deceiving James, 'elle s'en consoloit aisement.'[32]

Bolingbroke entered late into attempts to use the Jacobite Court's influence in his favour, and then on a defensive basis. His first contact with St Germain was through Gaultier in 1712, when he tried to wheedle the names of its Whig correspondents out of James under the thin pretext of co-ordinating all Jacobite sympathisers' attempts to restore James. James saw through this, and politely refused. Contact then lapsed until December 1713. Bolingbroke was at that time preparing to renew his campaign to oust Oxford, which his enemy had smartly checked in September. He had apparently got some inkling of Oxford's attempts to move James from Lorraine, and intervened to prevent his rival gaining such a valuable success by having Gaultier inform Torcy: 'Suivant le sentiment de la Reyne et de M. de Bolingbroke notre amy [James] restera tant qu'il voudra en Lorraine'.[33] Once he began his manoeuvres to win over the Country Tories, Bolingbroke's contacts with St Germain became more regular. His plans required him to be seen as the upholder of the cause each of the dissident Tory groups espoused. Thus for Jacobite consumption he adopted the position current among many of its British adherents: that James must convert or a restoration would be impossible. Like Oxford in 1711, he was mainly concerned to convince the Jacobite Court of his sincerity in the first instance, and carefully refrained from anything more than verbal commitment. Indeed, his proposals to James offered even less than those of his rival: James was to convert and then let the Hanoverian succession take place, in the sublime confidence that he had Bolingbroke's assurance that within a year or two a national rebellion would eject the German usurper. When St Germain rejected this proposal, Bolingbroke declared his inability to do more while loudly proclaiming his attachment to the Jacobite cause.[34] This convinced the Parliamentary Jacobites, though not those in exile, of his sincerity. At the same time Bolingbroke tried to use his Jacobite connection to provide proof of his attachment to the Hanoverian succession for the Hanoverian Tories. Like Oxford too, he began to urge James to leave Lorraine before the 1714 session began. Both men did this in the hope of thereby removing one of the Hanoverian Tories' major reasons for coolness towards the ministry:[35] Oxford, because a quiet session was the only type he could survive (short of a political miracle such as James's conversion), Bolingbroke in order to attach them to his cause. Bolingbroke did not succeed in persuading James to leave, and so was obliged to draw them to him more laboriously.

Bolingbroke's links with the Jacobite Court were significant only in 1714. They were established for domestic political reasons, but also with an eye to the future. If Bolingbroke succeeded Oxford as the head of the ministry, he would need as broad a base as possible in the Tory party. This was the principle attraction of the 'thorough' Tory policy he was offering the queen: a united and overwhelmingly strong Tory party crushing the Opposition whenever they dared oppose her Government. Establishing a reputation for sincere crypto-Jacobitism among the Parliamentary Jacobites was certain to stand him in good stead, whatever opinion St Germain held of him.

The Tory ministry's contacts with the Jacobite Court from 1710 to 1714 were founded on domestic political necessity. Starting with the simple intention of suppressing any embarrassing Jacobite activity, political or otherwise, at source, these links developed further in response to the gradual failure of Oxford's moderating management, the growth of internal conflicts within the ministry and the emergence of an independent Jacobite group. The only coin St Germain would accept was negotiations about a restoration, so this was the basis on which their relations were conducted. Neither Oxford nor Bolingbroke had any intention of bargaining seriously, hence their demands for extraordinary concessions, with nothing of substance offered in return. The whole process was designed to serve a turn, but in the eyes of posterity the words used and the people whom the ministers deliberately sought out carried it beyond the political context from which it stemmed. The internal political movements in which these negotiations originated were the crucial factor which has hitherto been ignored, and as a result a specious significance has been attached to contacts that were symptomatic rather than fundamental.

NOTES

1. AAE 230, f. 318: Gaultier to Torcy, 3 Oct. 1710 ns.
2. AAE 232, ff. 29 162: Gaultier to Torcy, 10 Feb. and 12 May 1711 ns; 230, ff. 319,323,410,411,440,441: Gaultier to Torcy, 7 and 10 Oct. and 2, 5, 28 and 30 Dec. 1710 ns; 235, f. 263: Gaultier to Torcy, 12 June 1711 ns.
3. AAE 230, f. 403: Torcy to Gaultier, 4 Dec. 1710 ns; 232, ff. 163,168,170,207: Gaultier to Torcy, 15, 19 and 22 May and 16 June 1711 ns; 235, ff. 253,257,262: Torcy to Gaultier, 31 May and 4 and 7 June 1711 ns.
4. Berwick, *Mémoires*, pp.126-8; Baschet 197, f. 387: Torcy to James, 5 Aug. 1711 ns; AAE 234, f. 217: Gaultier to Torcy, 4 Dec. 1711 ns.
5. Fieldhouse, pp.458-9: D'Iberville to Torcy, 6 Mar. 1714 ns. See also: p.457: D'Iberville to Torcy, 18 Feb. 1714 ns; Wickham-Legg, pp.508-10: Gaultier to Torcy, 6 Feb. 1714 ns.
6. Gaultier 122, ff. 5-6 24: Gaultier to Torcy, 23 Apr. and 10 May 1714 ns; Baschet 203, ff. 266-9: D'Iberville to Louis XIV, 16 Aug. 1714 ns.
7. AAE 232, f. 170: Gaultier to Torcy, 22 May 1711 ns.
8. AAE 249, ff. 29-30: Gaultier to James, 14 May 1713 ns. See also: Wickham-Legg, p.504: Gaultier memo [c.Mar. 1713]; Gregg, *Queen Anne*, pp.336-7.

9. AAE 249, ff. 84-5: James to Torcy, 23 May 1713 ns; Gaultier 139, ff. 334-6 265-85: Gaultier to James, c.6 and 19 Feb. 1714 ns.

10. AAE 234, f. 114: memo for Gaultier, 18 Nov. 1711 ns; 237, ff. 212-13: memo for Gaultier, 28 Mar. 1712 ns.

11. AAE 241, f. 5: Gaultier to Torcy, 27 Jan. [1713] ns.

12. AAE 249, ff. 29-30: Gaultier to Torcy, 14 May 1713 ns; 247, f. 50: Gaultier to Torcy, 18 Nov. 1713 ns; Wickham-Legg, pp.503,505: Gaultier to Torcy, 20 Mar., [25] Nov. 1713 ns; Gaultier 121: Gaultier to Torcy, 21 Dec. 1713 ns.

13. Salomon, *Geschichte*, p.333: James to Gaultier, 1 Jan. 1714 ns; Gaultier 139, ff. 113-17: Torcy to Gaultier [mid-Nov. 1713]; Wickham-Legg, p.507: Gaultier to Torcy, 5 Feb. 1714 ns.

14. AAE 261, ff. 177-8: Torcy to James, 25 Feb. 1714 ns. See also: AAE 262, ff. 35-6: Torcy to James, 18 Apr. 1714 ns.

15. Stuart, i, 309: Berwick to James, 25 Mar. 1714 ns; Gaultier 139, ff. 286-8, 320-7: Torcy to Gaultier, 19 Feb. and 25 June 1714 ns; 122, ff. 10-11,19-20,21,40-2; Gaultier to Torcy, 30 Apr., 3 May and 18 June 1714 ns.

16. Macpherson, ii, 465-6: Robethon to Grote, 6 Jan. 1713 ns; ii, 552-3: Schütz to Robethon, 29 Jan. 1714; Add. MSS 40621, f. 163: T. Harley's instructions, Jan. 1714; Wickham-Legg, pp. 508-10: Gaultier to Torcy, 6 Feb. 1714 ns.

17. Salomon, *Geschichte*, pp.335-6: James to Torcy, 26 Feb. 1714 ns.

18. Carte 212, ff. 57-8,61-2: Nairne to Menzies, 20 Aug. and 25 Nov. 1713 ns; Wickham-Legg, pp.511,512,516-17: Gaultier to Torcy, 19 and 26 Feb., 19 Mar. and 26 Apr. 1714 ns.

19. Hermitage GGG, ff. 365-6,391-2,407-8: 13 Oct. and 6 and 20 Nov. 1713; HHH, ff. 70-2: 9 Feb. 1714; Macpherson, ii, 545-6: Schütz to Robethon, 5. Jan. 1714.

20. Baschet 197, ff. 333-4: [Torcy to Louis XIV], 16 Apr. 1711 ns; Salomon, *Geschichte*, p.325: James to Torcy, 20 Aug. 1712 ns.

21. AAE 237, f. 109: memo by Gaultier, 28 Mar. 1712 ns; 241, f. 5: Gaultier to Torcy, 27 Jan. [1713] ns; Carte 212, f. 38: Middleton to 'Watson', 28 July 1712 ns.

22. Salomon, *Geschichte*, pp.339-41: James to Queen Anne, Oxford and Bolingbroke, 3 Mar. 1714 ns; Wickham-Legg, pp.516-17: Gaultier to Torcy, 19 Mar. 1714 ns.

23. Stuart, i, 247-8: Berwick to James, 23 Oct. 1712 ns; Baschet 200, f. 233: James to Torcy, 12 Oct. 1712 ns; Salomon, *Geschichte*, pp.327-8: James to Torcy, 4 Dec. 1712 ns; Fieldhouse, p.446: Torcy to James, 15 Dec. 1712 ns.

24. Gaultier 139, ff. 200-1: Torcy to Gaultier, 25 Jan. 1713 ns; ff. 208-20: Gaultier to Torcy, 15 Feb. 1713 ns; Salomon, *Geschichte*, pp.328-9,329: James to Torcy, 5 and 19 Jan. 1713 ns; Wickham-Legg, pp.503-4: James to Torcy, 18 Apr. 1713 ns.

25. Salomon, *Geschichte*, pp.334-5: James to Gaultier, 1 Feb. 1714 ns. See also: Gaultier 121: James to Torcy, 2 Dec. 1713 ns; Fieldhouse, pp.447-8: Torcy to Gaultier, 11 Dec. 1713 ns; Wickham-Legg, p.506: Gaultier to Torcy, 14 Dec. 1713 ns.

26. AAE 262, ff. 126,189-90, 351: James to Torcy, 16 May, 18 June and 3 and 13 Aug. 1714 ns; f. 196: Torcy to James, 25 June 1714 ns.

27. Berwick, *Mémoires*, pp.130-1; Stuart, i, 306-7,315-16: Berwick to James, 9 Mar. and 11 Apr. 1714 ns; AAE 255, f. 50: Torcy to D'Iberville, 18 Apr. 1714 ns; Salomon, *Geschichte*, p.331: Louis XIV to James, 26 Feb. 1713 ns. For another view, see: Gregg, 'Protestant Succession', pp.89-93,101-2,112-19,307.

28. Gaultier 120,121,122, *passim*.

29. AAE 250, ff. 86-7: Torcy to James, 21 Nov. 1713 ns; 262, ff. 344-5; Torcy to

James, 12 Aug. 1714 ns; Stuart, i, 282-3,284-5: Berwick to James, 21 Nov. and 12 Dec. 1713 ns.

30. Torcy, *Memoirs of the Marquis de Torcy* (1757), ii, 170: Baschet 196, ff. 319-24: Gaultier's instructions, 30 Oct. 1710 ns.

31. Stuart, i, 251-2,266-7: Berwick to James, 20 Nov. 1712 ns and 23 May 1713 ns; Baschet 200, ff. 235-6: Torcy to James, 17 Oct. 1712 ns; AAE 262, ff. 35-6: Torcy to James, 18 Apr. 1714 ns.

32. Berwick, *Mémoires*, p.132; Fieldhouse, p.445: D'Iberville's instructions, 26 Sept. 1713 ns; Baschet 200, ff. 266-7: D'Aumont's instructions, 6 Nov. 1712 ns.

33. Wickham-Legg, p.502: Gaultier to Torcy, 12 Oct. 1712 ns; Baschet 200, ff. 243-4: James to Torcy, 21 Oct. 1712 ns; Stuart, i, 286: Berwick to James, 17 Dec. 1713 ns.

34. Fieldhouse, pp.457,458-9: D'Iberville to Torcy, 18 Feb. and 6 Mar. 1714 ns; Gaultier 139, ff. 265-85: Gaultier to James, 19 and 22 Mar. 1714 ns; AAE 255, f. 215: Gaultier to Torcy, 15 May 1714 ns.

35. AAE 251, ff. 94,124,156: D'Iberville to Torcy, 2 and 16 Feb. and 1 Mar. 1714 ns.

Conclusion

Few political parties have ever looked so strong as the Tories did in the summer of 1714, following Bolingbroke's final eviction of Oxford. Equally few have ever been brought so low so swiftly as that same party was one year later. Such was the consequence of royal disfavour brought into play against them at all levels of the electoral and political process. This catastrophe for the Tory party has often been blamed on its covert Jacobitism, and this, it is alleged, touched all Tories to some extent. As proof of this assertion, the ministry's dalliance with the exiled Court is cited. According to this argument, the Hanoverian dynasty recognised the intrinsically equivocal feeling about the succession at the heart of Toryism, and regretfully but wisely cast the Tories aside. In retrospect the wisdom of their choice was duly demonstrated by Tory participation in the 1715 rebellion, Bolingbroke's flight to join James, and so on. What this line of argument completely fails to recognise is the discontinuity between the political worlds of 1714 and 1715, and quite how much of a trauma this was for the Tory party.

The Tory party underwent significant political development during the years 1710 to 1714. When Harley's predominantly Tory ministry came into office in 1710 it was on a floodtide of enthusiasm reflected both in the constituencies and among the M.P.'s and peers. As far as the mass of the Tory party — the Country Tories — was concerned, the Tory millennium had arrived and they were set to smite their party rivals hip and thigh. They looked with new respect on their former *bête-noire* and one-time despised apostate, Harley, and eagerly awaited his leading them into action. The majority of the Country Tories were not patient men, and as time went on and nothing was done, they grew first disappointed, then angry and finally determined. Denied leadership from any other source, they looked to men from their own ranks. Within a few months Harley's stubborn determination to retain his independence through a mixed administration (albeit as much forced on him by his need to retain the goodwill of Court Whigs in the Lords as by any ideological conviction) had effectively split the Tory party once again into two hostile camps. Harley could continue for a time to coax them into co-operating with his ministry by the need to ensure that it survived to complete the peace they so craved, and tempt them to obey him further by carefully manipulating their hopes of a golden future, but by 1712 his relations with his backbenchers more nearly resembled those of uneasy co-belligerents than members of the same party. Thus his need to cast the Country Tories an occasional sacrificial Whig, and to acquiesce in their intermittant bouts of ostentatiously Country zeal, such as the Land and Malt Tax episodes of 1713, despite the fact that such acts diminished the basis for his continued co-operation with moderate Whigs. By 1713 Oxford's methods of managing Parliament had created a very large and very hungry wolf at his door in the shape of his own backbenchers. He would not feed it, so it did its best to destroy him. One thing which all Country Tories could agree on in 1714 was the need to get rid of Oxford. Some were so determined that they were even prepared to threaten the Tory ministry by which they and the whole party had originally set such store. The Tory party was being wrecked on the rock of Oxford's moderation.

The barely suppressed hostility which characterised the Tory backbenchers' attitude towards their Court Tory fellows and leaders represented a superb opportunity for an ambitious and able alternative to Oxford to make a bid for the premiership, and Bolingbroke seized it with alacrity. By taking advantage of his superior's weakness among the Country Tory majority of the party, Bolingbroke was able to establish for himself a power base from which to push his opponent out of office and exhibit his own political skills to the one person whose support he had to have: the queen. Oxford could and did defeat Bolingbroke in Cabinet and at court on every occasion on which he challenged Oxford's supremacy before April 1714. But Oxford could not compete among the backbenchers, where his rival could outflank him ideologically by proclaiming the purity of his Toryism and make the kind of promises the Country Tories wanted to hear without the disadvantage of being automatically disbelieved. Bolingbroke's adoption of the role of militant saviour of the party definitely exacerbated the divisions Oxford had already created by intensifying the disenchantment the Country Tories felt with Oxford. In the end Bolingbroke's victory was certain to presage a Harleyite schism in the next session, had the queen survived that long. But in terms of the party, the loss of twenty to thirty Harleyites in the Commons and four or five in the Lords was far less serious than the much larger schism Oxford looked certain to create. In his frantic scramble for political survival at the end of the 1714 session Oxford appears to have been planning even to reinstall some of the Junto Whigs in office, and this would have created a division as bad as that of 1704–5 between the Court and Country Tories. Both elements of this scheme assisted Bolingbroke in winning the queen's confidence. When the price of keeping a prime minister (whose capacity for management seemed to be slipping anyway) was the permanent fracturing of the Tory party, which she by now saw as a bulwark against the Whigs who had become anathema to her, and the inclusion of their leaders in her Government, Anne's choice was clear. Oxford was dismissed. In many ways Bolingbroke's means of ousting his rival is one of the most interesting gauges of the development of the party system. Though premier ministers had been outflanked before by the creation of a Parliamentary Opposition, this had been on a 'national' or 'Country' platform, embracing all shades of Parliamentary opinion, as when the Cabal overthrew the earl of Clarendon in 1667. Bolingbroke was the first to do so on a strictly *party* platform, parading his purity and zeal as regards Tory principles as the standards round which to rally the internal opposition to Oxford.

By 1710 Oxford was the product of a bygone age. His skill as a political manager and his urbanity concealed the fact that he was basically out of touch with new political realities. Oxford had learned the arts of political management at the head of his Country party in the 1690s and continued to apply the same methods right up to his fall. Mendacity, vagueness and affability could only satisfy the requirements of management where most M.P.'s were seeking individual or connexion interest. In a situation in which party zeal, interest and uniformity were steadily displacing these characteristics, Oxford's capacities could only be less and less effective. The measure of his talent is that he kept them working for so long. The measure of his and their failure is that in the process he looked like destroying the ideological grouping the queen had chosen to depend on. Oxford was in effect trying to defy the advance of the party system with its logical concomitant of party Government.[1] The Whigs had recognised this development in 1708-10,[2] and the Country Tories already understood it when they came up to Westminster in 1710, as did high Tory chieftains like Nottingham. The Junto and Walpole were to demonstrate how easily the party system could be harnessed to the needs of Government by tying it in at every level, on the basis of spoils only for the faithful, but they only just preceded Bolingbroke.[3] Bolingbroke understood the potential utility of the party system where Oxford seems to have been incapable of doing so, and it is clear that had he had more time as prime minister he would have done to the Whigs what they later did to the Tories: proscription in Church and State, with the possible exception of the Army. Political stability in the form of one-party Government was steadily becoming the only option for a monarch who wanted a quiet life; even Anne had been brought reluctantly to realise that by 1714. There was, of course, no need for it to be Whig one-party Government.[4]

Parliamentary Jacobitism was a unique phenomenon evolved out of a rich mixture of hope, delusion and political circumstance. There had been Jacobites in Parliament since 1688, and would be into the 1760s. What was unusual about the Parliamentary Jacobites between 1710 and 1714 was their sudden importance in their own eyes and those of the rest of the Jacobite movement. Previously, it had been plain that James's only hope of restoration lay in a French-backed invasion supported by an uprising — a purely military matter. This meant that the numbers and actions at Westminster of Jacobite sympathisers were of little or no significance, except insofar as most of them were believed to have strong local influence which could be useful in activating rebel forces. The presence in office of a Whig ministry reinforced this attitude, and, while this remained the case, there was patently no possibility that James could succeed peacefully. This assessment changed entirely when a predominantly Tory ministry came to power in 1710. Suddenly there seemed to be a chance that James could simply succeed his sister, who, the Jacobites doggedly believed, would acquiesce in this if she could. This illusory belief in

Anne's concern for her exiled brother engendered hope at St Germain and this, combined with France's evident incapacity to indulge in military adventurism, served to create and maintain a faith in a two-tier political initiative. On one level the Jacobite Court fondly imagined itself to be actually negotiating with the Government, despite the fact that bargaining in the form of an exchange of political goods was notably absent from their relationship. On the other, Jacobite Parliamentarians were directed to support this process by their ostentatious co-operation with, and support of, the ministry. This was a novel departure, and carrying it into practice created something new at Westminster: a sense of unity and identity among the disparate strands of Jacobitism. This in turn was enhanced and tempered by the experience of action in the van of united Country Tory activity between 1710 and 1713 — an experience, too, which engendered a determination at Westminster among the Jacobite M.P.'s to force their own solution to the problem of James's restoration on the ministry. They were encouraged in this by false hopes of more general support from the rest of the Country Tories than was actually the case. This stemmed from the mainstream of Country Tory opinion's growing embarrassment and exasperation with the behaviour of the house of Hanover. As Sir John Percival observed:

> Jacobitism has undoubtedly gott ground; But I have great reason now to hope that the Constitution will be preserv'd, towards which it will not contribute a little, that honest men declare freely they are for the Protestant Succession,... but there is an unaccountable obscurity in some men's discourse which has giv'n ye Jacobites hopes that more are in their Master's interest than I am persuaded will be found really so.[5]

It only remained for the Parliamentary Jacobites to be unleashed by St Germain, disappointed and angry at the failure of its hopes on the diplomatic level, to produce the final stage of their development as a united, independently operating faction in the Tory party.

The influence of the developing Jacobite group, initially as a mass of individuals with only tenuous connections spread throughout the body of the Country Tories, then as a pressure group in their own right, was diffuse but in places profound. In terms of the development of the Tory Party the Jacobites were a catalytic element, speeding the process through which Oxford's moderate stance was rejected in favour of single-party domination of Church and State. This stemmed from the radical position which the Jacobites, and interestingly, the Hanoverian Tories too, represented in Country Tory circles. Jacobites were at the sharp end of all the October Club's battles with the Government. When co-operating with either the ministry or other backbenchers they always tried to take things to extremes, exhibiting an almost puritanical zeal about carrying party principles into practice. Indeed, from their point of view they could act no other part: since God was on their side they must be in the right and therefore opposition to them deserved only to be thoroughly blasted. From this stemmed their willingness to savage whatever they conceived of as an obstruction, be it Government, Opposition or fellow backbenchers. As the Jacobites increasingly drew together, their influence on the rest of the Country Tories diminished — a development that affected the Hanoverian Tories too — but their extremism was allowed full rein. Thus both the Jacobites and their pro-Hanoverian rivals had few qualms about ambushing Government Supply Bills in a way that the Country Tories as a whole would only rarely contemplate. The net effect of this fiercely pure attitude to party principle and the practice of Government was to drive the ministry into seeking ways to control them. The Jacobites were especially vulnerable in one area: their loyalty to the exiled Stuarts. Oxford, and later Bolingbroke, accordingly constructed links with St Germain through the French Court, and sought with some success to tame the Jacobite movement in general and the Parliamentary Jacobites in particular. This was the most concrete impact the Jacobites in Parliament had on the Tory party.

For between forty-three and fifty-seven M.P.'s to force a British ministry into illicit and dangerous negotiations was a remarkable achievement. However, like so much Country Tory and Jacobite activity it seems distinctly negative. Because the Jacobites threaten to create such trouble they must be silenced, so the ministry, defensively, embarks on bogus negotiations to induce their masters to shut the Jacobites up or at least restrain them. This negative aspect is in fact only superficial, and entirely founded on the tactics used by the Jacobites and their fellows. Since they rarely got beyond the tactical stage, the historian is left with the impression that they were merely a set of wreckers. This was emphatically not the case. All they were trying to do, in the same vein as Tory rioters in 1715 who pulled down Dissenting chapels to remind their social superiors of their duty, was to guide the ministry back to the true path as they saw it. None of the backbench groups which opposed the Harley ministry wished to take control of it. They were fully aware of their own incapacity in the form of interest and inexperience, and simply wished to prod it into going in a direction that accorded with party principle. Lockhart's plan for independent action by the Jacobites in 1714 failed to gain acceptance precisely because it aimed to divorce the Jacobites from the central direction of the Tory party. From the Country Tories' point of view the need for their action came solely from Oxford's betrayal or neglect of what they regarded as fundamental necessities. The only means they had of showing their displeasure and making him listen to them was by wrecking or obstructing Government legislation. Through his resistance to their demands, themselves originating in the compelling logic of the developing party system, Oxford brought on the incipient backbench rebellion which plagued his ministry. Thereby Parliamentary Jacobitism became a power in its own right and something he had to appease.

Jacobitism was an integral part of the Tory party and so of Tory politics from 1689 onwards. Yet, though the Jacobite presence in the first Tory party was a constant until its break-up in the 1750s, presence should in no way be taken to mean dominance or even, necessarily, significance. The mass of the Tory party was committed to the Hanoverian succession before 1714. Any coolness the party as a whole may have manifested towards the electoral family from 1711 onwards arose simply from embarrassment and exasperation at its behaviour over Britain's negotiations leading to the Peace of Utrecht in 1713. The Tories also suffered by comparison with the shameless servility of the Whigs in their determination to secure the reversionary interest. The Jacobites were *a* radical element in Tory politics, but their significance at Westminster between 1710 and 1713 rested almost entirely on their acting as the cutting edge of most of the Country Tory radicalism engendered by the developing party system. It was typical of Oxford that he should try to deal with the problem of intensifying party feeling by manipulating the Jacobites' principles and loyalty in order to silence them. Equally predictably given the Country Tories' real commitment to their principles, this expedient failed. Oxford was merely suppressing the symptoms of discontent, and failure to get to the root of the problem left him trying to deal with a Hydra. No sooner had he dealt with the Jacobites than the Hanoverian Tories began making trouble, and when he tried to deal with them the Jacobites began to stir menacingly, and so on. Jacobitism became a problem in the Tory party before 1714 only when circumstances acted to create a coherent unit out of the diffuse mass of backbench opinion. These circumstances arose in part from the queen's deteriorating health, in part from Jacobite impotence in other spheres and in part from the internal momentum of the developing party 'system' as politics in Britain steadily became more tense and violent. All of these factors, however, were subject to the most important influence of all: the Harley ministry. Without its intervention, politics and policies, Jacobitism could never have assumed the significance it did in the last years of Queen Anne.

NOTES

1. Holmes, *Politics*, pp. 415–17.
2. Plumb, *Stability*, p. 157; Bennett, *Tory Crisis*, p. 101; C. Jones, 'Godolphin, the Whig Junto, and the Scots', *Scott. Hist. Rev.*, 58 (1979), 158–74; H.L. Snyder, 'Queen Anne versus the Junto: the Effort to Place Orford at the Head of the Admiralty in 1709', *Hunt. Lib. Quarterly*, xxxv (1971–2), 323–42.
3. Plumb, *Stability*, pp. 159–89 and *passim*.
4. For another view, see: Plumb *Stability*, pp. 153, 156–8.
5. Add. MSS. 47087, f. 66: Percival to Philip Percival, 3 Apr. 1714.

Appendix 1: *M.P.'s and peers with probable Jacobite leanings, 1710–14*

The lists of M.P.'s and peers below are the results of my work in the sources. Because of this they are neither definitive nor exhaustive, but simply my interpretation of the evidence. Since their origins are so subjective, I have split them into two categories for each House: 'Probables' and 'Possibles'. A 'probable' is someone whom I believe did, or would have, voted against the ministry on an issue felt to be Jacobite. A 'possible' is someone I consider might have done so. This appendix is in no sense the last word on the subject and is simply intended as an aid to researchers.

Probable Jacobite M.P.'s, 1710–14

1. Charles Aldworth — New Windsor 21 Jan. 1712–1714
2. Sir Alexander Areskine (Lord Lyon King of Arms) — Fifeshire 1710–14
3. Abraham Blackmore — St Michaels 1710–13, Newton 1713–14
4. John Bland — Lancashire 1713–27
5. Richard Bulkeley, viscount Bulkeley — Angelsey 1704–15 and 1722–24
6. James Bulteel — Tavistock 3 Feb. 1711–14
7. Benedict Leonard Calvert — Harwich 17 May 1714–15
8. Henry Campion — Bossiney 1710–13, Sussex 1713–15
9. Sir William Carew — Saltash 17 Jan. 1711–13, Cornwall 1713–8 Mar. 1744
10. John Carnegie — Forfarshire 1708–16
11. William Cochran (of Kilmaronock) — Wigton Burghs 1708–13
12. Sir John Cotton — Huntingdonshire 1710–13
13. Rowland Cotton — Newcastle-under-Lyme 1699–1706, 1708–9, 1710–15
14. Richard Cresswell — Bridgenorth 1710–13, Wootton Bassett 1713–15
15. Sir Alexander Cumming — Aberdeenshire 1709–22
16. George Douglas (Colonel) — Linlithgow Burghs 1708–13, 1715–22, Orkney and Shetland 1713–15, 1722–30
17. Charles Eversfield — Horsham 1705–10, 1713–16 June 1715, 12 June 1721–41, Sussex 1710–13, Steyning 1741–7
18. Henry Fleetwood — Preston 1708–22
19. Thomas Forster (junior) — Northumberland 1708–16
20. Sir James Hamilton (of Rosehall) — Lanarkshire 1710–15, 1735–50
21. Simon Harcourt — Wallingford 1710–13, Abingdon 1713–15

22.	John Houston (junior)	Linlithgow 1708–14
23.	Sir John Hynde-Cotton	Cambridge 1708–22, 1727–41, Cambridgeshire 1722–27, Marlborough 1741–52
24.	Sir Charles Kemys	Monmouthshire 1713–15, Glamorgan 1716–34
25.	George Kenyon	Wigan 22 Apr. 1713–1714
26.	Corbet Kynaston	Shrewsbury 27 May 1714–1723, Salop 1734–40
27.	John Kynaston	Shrewsbury 1695–1709, Salop 1710–15
28.	John Lade	Southwark 1713–20 Apr. 1714, 3 May 1714–1722, 1724–27
29.	Thomas Legh	Newton 1702–13
30.	William Livingston	Aberdeen Burghs 1710–13
31.	George Lockhart	Edinburghshire 1708–14
32.	Richard Lockwood	Hindon 1713–15, London 1722–7, Worcester 1734–41
33.	Alexander Mackenzie (of Fraserdale)	Inverness-shire 1710–14
34.	George Mackenzie (of Inchcutre)	Inverness Burghs 1710–13
35.	Sir Thomas Mackworth	Rutland 1694–5, 1701–8, 1721–7, Portsmouth 1713–15
36.	Sir John Malcolm	Kinross-shire 1710–13
37.	James Murray (son of viscount Stormont)	Dumfriesshire 22 Feb. 1711–1713, Elgin Burghs 1713–15
38.	Lord James Murray (the duke of Atholl's brother)	Perthshire 1710–14
39.	William Newland	Gatton 1710–38
40.	Theophilus Oglethorpe	Haslemere 1710–13
41.	James Oswald	Dysart Burghs 1710–14
42.	Sir John Pakington	Worcestershire 1690–95, 1698–1727
43.	Sir Hugh Paterson	Stirlingshire 1710–14
44.	John Pugh	Cardiganshire 1705–8, Montgomery Boroughs 1708–27
45.	Samuel Rolle	Callington 1665–79, 1701–19, Devonshire 1680–1, 1689–1701
46.	Charles Ross (Lieutenant-General)	Ross-shire 1709–22, 1727–32
47.	William Shippen	Bramber 1707–9, 1710–13, Saltash 1713–15, Newton 1715–43
48.	Thomas Strangways (junior)	Bridport 1705–13, Dorset 1713–26
49.	Thomas Strangways (senior)	Poole 1673–9, Dorset 1679–1713
50.	Sir Simeon Stuart	Hampshire 1710–13
51.	Sir William Whitlock	West Looe 1659, Great Marlowe 1689–95, Oxford University 1703–17

Possible Jacobite M.P.'s, 1710–14

1.	Sir William Barker	Ipswich 1708–13, Thetford 1713–15, Suffolk 31 Oct. 1722–1731
2.	John Berkeley	Gloucestershire 1710–14
3.	Charles Caesar	Hertford 1701–8, 1710–15, 1722–3, Hertfordshire 1727–34, 1736–41
4.	John Codrington	Bath 1710–27, 1734–41
5.	Robert Ecklin (Lieutenant-General)	Sudbury 1710–14
6.	Sir Henry Goring	Horsham 1707–8, 26 Jan.—16 June 1715, Steyning 1 Feb. 1709–15
7.	Edward Harvey	Bletchingley 1679, Clithero 1705–13, 1715–22
8.	Richard Jones	Salisbury 1713–14
9.	Sir Alexander Maxwell	Wigton Burghs 1713–15
10.	Clayton Milborne	Monmouth Boroughs 1710–14
11.	Charles Oliphant M.D.	Ayr Burghs 1710–19
12.	Sir Alexander Ramsay	Kincardineshire 1710–13
13.	James Scott	Kincardineshire 1713–34
14.	John Stuart (of Sorbie)	Wigtonshire 1708–10, 1711–27
15.	George Yeaman	Perth Burghs 1710–14

Probable Jacobite Peers, 1710–14

1.	Lord Balmerino	Scots Representative Peer 1710–14
2.	Duke of Beaufort	
3.	Lord Blantyre	Scots Representative Peer 1710–13
4.	Earl of Breadalbane	Scots Representative Peer 1713–14
5.	Duke of Buckinghamshire	
6.	Earl of Clarendon	
7.	Earl of Dundonald	Scots Representative Peer 1713–14
8.	Earl of Eglinton	Scots Representative Peer 1710–14
9.	Lord (from 1711, Earl) Ferrers	
10.	Duke of Hamilton	Scots Representative Peer 1708–12
11.	Earl of Home	Scots Representative Peer 1710–13
12.	Viscount Kilsyth	Scots Representative Peer 1710–14
13.	Marquis of Carmarthen (Duke of Leeds from 1712)	
14.	Earl of Linlithgow	Scots Representative Peer 1713
15.	Earl Marischal	Scots Representative Peer 1710–12
16.	Lord North and Grey	
17.	Duke of Ormonde	
18.	Earl of Scarsdale	
19.	Earl of Yarmouth	

Possible Jacobite Peers, 1710–14
1. Viscount Hereford
2. Lord Lansdowne (created Dec.
   1711 – one of Oxford's 'dozen')
3. Earl Poulet

For more precise information regarding my categorisation of the Jacobite peers and M.P.'s, see: Szechi, Appendix 1.

Appendix 2: 'Computation of peers 30 Aug 1710 by Mr Thomas Bruce son to the Earl of Kincardine.'

The following list and computations are part of the Mar and Kellie MSS. deposited at Register House, Edinburgh (GD 124/10/14/5). They were probably compiled to aid Mar in his negotiations with the various parties into which the Scots peerage was divided. Thomas Bruce, though a younger son, eventually inherited his father's title and became a notorious Jacobite and adviser to Charles Edward Stuart. In 1710 he was probably in friendly contact with many of the peers mentioned on the list, but is likely to have known the Jacobite and Court peers better than the others. All those in italics were elected as Representative peers in 1710.

Hamilton	Queens List	Squadrone	Non Liquets
Hamilton	Argyle	Lenox	*Atholl*
Annandale	Lanthiem	Montrose	Keithness
Craufurd	*Marr*	Roxburgh	Winton
Erroll	Mertoun	Tuedale	*Home*
Mareshall	*Kinnoull*	Sutherland	Abercorn
Glenravin	*Laudunn*	Rothes	Sterling
Eglinton	Weems	Buchan	Elgine
[Lin]lithgow	*Northesk*	Haddington	Carnwath
Wigtoun	Kincardine	Lauderdale	Dysart
Strathmore	Balcarres	Finlaytor	Hyndford
Galloway	Forfar	Leven	Delorani
Airlie	Dumbarton	Kilmarnock	Dumbar
Selkirk	Kintor	Marchmont	Kingstoun
Dundonald	Cromartie	Seafield	Irving
Braidalbane	*Roseberrie*	Stair	Preston
Aberdein	Glasgow	Hopetoun	Newhaven
Dinmor	*Isla*	Gray	Tiviot
Orkney	Dumblain		
	[Carmarthen]	Cathcart	Forbes
Ruglen	Semple	Ross	Sinclair
Falkland	Elphinston	Torpichen	Mordingtoun
Stormont	*Balmirino*	Burlie	Pitsligo
Kilsyth	*Blantyre*	Rae	Fraser
Salton	Cranstoun	Ballenden	Bamfe
Oliphant	Elibank	Eymouth	
		[Marlborough]	Colvill
Linidors	Portmor		Rutherford
Forrester	Duffus	24	Kinaird
Burgany			

Belhaven   26   26
Rollo

29
[Number of Representative peers elected from each group:
Hamilton: 6   Queens: 8   Squadrone: 0   Non Liquets: 2]

Supposing d:Hamilton brooke off from the queens measures and joyns with d:Marlburrow and the treasurer, laying asyde the Squadrone, he gets 15 votes which increaseth that list to 44.
The 15 he getts are
Lennox
Southerland
Buchan
Lauderdale
Findlator
Leaven
Kilmarnock
Seafield
Stair
Gray
Cathcart
Ross
Burleigh
Rae
Eymouth

Supposeing at the same tyme the queens list takes in the Squadrone it gets nyn votes which increaseth that list to 35.

The nyn Squadrone votes are
Montrose
Roxburgh
Tweedale
Rothes
Hadington
Marchmont
Hopton
Torpichen
Bellenden

Supposeing that d:Hamilton joyns the squadrone togither with E:Stair, Lord Gray, Cathcart, and Eymouth, being 13 in all, his list comes to 42

Supposeing att the same time the queens list should be joyned by the Earle of Seafield, and these others mentiond in the Squadrone list (excepting the nyn originall Squadrone men, and the four mentioned on the other syde which four are considered as freis [sic] d:Marlburrow) in that case the queens list amounts to. . .37

Supposeing only these 4 viz Stairs, Gray, Cathcart, and Eymouth shall joyn d:Hamilton's list in that case it amounts to. . . 33

Supposeing att the same tyme the squadrone with the Earle of Seafield, and such others as may be brought off from the duke of Marlburrow, shall joyn the queens list it will amount to. . .46

The aforsaid computation is made without regard to the 26 non-liquets.

Bibliography

1. *Manuscript Sources*

Bodleian Library, Oxford:
MSS. Additional
    D. 26   Colonel Nathaniel Hooke
    D. 79   John Cotton
MSS. Ballard
    9–10, 12, 18, 21, 31, 38   Arthur Charlett
MSS. Carte
    117, 180, 198, 210–12, 231, 237–8   David Nairne
MSS. Eng. Hist.
    c. 974
MSS. North
B2, A3   Lord North and Grey
MSS. Rawl.
    D.: 153, 170, 198, 373, 835, 848
    Letters: 42, 87
    C.: 584

British Library, London:
Additional MSS.
    17677 DDD-HHH YYY   L'Hermitage despatches (transcripts)
28055   Earl Godolphin
20296–7, 20310–1, 31245,
    31254–9, 31267, 46494–5   Cardinal Gualterio
    32686   Duke of Newcastle
    47026–7, 47072, 47087   Sir John Percival
    22202, 22211, 22220–2
    22228, 31135–9, 38851   Earl of Strafford
    33273, 42176   Henry Watkins
    32686
    34077
    40621   Thomas Harley
    49360
Blenheim Papers
    61125, 61127, 61134, 61136,
    61461, 61495, 61632, 61684   Arthur Maynwaring
Lansdowne MSS.
    885

Loan 29 (Portland)
  7, 10–1, 125, 127–38, 143, 146,   Robert Harley
  148–56, 158–64, 307–8, 310, 371–3, 375,
  395, 45I, 45A, 45J

Cambridge University Library:
Cholomondeley (Houghton) MSS.   Robert Walpole
Stuart Papers Microfilm
  1214–5   Duke of Berwick

History of Parliament Trust, 34 Tavistock Square, London:
Transcripts
  Archives du Ministère de la Guerre
  Beaufort MSS.   Duke of Beaufort
  Blackett Diary
  Bute (Loudoun) MSS., Loudun MSS.   Earl of Loudoun
  Chatsworth MSS.   Lord Guernsey
  Erle MSS.   Lieutenant-General Thomas Erle
  Fox-Strangways MSS.   Sir Charles Fox
  Gurdon MSS.   Richard Berney
  Isham MSS.   Sir Justinian Isham

  Jervoise MSS.   Thomas Jervoise
  Kay Diary   Sir Arthur Kay
  Ketton-Cremer MSS.   Ashe Windham
  Levens MSS.   James Grahme
  Montrose MSS.   Mungo Graham
  Nicolson Diary   William Nicolson, Bishop of Carlisle
  Nottingham University,   Earl of Oxford
  Portland MSS.
  Rashleigh MSS.
  Roxburghe MSS.   William Ker
Microfilms
  Staatsarchiv Hannover, Calenberg Briefe 24 England 99 107a
113a   Kreienberg
                                                despatches
  Zentrales Staatsarchiv, Dienstelle Merseburg, Rep. XI (England)
37B 38A 38C 39A   Bonet despatches

National Library of Scotland, Edinburgh:
Wodrow Papers
  Folio 35
Wodrow Letters
  Quarto 5–8   Thomas Smith
Newhailes Papers
  Acc. 7228   George Lockhart
Fletcher of Saltoun Papers
  16503, 16746   Lord Saltoun

National Library of Wales, Aberystwyth:

Bettisfield MSS.	Sir Thomas Hanmer
Chirk Castle MSS.	Sir Richard Myddelton
Ottley MSS.	Thomas Strangways
Penrice and Margam MSS.	Sir Thomas Mansel
Tredegar MSS.	John Morgan

Public Record Office, Chancery Lane, London:
State Papers 44/106/218, 34/13 23
Baschet Transcripts 31/3/196–203

Quai D'Orsay, Paris (Archives du Ministère des Affaires Etrangères):
Correspondance Politique, Angleterre 230 232–9 241–53 255–6 261–2
Mémoires et Documents, Angleterre 24 138

Scottish R.O., Register House, Edinburgh:

Clerk of Penicuik MSS.	
GD 18/3148–50	John Pringle
Shairp of Houston Muniments	
GD 30/1562	John Houston
Dalhousie MSS.	
GD 45/14/: 321, 323, 326, 336–8,	
340, 348, 352–3, 362, 364–5	George Lockhart, lord Balmerino
Breadalbane Papers	
GD 112/45; 112/40/7/1, 3–8;	
112/40/8/1, 3, 5	Earl of Breadalbane
Mar and Kellie MSS.	
GD 124/10/14; 124/15/989, 1001–2,	
1011, 1017, 1020, 1024, 1099, 1143	Sir James Dumbar
Morton Papers	
GD 150/2375, 3461, 3466	Colonel George Douglas
Home of Marchmont MSS.	
GD 158/1117	Earl of Home
Seafield MSS.	
GD 248/560/44–6; 248/561/47–50;	
248/566/87; 248/571/6	Earl of Seafield

Other Collections

Baron Hill MSS.	University College of North Wales, Bangor (Viscount Bulkeley)
Blackett (Maften) MSS.	Northumberland R.O. (Sir William Blackett)
Blair Castle MSS.	Duke of Atholl, Blair Atholl Castle, Perthshire (Duke of Atholl)
Blair Letters	Scottish Catholic Archives, Columba House, Edinburgh (James Carnegy)
Chaytor Papers	North Yorkshire R.O., Northallerton (Sir William Chaytor)
Claydon House Letters	Buckinghamshire R.O., Ailesury (Sir Thomas Cave, Viscount Fermanagh)

Dartmouth MSS.
  Bradford Muniments

Ducie-Morton MSS.

Finch-Hatton MSS.
  Isham Letters

Forester MSS.

University of Pennsylvania, MSS.
French 120-2, 139 (Gaultier Papers)

Grey-Neville MSS.

Hamilton MSS.

Kenyon MSS.

Massingberd-Mundy MSS.
  Massingberd MSS.
  Massingbert of Gunby MSS.
  Monson MSS.

Legh of Lyme MSS.

Pakington Papers
  Somers Papers

Panshanger MSS.

Renaudot Collection

Throckmorton Muniments

Wake MSS.

Witley—Beaumont MSS.

Staffordshire R.O., Stafford (Earl of Dartmouth, Sir Arthur Kay)
Gloucestershire R.O., Gloucester (Matthew Ducie-Morton)

Northamptonshire R.O., Northampton (Earl of Nottingham, Sir Justinian Isham)
Salop R.O., Shrewsbury (Sir William Forester)

Microfilm in possession of Mr D. Szechi, Dept. of History, University of Sheffield (Abbé Gaultier)
Berkshire R.O., Reading (Charles Aldworth)
Duke of Hamilton, Lennoxglove (Duke of Hamilton)
Lancashire R.O., Preston (George Kenyon)

Lincoln Archives Office, Lincoln (Sir William Massingberd)
John Rylands Library, Deansgate, Manchester (William Shippen)

Worcestershire R.O., Worcester (Sir John Pakington, Lord Somers)
Hertfordshire R.O., Hertford (Earl Cowper)
Bibliothèque Nationale, Paris (Abbé Renaudot)
Coughton Court, Warwickshire (Sir William Throckmorton)
Christ Church, Oxford (Richard Dingworth)
Kirklees Libraries and Museum Service, Huddersfield (Sir Arthur Kay)

2. Printed Primary Sources
The Lockhart Papers, ed. A. Aufrere (1817).
Berwick, *Mémoires du Maréchal de Berwick* (Switzerland, 1778).
Quadriennium Annae Postremum; or the Political State of Great Britain, ed. A. Boyer, iii and vii (1718-19).
The Correspondence of Sir Thomas Hanmer, Bart., ed. Sir Henry Bunbury (1838).
G. Burnet, *History of My Own Time* (2nd ed., Oxford, 1833).

Calender of Treasury Books (1969), xvii.

The Wentworth Papers, 1705-39, ed. J. J. Cartwright (1882).

A Character of John Sheffield, Late Duke of Buckinghamshire (1729).

W. Cobbett,_Parliamentary History of England_ (1806-20) vi.

A Collection of White and Black Lists (1715).

Commons Journals (1710-14) xvi-xvii.

Diary of Mary, Countess Cowper, 1714-20, ed. S. Cowper (2nd ed., 1865).

G. Davies and Marion Tinling, 'Letters from James Brydges, created duke of Chandos, to Henry St John, created viscount Bolingbroke', _Hunt. Lib. Bull._, ix (1936) 119-66.

[D. Defoe], _A Letter from a Member of the House of Commons to his Friend in the Country Relating to the Bill of Commerce_ (1713).

The Correspondence of Sir James Clavering, ed. H. T. Dickinson (Gateshead, 1967).

The Letters of Henry St John to the Earl of Orrery, 1709-11, ed. H. T. Dickinson (Camden Soc., 4th Ser., xiv, 1975), pp. 137-200.

H. N. Fieldhouse, 'Bolingbroke's share in the Jacobite intrigue of 1710-14', _Eng. Hist. Rev._, lii (1937), 443-59.

The Letters of Joseph Addison, ed. W. Graham (1941).

Clerk of Penicuik's Memoirs, ed. J. M. Grey (Scott. Hist. Soc., xiii, 1892).

The Harcourt Papers, ed. E. W. Harcourt (Oxford, 1880).

The Private Diary of Lord Chancellor Cowper, ed. E. C. Hawtrey (1833).

The Diary of John Hervey, First Earl of Bristol, ed. W. Hervey (Wells, 1894).

Historical Manuscripts Commission:

  Bath MSS, i. 2.

  Baccleuch MSS, iii.

  Dartmouth MSS,

  Downshire MSS, i. 2.

  4th Report, Fitzhardinge's Papers.

  Hodgkin MSS.

  Kenyon MSS.

  Laing MSS, ii.

  Mar and Kellie MSS.

  Portland MSS, iv-v, vii, x.

  Rye and Hereford MSS.

  Stuart Papers, i.

N. Luttrell, _A Brief Relation of State Affairs_ (Cambridge, 1847), vi.

Original Papers; containing the secret history of Great Britain from the Restoration to the accession of the House of Hanover, ed. J. J. Macpherson (1775).

A. N. Newman, 'Proceedings in the House of Commons, March–June 1714', _Bull. Inst. Hist. Res._,xliii (1970), 231-3.

The Old Wives Tales (1712).

R. Patten, _The History of the Late Rebellion_ (1717).

The Diary of Sir David Hamilton, 1709-14, ed. P. Roberts (1975).

The Marchmont Papers, ed. Sir George Rose (1831).

The House of Commons, 1715-54, ed. R. Sedgewick (1970).

Letters of the Sitwells and Sacheverells, ed. Sir George Sitwell (Scarborough, 1901).

The Marlborough-Godolphin Correspondence, ed. H. L. Snyder (1975), iii.

Marquis de Torcy, _Memoirs of the Marquis de Torcy_ (1757) ii.

L. G. Wickham-Legg, 'Extracts from Jacobite correspondence, 1712–14', *Eng. Hist. Rev.* xxx (1915), 501–18.

Journal to Stella, ed. H. Williams (1958).

The Correspondence of Jonathan Swift, ed. H. Williams (1963).

3. *Secondary Sources*

P. M. Ansell, 'Harley's Parliamentary Management', *Bull. Inst. Hist. Res.*, xxxiv (1961), 92–7.

J. Baynes, *The Jacobite Rising of 1715* (1970).

G. V. Bennett, *White Kennett, 1660–1728, Bishop of Peterborough* (1957).

_____, 'Robert Harley, the Godolphin Ministry, and the Bishophrics Crisis of 1707', *Eng. Hist. Rev.*, lxxxii (1967), 726–46.

_____, 'Jacobitism and the Rise of Walpole', in *Historical Perspectives in Honour of J. H. Plumb*, ed. N. McKendrick (1974).

_____, *The Tory Crisis in Church and State, 1688–1730: the Career of Francis Atterbury, Bishop of Rochester* (1975).

I. F. Burton, P. W. J. Riley and E. Rowlands, 'Political Parties in the Reigns of William III and Anne: the Evidence of Division Lists', *Bull. Inst. Hist. Res.*, li (1977–8), 206–9;

J. Cannon and W. A. Speck, 'Re-Election on Taking Office, 1706–90', *Bull. Inst. Hist. Res.*, li (1977–8), 206–9.

The Whig Ascendancy, ed. J. Cannon (1981).

Earl of Cardigan, *The Life and Loyalties of Thomas Bruce* (1951).

E. K. Carmichael, 'Jacobitism in the Scottish Commission of the Peace, 1707–60', *Scott. Hist. Rev.*, 58 (1979), 58–69.

J. Carswell, *The Good Old Cause* (1953).

D. Chandler, *Marlborough as Military Commander* (1973).

_____, *The Art of Warfare in the Age of Marlborough* (1976).

J. Child, *The Army of Charles II* (1976).

_____, 'The Army and the Oxford Parliament of 1681', *Eng. Hist. Rev.*, xciv (1979), 580–7.

J. C. D. Clark, 'A General Theory of Party, Opposition and Government, 1688–1832', *Hist. Journal*, xxiii (1980), 295–325.

_____, *The Dynamics of Change* (1982).

P. Clark, 'Migration in England During the Late Seventeenth and Early Eighteenth Centuries', *Past and Present*, 83 (1979), 57–90.

G. E. Cokayne, *The Complete Peerage* (1900).

Linda Colley, 'The Loyal Brotherhood and the Cocoa Tree: The London Organization of the Tory Party, 1727–60', *Hist. Journal* xx (1977), 77–95.

_____, *In Defiance of Oligarchy* (1982).

Eveline Cruickshanks, The Tories and the Successsion in the 1714 Parliament'. *Bull. Inst. Hist. Res.*, xlvi (1973), 176–85.

_____, *Political Untouchables* (1979).

Eveline Cruickshanks, D. Hayton and C. Jones, 'Divisions in the House of Lords on the Transfer of the Crown, and Other Issues, 1689–94, 10 New Lists', *Bull. Inst. Hist. Res.*, liii (1980), 56–87.

G. Davies, 'The Seamy Side of Marlborough's War', *Hunt. Lib. Quarterly*, xv (1951–2), 21–44.

H. T. Dickinson, 'The Attempt to Assassinate Harley, 1711', *Hist. Today*, xv (1965), 788–95.

_____, 'The Mohun-Hamilton Duel: Personal Feud or Whig Plot', *Durham Univ. Journal*, 57 (1965), 159–65.

_____, 'The Tory Party's Attitude to Foreigners: a Note on Party Principles in the Age of Anne', *Bull. Inst. Hist. Res.*, xl (1967), 153–65.

_____, 'The Poor Palatines and the Parties', *Eng. Hist. Rev.*, lxxxii (1967), 464–85

_____, 'The October Club', *Hunt. Lib. Quarterly*, xxxiii (1969–70), 155–74.

_____, *Bolingbroke* (1970).

_____, *Liberty and Property* (1977).

R. Downie, *Robert Harley and the Press* (1979).

P. Earle, *Monmouth's Rebels* (1977).

K. G. Feiling. *A History of the Tory Party, 1640-1714* (Oxford. 1924).

K. G. Feiling, *The Second Tory Party, 1714-1832* (1938).

H. N. Fieldhouse, 'A Note on the Negotiations for the Peace of Utrecht', *American Hist. Rev.*, 40 (1934–5), 274–8.

_____, 'Oxford, Bolingbroke and the Pretender's Place of Residence, 1711–14', lii (1937), 289–96.

P. S. Fritz, 'The Anti-Jacobite Intelligence System of the English Ministers, 1715–45'. *Hist. Journal*, xvi (1973), 265–89.

_____, *The English Ministers and Jacobitism Between the Rebellions of 1715 and 1745* (1975).

L. J. Glassey, *Politics and the Appointment of Justices of the Peace, 1675-1720* (Oxford, 1979).

E. Gregg, 'Was Queen Anne a Jacobite?', *History*, lvii (1972), 358–75.

_____, 'Marlborough in Exile, 1712–14', *Hist. Journal*, xv (1972), 593–618.

_____, *Queen Anne* (1980).

M. Haile, *James Francis Edward the Old Chevalier* (1907).

Elizabeth Handasyde, *Granville the Polite* (1938).

Ragnhild M. Hatton, *George I* (1978).

Studies in Diplomatic History, ed. Ragnhild M. Hatton and M. S. Anderson (1970).

R. L. Hayley, 'Cibber, Collier, and the Non-Juror', *Hunt. Lib. Quarterly*, xliii (1979), 61–76.

D. Hayton, 'The Crisis in Ireland and the Disintegration of Queen Anne's last Ministry', *Irish Hist. Studies*, xxii (1981), 193–215.

B. W. Hill, 'Oxford, Bolingbroke and the Peace of Utrecht', *Hist. Journal*, xvi (1973), 241–63.

_____, 'The Change of Government and the 'Loss of the City', 1710–11', *Econ. Hist. Rev.*, xxiv (1971), 395–413.

_____, *The Growth of Parliamentary Parties* (1976).

G. S. Holmes, 'The Commons Division on "No Peace Without Spain" ', *Bull. Inst. Hist. Res.*, xxxiii (1960), 223–34.

_____, 'The Hamilton Affair of 1711–12: A Crisis in Anglo-Scottish Relations', *Eng. Hist. Rev.*, lxxvii (1962), 257–82.

_____, 'The Attack on the Influence of the Crown 1702–16', *Bull. Inst. Hist. Res.*, xxxix (1966), 47–68.

_____, *British Politics in the Age of Anne* (1967).

Britain After the Glorious Revolution, 1689-1714, ed. G. S. Holmes (1969).

G. S. Holmes, *The Trial of Dr Sacheverell* (1973).

_____, 'The Electorate and the National Will in the First Age of Party', Inaugural Lecture, *Lancaster Univ. Pamphlet* (Lancaster, 1975).

_____, 'Religion and Party in Late Stuart England', *Hist. Association Pamphlet G 86* (1975).

G. S. Holmes, 'Gregory King and the Social Structure of Pre-Industrial England', *Trans. Royal Hist. Soc.*, 4th Ser., xxvii (1977), 41–68.

G. S. Holmes and W. A. Speck, 'The Fall of Harley in 1708 Reconsidered', *Eng. Hist. Rev.*, lxxx (1965), 673–98.

H. Horwitz, 'Parties, Connections and Parliamentary Politics, 1689–1714: Review and Revision', *Journal of Brit. Stud.*, vi (1966–7), 45–69.

_____, *Revolution Politicks* (1968).

_____, *Parliament, Policy and Politics in the Reign of William III* (1976.)

E. Hughes, *North Country Life in the Eighteenth Century* (1952).

J. J. Hurwich, 'Dissent and Catholicism in English Society: A Study of Warwickshire, 1660–1720', *Journal of Brit. Stud.*, xvi (1976), 24–55.

F. G. James, 'The Active Irish Peers in the Early Eighteenth Century', *Journal of Brit. Stud.*, xviii (1979), 52–69.

R. C. Jarvis, *Collected Papers on the Jacobite Risings* (Manchester, 1972).

J. P. Jenkins, 'Jacobites and Freemasons in Eighteenth Century Wales', *Welsh Hist. Rev.*, ix (1979), 391–406.

C. Jones, 'Debates in the House of Lords on the "Church in Danger", 1705, and on Dr Sacheverell's Impeachment, 1710', *Hist. Journal*, xix (1976), 759–71.

_____, 'Godolphin, the Whig Junto, and the Scots', *Scott. Hist. Rev.*, 58 (1979), 158–74.

_____, 'The Impeachment of the earl of Oxford and the Whig Schism of 1717: four new Lists', *Bull. Inst. Hist. Res.*, lv (1982), 66–87.

P. D. Jones, 'The Bristol Bridge Riot and its Antecedents', *Journal of Brit. Stud.*, xix (1981), 74–92.

G. H. Jones, *The Mainstream of Jacobitism* (Harvard, 1954).

_____, *Charles Middleton* (1967).

J. P. Kenyon, *Revolution Principles: the Politics of Party, 1689–1720* (Cambridge, 1977).

N. Landau, 'Independence, Deference, and Voter Participation: the Behaviour of the Electorate in Early Eighteenth Century Kent', *Hist. Journal*, xxii (1979), 561–83.

B. Lenman, *The Jacobite Risings in Britain, 1688–1745* (1980).

A. McInnes, *Robert Harley, Puritan Politician* (1970).

D. McKay, 'Bolingbroke, Oxford and the Defence of the Utrecht Settlement in Southern Europe', *Eng. Hist. Rev.*, lxxxvi (1971), 264–84.

W. Michael, *England Under George I: The Beginnings of the Hanoverian Dynasty* (1936).

J. Miller, *James II: a Study in Kingship* (1978).

J. J. Murray, *George I, the Baltic and the Whig Split of 1717* (1969).

Sir Lewis Namier, *The Structure of Politics at the Accession of George III* (1957).

_____, *England in the Age of the American Revolution* (1961).

A. N. Newman, 'Political Parties in the Reigns of William III and Anne: the Evidence of Division Lists: A Supplementary Note', *Bull. Inst. Hist. Res.*, xliii (1970), 231–3.

J. B. Owen, *The Rise of the Pelhams* (1957).

Sir Charles Petrie, 'The Jacobite Activities in South and West England in Summer 1715', *Trans Royal Hist. Soc.*, 4th Ser., xviii (1935), 85–106.
――――――――――――, *The Jacobite Movement* (1959).
Studies in Social History, ed. J. H. Plumb (1955).
J. H. Plumb, *Walpole: the Making of a Statesman* (1956).
――――――――, *The Growth of Political Stability in England, 1675-1725* (1967).
P. W. J. Riley, *The English Ministers and Scotland, 1707-27* (1964).
N. Rogers, 'Aristocratic Clientage, Trade and Independancy: Popular Politics in pre-Radical Westminster'. *Past and Present*, 61 (1973), 70–106.
――――――――――, 'Popular Protest in Early Hanoverian London', *Past and Present*, 79 (1978), 70–100.
D. Rubini, *Court and Country, 1688-1701* (1967).
F. Salomon, *Geschichte des Letzen Ministeriums Königin Annas von England, 1710-14* (Gotha, 1894).
Dorothy H. Somerville, *King of Hearts, Charles Talbot duke of Shrewsbury* (1962).
H. L. Snyder, 'Godolphin and Harley: A Study of their Partnerhip in Politics', *Hunt. Lib. Quarterly*, xxx (1967), 241–72.
――――――――――, 'The Formulation of Foreign and Domestic Policy in the Reign of Queen Anne: Memoranda by Lord Chancellor Cowper of Conversations with Lord Treasurer Godolphin', *Hist. Journal*, xi (1968), 144–160.
――――――――――, 'The Defeat of the Occasional Conformity Bill and the Tack: A Study in the Techniques of Parliamentary Management in the Reign of Queen Anne', *Bull. Inst. Hist. Res.*, xli (1968), 172–92.
――――――――――, 'The Last Days of Queen Anne: The Account of Sir John Evelyn Examined', *Hunt. Lib. Quarterly*, xxxiv (1970-1), 261–76.
――――――――――, 'Queen Anne versus the Junto: the Effort to Place Orford at the Head of the Admiralty in 1709', *Hunt. Lib. Quarterly*, xxxv (1971-2), 323–42.
――――――――――, 'Party Configurations in the Early Eighteenth Century House of Commons', *Bull. Inst. Hist. Res.*, xlv (1972), 38–72.
――――――――――, 'A New Parliament List for 1711', *Bull. Inst. Hist. Res.*, 1 (1977-8), 185–93.
W. A. Speck, 'The Choice of Speaker in 1705', *Bull. Inst. Hist. Res.*, xxxvii (1964), 20–46.
W. A. Speck, *Tory and Whig* (1970).
――――――――, 'Brackley; the Growth of Oligarchy', *Midland History*, iii (1975), 30–41.
――――――――, 'The General Election of 1715', *Eng. Hist. Rev.*, xc (1975), 507–22.
――――――――, 'The Whig Schism under George I', *Hunt. Lib. Quarterly*, 1 (1976-7)
――――――――, *Stability and Strife, 1714-60* (1977).
W. A. Speck and W. A. Gray, 'Computer Analysis of Poll-Books: an Initial Report', *Bull. Inst. Hist. Res.*, xliii (1970).
J. A. Sperling, 'The Division of 25 May 1711 on an Amendment to the South Sea Bill: A Note on the Reality of Parties in the age of Anne', *Hist. Journal* iv (1961), 191–202.
Lucy S. Sutherland, *The East India Company in Eighteenth Century Politics* (Oxford, 1952).
D. Szechi, 'Some Insights on the Scots Peers and MP's Returned in the 1710 General Election', *Scott. Hist. Rev.*, 1x (1981), 61–75.

_____, 'The Duke of Shrewsbury's contacts with the Jacobites in 1713', *Bull. Inst. Hist. Res.* (forthcoming).

P. D. G. Thomas, 'Jacobitism in Wales', *Welsh Hist. Rev.*, i (1963), 279–300.

E. P. Thompson, *Whigs and Hunters* (1975).

M. A. Thomson, *The Secretaries of State, 1681–1782* (1932).

G. M. Trevelyan, 'The Jersey Period of the Negotiations Leading to the Peace of Utrecht', *Eng. Hist. Rev.*, xlix (1934), 100–5.

_____, *England Under Queen Anne: the Peace and the Protestant Succession* (1948).

R. R. Walcott, *English Politics in the Early Eighteenth Century* (Oxford, 1956).

_____, 'The East India Interest in the General Election of 1700–1', *Eng. Hist. Rev.*, lxxi (1956), 223–39.

W. R. Ward, *Georgian Oxford: University Politics in the Eighteenth Century* (1958).

J. R. Western, *The English Militia in the Eighteenth Century* (1965).

_____, *Monarchy and Revolution* (1972).

B. Williams, *Stanhope* (Oxford, 1968).

Index